SEEKING THE HIGH GROUND

Seeking the High Ground

Slavery and Political Conflict in the British Atlantic World

Matthew Mason

University of Virginia Press
Charlottesville and London

The University of Virginia Press is situated on the traditional lands of the Monacan Nation, and the Commonwealth of Virginia was and is home to many other Indigenous people. We pay our respect to all of them, past and present. We also honor the enslaved African and African American people who built the University of Virginia, and we recognize their descendants. We commit to fostering voices from these communities through our publications and to deepening our collective understanding of their histories and contributions.

University of Virginia Press
© 2025 by the Rector and Visitors of the University of Virginia
All rights reserved
Printed in the United States of America on acid-free paper

First published 2025

1 3 5 7 9 8 6 4 2

ISBN 978-0-8139-5341-0 (hardback)
ISBN 978-0-8139-5342-7 (paperback)
ISBN 978-0-8139-5343-4 (ebook)

Library of Congress Cataloging-in-Publication data is available for this title.

Cover art: Background, W. Phokin/Shutterstock.com; chains, Layerform Design Co./Shutterstock.com
Cover design: Susan Zucker

CONTENTS

Acknowledgments		vii
Introduction		1
Part I. The Colonial Period		7
1	The Politics of Servitude in the Seventeenth-Century English Empire	9
2	Slavery and Politics in the British Atlantic, 1680s–1764	20
Part II. Imperial Crisis and War		51
3	Stakes	59
4	Consistency	75
5	Humanity	99
6	Honor	139
7	Impacts on Slavery	173
Epilogue		215
Notes		219
Bibliography		285
Index		327

ACKNOWLEDGMENTS

I am grateful for some space in which to say I am grateful to a host of individuals and organizations who helped this book project along its way. David Waldstreicher deserves singling out for his friendship and for being an extraordinarily generous and formative critic of this work. For conversations both about our ongoing scholarly collaborations and directly about this manuscript, and in extraordinarily helpful and detailed written comments on the entire manuscript, he has my very great thanks.

Covid brought very few good things to the world, but in some contexts even the likes of me gaining facility with Zoom has proven helpful. So I was honored to join a political historians' virtual writing group midproject. Comprising Erik Alexander, Rachel Shelden, Adam I. P. Smith, Frank Towers, and Michael Woods, it was a formidable group to join that has proven to be very fun, collegial, and helpful. I am deeply grateful for their careful reading of most of the chapters of this book despite the constant violence they did to the nineteenth-century history nature of the group. Our discussions helped me think much more clearly about how best to frame the full significance of my arguments.

Various portions of this manuscript, in various states of completeness and coherence, have derived great benefit from scholars I respect in venues in which I have been honored to workshop them. The Front Range Early American Consortium (especially Eric Hinderaker, Jenny Pulsipher, Michelle Orihel, and Seth Archer) provided excellent early feedback. The Washington Early American Seminar (especially Leslie Rowland, Hannah Nolan, Christopher Bonner, Zachary Dorner, and Holly Brewer) and a meeting of the Seminar Series of the David Center for the American Revolution at the American Philosophical Society (especially Kevin Murphy, Sean Gallagher, Breanna Holland, and Nic Wood) offered sage advice and helpful critiques of more advanced chapter drafts.

Several individuals have also offered comments and leads on sources for various parts of the manuscript. Holly Brewer, Brian Cannon, Rebecca de Schweinitz, Amy Harris, Jenny Pulsipher, Neil York, and Jonathan Sassi all fall into these categories.

In addition to gainful employment and access to an excellent library at Brigham Young University throughout the years of researching and writing this book, I am grateful to various BYU entities for research funding and support. The Department of History, chaired by Eric Dursteler and Brian Cannon during the years of this study, has been an ongoing source of support. I also am grateful to the College of Family, Home, and Social Sciences and to the David M. Kennedy Center for International Studies for funding.

I have also been grateful for the early enthusiasm, helpful comments and interventions, and sustained support of Nadine Zimmerli at the University of Virginia Press. Critiques and suggestions from the anonymous readers she lined up improved this book in multiple ways.

It probably goes without saying that my family, headlined by my wife, Stacie, and my daughters, Emily, Hannah, and Rachel, deserve enormous thanks. But I will say it anyway. They have all blissfully been spared reading any part of this manuscript, but their contributions to my quality of life while also researching and writing this thing have been immeasurable.

SEEKING THE HIGH GROUND

Introduction

※

On the evening of October 5, 1777, itinerant Presbyterian preacher Abraham Keteltas stepped up to the pulpit in the Presbyterian church in Newburyport, Massachusetts. Gazing out not only on the congregation but also on the grave of evangelical superstar George Whitefield, Keteltas summoned the spirit of religious certitude natural to this setting as he delivered a heavily political sermon. "The cause of this American continent, against the measures of a cruel, bloody, and vindictive ministry," he pronounced, "is the cause of God." Given that the American Patriots contended "for the rights of mankind, for the welfare of millions now living, and for the happiness of millions yet unborn," theirs was manifestly "the cause of truth" as well as of "righteousness," verily the "cause, for which the Son of God came down from his celestial throne, and expired on a cross."[1]

But as arresting as Keteltas's language was, he hardly invented the idea that the stakes of the conflict begun with the Sugar and Stamp Acts more than a decade previous were of cosmic proportions. By 1766, for instance, erstwhile governor of Massachusetts and eminent commentator on relations between Great Britain and its North American colonies Thomas Pownall had become thoroughly alarmed by the state of those relations. That was in part because, in his mind as in those of others loyal to the ministry's policies, the issues of taxation and consent in question applied not only to "the present age" but also "to the future liberties of mankind."[2]

Embracing such lofty notions, both sides in the political struggle of the American Revolution attempted to seize every square inch of the moral high ground for their respective sides, and of course to deny it to the other. Slavery, both as an idea and as a reality, made up more than one of the strands they wove into a rope to help them scale those heights. That was because it wove so tightly, and so easily, into all the other strands. Thus, this period of political conflict only intensified the political salience of an idea and an institution that had been thoroughly political from its first appearance in the English Empire. Lofty ideals linked to liberty constituted the moral and political high ground for which British people throughout the Atlantic strove, especially but not only in the American Revolutionary conflict. Slavery proved politically valuable in multiple ways to those who jockeyed for that high ground. And as this book's cast of characters reveals, those who leveraged slavery to gain that high ground, and vice versa, ranged from the most elite policymakers to the most marginalized people in the British Atlantic. For instance, multiple Black people, whether addressing Patriot legislatures or British commanders, made use of the buzzwords of the day in appealing for liberty. As a result, that extended political conflict had numerous, if terribly complex, impacts on the lives of the enslaved and the institution of slavery both in the new United States and in the remaining British Empire.

This sense of the multiple interconnections between slavery and politics throughout the colonial era and American Revolution provides the framework within which I pursue the politics of slavery in this book. By "the politics of slavery," in other words, I mean both the ways in which political conflict put its imprint on slavery itself and debates surrounding its future, and the ways in which slavery put its imprint on political conflicts that not all historians have seen as relevant to slavery.

The Anglo-American politics of slavery stretched from the colonial period to past the American Civil War. The impacts of the American Revolution on slavery were thus very much in gestation rather than completion in 1783 with the advent of American independence. That end date for this volume, however, stems from my sense of urgency to intervene in the historiography of the American Revolution, both for British and especially for American historiography. Those interventions center on chronology, geographical scope, and most of all contestation. This book is dedicated to the proposition that for as much as the American Revolution was a crisis and disjuncture, certain key continuities in the transatlantic politics of slavery connected the colonial and Revolutionary eras. Furthermore, seeing the politics of slavery in the American Revolutionary era on a truly transatlantic stage, in addition to the continental one dominating current scholarship, helps us see them in their full complexity. Viewed through that lens, it becomes clearer that neither American Patriots nor Loyalists nor their allies in Britain developed fully consistent stances on slavery or could lay exclusive claim to the high ground. Indeed, complexity and division, rather than uniformity and consensus, characterize the impact of the American Revolution in my narrative, for both the United States and the remaining British Empire.

For a political historian to structure an argument around division, especially with Americans and slavery as the subjects, might not seem especially groundbreaking. But in recent years, both in the historiography and even in popular culture, historians and commentators have often portrayed both the causes and consequences of the American Revolution in monolithic terms. I engage in depth with this literature in the introduction to part 2 and in chapter 7. Suffice it here to say that both in the historiography and in popular culture, many commentators have emphasized "white America's" proslavery or antislavery tendencies, rather than depicting white Americans as a complex and quarrelsome bunch. Academic historians of all stripes might nod in agreement when they read medievalists Matthew Gabriele and David M. Perry caution that "as historians, it's always our job to remind people that anyone who offers" any "type of simplistic narrative is selling something. It's always the historian's job to say 'it's more complicated than that.'"[3] But in relation to some of the themes in this book, many academic historians have not heeded this maxim. As obvious as my tale of conflict might seem, therefore, it swims against various scholarly tides.

It does not swim alone, to be sure. Van Gosse, for instance, has pushed against the unitary view by positing "racial politics" in the early American republic not as dominated by an all-encompassing white supremacist order but rather "as a field of *dis*-order, contestation, and persistent opportunity for Americans of African descent." "The number of jurisdictions involved," stretching from the international to the national to the local, multiplied the cacophony of discord over not only slavery but Black people's rights in general. "Traversing this patchwork," Black political activists' vision thus by necessity extended "over great distances and borders"—including to the United States's many borders with the British Empire, which they saw as an "aid" in their quest for full freedom. Contentious politics, then, rather than white unanimity or social and cultural construction alone, made and remade slavery and race in multiple images.[4]

It is also true that some influential interpretations that might be read as unitary are in fact more complex. For instance, the title of Ibram X. Kendi's *Stamped from the Beginning* would seem to suggest a totalizing ideology of whiteness dominating American history across time. But his is a tale of "heated argument" and in fact a three-way debate involving antiracists, segregationist racists, and assimilationist racists. Therefore, "there was nothing simple or straightforward or predictable about racist ideas, and thus their history."[5] This book helps develop that insight by demonstrating the long-running importance of the British Atlantic sphere as one such important arena in which Americans and Britons, both Black and white, negotiated and remade race and slavery, in the process defining their multiple doctrines and practices. Transatlantic Anglophone print culture, as well as colonial governmental structures before 1783, put Britain's North American colonies squarely in that British Atlantic sphere.

I also am attempting to suggest a way forward for a literature on slavery and the American Revolution that seems to have settled into a stalemate of sharply divergent emphases and interpretations. The introduction to part 2 goes further into this historiography, but suffice it here to say that an older literature—and its contemporary proponents—emphasized the political events, centered on issues like taxation and representation, that fueled the imperial crisis and American independence movement. Accordingly, these historians have paid careful attention to analyzing the ideological content of the American Patriot movement and typically less attention to issues surrounding slavery and race except as they were impacted by the contagion of liberty flowing from the Revolution. Much contemporary academic literature on this issue tends to downplay—if not completely dismiss as window-dressing—the ideological origins and impacts of the American Revolution, seeing the defense of white supremacy and slavery as much more potent fuel for white Americans' resistance. My interpretation seeks to synthesize these approaches by taking the political rhetoric and ideological commitments of all participants (including but well beyond Patriots) seriously while also illuminating how very unlikely it was that slavery would not be implicated in every part of that rhetoric and those commitments. That was because it had become so thoroughly intertwined with British Atlantic ideas and practices surrounding freedom, sovereignty, and so on that it would have taken supreme effort to exclude it from the debates of the 1760s to the 1780s, let alone the conduct of the war. Also, it proved far too useful to political as well as military combatants for many of them to launch such an effort to exclude it.

Similarly, because Britons found themselves so divided over the state and desired trajectory of their domestic society and politics, they never projected one view on their empire, including North America. English and British commentary on the English and British Empire proved thus as consistently contentious as did the domestic English and British politics to which it was inextricably bound.

In relation to chronology, part 1 of this book finds more of political significance for slavery in the colonial period than have many historians, while part 2 argues that the American Revolution was nonetheless in key ways a departure from what came before. One especially influential historical interpretation downplays or denies colonial-era contestation over slavery because this interpretation posits the absolute novelty of antislavery beginning with the American Revolution. Gordon S. Wood has been a powerful and persistent advocate of such a view since at least 1991. The American Revolution, in his telling, "made possible the antislavery" movements of subsequent generations, "and in fact all our current egalitarian thinking." Wood's favorite phrasing for this point, repeated in multiple books, is that "black slavery had existed in the colonies for several generations or more without substantial questioning or criticism," until the Revolution.[6] But part 1 posits that slavery was much more contested, and contested in ways that contemporaries understood to be fundamentally political, than such literature grants. Although I develop the reasons more in later passages, it is worth noting here that I have chosen to treat the imperial crisis of 1764–75 and the Revolutionary War of 1775–83 as one period, devoting part 2 to thematic rather than chronological chapters. That is in part because I contend that while key issues emerged or changed during the war, the core political ideals that constituted the high ground in the imperial crisis persisted rather than disappeared with the advent and progress of the war.

In a sense, this volume fits with a trend in contemporary scholarship on the American Revolution identified by Trevor Burnard's recent historiographical survey. Burnard highlights a "current consensus" that emphasizes evolutionary development rather than dramatic and sudden turning points. This literature has placed "the American Revolution in a longer and more global context" than did previous scholarship. The point is less that the American Revolution was unimportant in absolute terms than that its significance as a milestone and its impact were complex and in ways limited.[7] Indeed, the Revolution did prove a rupture in the politics of slavery but more of degree than of kind. With previous political usages of and debates over slavery in the British Atlantic to draw on, contestants both intensified and extended the range of slavery's purchase in the political contests of the imperial crisis and Revolutionary War years. They also hoped, with good reason, to find an expanded audience via their skill in connecting slavery to the pervading sense of crisis in their day. The arguments changed far less than the breadth of the appeal.

The thought-provoking work of Kirsten Sword bridges this book's temporal and geographical points. As she demonstrated in an important 2010 article, the commonplace idea that effective antislavery action began only after the American Revolutionary War, and the commonplace focus on the politics of antislavery along national lines (American and British), began as products of the abolitionists' late eighteenth-century self-produced narratives. "Antislavery activism" before the Revolution "appears disconnected and ineffective at least in part because eighteenth-century propagandists portrayed it that way," in order to portray their respective American and British movements as fully aligned "with emerging national agendas." Quakers of dubious nationalist credentials "staged a disappearing act" in both Britain and the new United States, "rebranding" abolitionism to fit into "the national projects of the 1780s." For similar reasons, Sword argues, historians tend to "gravitate toward national antislavery stories" delimited by national boundaries.[8]

This nationalist pattern is especially true along the poles of the debate among American historians over the nature of the American Revolution respecting slavery. These competing narratives paradoxically consider the new United States in isolation from other nations yet pronounce the nascent nation exceptional either in its commitment to antislavery or in its commitment to white supremacy and slavery. Such narratives fit with the idea of the American Revolution as a beginning: either of a sovereign nation crippled by white supremacist dogma or of a sovereign nation inventing antislavery commitment.[9] But it helps us understand the roles of slavery in colonial politics to see that a truly transatlantic debate drove those politics from the beginning. Likewise it helps us more fully understand the American Revolution itself, and its relationship to the politics of slavery, to see it as the continuation and intensification of that long-running set of contests over slavery and freedom, waged on a canvas stretching far beyond the future borders of the United States of America.

PART ONE

The Colonial Period

1

The Politics of Servitude in the Seventeenth-Century English Empire

೧೨

THE RISE and growth of African slavery and other forms of bound labor in England's and then Britain's empire proved to be a thoroughly political process at every stage. As Christopher L. Brown has suggested, slavery was always political in the British Empire because "it produced political power, defined political interests, generated political conflicts," and "shaped political thought." It accomplished the first three by creating, and being created by, a planter class in multiple colonies whose political interests centered on defending against multiple possible threats to the burgeoning institution. Those threats included not only that of slave resistance but also "competing economic interests in the metropole" and in North American colonies that were less reliant on slavery.[1] But there were other reasons for slavery's politicization in addition to Brown's suggestive framework. Slavery and other forms of servitude played a key role in the bitter, long-running contests in the metropole about the proper nature of the empire, debates that were moral as well as economic in nature. In the process slavery and servitude powerfully shaped metropolitan views of the colonies. Furthermore, the rise of New World bondage gave added power to the use of slavery as a metaphor in political and social debates in the metropole. Finally, Brown's intimation of political divisions between different colonies only scratches the surface, because as some colonists joined in condemning slavery, that action rendered some of those colonies divided among as well as between themselves. In the imperial crisis beginning in the 1760s, then, North Americans and Britons expanded debates over slavery and weaponized slavery in other debates, but that crisis was not responsible for or pioneering in the process of slavery being a thoroughly political institution and playing a key political role in the empire.

From its slow-rolling inception forward, the English Empire featured contestation in the metropole about its nature and purposes. Indeed, long before England became a player in European colonization, among Europeans that process had pitted moral critics against backers of the economic and nationalist interests furthered by colonial exploitation.[2] Given that Protestant English subjects conceived of their nation as locked in an apocalyptic struggle with the great Catholic imperial powers, many hoped that the imperatives of national glory, national profit, and national morality might reinforce rather than compete with each other. Profitable and sustainable colonies might contribute to the glory of Protestantism and the expansion of civilization properly understood. But manifestly exploitative colonies would cloud this moral vision. And given the traditional English scorn for Spain's empire of conquest, such rapacious colonies would rob England of the moral high ground. While other English observers pushed back against such hopes as impracticably high-toned, many among the wide range of English people who closely attended to England's nascent colonial settlements shared the fear that this empire's moral legitimacy was not a sure thing.[3]

Thus, many seventeenth-century observers wrung their hands when they perceived their earliest colonies as depots of disorder and degeneracy. They worried that whether in Ireland or in Virginia, the English settlers were de-civilizing themselves rather than civilizing the natives. Alarmed because it was their countrymen rather than those they deemed foreign savages exhibiting this civilizational backwardness, they fell back on a class analysis of this phenomenon. Disorder and suspect loyalties were what one should expect, they sighed, from creating these colonies as "the sincke of England."[4] Londoners attending plays would have had seen all these anxieties and more acted out, as scholar Bridget Orr has demonstrated. English dramas and satires produced after the Restoration of 1660, she has found, revealed "considerable ambivalence about aspirations to empire" in their depictions of the "novel social types"—pirates, planters, Indian nabobs, and the like—"produced by colonial expansion and settlement." While many such plays also celebrated English greatness, they raised serious questions about how sustainable English civilization and liberty would be given such moral degeneration.[5]

These anxious depictions stood on strong evidentiary ground. Joseph Kelly's recent study of Jamestown, for instance, shows that it is entirely possible to tell the story of Jamestown's early years as a recurring scene of disorder, desertion, and rebellion. Indeed, as Bernard Bailyn has shown, one can build a convincing narrative of seventeenth-century North America—for both Native and new inhabitants—largely in terms of "confusion, failure, violence, and the loss of civility." "A degenerative spiral" was more common than triumph in Bailyn's interpretation.⁶ Of course, accounts of North America as a naturally abundant paradise sought to assuage all such fears, and historian Lauren Working has demonstrated how many metropolitan gentlemen proved impervious to them. Yet even some of these tracts granted that the remoteness of these settlements, and their being "situate among so many barbarous nations" as well as "pyrates and robbers," meant that invasions and other disorders "may probably be feared." As royal officials received and distributed accounts of recurrent major rebellions in the seventeenth-century colonies, they confirmed for readers this set of pejorative images of English colonies.⁷

Nothing did more to render the nascent American colonies proverbial for barbarity than the forms of labor exploitation their elites practiced.⁸ Proliferating colonial produce made constantly visible the fruits of bound labor in the colonies. More importantly, kidnapped and otherwise coerced English men, women, and children haunted the colonial image in the seventeenth-century English mind. Leading labor and legal historians have compellingly characterized both the law and the lived experiences of early modern English and Scottish labor arrangements as a spectrum of largely unfree statuses rather than a stark divide between unfree and free. Moreover, bound labor was widely accepted as a punishment for crime and even vagrancy. And as literary scholar Urvashi Chakravarty has demonstrated, the fact that "early modern England was keenly concerned with the politics of servitude" meant that tensions between England's celebrated love of liberty and the nature and practice of servitude can be found in places stretching from the classroom to the stage as well as the household.⁹ But as Michael J. Guasco's masterful study of sixteenth- and early seventeenth-century English attitudes toward slavery has demonstrated, the dominant rhetoric was of "the mythological freeborn Englishman who would rather suffer death than endure bondage." So, "if English men and women were to be enslaved, there had better be a good reason why," and the practices of the Spanish toward Indians and especially North Africans toward Englishmen were indefensible. How all this applied to English people's complex interactions with Others like Native Americans or Africans or even the Irish remained unclear. And early ideas on Native American slavery echoed the conceptual framework of penal bondage meant to reform the enslaved. Still, playing a clear role in "making slaves was not" acceptable to most English subjects. English ideas surrounding servitude in the nascent English Empire would therefore be best characterized as an English debate.[10]

While English political culture thus ensured that servitude in the empire would never prove uncontroversial, revealingly enough it was a period of political ferment that provoked an unusually intense debate about the role of unfree labor: the English Civil War and Revolution of the 1640s. Amid the fury of this period, some thought of their political enemies as deserving of servitude. And some opportunistic Englishmen thought nothing of kidnapping or otherwise coercing the most vulnerable of their fellow subjects into the growing trade in colonial servants. Still others welcomed these transportations as a means of ridding the realm of its undesirables. Revolutionary chieftain turned lord protector Oliver Cromwell pursued ambitions of an Atlantic empire that dwarfed those of previous regimes. The large-scale transportation of Irish Catholic prisoners of war, plus expanded English participation in the transatlantic slave trade, were major results of its conquests in Ireland and the Caribbean. Many in Cromwell's Puritan base cheered on and joined in the profits of an expanding empire, seeing the expansion of English wealth and power as success for the worldwide Protestant cause.[11]

But all these practices also provoked pointed protest in England and in the empire. They contributed directly to "the fragmentation of the Revolutionary coalition," as John Donoghue has written. The most radical members of that coalition vigorously protested against "the massive scale of corruption, slavery, and carnage that accompanied the Revolution's imperial progress." In a preview of coming arguments, they also insisted that this all exposed the would-be godly republic to charges of rank hypocrisy. Proponents benignly passed off the building of "a freedom loving empire" on the backs of "forced labor and slavery" as a "paradox," but their opponents saw it as an outright contradiction and crime against their revolution.[12]

These opponents made sure that in 1643, 1645, 1647, 1660, 1661, and 1670, Parliament debated and at times passed regulations aimed at stamping out illicit kidnapping and other abuses. Many members of Parliament refused to see the difference between the kidnapping of children and the transportation even of their political foes. The state lacked the regulatory capacity to enforce the laws Parliament passed, but the rhetoric in the debates was telling. One MP, for instance, protested against the transportation of his Royalist enemies because "I consider them as Englishmen." "We are the freest people in the world," he continued, and transporting political prisoners violated that self-concept. That self-image led a band of sailors to resist impressment to staff naval ships as "inconsistent with the Principles of Freedom and Liberty."[13]

Indentured servants themselves likewise vigorously resisted their servitude, not only on the ground but also in the public political sphere. A preeminent example is a 1659 pamphlet written by transported English prisoners to "remonstrate on behalf" not only of themselves but also of other prisoners whose transportation had put them in a "most deplorable (and as to *English*-men unparallel'd,) condition." It was only by the exercise of "arbitrary power," they protested to Parliament, that "so great a breach is made upon the free People of *England*." They proved politically savvy enough to shame the perpetrators with the habitual English pride in superior national freedom. It was "a thing not known amongst the cruell *Turks*," they jabbed, "to sell and enslave these of their own Countrey and Religion."[14]

This pamphlet also functioned as a petition for freedom to Parliament, one that provoked an extensive debate which implicated many of the core political issues of the era. To the charge that these political exiles had been the victim of the "unlimited power" of Puritans in Parliament as well as their masters in the West Indies, one defender of their status insisted that "none are sent without their consent." When that flimsy claim broke down rather quickly, other opponents of the petitioners cried that this "is a Cavalier's petition" which, as such, could produce no good. Indeed, "encouraging petitions" from such a source, many MPs charged, would only further divide Englishmen as well as countenancing the Royalist party that remained a very real threat to national security. Others retorted that this was not so much "a Cavalierish business" as it was "a matter that concerns the liberty of the free-born people of England." "Slavery is slavery," they insisted, and should the victors in the Civil War inflict it on their defeated enemies, they would be in effect embracing Stuart principles. So dire was the petitioners' plight, claimed one MP, that "I could hardly hold weeping when I heard the petition.... I desire not to live if" this became a precedent that Cavaliers could at some point visit on Roundheads. The men on this side of the debate claimed the mantle of true conservatives, for "our ancestors left us free men" by such instruments as the Magna Carta, and those who favored political transportation had practiced "innovations upon the people's rights and liberties." If by rejecting the petition they delivered "our sons into slavery, we are of all men most miserable."[15]

As these arguments resounded not only within the walls of Parliament but throughout the English Empire, they furthered the growth of racial thinking among those increasingly defining themselves as white. An MP in the 1659 petition debate insisted that the complainants' lot could not have been so hard as represented, reassuring Parliament that "the work" in the West Indies "is mostly carried on by the negroes." An opponent in this debate, while disclaiming that he was "as much against the Cavalier party as any man in these walls," argued that slavery should not be the lot of freeborn English people any more than it was for Roman citizens in ancient times. Indeed, he pursued, if English subjects could be enslaved, "our lives will be as cheap as those negroes," whom colonial slaveholders looked upon "as their goods." Likewise, a series of Irish travelers expressed shock at white Irishmen being treated like Black slaves.[16] However, the racial nature of this reaction often still took protean rather than solid form. For instance, Virginia's "Act for Repealing an Act for Irish Servants," passed during the 1659–60 session, decreed that "no servant comeing into the country without indentures, of what christian nation soever, shall serve longer then those of our own country." It thus emphasized religion rather than race.[17]

Barbados's legislators blazed the most influential trail by explicitly distinguishing between the law for African slaves and the less draconian law for white servants, but even that proved highly controversial within the empire. Even before it became a center of sugar production, Barbados received a disproportionate share of white bound emigrants. Most landowners in that colony, as Simon P. Newman has written, considered the "vagrants, criminals, and prisoners" in their workforce as having forfeited the claim to "traditional English liberties." And then, Edward B. Rugemer has illustrated, by the mid-seventeenth century these Barbadians had opened a clear legal gap between servants "subject to the laws" and Africans who "stood outside the law." Especially with its laws of 1661 for servants and slaves, "the Barbados Assembly laid the empirical foundation for racial ideology."[18] But this rising planter class quickly learned that influential metropolitans had made neither of these mental adjustments and demanded explanations for what they saw as extreme variations from English traditions. As Susan Dwyer Amussen has demonstrated, early English travel accounts of Barbados were "saturated with perceived difference and strangeness," and metropolitan suspicions raised a real possibility that Barbados's pioneering slave codes would be vetoed in London. In all their correspondence with London, planters used the term "Negro" to foreground their slaves' origins rather than their legal status, because "slavery had no counterpart at home, and its legitimacy was doubtful if the question of its legal basis was faced squarely." They were right to suspect this. In 1676, for instance, the Council for Trade and Plantations, in its reply to Barbados's slave legislation, expressed itself "not pleased with the word (servitude) p. 26 as being a mark of bondage and slavery." Council members thought it "fit rather to use the word (service)." Rugemer has shown a similar back and forth between Jamaica's legislature and the Lords of Trade throughout the late seventeenth century over its slave laws.[19]

Exchanges of this sort intensified rising colonial elites' determination to assert the right to control their unfree labor force as they saw fit. The English settlers of Providence Island, for instance, very quickly adopted African slavery because the profits and power that system provided "made up for their status as tenants" on land owned by the Providence Island Company.[20] Colonists like this discovered and then insisted that the human bondage about which metropolitans had their qualms was in fact vital to their own definition of freedom.

Some therefore experimented with defending slavery, at least as they practiced it. In 1657, Richard Ligon's travel and settler narrative depicted Barbados as "this happy Island" and minimized differences between it and England. He granted that white servants sometimes received harsh treatment depending on their masters' whim and character but assured his readers that Black slaves "are happy people" contented with their lot.[21] A 1666 narrative by former indentured servant George Alsop offered a rosy picture of servitude in Maryland, specifically to refute the colony's bad reputation in that regard.[22]

Another major effect of the politics of slavery in the English Atlantic, and yet another key preview of coming attractions, was that they gave an extra punch to political usages of terms like "slavery." English political culture, especially but not only of the radical variety, has since at least the Middle Ages nurtured a hostility to bondage as unnatural and un-English. Peasant rebels repeatedly asserted that God and "Christ made free men" and only extortionate earthly lords "maken bond." Therefore, holding their lands at the pleasure of English lords struck them as "miserable and slavish." Thus, decrying "slavery" came easily to a 1621 petitioner to Parliament against what he deemed "tirannical government" in Virginia.[23] That tradition gave an edge to any and all political uses of the s-word in English political discourse.

But the rise of New World servitude and slavery sharpened it. This was in part because, as scholars Holly Brewer and John N. Blanton have persuasively argued, there was at the very least a broad cultural resonance between Stuart absolutism and colonial slavery on the one hand and principles of parliamentary consent and a sort of antislavery on the other. The Stuart kings and their adherents, as Brewer has written, "legitimated slavery both in England and its colonies with the same kind of arguments that they used to justify the king's divine right to rule." Deploying the s-word thus came naturally to those who vigorously denied divine right and wished to dramatize that threat.[24] Furthermore, from the Civil War years forward, as Carla Gardina Pestana has convincingly argued, the concomitant rise of chattel slavery in the New World and of assertions of rights by English subjects caused all English regimes (whether metropolitan or colonial) to be "sensitive to accusations that they had denied liberties" to those subjects.[25] Individuals also recoiled from being labeled slave drivers. Diarist Samuel Pepys, for instance, recorded sharply chiding his servant Will for "telling his mistress that he would not be made a slave of, which vexes me."[26]

This rhetoric proved plastic, but not endlessly so. Mary Nyquist, in her perceptive study of the rhetoric of political slavery in Western culture since ancient Greece, has pointed out that that rhetoric "has its own unique logic and codes, none of which arise from concern for those who are actually enslaved." However, "political servitude is not inherently independent of chattel slavery or indifferent to its legitimacy." The relationship between the free and enslaved communities in any society in which this rhetoric has been wielded has set parameters on that wielding.[27]

Therefore, it took the expansion of attention to servitude in the English Atlantic, together with white-hot political debates in the metropole, to create what seems to have been a massive uptick in the usage of the term in the Civil War era. This flowering of slavery rhetoric was rooted in questions surrounding the degree to which the government should be answerable to the people. In 1646, radical Richard Overton argued that if government was not to flow from "*the choice of the people, from whom the Power that is just must be derived,*" the usurpers should just be honest and "tell us that it is reasonable we should be slaves." In 1647, at momentous debates over democracy at a church in Putney, Thomas Rainborough thundered that "that which enslaves the people of England" was the principle "that they should be bound by laws in which they have no voice at all." Given all these connotations of absolute power, the metaphor made itself available to Digger leader Gerrard Winstanley to argue that unchecked economic power in landowners meant that if the poor "cannot work like slaves, then they must starve." Hence the proliferation of this analogy in this time of religious/political/economic strife.[28] Across the Atlantic, when passing a 1652 law limiting all servitude to ten years, the legislature of the Separatist Puritan colony of Rhode Island proudly contrasted this with the "common course practised amongst" less godly "English men to buy negers" as slaves for life.[29]

Slavery rhetoric proved useful not only to radicals and Whigs but also to those who leaned Tory. For instance, a group of New Yorkers who wrote to vilify a rebellion led by Jacob Leisler charged that Leisler's rebels desired "to enslave them and their posterity" by usurping the power to tax them.[30] After the Restoration, historian Nicholas Hudson has written, "royalist authors widely decried the 'slavery' imposed on the British people by the Puritans." Although (or perhaps because) they knew that this use of the term "slavery" would be provocative, they employed it widely to depict the dark times in which "Sanhedrin and Priest inslav'd the Nation." Aphra Behn and the adapters of her tragic tale of Oroonoko, a wrongfully enslaved African prince, came from this Tory tradition, seeing royalty wronged as analogous to the Stuarts' fate after the Revolutions both of 1649 and 1688. One "crypto-Jacobite novel" pointedly had its protagonist, "a young English nobleman named 'Chevalier James,'" sold into all "the Hardships of an *American Slavery.*"[31] In her *Reflections on Marriage*, Mary Astell offered a feminist argument that also served as an effective Tory assault on Whigs' hypocrisy. Being against "sedition of any sort," she "heartily" wished that men as masters of their households "would pay their civil and ecclesiastical governors the same submission which they themselves exact from their domestic subjects." "For if," as the Whigs endlessly argued, "arbitrary power is evil in itself, and ... *all men are born free,* how is it that all women are born slaves? as they must be if the being subjected to the *inconstant, uncertain, unknown, arbitrary will* of men be the *perfect condition of slavery?*" In short, Astell drove home, "why is slavery so much condemned and strove against in" the political sphere by Whigs, "and so highly applauded and held so necessary and so sacred in" the domestic?[32]

This hatred of political slavery intertwined with a strong revulsion of those who would willingly submit to it.[33] In 1660, John Milton fretted that the drive to restore the Stuarts manifested "a strange, degenerate contagion suddenly spread among us, fitted and prepared for new slavery." For this nation newly "possessed of their liberty" to choose slavery "will render us a scorn and derision to all our neighbours."[34] John Locke wielded the s-word repeatedly in his famous refutation of Tory writer Robert Filmer, assaulting him as "an advocate for slavery." Slavery was "so directly opposite to the generous temper and courage of our nation" that he marveled "that an Englishman, much less a gentleman, should plead for it."[35]

The complexity of these political usages of the s-word makes it difficult to ascertain the impact of this rhetoric on the users' attitudes toward chattel slavery. All the disdain for slavishness, for instance, did not encourage a charitable attitude toward enslaved people. And Locke, to take one giant of an example, came to rather complex conclusions when he contemplated the power of West Indian slaveholders in the context of his overall discussion of political slavery. He granted their legal power over their slaves but denied that that power equated to sovereignty in any legitimate political sense or setting. He proclaimed that "freedom from absolute, arbitrary power" was so necessary that no man could "part with it," and even submission to "a lawful conqueror" did not legitimize absolute, inheritable slavery. But despite this limit, the enslaved fell outside his notion of the social compact, for "as soon as compact enters, slavery ceases."[36] Although touching on the pejorative view of West Indian planters, and leading with the standard English horror at slavery, this formulation at least potentially insulated chattel slavery as a separate issue from political slavery. And while Locke's treatises were crystal clear against political slavery and on the novelty of rising chattel slavery in the colonies, they were muddled in relation to the legitimacy of chattel slavery. That clarity differential applied to most, if not all, of the deployers of slavery rhetoric in politics quoted above.

No wonder scholars of British thought about slavery in the colonial period have emphasized its limits. Christopher Brown, for instance, has characterized it as "antislavery without abolitionism" until the 1780s. "Antislavery thought in the eighteenth century," he has argued, "did not build cumulatively, block by block, to a higher stage of moral consciousness," because the disconnect between this discourse and politics rendered it "the history of isolated moralists" until the 1760s.[37] However, as I have attempted to demonstrate in this chapter and will continue in the next, there was no disconnect between the rhetoric of slavery, or even the reality of slavery, and politics in the English and then British Atlantic. In fact, it was the multiple, complex interconnections between slavery and politics throughout the seventeenth century that both gave the analogy political punch and clouded the picture of what it all meant for actual slaves. That complexity would only continue as the expansion of African slavery's role in the English Empire transformed it into something recognizable from an eighteenth-century point of view.

2

Slavery and Politics in the British Atlantic, 1680s–1764

୧୨

THE CONTINUAL expansion of sugar cultivation by African slaves in the last third of the seventeenth century both solidified and fundamentally reordered the English Empire. The expansion of sugar cultivation accelerated a massive influx of enslaved Africans to Barbados and Jamaica. This development expanded and intensified the debates discussed in chapter 1. It created a new and powerful planter class running obscenely profitable colonies in the West Indies. Furthermore, supplying the West Indies proved a major boon for British merchants, the economically fragile colonies in New England, and the new English colonies of the Mid-Atlantic region. It led indirectly to the rapid adoption of African slavery in Carolina. This all made the West Indies the jewel in the crown as well as the economic engine of the empire from the Restoration forwards, and put an increased emphasis on trade and profits as the very reason for the empire.[1]

Another impact of these staple crop revolutions and the boom in the transatlantic slave trade was that in the metropolis and throughout the empire, the political face of colonial bondage gradually shifted from the white servant to the Black slave. It is worth noting that in the metropolis, that face—politically speaking—had never been Indigenous. Almost all of the legislative and legal history of Indian slavery and slave trading in colonial North America was local rather than imperial. The pattern of what little attention imperial officials seem to have paid to this form of slavery and slaving seems to be well summed by Alan Gallay: "Imperial officials beckoned their agents and their colonists to treat aboriginal peoples with justice," which even in the case of proprietary instructions in Carolina came in the form of "a moral and ethical framework for intercultural relations, not a detailed blueprint." Even in the rare cases where those instructions were insistent, officials in London backed off quickly, accepting white colonists' arguments that their security was involved and trumped all.[2]

To be sure, this was a shift in emphasis to African slavery rather than a stark line, as hand-wringing about white servitude continued into the eighteenth century. Indeed, protest literature written by ex-indentured servants continued well into the eighteenth century, depicting Britain as the land of (initially lost and then regained) liberty and America as the land of slavery.[3] And in the 1730s, the Irish Parliament investigated claims of Irish Protestants seduced or coerced into oppressive service in North Carolina. Explosive words like "tyranny" and "slavery" abounded in petitions meant to dramatize these unfortunates' plights. But for full effect, they complained of being "set to work . . . in the field with the negroes." Worse, "the planters there are more careful of" the well-being of "the negroes" than "of their white slaves."[4] As this concluding move of the petitioners suggests, however, the sheer number of Africans both in Britain's colonies and in Britain itself forced itself on the British popular consciousness in the eighteenth century. That latter number was reckoned in the thousands in the late colonial period, concentrated in but not limited to London. The former, by Philip D. Morgan's estimates, exploded from about 86,000 Black people throughout the empire in 1680 to around 555,000 in 1750.[5]

Critics of this new imperial emphasis and reality proved many and vocal. This was linked to the fact that not long after these West Indian developments the empire became British rather than English. After union with Scotland in 1707, ongoing debates about the legitimacy of empire became integral to the ongoing construction of British national identity through much of the eighteenth century. As Kathleen Wilson has put it, "Britain's growing imperial possessions" shaped "the way that national identity was conceived, understood and defended." Debates about how civilized white Americans were, for instance, carried tremendous salience to British claims to civilizational superiority over Catholic European rivals, as well as to nascent notions of racial superiority. Britons also took the state of their colonies "to be a barometer of the effectiveness and legitimacy of domestic political institutions" and ministries.[6]

These newly minted Britons conducted that debate, as those contesting the English Empire had before them, on the grounds of moral legitimacy as well as of material benefit. As David Armitage's rightly influential analysis of this contest has argued, "The constitutive elements of various conceptions of the British Empire arose in the competitive context of political argument." By the 1730s, many imperial officials and colonial elites had agreed on a "unifying concept" in which the British might balance empire with liberty by being at its heart "Protestant, commercial, maritime and free." But that broad concept, Armitage hastens to add, "left generous room for different conceptions of that Empire," as well as for different assessments of how well it met those criteria.[7] And then after midcentury, with the expansion of the power of the East India Company and of British trade and exploration in the Pacific, the mainstream conception of a commercial, maritime, Protestant, and free empire came under major "reconsideration," as P. J. Marshall has pointed out. In its new global guise, "the British empire was now territorial as well as maritime, based on military in addition to naval power, and it increasingly involved autocratic rule over peoples who were neither Protestant nor, in the British view, suited to a free government."[8]

Many eighteenth-century Britons were satisfied that their empire met those tests. By then, as Catherine Hall and Sonya O. Rose have argued, "There were few if any voices arguing the Empire should be disbanded," and the idea of a moral cordon between the metropole and colonies helped preserve in most minds the idea that Britons at home were modern and civilized no matter what happened in the empire.[9] More enthusiastic backers of empire could be found among scientists, who valued the empire as a vast source of new knowledge and thus tended to see it as a tool of benevolent progress.[10] Wilson's scholarship has shown that many eighteenth-century provincial Britons effaced "the crueler aspects of empire" by nurturing "a commercial and 'patriotic' vision of the British empire" that endowed them with "the power of possession," which gave rise to language like "*our* colonies, ships," and so on. The main point for them, Wilson has suggested, was "to be on the right side of the vast social and cultural chasms between those who profited from the processes of imperial expansion and those who did not."[11] The most vocal and influential proponents of the British Empire were those who sought to make sure Catholic France rather than Protestant Britain fell on the wrong side of that chasm. Historian Paul Langford has revealed that for eighteenth-century Britons, "commerce did not merely signify trade. Rather it suggested a definitive stage in the progress of mankind," the essence of modernity.[12] As a member of Parliament put it in 1738, ocean-borne trade was nothing less than "the life and soul of this nation." In 1754, one writer gushed that Britain's commerce constituted nothing less than "the Basis of our Liberty and Happiness, the Support of the State, the Bulwark of our Religion, and the Source of our Wealth." Commerce was thus inseparable from the imperial rivalries of the century. Seen in this way, Britain's colonies constituted a great enabler of, rather than an embarrassment to, Britain's claim to lead the forces of freedom in the world. As a later speaker in Parliament put it succinctly, everyone knew that amid the enormously costly wars of the eighteenth century, "power lies in riches, and that the source of the English riches lies in America."[13]

Still, the consciences of a wide range of Britons were not so easily salved. A religious revival within the Anglican Church from the 1680s through the 1730s created a strong desire to make the eighteenth century "an age of benevolence" in the British Atlantic. A "rise to national goodness" must complement the rise to national greatness in vindicating the principles of the Glorious Revolution of 1688. The widespread popular revulsion at Bernard Mandeville's 1710s writings, which vindicated the pursuit of self-interest against the hypocrisy of pious notions of private and national morality, spoke to the power of these moral aspirations. And apropos of slavery specifically, the Whiggish principles of the Glorious Revolution had complex rather than simple implications, setting up conflict rather than consensus.[14]

In that light both the history and current practice of British colonialism troubled many who were not distinguished for their religiosity. In parliamentary debates about military discipline at midcentury, for instance, America repeatedly figured as a savage land from whence variations from the normal rules of warfare might infect the British armed forces. One speaker averred that "the whole tenor of our American history" had been marked by "wars more cruel . . . than any we have in Europe." In that same decade, William and Edmund Burke's history of American colonization recoiled at conquests enacted "with as little colour of right as consciousness of doing any thing wrong." They pictured North America as a receptacle for religious fanatics, and the West Indies as that for people of "fiery, restless tempers," all of whom had made themselves troublesome in Britain.[15] Anglo-Irish poet Jonathan Swift vigorously satirized empire as barely disguised plunder, and white Americans themselves as the most extreme avatars of this exploitative world order. In his epic piece *Gulliver's Travels*, Swift challenged all manner of assumptions of superiority on the part of Europeans, nobles, and even humans over other species. At one key moment, for instance, his hero Gulliver reflects that the would-be victims of even the best-intentioned empires "do not appear to have any desire of being conquered, and enslaved, murdered, or driven out by colonies." Moreover, Swift's angry parody of British policy in Ireland, *A Modest Proposal*, put to good effect American colonists' reputation as extreme exploiters. Swift launched his sardonic proposal to raise Irish children for food by pointedly noting, "I have been assured by a very knowing American of my acquaintance in London, that a young healthy child, well nursed, is at a year old a most delicious, nourishing, and wholesome food."[16]

That said, it was the most earnestly religious Britons who found the most to protest against when directly encountering or reading about the new colonial regimes. The Anglican revival coincided with the explosive growth of the empire's Black population, so one "increasingly pressing" concern of that revival, as Travis Glasson has written, was "defining the place of black people in colonial societies" and in the Church of England. The missionary wing of this revival, the Society for the Propagation of Gospel (SPG), posited that the conversion of white masters as well as of African slaves and Indians would further both the humanity and orderliness of Britain's empire. Those conservative goals did not dispose SPG ministers to reject slavery as an institution, and indeed the SPG famously owned slaves. But in colony after colony slaveholders resisted baptizing slaves as a fundamental threat to their control, and their fervent resistance to their activities elicited strong religious critiques that bolstered the planters' negative image. SPG moralists could see nothing but "vulgar Prejudice" as actuating planters' perverse resistance to Christianizing slaves.[17]

They made this case early and often. As early as 1680, reformist Morgan Godwyn issued a book-length exposition of the argument that only unchristian and unreasonable prejudice by the planters of Barbados and Virginia kept the gospel from going to their slaves. Africans "*have naturally an equal Right with other Men to the Exercise and Privileges of Religion*," he insisted. At his most indignant Godwyn upbraided the planters' treatment of "not only their Souls but their Bodies also" as flowing from racist ideas "without doubt contrived in Hell."[18] In 1708, SPG activist Francis Brokesby echoed Godwyn when he damned all colonial slaveholders for their racial prejudice: these "Hellish Principles" typified the overall pattern of irreligion, religious chaos, and self-seeking that the SPG encountered throughout British America. Both Brokesby and an anonymous newspaper writer the next year sought to "put all *English*-men to the Blush" by contrasting them with the Catholic French and Spanish who did baptize their slaves. Planters' anti-Christian stance, the latter essayist insisted, was symptomatic of why slavery was "so dishonourable to human Nature, that in *Europe*, where Men pretend to much Reason and Civility, they grew asham'd of it, and lay'd it aside."[19] In 1748, a frustrated Anglican priest in Delaware decried slaveholders as "utterly destitute of common humanity," differing "in nothing but complexion and free estate from the most abject slave."[20]

This ongoing SPG critique of slaveholders added up to a fascinating mix of a narrow policy focus (baptism not emancipation of slaves) with rather advanced antislavery and antiracist rhetoric.[21] That mix continued in the explosive writings of yet another Anglican religious reformer, George Whitefield. His evangelical travels in the 1730s in the Chesapeake and Carolinas had touched him "with a Fellow-feeling of the Miseries of the poor Negroes," and in 1740 he published his extensive thoughts on their state in an open letter to their captors. The burden of Whitefield's message to these slaveholders was that "God has a Quarrel with you for your Abuse of and Cruelty to the poor Negroes." He steered clear of the question of whether buying slaves was "lawful," but he was certain that "it is sinful, when bought, to use them as bad, nay worse, than as though they were Brutes," as "the Generality" of American slaveholders did. After the standard refutation of slaveholders' qualms about Christianizing their slaves, he offered a less predictable passage. "Considering what Usage they commonly meet with," Whitefield marveled that slaves committed suicide and rose in rebellion so infrequently. "Tho' I heartily pray God they may never be permitted to get the upper Hand" in the revolts that did occur, he warned that "should such a Thing be permitted by Providence, all good Men must acknowledge the Judgment would be just." He reiterated at the end that "God has already began to visit" Carolina in particular, not only with disease but also with slave revolt, and only repentance would save that colony.[22] Focusing only on the limitations of Whitefield's focus on slave treatment rather than emancipation would be to miss the significance of much of this. In 1740, and in particular in the aftermath of the highly threatening Stono Rebellion in South Carolina, to class slave rebellion as divine punishment on the slaveholders was provocative in the extreme. And the whole pamphlet reinforced, with all the weight of this transatlantic religious celebrity, the building image of unregenerate, cruel planters.

Religious Dissenters also provided important censors of the rising colonial slave regimes. None was more vocal than the religious independent and multipurpose English activist Thomas Tryon, who published a severe critique of slavery in 1684. Slaves, he insisted, had every right to complain against "their *Hard Servitude*, and the CRUELTIES Practised upon them by divers of their Masters professing *Christianity* in the *West-Indian Plantations*." Having created societies devoid of "Compassion and Charity," the planters had good reason to fear the Christian precept "*that the Lord will Retaliate every man according to his Work.*" Every "Person whom our Creator hath endued with a rational Soul" who did not "willfully quench and extinguish" his conscience knew these charges to be true. Although Tryon challenged racial discrimination as a just basis for slavery and sympathized with runaway slaves (albeit not with violent slave rebels), his prescription was for better treatment rather than emancipation.[23] Tryon thus fit with the larger pattern of narrow policy recommendations combined with scorched-earth—and politically and culturally damaging—depictions of the planters.

Although some of these critics, being religious enthusiasts or Dissenters, might seem marginal to the rational Enlightenment culture of eighteenth-century Britain, this drumbeat of criticism pervaded metropolitan political culture. Servitude proved the most reliable "marker of incivility and oppression" in the fashionable post-Restoration London plays analyzed by Bridget Orr. Their authors worried about the "degradation" of both "slave-owner and slave."[24] Metropolitan readers of travel accounts from the West Indies encountered a supremely dark picture, with the harsh labor regime as the distinguishing feature. For instance, in his travel account published in London in 1740, Charles Leslie contrasted Britain, "with native Freedom blest," with Jamaica, "where Slavery was established" with all its horrors. He provided a catalog of those horrors inflicted by an endlessly greedy and ambitious master class, concluding that "no Country exceeds them in a barbarous Treatment of Slaves." Slave revolt, maroon war, piracy, and near-constant imperial rivalries and wars stalked Leslie's history of Jamaica, from which he recoiled as a lover of order. But he saw the long warfare of the island's maroons against "a superior Force" as evidence of "how strongly the Love of Liberty prevails in the Breasts of Men, notwithstanding the most wretched Circumstances." Unable to square slavery with his idea of natural rights, he once again reveled in the contrast between Jamaica and "happy *Britannia!* where Slavery is never known, where Liberty and Freedom chears every Misfortune."[25]

Readers of London's eminently fashionable *Gentleman's Magazine* encountered sometimes surprisingly stark antislavery sentiments. In 1735, this journal reprinted a remarkable antislavery essay arguing that it was the very picture of "Truth, Justice, and Morality" for colonial slave rebels "to struggle for Deliverance (for themselves and their Posterity) from a Condition worse than Death." The essayist added the supposed "Speech of *Moses Bon Saam*, a Free Negro," to some West Indian slave rebels. This speech expounded on the wretchedness and oppressions of slavery, and challenged the ideology of white supremacy "that bids a *White* Man, despise and trample on a *Black* one."[26] In 1740, the same magazine published an earnest essay by "Mercator Honestus" protesting against the brutalities of the slave trade and the "shocking" treatment of slaves in the West Indies. "Mercator" found it all so revolting that they wondered whether the perpetrators had "now quite put off their Nature? Is Humanity no more?"[27] Defending slave rebels and reading planters rather than slaves out of the ranks of humanity constituted strong antislavery medicine.

This tone extended to leading writers in the Scottish and English Enlightenments. William and Edmund Burke's history of European colonization conveyed the mainstream view of planters' cruel mismanagement of their slaves. This led to the startling conclusion that "the negroes in our colonies endure a slavery more compleat, and attended with far worse circumstances, than what any people in their condition suffer in any other part of the world, or have suffered in any other period of time."[28] Similarly, Adam Smith lamented that such unworthy souls as made up the planter class would wield absolute power over the noble souls of Africans. "Fortune never exerted more cruelly her empire over mankind," he rued, "than when she subjected those nations of heroes to the refuse of the jails of Europe, to wretches" whose distinguishing characteristics were their "brutality and baseness."[29] While Smith saw the master class as degenerate from the moment their progenitors left Britain, other observers, such as the massively influential French philosophe the Baron de Montesquieu, believed that slavery itself had wrought their declension from European civilization. Slavery, Montesquieu argued, might be theoretically defensible in the savage climate of the tropics, but it warped the masters' character by giving them "a power and a luxury they should not have."[30] Scottish legal thinker George Wallace was among the many British disciples of Montesquieu, whom Wallace termed "the greatest and the most humane politician of this, or perhaps of any age." Following in

Montesquieu's wake, Wallace branded slavery "horrid," "contrary to the feelings of humanity," "absurd," "barbarous," "cruel," "inhuman," "unnatural," and "irrational." As such, "it ought to be destroyed."[31]

This protest literature, among travelers as well as sedentary metropolitans, rising in a crescendo throughout the long eighteenth century, suggests that the common historical portrait of antislavery before the Age of Revolution as tepid or ineffective is overdrawn. Historian Jack P. Greene, for instance, has contended that before the 1760s, "few people explored the relationship between Englishness and slaveholding" or used slavery to raise "questions about the credibility of settlers' oft-claimed identities as English people" in the West Indies.[32] Robin Blackburn has gone so far as to say that "for nearly 400 years, struggles over slavery" in the Atlantic world "take place, as it were, offstage" until the Age of Revolution and its "rival conceptions of modernity" put slavery center stage politically. Thus, in Blackburn's judgment, one must wait until late in the eighteenth century to even see "any real philosophical and theoretical rejection of slavery."[33] But it all felt quite real for the targets of all the metropolitan rejections of slavery quoted above. To be sure, these appraisals across a long period and from multiple British appraisers certainly had their programmatic limits. But they had found slaveholders wanting as Britons, as participants in broader Enlightenment European civilizational norms ("conceptions of modernity" in Blackburn's terms), and even as Christians.

It also felt eminently political precisely because it was political as well as cultural. One political consequence was that it put white colonists, both in North America and the West Indies, very much on the defensive. Key metropolitan voices had challenged their Britishness and all that went with that cherished identity, and that caused them real cultural and political anxiety. As a rich historical literature has demonstrated, this challenge to their authority and gentility wove into the challenges they also perceived from below in their own colonies and households. And their defensiveness seems only to have increased from the seventeenth to the eighteenth centuries, whether traveling to Britain, receiving British visitors, or simply reading the metropolitan view of themselves. Their hunger for the kind of respectability that only the "metropolitan arbiters of fashion" could confer grew alongside the antislavery criticisms from those arbiters.[34] As Sean D. Moore has pointed out, there was a strong irony here given that the ownership of slaves had funded the subscription libraries in which so many aspiring colonial gentlemen read British and European criticisms of themselves. It is unsurprising, then, that the reflex of many white Americans was to defend slavery "as crucial not only to their economy" but also "to their sense of themselves as enlightened cosmopolitans" that had been integral to their pursuit of these libraries in the first place.[35]

Planters visiting or living in Britain may well have felt all this even more keenly than those living in the colonies. Among North Americans, aside from the (also often snubbed and frustrated) official colonial emissaries, it was elite Virginians and South Carolinians who were most likely to fit into this category.[36] The diary of the young William Byrd II, who lived in England from 1681 to 1705, provides a poignant portrait of the pursuit of acceptance and the experience of rejection, usually because he was a colonial. Similar themes dominated his return sojourns in the 1710s and 1720s.[37] In the next generation, Landon Carter studied in England for eight years, then sought to make his Virginia plantation the very image of enlightened Old World patriarchy.[38]

West Indian planters were even more likely than Virginians to be absentees in England, which is part of why they also proved touchy about the ongoing criticisms they received. William Beckford, an oft-absentee Jamaican planter who rose to political prominence in London in the 1740s and 1750s, knew that to complete that rise, his "imperial wealth" would have to be "mediated through traditional channels of influence," such as purchasing a country estate and entering party patronage networks. Yet for all those efforts, his political opponents found him an easy target to brand as "the king of negroe-land" who "hath been accustomed to the exercise of absolute dominion" over "his fellow creatures" and sought to import such Jamaican practices into London. As a result, he complained that Jamaica had "been grossly abused and misrepresented" in the metropole.[39] When Beckford became lord mayor of London in 1762, for instance, it was an easy move for a satirical writer in the *Gentleman's Magazine* to claim that his Jamaican background, complete with "a parcel of negroes" ready to "attend his will and pleasure," had prepared him "for the insolence of office." This piece was not ultimately about Beckford as a slaveholder; the main point was to protest the corruption of contemporary English politics. But the ill-gotten nature of his colonial wealth fit perfectly into the article's portrait of a corrupt class ready to abuse power. Editor Edward Cave dissented from this piece but had uphill work in countering the use of slavery in the essay; he could only weakly offer that Beckford "may make a good governor of freemen, though he is a lord of slaves."[40]

The responses of planters in the British Atlantic took multiple political forms. One was simply to insist, in all available channels, on more respect than the critics gave them. As Winthrop D. Jordan pointed out, this resulted in part from the religious nature of much of the criticism, which came across to touchy colonists as insufferably "holier-than-thou."[41] In the 1720s, Virginia grandee Robert Carter severed ties with a London merchant who had had care of his sons' education, but not before rebuking him for using "language that was hardly fit for your footman" in his letters to Carter. He finished this missive with the declaration that he "will be treated with respect by those that do my business."[42] In 1740, an anonymous West Indian writer complained that writers like "Mercator Honestus" had exaggerated the plight of the sugar islands' slaves and further groused that "their Misrepresentations" had been "too easily credited by others, in *England*." This was a "foul and abominable Injustice."[43]

A more obviously political version of this demand for respect was the constant and vehement assertions that white colonists deserved all the same political rights as did Britons at home. At its most extreme this feeling provoked violence, such as the 1710 murder of the Bermuda governor who had believed colonists in the Leeward Islands "possessed no English rights that he was bound to uphold."[44] A frustrated Maryland planter in the 1750s offered a highly racialized version of this lament. He longed for the day when English gentlemen would "hear that we are not all black, that we live in houses, speak English, wear clothes, and have some faint notions of Christianity," and would accordingly grant colonial whites the privileges their whiteness made their due.[45] To grouse that metropolitans saw colonists *as* Black rather than fixating on the colonists' treatment *of* Black people was a sleight of hand use of race that revealed the high degree to which this writer felt under attack.

In the eighteenth century, white colonists expanded cultivation of the positive portrait of slavery that had germinated in the seventeenth. Early eighteenth-century histories of Virginia published in London, for instance, lamented how "few people in England" entertained "correct notions of the true state of the Plantations" and pointedly depicted slavery in Virginia as idyllic.[46] William Byrd II, in letters to English aristocrats in the 1730s, developed such points into an insistence that Virginia planters constituted no exploitative master class. They lived on their plantations "in all the innocence of the patriarchs," he insisted, surrounded like the English gentry by "rural and domestick joys." He reiterated that those joys "are innocent," in part because the enslaved people's labor consisted basically of "gardening," which was less strenuous "by far, than what the poor people undergo in other countrys."[47]

Some granted slavery's violence but deployed maturing ideas of race to justify it specifically for Africans. Barbadians proved pioneers in this field as in so many others. Colonial authorities, such as Governor Jonathan Atkins in 1678, while acknowledging Barbados's laws as "being dissonant so much from the laws of England," pointed to "the severity of them being necessary here." A lawyer's report for the Privy Council in 1680 explained that harsh measures "not consonant" with English law were necessary because enslaved Africans were "a brutish sort of People and reckoned as goods and chattels in that island." And the colony's 1688 slave code put these ideas into law by decreeing that Africans "are of such barbarous, wild and savage nature" that they were "wholly unqualified to be governed by the Laws, customs and Practices of our nation."[48] In the eighteenth century, this strong association of Africans with savagery and disorder became an entrenched position of many whites from Boston to Barbados to Britain. Metropolitan John Oldmixon, for instance, explained away colonial slavery's severe laws and punishments by stating that African slaves were "very stubborn, are sullen and cruel, and their Masters are almost under a fatal Necessity to treat them inhumanely, or they would be ungovernable."[49] This was a far cry from later centuries' argument that slavery was such a positive good that slaves would never revolt; indeed, all such arguments and legislation flowed from the well-justified fear of slave resistance. Such an emphasis certainly did little to combat outside observers' sense that slave colonies were places of violence and disorder.[50] But these racial arguments combated the depictions of planters themselves as savages. And these experimental defenses were of real significance in the history of race as well as of slavery in the British Atlantic. As an absentee West Indian planter put it in 1764, "surely God" had ordained Africans "for the use and benefit of us." If God had not, "his Divine Will would have been manifest by some sign and token."[51] Such formulations in turn raised the stakes of religious and other opponents' repeated attacks on racial prejudice.

In 1735, "M" brought the racial and idyllic defenses of colonial slavery together in a letter to the *Gentleman's Magazine* in response to the Moses Bon Saam essay. After questioning the patriotism of a Briton who would cheer on slaves' resistance to His Majesty's forces, the writer declared that their purpose was "to convince the World of a common *Mistake, that those Negroes are under the most miserable Slavery.*" Slaves in the British West

Indies were far happier than rumored, for two reasons. First, the planters of British America, far from being petty tyrants, were "the most generous, humane, hospitable People in the World." Second, the transatlantic slave trade had "redeemed" Africans "from *native Slavery* to *savage Tyrants* of your own Complexion, and planted you here in easy Servitude" in which paternalistic masters provided for their wants. Bon Saam's motive, then, could only have been "to gratify his Lust of Rule, and make" his dupes "tenfold more his Slaves!"[52] This essay also joined the defense of slavery in the British Atlantic with the defense of the Britishness of the slaveholders, a natural result of metropolitans having arraigned both.

Another way in which eighteenth-century defenders of slavery linked it to Britishness was to offer a full-throated defense of its contributions to national greatness. This was a continuation of the belief among early English slave traders that allowed them to beseech and perceive God's blessings on their enterprises.[53] Especially amid the near-constant imperial war and constant imperial rivalries with the Catholic powers Spain and France sparked by the Glorious Revolution, anything that advanced Britain's power and ability to wage war could be seen to advance the cause of liberty and Protestantism. For nationalists thinking in this vein, expanded access to the transatlantic slave trade and newly acquired plantation colonies were to be celebrated as triumphs in the zero-sum jockeying for national advantage.[54] As historian Catherine Molineux has illustrated, the obvious material benefits of slavery induced many metropolitans, such as those selling colonial staple goods, to depict slavery with a certain "fuzziness" that "obscured" the "brutal realities" of what produced all that wealth.[55] This mental framework also convinced many planters that their plantations' productivity proved they were engines of both "moral and economic progress."[56] No one provided a better encomium to imperial trade than Sir William Keith, who in a 1738 pamphlet rhapsodized on "the impenetrable Connection wherewith the Interest of all" the members of "a Commercial State" were "cemented together into one firm united Body," and contrasted that with the "Slavery and Oppression of Men" under an arbitrary government. Trade thus worked "to secure and promote Peace and Prosperity to Mankind in Society, and all other rational Enjoyments of Life," including freedom itself.[57] It was a formula in which slave-trading Britain embodied freedom and its Catholic rivals embodied slavery.

In a series of pamphlets published in context of ongoing war against France and its allies, staunch British imperialists made explicit the link between the transatlantic slave trade and national greatness and even survival. In 1708, right in the heart of the first series of wars touched off by the Glorious Revolution, Oldmixon had lost patience with "the Scandal which the Enemies of the Plantations maliciously throw upon them." The "Prejudice" and "Ignorance" of these calumniators led them to miss the great economic contributions of especially the sugar islands. The fierceness with which the Spaniards and the French fought the British for possession over West Indian islands revealed their national importance. Therefore, "there are no Hands in the *British* Empire more usefully employ'd for the Profit and Glory of the Common-Wealth" than the sugar and tobacco planters. Oldmixon made no moral case for the colonies but rather this economic one, combined as it was with all the high ideals at stake in these wars. He even thought slave rebels should consider the Anglo-French conflict as central. If insurgent Africans in places like Barbados had succeeded, he lectured, European powers would never "have suffer'd them to set up a Negro Monarchy, or Republick, in the midst of their Governments." So most likely, rebels who cast off English masters would, "instead of serving Free-men, have been Slaves to Slaves, the French."[58]

Participants waged one of early modern England's great political disputes over slavery within this nationalist framework. From the 1680s to 1712, supporters of the monopoly of the Royal African Company (RAC) over English slave trading fought off those who pushed for a deregulation of this lucrative human traffic. As historian William A. Pettigrew has demonstrated, this long, hot debate took on a strong partisan hue, with Tories attacking the demands to dismantle the RAC monopoly as "questioning the very foundations of the empire and the royal prerogative upon which it was based," and seeing in them the specter of "phanatick principles" from the Civil War era. Equally predictably, Whig attackers argued that the monopoly was a symptom of the Stuarts' "arbitrary government," and claimed "the right to trade in African slaves as a deeply cherished English liberty." One writer got downright Orwellian, advocating the lifting of the RAC monopoly by blustering that monopolies "were always esteem'd the greatest Badges of Slavery and Oppression." Lobbyists for slaveholders and would-be slaveholders, especially from the Chesapeake colonies, found themselves working closely with metropolitan opponents of the RAC monopoly. At least on this side of this debate, then, "American slavery was the product of intentional, political interventions" that broke down the divide between imperial peripheries and center.[59]

For all its considerable divisiveness, this debate took for granted that the transatlantic slave trade and the resultant trade in slave-grown staple crops were a profit rather than a disgrace for the British Empire. Thus a group of slavers could complain, with no sense of irony or self-consciousness, to Parliament of the "unkind treatment" they had received from governors of slaving forts on the coast of Africa.[60] Precisely because the slave and staple trades were "the great Causes of the Increase of the Riches of the Kingdom," Joshua Gee wrote as late as 1738, attempts to reinstate the RAC monopoly should be resisted for the national good.[61] But the long-term victory of the deregulators hardly struck a blow for antislavery; it made Britain easily the leading slave-trading power in the world in the eighteenth century. The link between Britain and slave trading was so strong that planters in Guadeloupe and Cuba found it to their benefit to have Britain occupy their islands during the Seven Years' War.[62]

Other treatises linking slavery to nationalism were published in the 1740s, even deeper into the era of imperial wars. Britain "derives some of her chief Advantages" over rival powers from its preeminence in the slave and sugar trades, wrote an anonymous London essayist in 1741. To benefit from it but protest against it in principle, and insult the prosecutors of it, this writer pertly challenged, smelled "rank of a Spirit of Prevarication, and foul Attachment to the temporizing Way." It would be far better and more honest to embrace it openly and seek to expand Britain's participation as much as possible.[63] In 1745, the pseudonymous "British Merchant" treated it as self-evident that the trade in slaves and staple crops constituted "a Trade of such essential and allowed Concernment to the Wealth and Naval Power of *Great Britain*." Indeed, "it would be as impertinent to take up your Time in expatiating on that Subject as in declaiming on the common Benefits of Air and Sun-shine in general." Their real subject, then, was to inquire how Britain had let France impinge on British dominance in the trades in "those valuable People, the *Africans*," and in the resultant *"Plantation Produce."* "None but the greatest Enemy to his Country," the essayist charged, would make Britain helpless against France by ceding to them "the Riches of *Africa* and *America*, to support their *mighty* ARMIES and their NAVAL POWER."[64] The next year, Malachy Postlethwayt began his own essay by pronouncing that "our *West-India* and *African Trades* are the most nationally beneficial of any we carry on," and that the transatlantic slave trade was the lynchpin of it all. After a brief attempt to refute common British notions that the trade was inhumane, he moved from this consideration of "the welfare of the *Negroes*" back to his central consideration, the benefits to British shipping and manufacturing. If the government would press its advantages against "our Competitors" in Africa and the New World, France's "Naval Strength [would] be so reduced as never again to have it in their Power to insult us with Invasions, and threaten us with the Subversion of our happy Constitution." In short, all true patriots must see that "the INTEREST of the Nation in general" was "essentially connected with the Trade to *Africa*."[65]

This line of argument proved persuasive to Britons of widely varied ranks. For instance, as Abigail L. Swingen has shown, the South Sea Company scheme to rescue Britain from its wartime debt crisis in the 1710s was based entirely on the prospect of that company fulfilling Britain's newly won right to sell slaves to the Spanish Empire. The company's boosters counted on "a widespread perception among the British public that slavery and the slave trade provided" such economic strength to Britain that it "could even solve a vexing and potentially dangerous credit crisis."[66] Even many radical critics of the regime in England, from John Trenchard and Thomas Gordon in the 1720s through John Wilkes in the 1760s and 1770s, saw no need to question the economic and geopolitical value of the empire, including the trades in enslaved people and staple crops.[67] A very early slave narrative, the 1760 account of the life of enslaved black Bostonian Jupiter Hammon, also confirmed rather than contested this complex of ideas. From the point of view of later slave narratives Hammon's was an inverse tale of deliverance, telling of long captivity and servitude among Indians in Florida and the Spanish in Havana and of repeated attempts to escape home to Boston or at least to English territory. The climax of the narrative was when he was providentially reunited with "*my good Master*" on board a ship sailing from London to Boston. The moral of the story was thus that "*the Providence of that GOD*" had freed him "*from a* long *and* dreadful Captivity, among ... Savages," and returned him "*to my* own Native Land."[68] He would continue in bondage in Massachusetts, but the narrative celebrated Britain and its colonies as the epicenter not of slavery but of true religion and civilization, in contrast to Spanish and Native American barbarity.

But even this nationalist defense of the imperial slave system did not go unchallenged. As Paul Langford has written, the reform efforts of eighteenth-century British evangelicals "had more than a tinge of patriotic ardour." They refused to believe that unfettered pursuit of profit, without regard to social consequences, would actually "increase the nation's manpower at a time of growing international insecurity."[69]

"Mercator Honestus" made this link by insisting that the slave trade and slavery would ultimately prove self-destructive. "It is a Maxim with me," they preached, "that whenever a Man acts wrong, I mean knowingly, he acts contrary to his true Interest."[70] In the midst of the titanic Seven Years' War, George Wallace also rejected as horribly selfish the objection that "our colonies would be ruined, if slavery was abolished." It was the logic of the highwayman to insist "that the bulk of mankind ought to be abused, that our pockets may be filled with money, or our mouths with delicates." Moreover, Wallace insisted, "it is false, that either we or our colonies would be ruined by the abolition of Slavery." There might be some short-term "stagnation of business," but the benefits would be long-term, and the British economy would still prosper so long as Britons were "industrious."[71]

Enslaved people themselves played a major role in this debate, given that ongoing slave resistance proved a lynchpin of this refutation of the national advantages of slavery.[72] Africans' resistance was especially strong in Jamaica, whose strong maroon communities posed a special ongoing challenge to the plantocracy. As Edward B. Rugemer has written, the security threat dramatized by extensive London press coverage of "the protracted military conflict between colonial forces and the Maroons" in Jamaica contributed "an additional line of antislavery argument" that resonated throughout the Atlantic. Even Jamaica's Governor Edward Trelawny wrote to a London friend that the threat and actuality of race war on the island had stirred in him "loose thoughts" about abolishing slavery there. He shelved these ideas for a time, but in 1745 anonymously published a pamphlet centering on the enormous national security threat that unlimited trafficking in slaves posed to the colonies. Even amid maroon warfare, he lamented, the planters "cannot forbear indulging themselves both in their Indolence and fond Desire of more and more Negroes." So Trelawny had become convinced that "the Parliament at Home should interpose" just as would any parents "out of Pity to these their Children, who know not what they do, who are playing with Edge-Tools, which they cannot manage, and should be prevented from cutting themselves." In short, "I cannot think that the Parliament of *Great-Britain* ought to risqué the Security of so valuable an Island as *Jamaica*" by indulging the imbecility and inhumanity of the planters by continuing the slave trade apace.[73] The hazard and violence that was Jamaican slavery became even clearer in 1760–61 with Tacky's Revolt. This eighteenth-month-long war between enslaved insurgents and the Jamaican slave regime cost Britain the most lives of any engagement in the American hemisphere during the Seven Years' War except the Battle of Ticonderoga. Slave resistance on this scale thus gave a stronger impetus to those who sought to restrict the slave trade. Especially North American colonial legislators argued that such disastrous internecine warfare meant that "the interest of the Country" was not served by increasing the enslaved population.[74] Manifestly, Britons could not agree on issues surrounding slavery, even on the point of slavery's contribution to national security and even amid cataclysmic wars against a hated foreign enemy.

All these debates about the legitimacy and future of slavery in the British Atlantic created yet another story of division: of white colonists among themselves. Defenders of slavery and slaveholders' Britishness were at least matched in numbers and vociferousness by critics of both from within the ranks of colonial whites. One key political impact of this development was that residents of different colonies articulated regional distinctions within the British Empire to distance themselves from regions and colonies with which they had no desire to be aggregated.

Several strongly religious colonists joined the SPG and metropolitan Quakers in the chorus of critics of racism as well as of slavery. A 1710 pamphlet from Jamaica created a speech for an enslaved African complaining that "the *European* World" had declared that "we're of such base, such brutal Natures, that nought will govern us, but downright Force and Fear." But this was an "abominable Forgery! Hated Imposture! What, are we not Men?" In reality, "our Lords who call themselves Whitemen and Christians" had made themselves "barbarous" by daily subverting "the Laws of Nature, and the Order of Creation."[75] In a 1746 pamphlet, Pennsylvania Quaker John Woolman urged readers to "consider mankind as brethren."[76] Philadelphia's Anthony Benezet, Woolman's fellow Quaker abolitionist, also strongly contended for the intellectual and moral equality of Africans to Europeans. One of Benezet's pamphlets, for instance, included extended extracts from a London essayist who could only explain colonial planters' "cruel, barbarous" treatment of their slaves by race prejudice having warped their hearts and minds. Likewise, all perpetrators of the transatlantic slave trade allowed themselves to become veritable "Monsters in Nature," "destitute of all Humanity and Compassion."[77] Precisely because planters and slavers had defined Africans as subhuman, they themselves had drifted beyond the pale of humanity.

Colonial religious protesters also challenged the idea that the slave trade and slavery were in the national interest by making early forays into the argument that it provoked God's judgment.[78] As literary scholar Brycchan Carey has shown, fierce debate characterized the first century of Quakerism's interaction with slavery, but by 1758 "antislavery Friends had won the debate and were able henceforth to begin and sustain a debate with others beyond the Society." One impact of the length and intensity of that debate was that antislavery Quakers "had already developed, tested, and refined a sophisticated rhetoric of antislavery" combining altruistic with "more self-interested" appeals.[79] In 1754, the Pennsylvania Yearly Meeting warned that since slaveholding was consistent with neither "Christianity, nor common Justice," it "draws down the Displeasure of Heaven" on societies that tolerated it.[80]

Benezet proved especially important in developing both a set of ideas and the transatlantic infrastructure necessary to take an antislavery message well beyond the Quaker communities. It takes mental gymnastics with a high degree of difficulty, it seems to me, or at least a very narrow definition of the political, to see the work he and his collaborators were doing as apolitical. As Kirsten Sword has pointed out, depictions of colonial-era Quaker abolitionists as "ideologically pure but culturally insular and politically naïve" do not fit with the organizational work and political acumen of the likes of Woolman and Benezet. Likewise, David Waldstreicher has argued persuasively against the scholarly urge to dismiss these early Quaker abolitionists as "pious exotics who influenced no one because slavery was simply common sense" in the colonial period. Even their "pose of humility," in Waldstreicher's careful reading, "covers a multitude of politics." They should thus be taken seriously, he has rightly insisted, for their political acumen as well as the cross-generational influence of their arguments.[81]

Benezet's rhetorical work was also carefully targeted to his specific political milieu. In 1760, deep into the Seven Years' War, he connected Quaker pacifist and antislavery beliefs by suggesting that slave trading was at least "one Cause of the Calamities we at present suffer." "When a People offend" God "as a Nation, or in a publick Capacity," he admonished, God's justice "requires that as a Nation they be punished, which is generally done by War, Famine or Pestilence." Especially given "the number of natural Enemies" held in bondage in the land, then, the slave trade was "inconsistent with the Peace and Prosperity of a Country." In 1762, as the war still dragged on, Benezet included the idea of divine judgment in yet another antislavery essay.[82] Also during this war, Woolman warned that God "cannot be partial in our favour" when the cries of the enslaved "have reached the ears of the Most High!" God's judgment, therefore, was a key reason that "the effects" of the slave trade "are detrimental to the real prosperity of our country." And the instrument of that judgment would likely be "the Desire of Revenge" in slaves, "till the Inhabitants of the Land are ripe for great Commotion and Trouble."[83]

Colonists of other religious persuasions joined in this indictment and warning. In his letters from South Carolina to the SPG secretary between 1706 and 1717, Anglican minister Francis Le Jau tried his very best to limit his focus regarding enslaved Africans and Indians to their spiritual welfare. But he marveled that white Carolinians had convinced themselves "that we answer not before God" for atrocities such as "the Barberous usage of the poor Slaves." He thus strongly believed that both diseases and slaves' plotted rebellions constituted God's judgments; indeed, in 1713 he reflected that since arriving in Carolina, he had seen "Nothing Else almost but" "very Severe Judgments" for that godless colony's "Crying Sins."[84] A white Jamaican essayist thought that only "Divine Goodness and Forbearance" could explain why that colony had not yet experienced more "publick Calamitys."[85] Antislavery petitioners amid Georgia's serious internal debate in the 1730s and 1740s over adopting slavery appealed first and foremost to security concerns. They pled that on their unstable frontier with Spanish Florida, introducing more slaves would be "to have one Enemy without, and a more dangerous one in our Bosoms!" African slaves would "be our Scourge one Day or another for our Sins; and as Freedom to them must be as dear as to us, what a Scene of Horror must it bring about!" The protest from Darien, Georgia, was dated January 1739; colonial South Carolina's largest slave uprising, the Stono Rebellion, took place in September of that same year.[86]

Still other white colonists lamented slavery as the cause of the colonies' image problem rather than defending that image. As Katharine Gerbner has argued, the famous 1688 protest against slavery from Mennonites and Friends in Germantown, Pennsylvania, stemmed in large part from German-Dutch Quakers' worries about attracting new emigrants from Europe. "The 'marketable' aspect of Pennsylvania was its pure wilderness," she has pointed out, "and the institution of slavery worked against this image." But these protesters also leveraged another reputational idea that was calculated to appeal to a broader audience of European Christians. Christians at sea feared enslavement by Turks, but it was "worse for them, which say they are Christians" to themselves enslave Africans. Moreover, slave traders and slaveholders "surpass Holland and Germany" as persecutors, oppressing Black people for their skin color rather than their religion. "This makes an ill report in all those countries of Europe," they chided, "and for that reason some have no mind or inclination to come hither." "Especially whereas ye Europeans are desirous to know in what manner ye Quakers doe rule in their province," to outlaw slavery would satisfy not only the Germantowners' consciences but also those of potential immigrants for whom "it is a terrour, or a fairfull thing that men should be handeld so in Pensilvania."[87] These memorialists deployed a tactic that is a major theme in this book: shaming their audience by unfavorable reputational reference to a despised Other. But they did it twice over, negatively contrasting slaveholding Mennonites and Quakers with both their erstwhile European persecutors and Muslims.

Multiple antislavery Quaker writers echoed this theme. Taken together, their targets of shaming constituted an amalgam of province, religion, and nation. In 1693, George Keith challenged Quakers to "discover themselves to be true *Christians*" by leaving off slave trading and slaveholding. For their treatment of Africans "doubtless is far worse usage than is practised by the *Turks* and *Moors* upon their Slaves. Which tends to the great Reproach of the *Christian Profession*." In 1715, New Jersey Quaker John Hepburn chimed that Christian slaveholders were "a perpetual Scandal" to the good name of Christianity and even gave Muslims an excuse to enslave Christians. In 1729, Ralph Sandiford repeated the charge that this stumbling block kept Pennsylvania Quakers from setting the best possible example "to the Nations throughout the Universe."[88] In 1737, Benjamin Lay's sprawling antislavery treatise charged that alleged Friends who held slaves were the worst of hypocrites—they "come the nearest the Scribes & Pharisees of any People in the whole World"—destroying the good example of the gospel. Their cruelty was worse than the Turks, so they "shall receive the greater Damnation" for "this soul Sin, Slave-keeping."[89] Woolman pointed out that while "the *English* Government hath been commended by candid Foreigners for the Disuse of Racks and Tortures," colonists to their shame had revived such tortures for resistant slaves.[90] For his part, Benezet applied this notoriety to the whole British Atlantic, lamenting that the transatlantic slave trade was "a Reproach" to Britain and "to Christianity." And he reprinted a London antislavery piece whose author trembled at the "Load of Guilt" that lay "upon this Nation" on account of slavery and the slave trade. Those practices held up all Britons who enabled them "as a very bloody, cruel, barbarous People," even worse than the Spaniards, whom they were accustomed to "exclaim against."

"We reckon ourselves to be a brave, generous, humane, civilized People," this essay pursued, but slavery and the slave trade belied that so badly that they were "the greatest Scandal and Reproach that lies upon this Nation."[91]

More than Quakers bitterly conceded that slavery meant the colonies had earned their poor reputation throughout the British Atlantic. In 1700, Massachusetts Puritan Samuel Sewall also deployed the invidious Turkish distinction.[92] In 1710, a white Barbadian wrote an acrid little doggerel depicting "Barbadoes Isle inhabited by Slaves, / And for one honest man ten thousand knaves. / Religion to thee's a Romantick storey, / Barbarity and ill-got wealth thy glory."[93] Also in 1710, a pamphleteer writing as a Jamaican planter cried that cruelty to the enslaved presented a "miserable Spectacle in the face of the Sun and the World, . . . to the *shame* of those who call themselves *Men, good-natur'd Men*, and *Christians*." Moreover, this pamphlet hit where it hurt by arguing that British planters were even worse than French sugar planters because the latter but not the former allowed their slaves Christian baptism.[94] John Dickinson's letters to his parents during his time studying law at the Middle Temple between 1754 and 1756 provide an especially strong example of the ambivalence colonists felt about and in the metropolis. On the one hand, he found corruption in England's electoral politics disgusting. In that light, "America is, to be sure, . . . rude, but it's innocent." Yet one letter contains a remarkable passage casting massive doubt on that innocence. He saw that far too many young Americans in London showed themselves prickly upon finding that they did not enjoy "the respect & place they had at home," and he traced this to "their childhood. What a nest of vices shall we find in the education of a gentleman's son in America? The little mortal can no sooner talk than he is exercising his commands over the black children about him; no sooner walks, but he is beating them for executing his orders too slowly or wrong." "Governing slaves from his infancy" sowed in the young white American vast "crops of pride, selfishness, peevishness, violence, anger, meaness, revenge & cruelty."[95] Slaveholding in this rumination served as the worst marker and corrupter of provincialism.

The fact that Dickinson, scion of a slaveholding family whose holdings sprawled throughout the Mid-Atlantic, wrote about children raised in such families in the third person pointed to yet another political reaction to the British Atlantic's overall disdain for slavery: defending one's region by declaring other regions to be the true outsiders. One of the key fault lines, in part because it was firmly based in political and social realities, was between the West Indies and British North America.⁹⁶ In large part because of the menace of both the enslaved population and the French enemy, West Indian whites' powerful lobby in London had for decades pursued active support from the metropolitan government. They received it in the form of military aid and support for slave imports and sugar exports. The West Indies' tremendous economic importance to the empire explains this response. For instance, in the mid-eighteenth century, West Indian imports equaled 74 percent of Britain's total from the New World.⁹⁷

North Americans, especially in New England, understood the vital importance of their trade with the West Indies, but they resented the West Indians' outsized power in London and how that could impinge on their own sovereignty and interests. For instance, when North American legislatures like Virginia's enacted prohibitively high duties on imported slaves, the Board of Trade rather easily acquiesced to West Indian planters and British slave-trading merchants who demanded that the Board of Trade veto these laws.⁹⁸ These tensions came to a boil in Parliament in debates stretching from 1731 through 1733, lit by a bill tightening imperial trade restrictions in ways that would benefit the sugar islands. Petitioners from and advocates of the North American colonies and even Ireland did not hesitate to employ terms such as "impoverishment" and "ruin" in describing the bill's effects for them. They protested that this law would not only "absolutely ruin their trade" but also trample on their charter rights, whimpering that "they were subjects of England" and "should be heard" just as the West Indian lobby were. Were the West Indies to rule over all other colonies, they essentially asked, to the detriment of all? In one MP's stark formulation, the question at the heart of this debate was "whether the northern colonies, or the sugar-colonies ought most to be encouraged by this House." The delays in the success of this bill—from introduction in January 1731 to passage in May 1733—would have come as no consolation to its foes when it did pass.⁹⁹

New England probably constituted the region most different from the West Indies within the culture and politics of the empire. In eighteenth-century London, the planters of North America's southern colonies mixed easily with West Indian absentees, but neither mixed well with puritanical New Englanders, who tended to stand out as rustics. And as Adrian Chastain Weimer has recently shown, both New Englanders' self-image and their image in the metropolis differed widely from other regions of the empire when it came to questions of sovereignty. Not only during the period of the English Civil War but also deep into the Restoration period, their "constitutional culture" seemed different even as questions of power and governance echoed throughout the empire.[100]

Perhaps because of perceived similarities to suspect West Indians, Virginians seem to have worked the hardest to distinguish themselves in the metropolitan mind. The broad similarity among planters is reflected in George Washington's diary of his journey to Barbados in the early 1750s, in which he betrayed no sense of any great dissimilarities between Virginian and Barbadian society.[101] In his 1724 history published in London, on the other hand, Hugh Jones attempted to throw all colonists but Virginians under the bus. "If New England be called a receptacle of dissenters," he wrote, "Pennsylvania the nursery of Quakers, Maryland the retirement of Roman Catholicks, North Carolina the refuge of run-aways, and South Carolina the delight of buccaneers and pyrates, Virginia may be justly esteemed the happy retreat of true Britons and true churchmen for the most part." Virginia "consequently should merit the greater esteem and encouragement."[102] In a 1736 letter to an English earl, William Byrd II lamented that the ever-increasing number of enslaved Africans in Virginia led to "the necessity of being severe. Numbers make them insolent, and then foul means must do, what fair will not." But he hastened to add that "we have however nothing like the inhumanity here, that is practiced in the islands."[103] Given the timing and audience, this was a key entry not only in the cultural politics of the empire but also in the imperial politics of Virginia's attempted slave trade bans and West Indian influence blocking them. But it was likewise part of an emerging pattern in which white colonists embraced a wide range of postures in response to metropolitan disdain for slavery, but very few if any of those postures created a sense of white colonial solidarity.

For all the fronts on which Britons besieged other Britons for slaving, for all the need of historians to appreciate that debate rather than consensus characterized the colonial English and then British Atlantic, at the level of policy the slavers piled up more wins than losses. A growing body of historical scholarship is highlighting how late seventeenth-century English people of various stripes in the metropole, not just in the colonies, benefited from and were complicit in creating an empire-wide system of slavery. As Simon P. Newman's bracing recent book has demonstrated, a wide variety of Restoration-era white Londoners constituted a "connected community of slave-ownership" whose power is best emblematized by their pioneering of the genre of the fugitive slave advertisement.[104] As the work of historians such as Holly Brewer has demonstrated, neither side won a final victory at any point, and that only fed the politicization of slavery in the empire as contestants sought for new venues—Parliament, the courts, the Board of Trade, and so on—where they hoped for a friendly hearing. But even in individual arenas of conflict victory could never be total or stable, for in the politically volatile atmosphere that was seventeenth- and eighteenth-century England, who commanded a majority or otherwise controlled the levers of power in Parliament, or the courts, or the Board of Trade, changed drastically over time. "It's crucial to note how political" not only the decisions of these bodies but also their interpretations were, Brewer has aptly written, which history of fierce debate and political fluctuations fits uncomfortably with interpretations that have posited the colonial era "to be a time when no one questioned principles of enslavement."[105] Nevertheless, human traffickers and enslavers won more often than the rhetoric of free Englishmen would suggest, for reasons including but beyond the stark economic interests of the empire, even as understood in light of all that meant politically and culturally. Those reasons also included the uncertain relevance for chattel slavery of the continued deployment of the rhetoric of political slavery, and the decentralized nature of power that allowed those slavers high levels of control over the enslaved and other enemies of slavery where they held sway locally.

The political deployments of the s-word only increased in complexity and volume in the eighteenth century.[106] One of the most influential sources that kept this rhetoric alive was Joseph Addison's play *Cato*, a smash hit throughout the British Atlantic. Written in 1712, this drama set in ancient Rome dramatized such contemporary Britain's concerns as the clashes of liberty versus slavery and of true versus faux patriotism. Addison rendered these themes in sufficiently memorable phrasings that the play was constantly quoted and paraphrased by Anglophone writers and speakers throughout the century. The basic plot features Cato fighting for "honour, virtue, liberty, and Rome" against the ravaging tyrant Caesar. In a Senate debate over how to respond to Caesar's approaching army, Cato's ally Sempronius exclaims, "Gods, can a Roman senate long debate / Which of the two to chuse, slavery or death!" Cato himself proclaims that "a day, an hour, of virtuous liberty, / Is worth a whole eternity in bondage." For all his immoderate rhetoric Sempronius turns out to be the chief of many traitors to the cause of liberty. Cato, however, remains so incorruptible that when his son dies fighting Caesar, he triumphs, asking, "Who would not be that youth? What pity is it / That we can die but once to serve our country!" He lives up to that creed in the final scene, falling on his sword rather than submit to Caesar.[107]

As with subsequent eras, the use of the s-word was so multifarious that many of its deployers paused to assure readers that they, at least, were using it precisely and appropriately.[108] These clarifiers agreed broadly that slavery, whether in politics or on a plantation, consisted of unchecked power in the master. In a 1689 political tract, Increase Mather groused that in the wake of recent imperial legislation revoking Massachusetts's charter and increasing the powers of the colonial governor, "the people in *New-England* were all *Slaves*." But without moving to a new sentence, he added the proviso that "the only difference between them and *Slaves* is their not being bought and sold."[109] In his influential 1698 pamphlet arguing for the legislative sovereignty of Ireland's Parliament, William Molyneux protested that "the Religion, Lives, Liberties, Fortunes, and Estates of the Clergy, Nobility, and Gentry of *Ireland* may be dispos'd of, without their *Privity* and *Consent*." Professing reluctance "to give their Condition an *hard Name*," he nevertheless concluded that "I have no other Notion of *Slavery*, but being Bound by a Law to which I do not Consent."[110] Viscount Bolingbroke, in influential essays in the 1730s, clarified that "tyranny and slavery do not so properly consist in the stripes that are given and received, as in the power of giving them at pleasure." Whether inflicted by a king or an individual subject, then, the essence of slavery was arbitrary power to which only "oriental slaves" and their ilk would submit.[111] South Carolinian Christopher Gadsden echoed this concept in 1763 when he lauded George III for desiring "to reign solely in the hearts of *free* people, not over a parcel of *slaves*." Free men, he specified, "have an *inherent* not *promissive* right to be so," as their very "birth-right" under their country's laws.[112]

Given that this was an era of imperial rivalry and war, many deployers of slavery rhetoric cunningly intertwined it with nationalism. Critics of British governments, for instance, employed multiple comparisons to slavery and tyranny elsewhere, never to the advantage of their British targets. As early as 1649, the radical Gerrard Winstanley demanded, "if the common people have no more freedom in England" than to work as subordinates for wages, "what freedom then have they in England more than we can have in Turkey or France?"[113] In a 1721 essay, Mary Astell protested that "in all the Eastern Parts of the World," women, "like our Negroes in our Western Plantations, are born Slaves," but that in Europe "our Condition is not very much better."[114] In 1762, a group of Scottish colliers connected their appeal to be released from bondage to British pride in being the land of liberty rather than slavery. The very first objection to their state, the address read, must be that "it is inconsistent with *British* Liberty, and repugnant to the Spirit of Christianity; which last Consideration has abolished Slavery throughout all *Europe*."[115] While leveraging the concept of slavery to shame fellow Britons, this rhetorical move by itself would have rendered African slavery in the New World impervious to critique, given its presumption that white Protestant Britons were the ones preeminently unsuited for slavery.

Similarly circumscribing the antislavery potential of this sort of rhetoric was its deployers' deep distaste for qualities they characterized as slavish. In the 1720s, influential opposition writers John Trenchard and Thomas Gordon stated that to please a particular party "is the base office of a slave, and he who sustains it breathes improperly English air." The air in France or Turkey "would suit him better." Taking "Cato" as their penname in the decade after Addison had written his play, they used slavery as an all-purpose central trope for the dangers of political tyranny, abusing tyranny's victims and perpetrators alike as slaves possessed of a slavish spirit. "A spirit that would not submit to slavery," indeed one that disdained "the odious company of slaves," was what they prescribed for Georgian England.[116] One writer gave particularly vigorous voice to Whigs who detested the Tory doctrines of passive obedience and nonresistance to government by proposing that the SPG send "our Apostles of Slavery and Passive-Obedience . . . to preach to the poor Negroes, who are so cruelly treated." Furthermore, they "should be liable to the same Treatment themselves, that they may have a little Taste of the Slavery they would so fain bring upon the *British* Empire."[117] Such dismissive or angry depictions of Britons surrendering their liberty continued throughout the century as a stock in trade among still others protesting the corruption of the Georgian regimes. One such usage, from Oliver Goldsmith in 1764, linked to colonial slavery by arguing that the rich ruled by way of "the wealth of climes where savage nations roam, / Pillag'd from slaves to purchase slaves at home."[118] English radical John Wilkes vented his fear and loathing of Scottish influence on British politics by remembering 1745 as an occasion on which "the *English* were so gallantly fighting for the liberties of Europe" but had to return to fight "their fellow subjects of *Scotland*, who were forging chains for both nations" by supporting the second Jacobite uprising. These Scots, then, "not only refused the liberty they might enjoy themselves, but endeavoured to entail *their* vassalage and slavery on the whole island."[119]

One structural political fact that also blunted the impact especially of metropolitan antislavery sentiment was that for much of the colonial period, the empire worked de facto as a sort of federal system in which colonists had tremendous control over institutions like slavery. As Peter S. Onuf put it so well, while the British Empire was "unitary in theory," especially at certain moments of attempted centralization of power, it was "'federal' in practice" for most of its history. "The central principle" of what Mary Sarah Bilder has analyzed as the "transatlantic constitution" of the empire was "that a colony's laws could not be repugnant to the laws of England but could differ according to the people and place" across colonies. This understanding was never fully stable, but it did develop from "a continuous conversation" between the metropolis and colonies as well as among the colonies. While British constitutional thinkers and policymakers tried to define the colonies as both separate from and dependent on Britain, colonists especially in their legislatures constantly probed where they fit on that spectrum in practice. When functioning smoothly, "transatlantic legal culture valued a certain pragmatism and flexibility" over "conceptual consistency." This led to a reliance on the consent of colonial elites rather than force in holding the empire together.[120] This had been true even before the union with Scotland in 1707, given the constitutionally anomalous situation of Ireland as neither an independent kingdom nor officially part of the empire. One scholar has aptly characterized English thought and practice toward Ireland's constitutional place across centuries as an "untidy jumble." But union with Scotland only increased the reality of multiplicity rather than uniformity within Britain itself, and by extension within the empire.[121]

Pressed to its conclusion, this federal logic could allow metropolitans to have their cake of antislavery sentiment and sweeten it with slave-grown sugar. Eliga H. Gould has shown that in a variety of imperial concerns, including the existence and legitimacy of slavery, cultural assumptions throughout the British Atlantic created a "legal geography" treating Europe as "a zone of law and civility" governed by international law, while the colonial zone lay beyond that line. In this conception, slavery with all its barbarity was actually appropriate to the New World in a way it could not be in the Old.[122] Even Charles Leslie, for all his revulsion for Jamaica, believed that the path to order there was for the colony to actually enforce its draconian slave laws. This attitude could extend to indentured servitude as well. In 1730, for example, the Pennsylvania Council defended the practice by pleading that "altho' in Britain they are wholly Strangers to Servitude as practised amongst us," the forms of unfreedom practiced in the colonies were "highly reasonable" for that context.[123]

As several scholars, led by Sue Peabody, have demonstrated, many European imperial powers practiced this compartmentalization between a free-soil Europe and a slave-soil New World. This concept of free soil had medieval roots but flourished with the rise of the transatlantic slave trade, particularly when enslaved people in metropolitan centers leveraged the concept to challenge their bondage. They and their representatives also proved adept at connecting the concept to all-important national pride. In 1759, the lawyers for a South Asian named Francisque pled for his freedom before the Parlement and public of Paris that "the natural and wise laws" of France should free Francisque. Significantly, these lawyers granted that "without a doubt" slavery was legal for Africans in the New World. This agreed with a French minister who had bluntly called the colonies "the place of slavery." And in France as in England, the desire for distance from slavery had the darker side among those who argued that Black people in general needed to be kept from the metropolis.[124] What it all added up to in the British Empire, as Seymour Drescher has put it, was a mix of plaintive metropolitan hopes for colonial laws to be "agreeable to the laws of England, and be not contrary to the Christian Faith," while in practice "the institution of slavery evolved with maximum legal protection and minimal legal hurdles for slave-owners" in English and British colonies.[125]

However, there were important moments of change, both potential and actual, in the ways this constitutional arrangement worked. After the Restoration, the Stuart regimes nurtured dreams of imposing the sort of authoritarian rule on their colonial possessions that eluded them in England itself. Stuart authorities represented in the Lords of Trade issued increasingly imperious dictates to colonial governments that repeatedly touched off open and serious conflicts both at home and in the colonies. Control over the transatlantic slave trade featured prominently in these debates, further confirming the politicization of that trade.[126]

Although the Glorious Revolution overthrew those Stuart dreams, its elevation of Parliament's authority to the supreme position within the English constitution created a great deal of momentum toward centralization of authority in that Parliament. "Whig regimes after 1688," J. C. D. Clark has summed, "progressively destroyed adjacent assemblies in the name of unified authority." Extinguishing Scotland's Parliament in 1707 with union was just one example of this drive. Eventually both imperial rulers and loyal colonial subjects rallied behind a concept in which the King-in-Parliament was sovereign, locals controlled day-to-day governance, and the empire would defend both the Protestant interest and the safety of its subjects. This consensus, helped along in white colonists' minds by fear of foreign and internal enemies, created more imperial stability than had the Stuarts' more heavy-handed attempts to centralize authority in London.[127]

The ultimate turning point in the imperial constitution came in the era of the Seven Years' War. Waging a global war on an unprecedented scale convinced imperial rulers of the need to command obedience rather than seek consent from colonial subjects. William and Edmund Burke bespoke these new metropolitan attitudes when they remarked on the levels of attention metropolitans now paid to their colonies, and described the New World as the outright "property" of the European powers to whose empires it belonged. After British victory in the war resulted in far-flung territorial acquisitions, "the American view of empire as a partnership between more or less equal communities enjoying the rights of Englishmen" seemed even less applicable to an increasingly multiethnic global imperium.[128] Centralization and political integration became the watchwords in Westminster and Whitehall. That ushered in a new chapter in not only the British Empire but also in the Anglo-American politics of slavery.

PART TWO

Imperial Crisis and War

In 1768, Benjamin Rush, a medical student and aspiring Enlightenment figure from Pennsylvania, visited the Palace of Westminster in London. In the House of Lords' chamber, he recalled to a friend, "I felt as if I walked on sacred ground. I gazed for some time at the Throne with emotions that I cannot describe." And after "importuning" their reluctant guide "a good deal," Rush was even able to sit reverently on that throne. But his years studying medicine in Edinburgh had hardly quelled his pride in being a North American; to the contrary, also in 1768 he had pledged "to devote my head, my heart, and my pen entirely to the service of America." So when his tour group entered the House of Commons, he could not say he felt he was treading "on 'sacred ground' here. This, I thought, is the place where the infernal scheme for enslaving America was first broached."[1]

Rush had such contrasting feelings because it was that House of Commons that had birthed the measures taxing and more firmly regulating the trade of Britain's colonies—starting with the Sugar Act of 1764 and the Stamp Act of 1765. These laws outraged this devoted British subject in part because they seemed to mark him and his out as provincials whose rights might well be inferior to that of full-fledged Britons. As one who was in about equal parts a committed abolitionist and a committed American Patriot (or opponent of the ministry's measures), Rush did not use the loaded term "enslaving" lightly. Indeed, the fact that he employed that word to communicate his full vehemence was entirely typical of the debate surrounding these controversial laws.

Britons and North Americans weaponized slavery as a concept and reality more extensively and intensively than ever before amid the political and military crises of the British Empire between 1764 and 1783. In this context, past themes in the imperial politics of slavery, such as the role unfree labor played in metropolitan disdain for colonists, gained a new edge. That prehistory mattered, however, because having the basic concepts and language in place enabled the combatants on both sides in the imperial crisis to go quickly from zero to sixty with the slavery rhetoric.[2]

Indeed, this crisis intensified or reintensified multiple previous themes in the politics of slavery. Using the term "slavery" and its cognates, for instance, became a way to signal one's perception of the enormity of the stakes involved in the controversy, much as it had been previously amid the white-hot politics of the English Civil War era. And the need to protect both individuals' and whole groups' images as true patriots and lovers of freedom carried greater urgency in the vortex of this long debate. The pressures of this unusually sustained and intense debate pegged the premiums for being seen as consistent, and for articulating one's points precisely, at an all-time high in participants' lifetimes. That was also true in part because all these debates and policy choices surrounding slavery touched on core ideals in the British Atlantic world beyond liberty, including honor and humanity.

In recent years, historians have debated the degree to which slavery drove the debates of the imperial crisis and Revolutionary War years, or featured as an adjunct to other issues. To paint broadly, a literature dating back at least to the middle of the twentieth century posited that the American Revolution resulted from American Patriots' dedication to a republican ideology through which they read imperial measures of taxation and control as so deeply threatening that only terms like "slavery" would suffice to dramatize that threat. In this formulation, actual chattel slavery might or might not have become a pressing issue during this era, but if it did that was as a result rather than a cause of the American Revolution.[3] Gordon S. Wood has ratcheted up the stakes of this emphasis on the Patriots' stated ideals by accusing those who accentuate sectional and class division, beginning with the Progressive historians but including many today, of perpetrating a "denigration of ideas."[4]

Other historians have begged to differ, and these are the loudest voices in recent years, at least within academia. They argue that the desire to protect American slavery and white supremacy from British threats comprised one if not the key Patriot motive from very early in the contest. Scholars including Robert G. Parkinson argue that the Patriots would not have embraced independence as a goal had not the British posed such a threat to slavery and white supremacy beginning in 1775. As Woody Holton has provocatively phrased it, "no other document—not even Thomas Paine's

Common Sense or the Declaration of the Independence—did more than" Lord Dunmore's Proclamation offering freedom to enslaved Americans "to convert" white Americans "to the cause of independence." Neither has Holton shied away from comparing the American Revolution to the American Civil War, both being battles "over slavery and sovereignty."[5] Beginning in 2019, the *New York Times*'s "1619 Project" gave a popular megaphone to this interpretation, depicting white American revolutionaries as unified by the threat they perceived the British regime posed to slavery and white supremacy.[6]

So influential is this interpretation that a recent historiographical essay positing that white men built American nationhood around the idea "that achieving 'life, liberty, and the pursuit of happiness' would be restricted to themselves" argues that those who highlight sectional and other divisions in the early American republic only do so because they "have not yet fully internalized" this interpretation. Nor does the condescension stop there: blinded by "hindsight," knowing that the American Civil War was coming, these scholars "still rehearse earlier myths," perversely resisting the idea that "when push came to shove," whites in early America "came together as a nation" strictly "for the benefit of white settlers."[7]

Even many scholars who have offered more nuanced portraits stress slavery as a causal factor for the Revolution. Jason T. Sharples, for instance, posits that "conspiracy scares accelerated political affiliation," rather than causing it. The "terrifying events" of mass slave flight and proliferating slave conspiracy scares "confirmed for white colonists exactly which center of power, provincial or imperial, they could rely on to safeguard their persons and privilege." Sharples also refines the Parkinsonian interpretation, in which defending slavery and white supremacy bound the Patriots together across regions, by differentiating the political effects of insurrection anxiety by region, arguing that "the conspiracy scares of the American Revolution accelerated political tendencies peculiar to each region" in which slaveholders were dominant. "The stable continuation of this exploitative system" seemed to fearful slaveholders to dictate more reliance on the empire in the West Indies and independence in North America. His discussion by emphasis, however, like so much other recent literature, is definitely in the Parkinson-Holton camp.[8]

The section of this book that follows this introduction, by contrast, tries to embody an answer to the following questions: What would the republicanism literature look like if it took slavery more seriously, exploring its full complexity as a political weapon? What if that literature had seen slavery as inevitably interwoven with, rather than a byproduct of, the headliner political issues analyzed in that historiographical tradition? What would the more recent scholarship emphasizing slavery as an issue in the American Revolution look like if it took political issues like taxation and representation more seriously? As Samuel Fisher has put it in relation to the role Britain's Native American allies played in Patriot grievances and political rhetoric, current historiography on the causes and consequences of the American Revolution tends to be too narrowly focused and reductive. That is, both the "'idealist' interpretations" stressing political ideas and marginalizing race, and scholars who reverse that by putting race alone at the center, oversimplify matters. In no way "peripheral" to nor "divorced from" the political questions driving Patriot resistance, Fisher has demonstrated, Britain's Indigenous allies proved "central to the American case." Thus, "we need not—in fact, should not—choose between a focus on Indians"—and, I would add, Black people enslaved and free—"and a focus on" the political debates of the era. "They cannot be divorced from each other."[9]

Indeed, far from cordoning slavery off as a separate issue, political combatants on both sides of the American Revolution connected it to all the headline issues of the conflict as well as all of their adjuncts. It would have been the most surprising outcome had they not done so. This extended, intense political conflict—in a way that should not surprise political historians of other similar eras of conflict, or any observer of our own hyperpartisan times in the twenty-first century—politicized all manner of issues that would seem to have been beyond the realm of politics. In the late 1760s in Virginia, for instance, the question of whether to inoculate against smallpox "became entangled with the imperial crisis," and who did and did not inoculate broke down along party lines.[10] Furthermore, it was no reach for participants to marshal slavery in these debates, given how central slavery was to the British Atlantic and how natural it had become by the 1760s to make such connections. As historian Kirsten Sword has pointed out, it is telling that these male Patriots chose not to resort to another analogy available to them: that they were being treated like wives. "Marriage worked better as a symbol of social order," she has suggested, "than as a metaphor for social injustice." So comparing themselves to wives would not only have unsexed them but also have failed to suggest the abuse of authority they wanted to dramatize.[11] Weaponizing slavery in this precisely targeted way both indicated how toxic the extended imperial crisis was and further poisoned it. In all these ways the politics of the American Revolution proved to be a hyper-dramatic opening act in the Anglo-American politics of slavery.

Paradoxically, this political war that trafficked in absolute statements of right and wrong incubated a bewildering proliferation of usages of the s-word that made its impact on actual chattel slavery far from clear, unitary, or predictable. Its complexity stemmed in great measure from the ways in which participants' stances on race and slavery interacted with other priorities and identities. Preexisting antislavery or proslavery commitments led some Britons and North Americans to approach the imperial crisis as an opportunity to raise awareness and support for their positions. But it worked the other way around with a much larger group: Patriots and Loyalists who initially did not seem to have thought much about slavery and race found rhetoric and policies in that genre to be useful to winning the core debates (and the war). The smaller band of participants who cared equally about their positions on slavery and on the mainstream political issues were left to decide which loyalty would take priority and what that would mean for the other. Just as the concept and reality of slavery, then, had a complicated impact on the imperial crisis and war, the imperial crisis and war had a complicated impact on the political situation of the institution of chattel bondage in North America and Britain by 1783. Contemporaries thus had no way of predicting the future of this institution or gauging how the course and outcomes of the crisis and war would shape that future.

3

Stakes

∽∾

THE IMPERIAL crisis and Revolutionary War alarmed and disoriented many contemporaries because these years seemed to comprise a series of crises whose seriousness ratcheted ever upward. Patriots found the rhetoric of slavery a perfect way to dramatize that seriousness. It was such a powerful rhetorical tradition in English and political tradition in the British Atlantic that Loyalists had to find ways to counter this Patriot appeal.

The initial stage of the controversy raised serious questions of sovereignty, power, identity, and self-interest. This phase of the crisis was headlined by the Stamp Act of 1765 but also included other monumental pieces of legislation such as the Declaratory Act asserting Parliament's sovereignty over the empire in 1766 and a series of tax measures known as the Townshend Acts in 1767. Many observers on both sides described the conflict over these acts in terms not usually reserved for normal legislation and evinced a clear understanding that they were living through such a major turning point it constituted what historians have called a "Moment." In 1768, for instance, a speaker in Parliament flatly declared that "the present state of our colonies ... is the most momentous subject ever under consideration."[1]

And then, beginning in 1769, the Patriots and their allies raised the stakes yet again. As scholar Eric Nelson has shown, in this second phase of the imperial crisis, they articulated a concept of empire in which the crown had sovereignty over the colonies but Parliament had none.[2] As George Grenville, the very author of the Stamp Act, put it in 1770, seeking to remove Parliament's but not the king's authority over the colonies would encourage absolutism's return to Britain. He would never "lend my hand to forge chains for America" in this way, "lest I should forge them for myself." Thus, especially after 1769, Loyalists could only see the Patriots and their sympathizers as guilty of sedition. In short, as Grenville put it on another occasion, "everything that was dear to us was at stake" in the imperial crisis.[3]

Much as the Patriots' position after 1769 escalated the Loyalists' sense of crisis, the British government's coercive response to the late 1773 Boston Tea Party heightened the opposition's fears for British liberty. The harsh measures toward the colonies known as the Coercive Acts (what Patriots called the Intolerable Acts) marked, as historian Bernard Donoughue put it, "the end of vacillation and compromise" by successive ministries since 1765, explicitly stating that the government sought to secure the submission of the colonists.[4] This development intensified the conflict even further. "To settle the Rights, & ascertain the privileges of a Continent like this" in an environment fraught with such risk, wrote Silas Deane in 1774, "is a Work of Time, & serious beyond the Conception of a bystander."[5]

Of course, the outbreak of war in Massachusetts in April 1775 represented a yet more serious escalation of the crisis. As the analysis of historians including Dror Wahrman has shown, in Britain the war brought to a head many of the most serious questions about identity in the British Empire, as both supporters and opponents cast about for how to conceptualize the American Patriots—were they brothers, cousins, foreigners? As a civil war, "the American war was irreducible to any reliable map of 'us' and 'them' based on a stable criterion of difference." As with any such crisis, "the American war brought to a cataclysmic head trends that had long been developing gradually and imperceptibly beneath the surface, turning them from tentative possibilities to overbearing actualities."[6]

It is worth emphasizing that both sides' purposes in waging the war remained essentially political, so the advent of war did nothing to lessen the significance of political rhetoric. Given that neither the British government at home nor especially the Patriots in North America had unassailable majority support, both sides saw waging effective ideological warfare as vital to both growing and unifying their ranks. In this setting, even military commanders valued propagandists and printing presses as highly as bullets and cannons.[7] For instance, Lord North's ministry showed itself fully willing to orchestrate demonstrations of "the British public's willingness to assist in the war effort," as Eliga Gould has written. They got up loyal petitions and addresses in addition to offering vigorous speeches in Parliament, in an effort to cultivate "the same national purpose that had carried the British through previous struggles." An ocean away, Lord Dunmore, beleaguered royal governor of Virginia, seized the Patriot printing press in Norfolk early in the war, citing the damage it had done "in exciting, in the minds of all ranks of people, the spirit of sedition and rebellion."[8] For his part, Patriot chieftain George Washington possessed a keen understanding of the political nature of the war. So he pored over British pamphlets and proclamations just as he did maps and military reports.[9]

And then in 1776, the American Congress's Declaration of Independence confirmed Loyalists' long-running charges that the professedly loyal Patriots had aimed all along at the power grab of separation from the empire. The issues had gone beyond even major adjustments in the imperial constitutional arrangement, although that reality dawned slowly on some British officials.[10] By its high-flying rhetoric of universal liberty and equality, the Declaration raised social and political questions that in the short run only further destabilized categories of difference in the British Atlantic and would drive Anglo-American conflict for decades thereafter.[11] This accumulating weight of issues led Samuel Johnson to remark in 1777 that "there was hardly ever any question of great importance before Parliament, any question in which a man might not very well vote either upon one side or the other," but "that respecting America," in all its ramifications, was an exception to that rule.[12] Johnson's sovereign agreed wholeheartedly, so much so that in spring 1782, when a parliamentary vote forced him to accept a new ministry pledged to negotiating independence with the United States, George III drafted documents abdicating his crown. In spring 1783, he once again drafted a resignation letter.[13]

Finally, the newly styled United Colonies' alliances with European powers, headed by Britain's bitter enemy France, raised the stakes for the British Empire yet again. This was such a dramatic shift in the nature of the war that it relegated the preservation of British control over North America to a lesser position than defending the West Indies, Gibraltar, India, and even at times the British Isles themselves.[14] Antiwar Britons, such as Edmund Burke, decried it in its new aspect as the climax of an "era of calamity, disgrace, and downfall, an era which no feeling mind will ever mention without a tear in England."[15] The prospect of French entry into the war led one opposition MP to execrate the ministry as having "precipitated this nation from the highest pinnacle of fame and happiness, to the lowest abyss of wretchedness and disgrace." "There may not be a week between us and total ruin," cried another.[16] Lord North, despite being the most powerful champion of the war in principle, did not disagree that another costly global war, this time with France's allies far outnumbering Britain's, might "undo" Britain. He repeatedly portrayed to King George III "the very alarming situation of the country" in this changed war situation.[17]

The monarch's response to North in this setting, that he trusted "in the justness of my cause and the bravery of the Nation," encapsulated the determination of many Britons to continue the war not despite, but especially in light of, the entry of France and its allies. That development had clarified that justice, for even those who had hesitated to fight Americans had no such compunctions about the French. As the parliamentary majority phrased it in their address to George III in November 1779, Britain now fought "to save not only their own rights, but the liberties of other free states, from the restless ambition and encroaching power of the house of *Bourbon*."[18] The widening of the conflict in this way made it at once more familiar and more existential for Britons.[19]

The ideas involved in these crises, at least as much as the events themselves, elevated contemporaries' sense of what was in question. The sense that the rights of subjects and the powers of governments were arguably being redefined by the ministry's taxation policies, and undeniably being redefined by new legislation for Quebec and Ireland, heightened the unease for all involved. Victory in the Seven Years' War transformed the empire by giving Britain claims to power over a much more diverse assortment of subjects—ranging from Canada to India—who were neither ethnically British nor Protestant. "Subjecthood" in this new British Empire, scholar Hannah Weiss Muller has written, "would be chosen, negotiated," and redefined by British policies toward these new subjects. The Quebec Act of 1774 proved particularly explosive as it sided with the French inhabitants' notion that subjecthood meant being "entitled to live under their ancient 'customs and usages' even if these were French."[20] The imperial crisis also intensified the determination of Anglo-Irish "Patriots" to protest London's control over Irish legislation in terms of sovereignty, rights, and liberty. These Irish Patriots consciously modeled their agitation on the tactics of the American Patriots and unapologetically leveraged the dire situation of the war for Britain. And they achieved concessions from London culminating in the 1782 repeal of the Westminster Parliament's veto power over the Dublin Parliament's legislation.[21]

These also seemed like no ordinary debates in part because of the leading role Britons expected their empire to play within the story of human liberty. Arthur Young was one who took a global view by calculating that only about 33 million of the Earth's 775 million inhabitants enjoyed the inestimable blessing of political freedom, "and of these few so large a portion as 12,500,000 are subjects of the British empire." This should inspire Britons to defend "this sacred temple of THE NATION'S HONOUR."[22] Many another writer and speaker (both in private and public) likewise urged their audiences to preserve the rights and earn the good opinion of posterity. On the current generation's political choices, scribbled one, "depends, under a superintending Providence, the fate of your posterity, perhaps your own fate."[23]

As that concluding suggestion demonstrates, participants conceived the stakes of this contest to be enormous for Britain itself, not just for its empire. Precisely because it struck home in so many ways, as Troy Bickham has written in his study of the volume (in both senses) of press controversies of 1763–83, "the American Revolution was perhaps the most nationally divisive event in Britain during the eighteenth century."[24] Losing the empire's grip on North America, many observers were convinced, would have dire consequences for Britain's ability to defend itself in a dangerous neighborhood full of enemies. One commentator declared this a question of "whether Great Britain shall be the first country in the world or ruined or undone."[25] In 1768, MP Isaac Barre warned the House of Commons against further alienating the colonies, in part because "this country can not last long, if we are reduced to our little insular insignificance."[26] George III shared this vision that losing North America amid military defeat meant "certain ruin" for Britain, sinking it to "a state of inferiority" within Europe.[27]

Loyalist Britons also believed that the very British constitution hung in the balance. Looking back from 1822, the British politician John Nicholls explained the French Revolution as a product of how the American Revolution "produced, through the whole of Europe, a discussion as to the rights of governors and governed." But it was more even than that, as historian Justin du Rivage has argued recently. "At stake were power and property, equality and inequality, sovereignty and subordination," and these big concepts had implications for more than the colonies.[28] Contemporaries said as much from the beginning. In 1766, the *Gentleman's Magazine* proclaimed that Parliament's debates on repealing the Stamp Act "relate to a subject of greater importance than ever engaged the attention of the public since the memorable question, Whether the subjects of *Great Britain* were to be bond or free." A group in the House of Lords opposed to the Stamp Act's repeal resolved that to admit any limit on

Parliament's supremacy would "not only surrender the honour and essential interests of the kingdom now and forever, both at home and abroad, but will also deeply affect the fundamental principles of our constitution."[29]

The war hardly decreased their self-image as defenders of the beleaguered British constitution. Kathleen Wilson likewise has made a vigorous case for this "war's profound impact on domestic political culture and the intensity of the rifts in the nation that it produced." This is because "the colonial conflict crystallized in England competing ideas about the nature of authority and liberty, the meaning of patriotism and the role of the people in the political process." These and related issues "would impact popular politics for the next half-century."[30] In 1777, a pseudonymous writer in the *Gentleman's Magazine* captured a major thrust of wartime Loyalist arguments when they starkly branded pro-American preacher and writer Richard Price "one of the most dangerous enemies of the constitution, and therefore eventually of liberty."[31] In 1780, a parliamentary reporter marveled that an administration supporter responded to a speech by an opposition MP with "the strongest language we ever heard made use of in a House of Parliament." And then in June of that year, when members of the House of Lords quite literally came to debate bearing "some marks of the resentment of a mob" during London's Gordon Riots, the hyperbole only increased. These riots, historian Matthew Lockwood has written, killed "as many as 700 men and women" and encapsulated the disorders, division, and resulting fears of anarchy and revolution in the British Isles during the Revolutionary War years. MPs loyal to the administration rushed to ascribe the riots to the opposition's "systematic plan, to destroy the Constitution," in Lord Mansfield's words. The king's resultant proclamation proroguing Parliament urged MPs to warn their constituents that agitating for political reform at this fraught moment would result "in the subversion of our free and happy constitution."[32]

The rise of a more disruptive radical politics in Britain in the 1760s and 1770s added to the challenge from the colonies to produce this existential constitutional dread. Centering on the figure of John Wilkes, this constitutional reform movement offered a more "overtly radicalized vision of the polity" than Britain had witnessed since the seventeenth century. "If acted upon," as John Brewer has written, the Wilkesite program of parliamentary and electoral reform promised/threatened "to change politics fundamentally." These radicals cared about the global cause of liberty in intellectual terms but linked their own cause most closely to that of

North America. Their feeling of kinship with American Patriots and open talk of resistance, and the resultant governmental repression, stoked the fears of both sides about the other in this tense moment in Britain's political culture. Wilkesites and other radical Whigs saw their opponents as authoritarians both at home and abroad, and administration supporters saw their opponents as undermining the parliamentary supremacy that was a key legacy of the Glorious Revolution. All this immediately—rather than gradually—rendered the imperial crisis a key component and indicator of a constitutional and political standoff of the highest order.[33]

Thus, the Patriots and their British allies fell not one step behind their foes in employing hyperbole to dramatize the ministry's threat to British liberty. An anonymous pamphleteer branded the principles of government supporters "a scandal and disgrace to the name of an Englishman." While they charged Patriots and their allies with endangering the constitution, "the very reverse is true," for "the rights and liberties of the people are in the utmost danger, of being destroyed by Tories and Jacobites" whose intentions were to change "the free constitution of this kingdom into a despotic Government." Not only the brave colonists but also "all English subjects have a right to resist" this drive against "their laws, rights and constitution."[34] Yet another anonymous writer raised the warning cry that the present government's determination "*to govern despotically through Parliament at the Will of the Minister*" beginning in America would "so weaken and destroy the Nerves and Sinews of the Constitution, as at length to put an End to its Existence." "Poor old England!" they lamented. "Here is the Mausoleum raised for the Sepulture of thy Liberties!"[35]

Parliament's flimsy expectations of decorum were no match for the opposition's passions. In February 1775, Wilkes touched off a fiery exchange in the Commons by wishing that "the loss of the first province to the Empire be speedily followed by the loss of the heads of those ministers, who advised these wicked and fatal measures."[36] The next month, MP Temple Luttrell offered a motion to have a bill closing North American trade and fisheries "burnt by the common hangman," given that it was "in its nature more treasonable, and in its tendency more dangerous," than Patriot pamphlets recently burned on Parliament's orders.[37]

The long and brutal war hardly blunted the rhetorical edge of the Patriots and their allies. One reporter of a parliamentary debate in March 1776 captured the polarization when he described an opposition MP's speech as having "bestowed almost every opprobrious epithet in the English language on the American war." Luttrell strung some such epithets together when he pronounced the war "the most unjust, barbarous, disgraceful and destructive war to be found in the annals of any civilized nation since the commencement of the world." "Every thing which is dear to a freeman is at stake," George Johnstone told the Commons on October 26, 1775. The government, led by "the natural Enemies of this Country," menaced both American and British freedom.[38] In November 1780, opposition members in the House of Commons sparked a sharp debate by opposing a vote of thanks to Lord Cornwallis for a victory in South Carolina. Wilkes would deny Cornwallis thanks because "he carried on a wicked war against the constitution of" Great Britain. "The American cause," Wilkes reiterated, was "the cause of every Englishman, who values our excellent constitution." Flare-ups like this spoke to opposition MPs' ongoing frustration at the ministry's unwillingness to listen to Britons' complaints against this unjust and ruinous war, which only increased their zeal for reform of Britain's political system.[39] In 1782, a London pamphleteer celebrated the fall of the North ministry as "not less a Revolution of system and government, than that of 1688," working "the emancipation of their Country" by true Whigs from the worst of Tories.[40]

Among the Americans, it was common late in the war to exhort that the Patriots' initial motivations for the war must remain their sustaining motivations. In general orders in January 1781, George Washington pointedly asked whether "we who aspire to the distinction of a patriot army," fighting "for everything precious in society against every thing hateful and degrading in slavery," would "discover less Constancy and Military virtue than the mercenary instruments of ambition?" That same year, Nathanael Greene exhorted his troops that "you have every thing that is dear and valuable at stake" in the contest. If they failed to fight to the finish, he warned, "you will deserve the miseries ever inseparable from slavery."[41]

As Greene's and Washington's rhetorical flourishes suggested, throughout this series of crises Patriots (especially in North America) expressed their understanding of and emotive response to these stakes by comparing Parliament's policies to slavery. The political usefulness of the s-word was slow to dawn on some elite Patriots. The earliest official resolves of colonial legislatures and the Stamp Act Congress offered vigorous, direct attacks on the constitutionality of the Sugar and Stamp Acts in the language of British rights and liberties but eschewed resorting to the s-word. Patriots resorting to venues like the press and town meetings proved far less reticent, which suggests that some legislators initially thought it unstatesmanlike to deploy loaded terms like "slavery."[42] But before long the flood of political usages of the s-word swept away all the committed Patriots.[43] As early as 1765, a Stamp Act protest in New York featured an effigy of the stamp collector, alongside one of "the grand deceiver of mankind, seeming" to the reporter "to urge him to perseverance in the cause of slavery."[44]

Among other purposes, the rhetoric of slavery served a key internal function within the Patriot movement as a shibboleth. As literary scholar Peter A. Dorsey has pointed out, "The slavery metaphor . . . often served a socializing function, indicating that its user had accepted the Whig position."[45] As the scholarship of linguistic anthropologist N. J. Enfield suggests, this was a variation on a broad theme in how language works. Language, he writes, is by its nature "a *social* tool," used primarily as "a coordination device" for "regulating social life" in multiple ways. Thus, "when you use language, you are never just saying something. You are doing something," acting on people around you to "influence them, build affiliations with them." Among the key roles of language among groups that are already built is "the management of *reputation*" for admittance to and continuing membership in that group.[46]

Willingness to compare parliamentary policies to slavery worked in all these ways for the Patriots by signifying that one had reached the proper level of outrage at those policies. A Connecticut Patriot, for instance, thundered that the imperial controversy comprised "the most important Case an *American Assembly* ever acted upon.—Slavery on the one Hand, the Resentment of Britain on the other.—Strange! that any should be at a loss which side of the Alternative to take.—What can be worse than Slavery? What more mean and abject than tamely to submit our Necks to the galling Yoke?"[47] In 1769, Christopher Gadsden in a newspaper essay attacked all those who would "divert us from the Grand *Common* concern, at this momentous crisis" by downplaying its gravity until "it is too late, and we are rivited in a Slavery beyond Redemption."[48] George Washington ratcheted up his resort to the s-word in his remarkable correspondence with the hesitant Bryan Fairfax. Washington implored Fairfax to both see and name the Coercive Acts as threatening "the most abject state of Slavery that ever was designd for Mankind." Could "a virtuous Man," he later demanded, "hesitate in his choice" between resistance and slavery?[49] "All the Horrors of a Civil War and even Death itself," Samuel Ward exhorted his fellow delegate to Congress John Dickinson in late 1774, "will be infinitely preferable to Slavery, which in one word comprehends Poverty Misery Infamy and every Species of Ruin and Distruction." He therefore earnestly hoped "no American will hesitate one Moment which to chuse."[50] Patrick Henry's most famous utterance was also meant to demonstrate that he felt the appropriate amount of alarm. The Redcoats' occupation of Boston, he clamored in March 1775, meant that "there is no retreat but in submission and slavery!" "Is life so dear, or peace so sweet," he emoted, "as to be purchased at the price of chains and slavery? Forbid it, Almighty God!" Therefore, "for me, give me liberty or give me death!"[51]

Repeatedly branding the ministry's as "the cause of slavery" encouraged in many Patriots the need to specify why this was the best, not just the most loaded, metaphor. A common answer was that those acts' very rationale was the colonists' inequality to and dependence on the imperial government. A 1764 resolution of Virginia's legislature, for instance, protested that the contemplated Stamp Act would "establish this melancholy Truth, that the Inhabitants of the Colonies are the Slaves of *Britons*, from whom they are descended."[52] John Dickinson used the s-word repeatedly in his *Letters from a Farmer in Pennsylvania*, a late 1767 series of essays that gained massive circulation throughout North America and the British Isles. One representative passage declared flatly, "*We are taxed* without our own consent, expressed by ourselves or our representatives. We are therefore—SLAVES."[53] In 1771, a Bostonian posited that "a free people" could only be "those who have a *constitutional check upon the power* to oppress." Whether "we are slaves or freemen," therefore, depended on whether the imperial constitution included such a check to protect colonists.[54]

The focus of all this rhetoric centered on the relationship, key to British political thought since John Locke, between property and consent.[55] A repeated rallying cry for Patriots was "Liberty, Property, and No Stamps." A Patriot letter to the editor declared that "*Liberty* and *Property*" were by "their own natures so nearly ally'd, that we cannot be said to possess the one without the enjoyment of the other."[56] Virginian expatriate Arthur Lee built on his understanding of "the original compact upon which, according to Mr. Locke," colonists as well as Britons had "entered into society," to explain why slavery was the appropriate analogy for Parliament's tax acts. Taking a people's property at will thrust them into the category of slaves rather than subjects. Writing anonymously and posing as a Londoner, he warned that "a serious system of slavery has ascended the back stairs" of the government, "the first line of which is to subjugate America."[57] Joseph Warren put it starkly in a Boston Massacre oration in 1772. Whoever defended the ministry's measures, he decreed, "must admit at once that we are absolute SLAVES, and have no property of our own." To say "that we may be FREE-MEN" with "PROPERTY OF OUR OWN, which is entirely at the disposal of another," was untenable.⁵⁸ This linkage persisted well into the war years among Patriots. For instance, in December 1775, Virginia's Patriot Convention railed that to submit to Lord Dunmore's Proclamation, which declared martial law and offered freedom to servants and slaves willing to fight for the crown, would be to "bend our neck to the galling yoke, and hug the chains prepared for us and our latest posterity!" For what better described a situation where "by his single fiat he can strip us of our property, can give freedom to our servants and slaves, and arm them for our destruction"?⁵⁹

Although slavery was useful in large part because it was a deadly serious word in the English lexicon, some Patriots found it helpful in mocking the absurdity of the ministry's position. In 1768, one Patriot writer recommended tongue-in-cheek to the ministry that "if the Property of the Americans is not sufficient to" retire the national debt, "let us make a Merchandize of their Persons. If they are to be Slaves, it little signifies who is their Master." Moreover, enslaving them outright would teach "our Trans-Atlantic Worthies" their subordinate place.⁶⁰ In 1774, while Parliament debated the Coercive Acts, Benjamin Franklin wrote a satirical public letter to the prime minister seeking to associate them with the hated West Indian planters. Parliament, this mock letter insisted, must treat the colonists as a "dastardly set of Poltroons," a "conquered People" "degenerated" from their British ancestors. "When all North America have thus bent their Neck to the Yoke designed for them," this lampoon proposed, Britain should adopt the West Indian practice of appointing "what they call a Negro Driver, who is chosen from among the Slaves."⁶¹ In short, white Patriots throughout the imperial crisis found the s-word to be precisely descriptive of their plight rather than histrionic.

The outbreak of war produced no diminution in the Patriots' resort to such rhetoric. To show how "greatly alarmed" and "shocked" they were by the ministry's resort to force, a town meeting in rural New York solemnly resolved "never to become slaves."⁶² In May 1775, Congress invited Canadians to show they belonged to the Patriot club by "rejecting, with disdain, the fetters of slavery, however artfully polished."⁶³ In Congress's July 1775 declaration of the causes for Americans' taking up arms, the peroration demonstrated that far from the war eclipsing prewar issues, it seemed to have ratcheted up the rhetoric associated with them. "We have counted the cost of this contest," Congress testified, "and find nothing so dreadful as voluntary slavery. Honour, justice, and humanity forbid us tamely to surrender that freedom which we received from our gallant ancestors, and which our innocent posterity have a right to receive from us." Given that "our cause is just," Americans were "with one mind resolved to die freemen, rather then to live slaves."[64] In 1776, Thomas Paine published a fictitious dialogue in which a member of Congress hesitated to embrace independence because of "the destructive consequences of war," to which a true Patriot responded, "I think of nothing but the destructive consequences of slavery."[65] Ethan Allen remembered joining the American cause because when he read "the history of nations doomed to perpetual slavery, in consequence of yielding up the tyrants their natural-born liberties," he felt "a sort of philosophical horror."[66]

As the war dragged on, key Patriots demonstrated that the political cause sustained their resistance to Britain and urged others to stay in the fold by appealing to the slavery trope. In 1777, after having sacrificed his health "and no small part of my fortune" to the cause, Brigadier General Alexander McDougall shook his head at the penny-pinchers who supplied the army. "What will our money avail us," he cried, "if we are enslaved?" And in 1778, Washington, while acknowledging Americans' war weariness, admonished them not to succumb to British temptations to a negotiated peace, as the only paths before them remained "to liberty, or to Slavery."[67] In 1778, Virginia Patriot Edmund Pendleton cheered on Washington for his work "rescuing" Americans "from Slavery." "In plain English," Pendleton reminded another Patriot commander that same year, "absolute slavery" was the "aim" of the British.[68] Also in 1778, a Massachusetts officer suffering with the army at Valley Forge, Pennsylvania, distinguished himself from "the cringing, non-resisting, ass-like fools of this State" by exclaiming, "Oh! horrid thought! To be a slave! Oh! base idea first conceived in hell!"[69]

As the reality of civil war confronted opposition MPs, they let loose a flurry of slavery rhetoric to convey their appreciation of the stakes for British and human liberty. To take just one example, in 1776 an opposition member of the House of Commons proclaimed that he had long believed the ministry's "system" had been devised "to compel America to consent to unconditional submission, which was, in other words, to consent to be slaves." The war confirmed that his faith was true.[70] Likewise, late in the war, opposition MPs signaled that its length had embittered rather than reconciled them to the British cause by continued usage of the language of slavery. The Marquess of Rockingham, for instance, provocatively exulted in the House of Lords that as of late 1779, "the attempt to enslave America had happily miscarried."[71]

This sort of deployment of slavery could also work on the international stage to show what side one was on. Irish Patriots often deployed the analogy of their subordinate condition with slavery. Patrick Griffin has helpfully pointed out that this rhetorical device functioned as much more of an abstraction for Irish than American Patriots, much as cries of the threat of "popery" tended more to the abstract for American than Irish Patriots. That said, it remains telling that the Irish Patriots did resort to the language of slavery as often as they did.[72] In December 1775, the Dutch baron Johan Derk van der Capellen used it for both a domestic and an international audience. The British government had requested that the Dutch Republic consent to the transfer of the Scotch Brigade from the Netherlands to North America, and van der Capellen appealed to other leading Dutch figures to say no. The Dutch would be cast in an "odious light" if they, "who were themselves once slaves" but had shown the "spirit to fight themselves free," joined George III in reducing his own subjects to bondage. Van der Capellen also proudly recounted his part in this debate to his British correspondent Richard Price. This was but one example of liberal Europeans using the language of slavery to signal that they were on the right side, with the appropriate amount of zeal, in this cosmically crucial contest.[73]

IN TURN, Loyalists throughout the Atlantic marked themselves in part by resisting the Patriots' application of the language of slavery to the situation. Given the political purchase of this Patriot rhetoric, one option was to dodge completely the charged concept and reality of slavery. In January 1776, undecided New Yorker Peter van Schaack reflected in his journal that he could not agree with the Patriots that Parliament's acts since 1765 "manifest a system of slavery." He imputed the policies instead "to human frailty and the difficulty of the subject."[74]

That might have suited van Schaack ruminating privately, but Loyalists arguing in the public sphere rather more vigorously sought to deny the Patriots the use of the s-word. An essay published in a Loyalist Boston newspaper adopted a relativist line regarding terms like "slavery" and "freedom." While "we hardly meet any one in the community who does not start at the mention of" terms like "slavery" or "oppression," "we find liberty to be so very uncertain a thing, and oppression a being of so many shapes," that thinking men could come to a "multiformity" of "notions of liberty and oppression." So such terms should be employed with much more care than the Patriots were using.[75] In an influential tract defending the Stamp Act, Soame Jenyns recoiled at the Patriots' wanton misuse of "several patriotic and favorite Words, such as Liberty, Property, *Englishmen, &c.*," and their cries that "they are all Slaves, and all is lost."[76] The Patriots' comparison of British taxes to slavery also deeply offended Hector St. John de Crèvecoeur. Given that actual chattel slavery in America was manifestly "more *compleat,* more *miserable,* more *disgraceful*" than anything ever endured by white taxpayers, he rebuked slaveholding Patriots for their "cavalier usage of the term."[77]

Methodist divine John Wesley proved a very important practitioner of this sort of conspicuous eye-rolling. In his influential 1775 pamphlet *A Calm Address to Our American Colonies,* Wesley argued that the Patriots were reading the idea of consent far too literally, given that very few people consent directly to the laws that bind them. People could not consent directly to laws made before they were born, and most English subjects' consent to laws currently being made "is purely passive." "Vainly do you complain of being 'made slaves,'" he concluded. "Am I, or two millions of Englishmen made slaves because we are taxed without our own consent?"[78] In a 1776 rebuttal to Richard Price's response to *Calm Address,* Wesley became rather more pointed. "Slavery," he lectured, "is a state wherein neither a man's goods, nor liberty, nor life, are at his own disposal." That description applied to "negroes in the American colonies," to be sure, but "are their masters in the same state with them? In just the same slavery with the negroes?" Surely any Patriot who would "face us down" with such an assertion could not be taken seriously.[79]

Wesley's defenders echoed and expanded his points in the pamphlet skirmish following *Calm Address.* For John Fletcher, the talk of slavery and tyranny among the Patriots and their allies was a function of their "inattention to the nature of civil government" and the nature of the British constitution. Moreover, Fletcher demanded, "Are you aware of the stab which you give the constitution; and of the insult which you offer, not only to your superiors, but also to millions of your worthy countrymen, whom you absurdly stigmatize as some of the *most abject slaves in the universe?*" When "impartial men" hear such histrionics, they "smile and say, What! is British liberty so mean a blessing, as to depend upon a couple of shillings" drawing the line between voter and nonvoter?[80] The anonymous author of a satirical "sketch" of North American Patriots set them down as so many "giddy, thoughtless, helpless Boys" who "damn as Slav'ry, just

Allegiance." They would apply the s-word in the imperial dispute far less liberally if they looked around the world and saw the prevalence of real slavery outside of Britain's blessed realms.[81] One writer encapsulated this Loyalist argument by decrying the Patriots' "profanation of language."[82]

The retort that the Patriots abused terms like "slavery" and "freedom" was a powerful element (even captured in its title) of the most influential of Loyalist pamphlets, Samuel Johnson's 1775 *Taxation No Tyranny*. He found it astonishing how petulant the Americans were, deigning to decide what they will "allow to the supreme power" based on a confused miscellany of appeals to natural rights and colonial charters. The more he read American demands, the more "we wonder at their shamelessness." He caricatured their position by putting it in the mouth of hypothetical Cornwall secessionists who declared, "While we are governed as we do not like, where is our liberty?" "It has been of late a very general practice," Johnson griped, "to talk of slavery among those who are setting at defiance every power that keeps the world in order." If Johnson had his way, he would ban this abuse of the s-word, substituting for it "the softer phrase of English Superiority and American Obedience." But he granted that "it will be vain to prohibit the use of the word *slavery*"; still, "I could wish it were more discreetly uttered" than the Patriots had done.[83]

Given that Patriot allegations of a ministerial plot to enslave white Americans persisted full force into the war years, so did the Loyalist counterthrust that this was a gross abuse of language. In Parliament in October 1775, Lord North bristled that he possessed "as great a veneration for liberty as any man in that House" and valued Britons' "glorious ancestors," who did not "hesitate a moment in their choice between slavery or war, between ignominy and death." But, he sighed, in the current conflict with North America, "there was no question of slavery." A year later, North reiterated that his government's war aim was "cementing a lasting unity and amity" with the American colonies, and certainly not "forging chains of slavery, or excuses for tyranny or oppression."[84] In a December 1776 fast sermon, a Loyalist English clergyman pronounced the Patriots' running enslavement rhetoric to be the "stale and gratuitous Assertions of those whose Business it seems to be to abuse and misrepresent."[85] Another Anglican Loyalist, Josiah Tucker, dismissed all the talk of "the *enslaving* Nature" of the ministry's acts as a shameless attempt to puff up the Patriots' "Catalogue of *pretended* Grievances."[86] And as late as 1781, Lord Westcote, speaking in Parliament, doubled down on such denials. Far from being "on our part, a wicked, an accursed, and diabolical war, . . . meditating the slavery of the vanquished," as charged by the opposition, the conflict was in fact "a holy war."[87]

In November 1777, in a debate over renewing an act suspending habeas corpus for rebels captured on the high seas, Edmund Burke implored the Commons to "crush the infamous bill that was to be the instrument of their slavery." Welbore Ellis responded with shock "that the honourable member should fly into such extremes." "Truth and virtue," quoth Ellis, "were generally to be found in the midway, between the two extremes."[88] However, dodging, denying, and even inculcating moderation made for neither a sufficient debating position against Patriots nor a rallying point for Loyalist community. Fortunately for them, other rhetorical tactics worked better to accomplish both purposes. None came more readily than to assault the Patriots as inconsistent.

4

Consistency

☙☙

For Loyalists on both sides of the Atlantic, pointing up the brazen hypocrisy of North American slaveholders branding parliamentary taxation as slavery proved the lowest-hanging fruit in their conflict with Patriots. Despite the obviousness of this move, it did produce a variety of intriguing adjunct issues. Those contests included who was a true patriot, who were the real rebels, and who had a claim on God's favor.

Both the pressures and the nature of the debate combined to create an obsessive drive for consistency, especially on the Patriot side. Political debates always tend to set a premium on consistency, but the length and intensity of this one multiplied it. As David Brion Davis phrased it decades ago, both sides feared paying "the penalty for being inconsistent," but the Patriots most of all, given that "few resistance movements have been so psychologically dependent on a consistent defense of abstract principles." More recently, David Runciman has illustrated that while hypocrisy is a timeless quality in politics, and "in liberal democratic societies it is practically ubiquitous," as an idea and practice it has taken different forms in different historical contexts. As such, he has shown not only how concerned leading American revolutionaries were with the issue of hypocrisy but also that they (and their enemies) thought of it as a specifically political as well as moral issue.[1]

That said, being consistent in one's stated moral principles was also about ensuring that one's cause got and stayed right with God. Evangelicals, New England Puritans, and Quakers all earnestly believed that Providence would sort out who deserved collective aid and who deserved collective punishment. But many people throughout the British Atlantic world shared the idea that "Communities, as *their* existence will cease with this world, can neither be rewarded or punish'd in the next," so they must be in this world. In 1774, for instance, Virginia Patriot Robert Wormeley Carter—not obviously a paragon of piety—entered into his normally prosaic diary his hope for "divine Assistance in this just cause." If "these our just endeavours may be approved of by Heaven," he continued, "we will not fear what man can do unto us."[2] And the Anglican vicar East Apthorp, a high churchman loyal to the ministry, told his English congregation in a 1776 fast sermon that this time of "awful suspence" could be explained only by "the vindictive providence of God, justly chastising a corrupted nation, both in its seat of empire, and in its distant dependencies." Thus, he called not only for peace and reconciliation with America but also and more pressingly for "a national and general reformation" of morals.[3] That same year, Dissenting English minister Joshua Tolman echoed such sentiments in a sermon, although he did add that the injustice of the war and inhumane way of prosecuting it on Britain's part "render some doubtful of the goodness of our cause." Such inhumanity and inconsistency "with the principles of our constitution" might well "check the aspirations of humble confidence in the *Lord of Hosts*" among Britons.[4] Anglican minister Andrew Burnaby, in a 1781 sermon, would have none of this, but he did not dissent from this broad doctrine of Providence. He granted that because "the vessel of the Commonwealth is in a great storm," Britain must look to "an over-ruling Providence" for aid. But in his judgment, it was America and its allies who "by open and avowed violation of public faith and treaties" had provoked this war.[5] Britons and Americans of every political and theological stripe, therefore, seem to have agreed that Providence favored the consistent and punished the hypocrite at a community level. Accordingly, for reasons secular and religious, both sides had a deep psychic as well as political need to prove their consistency.

North American Patriots began the cycle of charges and countercharges that came to implicate the virtue consistency by first introducing slavery as a rhetorical term and a reality into the conflict. This area became prime Loyalist territory, however, because their easiest retort was to tar the American Patriots as rank charlatans for resorting to the rhetoric of slavery. Briton William Allen invited all observers to "scrutinize their [Patriots'] Pretentions" in light of the fact that "no People ever so cruelly enslaved their Fellow-Creatures as the *Americans*." That grim reality rendered their soaring rhetoric "the most impudent Prostitution of Words that ever was, or can be."[6] A New Hampshire Loyalist thought a passage in Oliver Goldsmith's 1766 novel *The Vicar of Wakefield* an apt description of the Patriots: "I have known many of those pretended Champions for Liberty in my Time, yet do I not remember one that was not in his Heart and in his Family a Tyrant."[7] Another New England Loyalist was so embittered by Patriot pretensions and persecutions that in a letter to the Loyalist sheet the *Massachusetts Gazette,* he cheered on the arrival of British troops to not only put down America's "*Insolence*" but also hasten the day when "AFFRIC's *Race will cease as Slaves to toil, / And* EUROPE's *Sons will reap the golden Spoil.*"[8] A letter to a London newspaper capitalized on the fact that the poetic genius Phillis Wheatley remained enslaved in Boston. "The people of Boston boast themselves chiefly on their principles of liberty," he chided, but freeing Wheatley "would, in our opinion, have done them more honour than hanging a thousand trees with ribbons and emblems" of the Patriot cause.[9] A British pamphleteer drew on slaveholding and other metropolitan stereotypes to mercilessly mock American Patriots' claims to be "very sober and temperate." He memorably pronounced them "as sober, temperate, upright, humane and virtuous, as the posterity of independents and anabaptists, presbyterians and quakers, convicts and felons, savages and negro-whippers, can be."[10] Alarms that Parliament was the threat to liberty were doubly extravagant and puzzling coming from such a cast of characters.

Some Loyalists posited that American Patriots' slaveholding was actually consistent with their politics but not in a good way. Andrew Burnaby, whose travel narrative was published in 1775, suggested that white Virginians' racial prejudice toward "Indians and Negroes, whom they scarcely consider as of the human species," and their "public or political character," which was "haughty and jealous of their liberties, impatient of restraint" by "any superior power," both flowed from their ignorance of their true place in the global scheme of things.[11] For his part, Josiah Tucker proved his true Tory bona fides by insisting that the selective love of liberty among American Patriots and their British enablers should surprise no one. These same Whigs had for nearly a century feted John Locke as "the Friend of, and Champion for the Liberties of Mankind" despite his having drawn up Carolina's colonial constitution granting the slaveholder "ABSOLUTE POWER AND AUTHORITY over his Negro Slaves." No one should wonder at this, Tucker pursued, for "Republicans in general," from the ancient Romans and Greeks to the present, "are for leveling all Distinctions above them, and at the same Time for tyrannizing over those, whom Chance or Misfortune have placed below them."[12]

A pointed subtheme of this excoriation of hollow Patriot rhetoric was that Britons stood for true freedom while Americans' lust for enslaving others knew no bounds. An English pamphleteer charged that the Patriots' cry that Parliament meant to enslave America was manifestly mendacious because "Slavery is no Part of our Constitution. We have no Idea of it in our Country," he added, drawing on an exaggerated reading of the impact of the 1772 *Somerset* case. Lord Mansfield had limited his celebrated ruling to saying that the fugitive Black man James Somerset could not be forced into slavery while in England, but this pamphleteer was among many who greatly expanded its antislavery implications, in this case to score points against the Patriots. So superior was the British commitment to liberty that "we hang even Americans themselves if they murder those, whom they make Slaves" in Britain.[13] Apropos of *Somerset*, in 1779 exiled Massachusetts Loyalist Thomas Hutchinson had a long visit with the arch-Loyalist Lord Mansfield, in which the latter recounted one of his cases, wherein he had confirmed the freedom of two Black men who had been trafficked to the West Indies and then to Virginia but who subsequently stowed away for freedom in a ship bound for Bristol. Hutchinson recorded in his diary that Mansfield "seemed much pleased at having obtained their relief." Hutchinson also recorded how he went out of his way to tell Mansfield that all the Loyalist refugees like himself "who had brought Blacks" with them to Britain "had, as far as I knew, relinquished their property in them, and rather agreed to give them wages, or suffered them to go free."[14] Hutchinson thus demonstrated that he understood the simple Loyalist equation: American Patriots made slaves while true Britons freed them.

In this vein, during a long debate on the Townshend Duties in the Commons held on the same day as the Boston Massacre, Alexander Mackay made an explosive allegation that caused "no small disturbance in the House." One symptom of American misrule, he submitted, was that British military men "are deprived of the liberty of free-born subjects." As proof, he alleged that while he was stationed in Boston, "some of the troops under my command were sold as slaves." This referred to an incident detailed by historian Eric Hinderaker, in which a private named John Moise came before a local court in 1769 charged with joining five local laborers in burglarizing a Boston shop. Moise was unable to pay the fine the court levied, so "the court empowered the shopkeeper to sell him as an indentured servant for a term of three years." Colonel Mackay protested at the time that the court had "indented him as a Slave." General Thomas Gage fumed that "the Selling of a Soldier like a Negro for a Slave is beyond Comprehension," and that it "savours more of the Meridian of

Turkey than a British Province." Given that Moise had no normal route out of his lifetime enlistment in the army, he seems to have wagered that this three years' servitude was a better bargain, so his superiors in the army dropped the case.[15] But Mackay knew better than to let such facts get in the way of this potent political ammunition when he entered Parliament.

The most famous retort of this kind was Samuel Johnson's landmark pamphlet *Taxation No Tyranny*. But this polemic attacked Americans and their allies on multiple fronts, so it is worthy of analysis beyond its most famous line about slaveholders yelping for liberty. In it Johnson employed slavery as a concept to multiple purposes, all meant to make the Americans and their English friends look ridiculous at best. Johnson found the concept of mastery, although closely related to slavery, in no way dangerous or dodgy, provided that mastery had a natural basis. The problem with the Americans trying to dictate policy to Parliament was that they—a motley band of defaulters who made no real contribution to the security of their own colonies—sought to pervert right order by setting themselves up as Britons' masters. Therefore, Britons' proper response was "indignation, like that of the Scythians, who, returning from war, found themselves excluded from their own houses by their slaves." And "the threats hissed out by the Congress," he argued, amounted essentially to blustering that "if we do not withhold our King and his Parliament from taxing them, they will cross the Atlantick and enslave us." There were far too many Britons, he grumbled, "who startle at the thoughts of *England free and America in chains*." "*Chains* is undoubtedly a dreadful word," Johnson granted, but these political simpletons had missed the "gradations between chains and anarchy. Chains need not be put upon those who will be restrained without them," but the Americans as usual were calling into question whether they would fall into that category. America's British friends also wailed that the "subjection of Americans may tend to the diminution of our own liberties: an event, which none but very perspicacious politicians are able to foresee. If slavery be thus fatally contagious, how is it that we hear the loudest yelps for liberty among the drivers of negroes?"[16] The first usage above was of a piece with the bottomless disdain for Americans that was never far from the surface in Johnson's writings; these petty provinces forgetting their place were on the same level as ungrateful and restive Scythian slaves. Then Johnson walked a very thin tightrope by simultaneously pooh-poohing all the Patriots' rhetoric about slavery and tyranny while threatening "chains" for Americans if they continued to be ungovernable without them. So the "yelps" passage was a supremely effective jab, one that Johnson kept until (almost) last in his pamphlet because it was so good. But it appeared in the context of multiple usages of slavery not only in the larger debate but also in this pamphlet itself.

The Patriots' use of the s-word rang so false on all these levels for Loyalists that many thought there was no way the Patriots could be sincere. English traveler Nicholas Cresswell's diary recorded his impression in late 1774 that New England's Puritan "rascals" were seeking "by their canting, whining, insinuating tricks" to create a pan-colonial protest movement by means of the charge "that the Government is going to make absolute slaves of them."[17] "A FREEMAN" lamented in the *Massachusetts Gazette* that wily Patriot agitators appealed effectively to people's emotions, unchecked by reason. "When the threats of tyranny, and the terror of slavery, are artfully set before" the masses, the individual American embraced measures as a mob "from which a *little* reflection would have made him retract with horror."[18]

Such ostentatious shaking of Loyalist heads only increased in the war years. As Ruma Chopra has argued, even for moderates among them everything about the Patriots' war was unnatural, from rising up against the parent state to allying with the Bourbons. Loyalists therefore reacted with even greater vigor against the Patriots' "infidelity to American liberty" during the war than before it.[19] In a November 1775 debate in the House of Commons, William Innes showed in a remarkable speech just how aggrieved he was by the Americans' sedition having escalated to actual war. While "the grand claim of the Americans is liberty," he thundered that "a people who import slaves, and are despotic over them" had forfeited their "right to the freedom which the inhabitants of this country enjoy." Unlike the inhabitants of Britain, whose professions and practice of liberty harmonized, "the North American spirit and practice in this respect" diverged wildly. It would therefore be dangerous to "the mother-country" itself "to countenance" men whose "dangerous spirit" would spread from the tyranny of chattel slavery to "tyranny, over their present constitutional superiors." Driving home his metropolitan disdain for and fear of these colonial tyrants, Innes asked, "What claim can those persons have to an increase of liberty, who do not grant the smallest exercise of it to their neighbours?" Britons at home should never be so weak as to coddle rebel ringleaders, nor so muddled as to forget that "liberty, genuine liberty, if it exist at all, is confined to" the British Isles.[20]

The Declaration of Independence seemed to Loyalists to sink the Patriots' hypocrisy to yet lower depths. Josiah Tucker, for one, arraigned

Congress for a total failure to be "consistent and uniform," or "as strenuous Advocates for Liberty in other Cases, as you are in" claiming independence. They had declared themselves free by natural law, and that they had "never ceded to any Sovereign Power whatever, a Right to dispose of" their lives, liberties, or property without consent. "Permit me therefore to ask, Why are not the poor Negroes, and the poor *Indian* entitled to the like Rights and Benefits?" If these were truly "*immutable Laws* of Nature," Tucker demanded to know how they "are become so very mutable, and so very insignificant in respect to them? They probably never ceded to any Power,—most certainly they never ceded to you, a Right of disposing of their Lives, Liberties, and Properties, just as you please." Yet slaveholding Americans daily enacted "horrid Cruelties" on "the poor Negroes; over whom you can have no Claim, according to your own Principles." And American settlers likewise committed "Robberies and Usurpations" against the Native peoples of America. While white American Patriots, Tucker concluded, "are chargeable with so much *real* Tyranny, Injustice, and Oppression, you declaim with a very ill Grace against the *imaginary* Tyranny, and the pretended Oppression of the Mother-Country."[21] Somewhat less comprehensively but just as pointedly, "An Englishman" wrote to the *Gentleman's Magazine* to pronounce that the Declaration's introductory passage on universal equality and unalienable rights meant the "assigned cause and ground of their rebellion" rested on an outright lie. For "slaves there are in America, and where there are slaves, there liberty is alienated."[22] Also in 1776, John Lind and Jeremy Bentham gleefully highlighted how the Declaration's bitter complaint that George III had stirred up "domestic insurrections" was entirely inconsistent with its preamble. "How did his Majesty's Governors excite domestic insurrections?" they demanded. The government simply "offered *freedom* to the *slaves* of these assertors of liberty." It was those assertors' "boast that they have taken up arms in support of these their own *self-evident truths*—'that all men are endowed with the *unalienable* rights of life, *liberty*, and the *pursuit of happiness.*'" How could the Patriots then complain so bitterly of Dunmore's offer to restore to the enslaved of Virginia "those *unalienable rights*, with which, in this very paper, God is declared to have *endowed all* mankind?"[23]

These arguments hit the Patriots where it hurt. Thus, one earnest Patriot cried that North American planters were "quite inexcusable for not taking Cognizance of such Matters" as masters murdering their slaves, because it made them "appear destitute of Humanity, as well as neglectful of their Duty" as magistrates. Similarly, in 1770 a South Carolina legislative committee instructed their colony's London agent, Ben Franklin, to make it known in the capital that they had framed their new slave code "on the most humane Principles that the Nature of such a Law can admit."[24] Scholars have debated whether the Patriots in particular actually and sincerely subscribed to the moral positions they claimed, but Duncan J. MacLeod put a middle position well when he posited that "externally applied pressures" in the setting of this transatlantic debate "added momentum to the internal drive toward consistency."[25]

In this fraught environment, debaters on both sides evinced a veritable obsession with exposing their opponents' patriotism as fake while claiming authenticity for their own patriotism. This fixation had deep roots in eighteenth-century British society. Some of the most influential English writers of the age, like some seventeenth-century forebears, had not only recommended the virtue of true patriotism to Britons of all stations but also warned against fabrications. Hallmarks of actual patriotism included traits such as orderliness, moderation, humanity, benevolence, and honor, but especially a true rather than a selective or selfish love of liberty.[26] Phobia of the mask of patriotism increased in the imperial crisis in part because both sides saw the other as engaged in a deep-laid conspiracy against British liberty. As Bernard Bailyn put it, once the Patriots assumed a conspiratorial reading of the actions of the government in Westminster, "it could not be easily dispelled: denial only confirmed it, since what conspirators profess is not what they believe; the ostensible is not the real; and the real is deliberately malign." For their part, those loyal to the administration earnestly believed "as the crisis deepened that they were confronted by an active conspiracy of intriguing men whose professions" of loyalty to the crown "masked their true intentions" to sever ties between the colonies and Britain. It all added up to "an escalating mutuality of conspiratorial fears."[27] Likewise, in the cultural realm, the many in the Anglo-Atlantic world who subscribed to the cult of sensibility and its associated virtues such as humanity and philanthropy worried about and warned against "false sensibility." This was likely to be seen among "those whose tears" only flowed in relation to misfortunes that affected themselves.[28] Thus, no claim to be a true lover of one's country, or friend to humanity, could expect to be taken at face value.

It all led some commentators to throw up their hands in skepticism or confusion. One such assessment of "The Present State of Parties in England" concluded that "real Patriotism is unknown, and the Love of our Country is used as a Cover for a Principle of the basest Kind."

Another essay entitled "On Patriotism" argued that in a time in which self-proclaimed "Patriots rise up like Mushrooms" in England, "there is so much Nonsense and Contradiction in the Character of Patriots, in this Kingdom, that the Moment any One makes Pretences to the Virtue," they were dismissed "either as a visionary Fool or a designing Knave."[29] Yet other writers decried this sort of cynicism about the virtues of patriotism. One sighed that contemporary Britons too often "defy sentiment, and are eagle-ey'd to the frauds and impositions of patriotism." In 1780, "Caius" insisted that in reality, "enemies to corruption, champions in the cause of freedom" did exist. But if patriotism "is become a term of reproach" among Britons rather than something to which to aspire, "then farewell liberty!"[30]

But committed partisans were energized rather than paralyzed by these conflicting claims. On the Loyalist side, Samuel Johnson composed a pamphlet in 1774 entitled *The Patriot* with the express purpose of reclaiming "the original and genuine sense" of that term from its current connotation of opposition to the government by the supporters of John Wilkes and the Americans. True patriots, Johnson lectured, were vigilant for their country's rights and liberties but did not cry wolf or willfully manipulate popular fears: "That man therefore is no Patriot, . . . who endeavours to deprive the nation of its natural and lawful authority over its own colonies."[31] A composer of anti-Patriot doggerel branded his foes the "false Sons of Liberty." A Boston Loyalist dubbed them "the Sons of Tyranny" because of their mob rule.[32] A squib in a London paper gibed that all one had to do to pass as a Patriot was "to humour the popular Prejudices of the Times" and fight against the authority of the government.[33] The pseudonymous Massachusetts Loyalist "Chronus" suggested that "it would not be improper for some of the Publishers of weekly News, at the bottom of each page to subjoin in large capitals, TAKE HEED OF PRETENDED PATRIOTS."[34] A Loyalist writing from besieged Boston whose letter was published in a London newspaper in June 1776 shook his head that while Patriots claimed to be "fond of liberty and property," they were "more enslaved by their Congress than the subjects of Morocco." On the other hand, "the real sentiments of true Englishmen are liberal, open, and generous. They detest Slavery, and only contend for a just and equal" distribution of the empire's tax burdens.[35] A source of British intelligence showed that a sense that Patriots' patriotism was a sham could still have political and military salience late in the war. His 1780 report pinned his hopes for victory on large numbers of Americans ready to desert who "openly say the Country has been cheated by the Cry of Liberty, & that it is all a delusion."[36]

Many in the Patriot ranks seemed inclined to soul searching over whether their side was populated by pretended or actual patriots. The year 1774, as the imperial crisis veered toward war, proved especially fertile soil for such anxieties. A Maryland Patriot warned that there was no room for error: anything that smacked of "injustice and partiality" among Patriots' proceedings "will give a handle to our enemies to hurt the general cause."[37] "It is not Violence," Virginian Robert Beverley lectured ardent Patriot Landon Carter in 1774, "or a Declaration of our own Excellencies, wh. constitute Patriots." Those who "set up as Champions for Liberty" needed to "convince Mankind, that the pure Love of the Publick is the basis of their Conduct."[38] Others worried that intensifying nonimportation might involve some unjust consequences. Philadelphian Richard Wells disavowed Boston's proclamation of an embargo on trade with the West Indies to punish their backwardness in the cause of colonial rights. He admonished thinking that "by *their* sufferings, *we* might find relief" would make the Patriots the very textbook definition of false patriots. "Tho' we search with a jealous eye into our own rights," he urged, Patriots must "scrupulously divest ourselves of the most distant wish to invade the just claims of others."[39]

North American Loyalists repeatedly publicized their persecution at Patriot hands as yet another sure sign that their enemies' commitment to liberty was bogus. So aggrieved were these Loyalists that they equated their treatment to slavery. Even before the internecine violence of the war, prints like the *Massachusetts Gazette* abounded with charges that the Patriots were depriving opponents of free speech—and "what is this but taking away the boasted liberty of a Briton" or "enslaving every one to their own Opinions?" Allowing "the Tyranny of Patriotism" to run riot would "sometime end in the ruin or slavery of this unhappy kingdom."[40] Loyalist pamphleteer Samuel Seabury repeatedly demanded of his fellow New Yorkers whether they would "submit to" the decrees of the Continental Congress and local Patriot nonimportation committees: "Will you be instrumental in bringing the most abject slavery on yourselves?" As for himself, his answer was "no, if I must be enslaved, let it be by a KING at least, and not by a parcel of upstart lawless Committee-men."[41] An anonymous defender of the Stamp Act was among the earliest of the many Loyalists who arraigned the Patriot leaders for aiming at independence. "What a wretched exchange, then, would the Americans make! They would barter liberty for slavery," in part because the barbarous colonists needed the crown to protect them from each other. In the very likely event of American civil war colonists could not reasonably "expect to remain free from slavery" inflicted by other colonists.[42]

A defender of West Indian slavery offered an interesting variation on this theme in a 1772 treatise by warning that the real threat to liberty in their age was not absolutist tyranny but rather anarchy along the lines of the English Revolution of the 1640s. The author clearly wanted to damage both the antislavery and Patriot movements by associating their worst features with each other. The writer charged that the abolitionists' "unnecessary and impracticable scheme of universal freedom" was in fact "the device of the Puritans of North America." Both abolitionists and Patriots "now cry out for *perfect* liberty," just as the Puritans' seventeenth-century ancestors had cried out "for *perfect* purity, till they destroyed all real religion, and ruined both church and state." All of these malcontents, in sum, "must be declared a stranger to both ecclesiastical and civil polity, and an utter enemy" to Britain.[43]

With the advent and protracted prosecution of the war, Loyalists on both sides of the Atlantic escalated such rhetoric. They had long stigmatized Patriots as people "whose *liberty* is the *power of persecuting others*," and out of their ever-mounting bitterness amid the civil violence of what Maya Jasanoff has characterized as their "war of ordeals," they proclaimed their satisfaction at having been proven right.[44] In 1779, a Loyalist newspaper in British-occupied New York City illustrated how the rhetoric of slavery could be implicated in wartime when it published a complicated satire on the Patriots. The central premise was that their promises of freedom proved a sham for all, and that what they truly represented was an insatiable threat to property as well as true liberty. The piece's literary device was mock proposed legislation for Congress, including freeing all North American slaves—but then handing half of them over to the king of France as payment for his alliance. The other half would choose their own masters, but their wages would all go "into the public treasury" as repayment "for the great and valuable blessings of Freedom."[45]

Throughout the war years, British policymakers put forth protecting the king's friends from the Patriots as a key war aim. Therefore, equating their plight to slavery became even more useful politically. A London pamphleteer in 1776 lambasted both American Patriots and their British supporters as faux patriots who, "with the syren song of Liberty, ... seduce their followers to the worst of slavery," the "banishment" of freedom of thought. Britain must thus put down their "unjust usurpation, which under the cause of resisting slavery, erects the banners of tyranny" over North America.⁴⁶ This idea accorded with both the king's message opening Parliament in late 1776 and the speeches of government supporters in response. Countering the opposition charge that their war aim was "forging chains of slavery" for Americans, they insisting that it was in fact to restore to all Americans "the blessings of law and liberty, equally enjoyed by every British subject, which they have fatally and desperately exchanged for all the calamities of war, and the arbitrary tyranny of their chiefs."⁴⁷

Policymakers also saw fostering Loyalists as a vital strategic means of waging the war, and the idea that they were resisting Patriot-inflicted slavery proved appealing to such minds. In 1779, for instance, George III retained hope that the war could be won in North America based on a certainty "that the People of the Middle Colonies are tired of the Rebellion." His proposal for the pacification of North America centered on such subjects' sense of having "fallen from the highest Degree of Happiness under His Majesty's Government to the most abject Slavery."⁴⁸ Upon occupying Savannah, Georgia, a joint proclamation by British military and civilian officials invited true Loyalists to "repair without Loss of Time" to their protection, "whereby they may be enabled to rescue their Friends from Oppression, [and] themselves from Slavery."⁴⁹ Loyalist propagandists, for their part, sought to ensure their followers lived up to such British hopes. In 1776, James Chalmers urged that no American should submit to "the harrow of oppressive Demogagues" in place of Britain's mild and free government. "Those who wish for TRUE LIBERTY," he pled, should embrace "reconciliation to the authority of Great Britain," for "INDEPENDENCE AND SLAVERY ARE SYNONYMOUS TERMS." And in late 1781, a beleaguered Loyalist preacher in Connecticut urged his followers to maintain their resistance rather than accept being "slaves and living instruments of Congress, Washington," and their allies.⁵⁰

The thoroughly selfish love of liberty among the white American Patriots, some British officials were quick to argue, also manifested itself in their barbarity toward the Africans among them. A poem in the *Gentleman's Magazine* of June 1776 connected Patriots' mob law with their persecution of slaves. The Patriots, while "maintaining that all human kind / Are, and have been, and shall be, as free as the wind," "by force and oppression" had "compell'd" white Loyalists "to be free" by the Patriot definition.

They also set about "impaling and burning their slaves for believing / The truth of the lessons they're constantly giving."[51] Georgia's royal governor James Wright found this trope so irresistible that he spun an apparently antislavery act of Georgia's Provincial Congress into an act of cruelty toward enslaved Africans. In September 1775, that Patriot legislative body had forcibly turned away a slaving vessel, laden with over two hundred people, from selling its human cargo in Georgia. The "very tempestuous weather" at the time, which would lead to great mortality among those on board, was a grim testimony to "how far they have any regard to the true principles of either law or equity."[52]

Early in the war, panicked Carolina Patriots handed Loyalists an example requiring much less of a reach, with their hasty execution of the free Black man Thomas Jeremiah for allegedly stirring up slave rebellion. South Carolina's new royal governor Lord William Campbell narrated Jeremiah's execution in detail to Lord Dartmouth, in part to sum up "the spirit, my lord, of the party that now governs this province." By means of deliberate "falsehoods" they had usurped power, "which they exercise in the most arbitrary, cruel and wanton manner."[53] Hutchinson, in a diary entry surely inflected by his own experiences as a governor, found the mob's intimidation of Campbell to be the most alarming "tyranny" in this incident.[54] But in a heated Lords debate in December 1775, the Earl of Sandwich offered Jeremiah's execution, "attended with every circumstance of cruelty and baseness," as evidence "of the cruel and cowardly disposition of the Americans." By such incidents "the Americans had given examples of tyranny, not to be equalled in the annals of any civilized country," Sandwich thundered.[55] Railroading Jeremiah to his death thus played into the full range of Loyalist depictions of white American Patriots as petty tyrants to people of all races.

North American Patriots hardly wilted under these comprehensive charges of backwardness and inconsistency. Instead, they determined to contest these accusations in the courts of both metropolitan and provincial public opinion. Although the imperial crisis involved an empire-wide back and forth, British friends of American rights and Americans in London penned the most direct responses to Loyalists' arguments. For all the transatlanticism of British print culture, writers were most likely to respond directly to people in geographical proximity to them. There were many echoes of American Patriots' arguments in those of their friends and representatives in the metropole, a function of a strong network connecting them. This partnership offered North Americans a respectability they otherwise would have lacked, although that was relative given the prevalence of religious Dissenters and London merchants in their ranks.[56]

For their part, the British allies of North America's Patriots tended to dodge rather than directly refute Loyalist barbs about slaveholding American Patriots. Two anonymous pamphleteers and one magazine reviewer responding directly to Johnson's *Taxation No Tyranny* focused mainly on demolishing his constitutional position on taxation and representation as the "slavish tenets" of a ministerial lackey. Except for some rather vague praise for the Patriots' defense of British liberty, they skirted his famous passage about slaveholders yelping for liberty. It is very likely that this tack seemed like better politics in Britain than dwelling on the prevalence of slaveholding among their North American allies.[57]

Benjamin Franklin, in London as a sort of colonial ambassador in the tense prewar years, proved much more willing to directly engage the metropolitan critics. Indeed, Franklin made a cottage industry of deflecting the repeated charges of inconsistency on Americans and boasts of Britons' superior love of liberty that he heard and read all around him. To British and European audiences he presented North America—including its slavery—in as rosy a light as possible, and consciously contrasted it (with a strong emphasis on the northern colonies) with the West Indies. Especially to abolitionist correspondents he amplified all evidence of North American opposition to slavery, expressing optimism "that the Friends to Liberty and Humanity will get the better of a Practice that has so long disgrac'd our Nation and Religion." But if such expressions left unclear who precisely slavery disgraced, he clarified in a 1770 letter for a London newspaper. In a dialogue between and Englishman and an American, Franklin had the Englishman rehearse the inconsistency of slaveholding Patriots. But the American could not "approve of" the Englishman's "*general Reflections* on *all Americans*" as hardhearted slave drivers. It would be "particularly *injurious* to us at this Time," he pursued, "to encourage those who would oppress us, by representing us as unworthy of the Liberty we are now contending for." The American portrayed the northern colonies as bastions of free labor and asserted that the reliance of most southern families on slave labor had been exaggerated. Moreover, Britons "began the Slave Trade" and many Americans sought to abolish it, so "is American to have all the Blame of this Wickedness?" Given that the British government also foisted convicts onto the colonies, "you force upon us the Convicts as well as the Slaves." Adding to all this the outright slavery of Scottish colliers and the mistreatment of English sailors and soldiers, his clinching argument was that if it were "true, that those who keep Slaves have therefore no Right to Liberty themselves you Englishmen will be found as destitute of such Rights as we Americans."[58]

Franklin continued this line of argument in a 1772 newspaper article responding to the *Somerset* decision. He celebrated Mansfield's ruling but added that "it is to be wished that the same humanity may extend itself" to abolishing the slave trade and beginning a gradual process of emancipation. Mortified by metropolitan boasts over the colonies after *Somerset*, Franklin burst out, "*Pharisaical Britain!* to pride thyself in setting free a *single Slave* that happens to land on thy coasts, while thy Merchants in all thy ports are encouraged by thy laws to continue a commerce whereby so many *hundreds of thousands* are dragged into a slavery" that amounted to "a constant butchery of the human species."[59]

When, in late 1775, Virginia's royal governor Lord Dunmore proclaimed freedom to enslaved Virginians who rallied to his standard, the fact that he was himself a slaveholder gave Patriots an opening of this same sort. One newspaper squib quoted "an honest negro" as saying that "he did not know any one foolish enough to believe" Dunmore's blandishments. If he really wanted to play the liberator, "he ought first to set his own free."[60] Another piece's punch line read that "his Lordship has not been so very generous to his own bondmen as he wished to be to those who were the property of others."[61] Virginia Patriots would ascribe many other faults alongside personifying Franklin's Pharisaical Briton to their archenemy Dunmore. But Loyalists had upbraided them so often for their own inconsistencies that they could not refuse even the slightest opening to return fire.

Another key theater of the consistency war was which side were rebels against, and which side the true defenders of, the British constitution. The Patriots' allies in Britain led the forces on that side of this conflict. Advocating reforms to make the British system more directly representative, they recoiled from administration arguments that virtual representation was perfectly constitutional in the metropole as well as the colonies. Their opponents, of course, never conceded this point. As Peter Rushton and Gwenda Morgan have demonstrated, contestation of terms like "treason" and "rebellion" was a constant in the early modern British Atlantic. Although "Britain experienced at least five civil wars between 1642 and 1800," by the end of that period it was not close to clarity on the lines between or the precise definitions of these words, let alone lesser crimes like sedition. This was not for lack of trying; Parliament sought multiple times to clarify via legislation. But both within the United Kingdom and across the empire, it was up to local jurisdictions to prosecute such crimes, "each with their own legislative bodies and often unique configurations of classes and structures of domination," including the racialized structures of the colonies. Thus, Rushton and Morgan conclude, the law of treason "proved impossible to render consistently in so many different contexts."[62] Amid the polarization of the imperial crisis and war, then, rebellion was inevitably in the eye of the beholder. Indeed, as Kathleen Wilson has observed, both sides had a propensity "to describe current divisions in terms of seventeenth-century polarities." Those loyal to the ministry saw regicides in the opposition, while the opposition saw absolutists on the other side.[63]

Uses of the s-word flourished in this climate, beginning with the prewar battle for the mantel of true friends of the constitution. In early 1765, for instance, Charles Townshend blundered into a donnybrook in the Commons when he averred that he "would not have" the colonies "emancipated" from parliamentary supremacy. William Beckford, a leading London reform politician and absentee West Indian planter, objected that this phrasing "supposes them slaves." Notwithstanding Townshend's awkward attempt to explain away his wording, Beckford concluded that such talk "made his ears tingle."[64] One pamphleteer admonished that the government's drive "*to govern despotically through Parliament at the Will of the Minister*" comprised a dangerous "Perversion" of the constitution, being a veritable "Rod of Iron which our slavish Backs are about to feel." If they could establish this principle of government via American policy, they would achieve for despotism "what all the civil and foreign Wars against this Country could never accomplish: *Make Slaves of Britons*."[65] In a similar rhetorical flight, Dissenting preacher Joseph Priestley invited his congregation and readers to "suppose America to be completely enslaved" by the success of the ministry. Would they then accept having "their power confined *at home?*" Moreover, "can it be supposed that the Americans, being slaves themselves, and having been enslaved *by us*, will not, in return, willingly contribute their aid to bring us into the same condition?"[66] Probably inadvertently, Priestley in this dystopian fantasy offered a rather unflattering portrait of Americans' love of liberty, but the true enslavers in his tale were the ministry and their enablers.

The struggle to avoid labels like rebel or traitor reached a new level with the advent of the war. The very fact of that war changed Patriots in the Loyalist imagination from suspect opposition to outright traitors. More than ever before, their self-proclamations that they were the Patriots and the Sons of Liberty signified the opposite to Loyalists. As an aggrieved Connecticut man put it in late 1775, his fellow Loyalists had "the greatest abhorrence of treason and rebellion" and thus were not taken in by Patriots' "specious pretexts" of "exertions in the cause of liberty."[67] In March 1776, when Andrew Oliver, lieutenant governor in Massachusetts's royal government, fled Boston as it fell to the Patriots, he damned their cause as "the most unnatural, ungratefull, wanton, and cruel rebellion that ever existed." Indeed, it exceeded "in cruelty, malice, and infernal ingratitude, the united Rebellions recorded in history."[68]

Pro-ministry Britons likewise showed little wartime rhetorical restraint. One MP, for instance, branded the American Patriots "the worst sort of rebels; for not content with being rebels themselves, they want to spirit this country into rebellion too." Taking such a cue, others heaped up arguably stronger verbal abuse on the Patriots' British friends, who, "under a pretended regard for their country, encouraged, from the worst motives, an unnatural rebellion" against British liberty. In his October 1775 message to Parliament, George III proclaimed the American Patriots rebels and usurpers, and hoped that most of his American subjects would soon remember "that to be a Subject of *Great Britain*, with all its Consequences, is to be the freest Member of any Civil Society in the known World." Lord North added that the opposition supporters of the Patriot cause constituted "the real enemies of freedom."[69] In July 1775, British commander John Burgoyne, as part of a public epistolary debate with his former comrade Charles Lee, gave Lee a history lesson from the seventeenth century whose moral was that not all "resistance" was "justifiable." Some opponents to Stuart regimes across that century, Burgoyne granted, "resisted to vindicate and restore the Constitution." But others had "resisted to subvert it." He entreated Lee to "lay your hand upon your heart as you have enjoined me to do on mine, and tell me to which of these purposes do the proceedings of America tend?"[70]

The Patriots took great umbrage at being labeled with terms like "rebel" and "traitor," not only because of their dire legal consequences if they were defeated but also because of their political and cultural stigmas. Key to their wrenching shift of loyalties from George III to Congress in a very short period of time was the notion that the king had in effect abdicated his legitimate power by having "irrevocably broken the governmental contract" presupposed by Whig principles. Conceptualizing their enemies rather than themselves as the real insurrectionists against legitimate authority was thus key to their revolution.[71] As Henry Laurens put it pithily in a 1776 letter to his son, "Rebels are not here" among the Patriot ranks—"they surround the Throne & fill the Court."[72] Congressional proclamations thus directly refuted the ascription of the term "rebel" to the Patriots, and ascribed atrocities by British troops to their have been brainwashed into seeing Americans "not as freemen defending their rights on principle, but as desperadoes and profligates, who have risen up against law and order in general." In August 1776, the committee for devising a Great Seal of the United States proposed, on one side, a picture of Pharaoh being swallowed in the Red Sea, with the motto "Rebellion to Tyrants is Obedience to God."[73] At a rather more grassroots level, a 1776 Patriot song taunted, "We REBELS still live on." But it used that term ironically, for the ministry, "blind to England's Good," had "for thirty Pieces, betrayed your Country's Blood."[74]

The opposition in Britain contested the application of such terminology at least as vigorously as did North American Patriots. They like their North American allies recoiled at "the ugly word rebel," foreseeing dire political, cultural, and possibly even legal consequences if it stuck to them.[75] In 1775, the anonymous author of a British pamphlet tellingly entitled *Resistance No Rebellion* railed that progovernment writers had dredged up "old Tory principles of passive obedience and non-resistance" in order to brand the Patriots as rebels and traitors. Not only were those principles "slavish" but also their proponents "are certainly guilty of high treason against the Majesty of the people of England."[76] The authors of the opposition sheet *The Crisis*, which ran from 1775 to 1776, similarly drew on the concept of slavery as part of their repeated contestation of the government's nomenclature. They declared George III and his ministers "worse than the *Stuarts*; who / BORN SLAVES, tried to make slaves of FREEMEN too."[77] In 1778, Richard Price found the s-word useful in parrying government supporters' ongoing charges that he was a subversive. By rejecting the tenets "taught by Mr. Locke" at the time of the Glorious Revolution in their marginalizing the consent of the governed, he argued, the Loyalists had "given a definition of liberty which might as well have been given of slavery." Price asserted that all those facing down "arbitrary power have a right to emancipate themselves as soon as they can." "But alas!" he jabbed in a passage turning accusations of Patriots' inconsistency back on their accusers, "it often happens in the political world as it does in religion, that the people who cry out most vehemently for liberty to themselves are the most unwilling to grant it to others."[78] Also in 1778, an anonymous radical pamphleteer averred that since George III owed his throne to the Glorious Revolution, what his ministers "now call rebellion, should be stiled" instead "a necessary laudable spirit of resistance," upholding the core principles of said Revolution, "the right of assent and consent in taxation." Thus, the government's proclamations breathed "the dogmas and language of Turks, not of Britons."[79]

The opposition in Parliament likewise returned the ministry's volley of the term "rebel" chiefly by reference to the principles of the Glorious Revolution, as they understood them, as the measure of true loyalty. In response to the king's message in October 1775, for instance, Lord Shelburne declared that the ministry had committed "high treason against the constitution" by "fundamentally infringing the first principles of our government." Temple Luttrell told the Commons in the same day's debate that "it is the exertion of such power" as would infringe on "the original rights and liberties of the people" that "constitutes rebellion," "not the resistance to" such abuse of power. He later clarified that "the glorious founders of the Revolution in 1688 were patriots, not rebels," for when governments perverted their power, "resistance is not only pardonable, but praiseworthy." So, Luttrell directly stated, it was the government attacking the Americans, not the Americans defending themselves, that had committed "rebellion against the fundamental constitution of Great Britain."[80] The opposition's rejection of the applicability of the terminology of rebellion persisted throughout the war. In 1776, Edmund Burke professed himself disgusted by the government's proclamation of a fast day in support of the war, which put the churches in the posture "not as the temples of the Almighty, but the synagogues of Satan." That was in part because the proclamation asked subjects "to perjure themselves publicly by charging their American bretheren with the horrid crime of rebellion." In 1780, opposition firebrand Charles Fox made the explosive allegation that "the same men, who had fomented" the Jacobite Rebellion against the Hanoverian monarchy "in 1745, seemed to be at the bottom of the American war." In late 1781, upon receipt of the news from Yorktown, opposition MPs declared the ministry "state criminals who had ruined their country."[81]

"Rebel" was a loaded word for American Patriots' allies beyond Britain as well. In Dublin in 1776, for instance, "the spectators rioted" upon hearing an epilogue to John Gay's *The Beggar's Opera* performed in which "Americans were styled rebels." This may have been in part because they saw the logic of the American Congress's 1775 appeal for Irish Patriots' support by highlighting the atrocities implicitly authorized when the ministry had declared Americans rebels and traitors. It took no feat of imagination for Irish Patriots to fear the application of such terminology in their own island.[82] And a Dutch sympathizer wrote to Richard Price that it would be "very strange" for the Dutch, "who have also borne the name of *Rebels*, and who have gained their liberties by force of arms," to aid the British war effort.[83]

This dispute took on particularly vivid forms—and directly implicated slavery—beginning in Virginia in 1775 with royal governor Lord Dunmore's recruitment of slaves and indentured servants, but radiating throughout the British Atlantic thereafter. As early as May, Dunmore told both the Patriots menacing him in Williamsburg and his superiors in London that if the former persisted with "this present insurrection," he would "be forced and it is my fixed purpose to arm all my own Negroes and receive all others that will come to me whom I shall declare free." This drastic step, he assured Dartmouth, was justified because of "the rebellious spirit" enacted by the colony's Patriots. That same month, Lieutenant-General Thomas Gage, as chief British commander in America, noted approvingly in a letter to Dartmouth that Dunmore's statement "has startled the insurgents." In late June, Dunmore acknowledged to Dartmouth that his threat had "stirred up fears" strong enough to carry the leading Patriots "even to treason and the brink of rebellion." But he also insisted that it was their "insurrections," not his threats in response to them, that had "occasioned the commotions" in the colony.[84] In these formulations, the true insurrectionists were the white American Patriots, not any enslaved Virginians who would flee to His Majesty's standard to help put down their rebellion.

From that point of view, Patriot slaveholders should not have been surprised that their rebellion had given an opening for African American freedom. "The fatal effects of opposing superior authority," lectured a New York Loyalist in 1775, had already forced slaveholders "to relax the necessary severities exercised toward their slaves, who are become restive to those they formerly implicitly obeyed," just as white Patriots had done toward imperial officials.[85] In a similar vein, in South Carolina in late 1775, a British naval captain, John Tollemache, rejected white Patriots' complaints that British forces had "enticed" enslaved Americans into insurrection. Not only had fugitives come "as freemen" to his ship, he told a Patriot emissary, but more to the point, it was this emissary and those who sent him who "were all in actual rebellion."[86]

It was thus fully in character when, in November 1775, Lord Dunmore issued what would become his famous proclamation, he led with declaring the American Patriots "traitors" for whom martial law was necessary. Indeed, he advertised his sole purpose in recruiting slaves and indentured servants to be "speedily reducing this colony to a proper sense of their duty, to his majesty's crown and dignity."[87] Military and political setbacks thereafter did not dissuade him from his deeply paternalist view of his actions as governor. In January 1776, Dunmore, still writing from exile on a British ship, repudiated the Patriots' portrait of him "as an enemy to this Colony" by protesting that "every Transaction of my Administration Proceeded from a heart that" had always cherished "the Real happiness and well being of this Colony." Therefore, he wrote, "I wish to god" that the rebel leaders would abandon their "Undutyfull and ungratefull" course and reconcile with the empire "that has fostered them with the most Parental Care."[88] As Dunmore combated rebellion in the belly of the beast, he became a hero for Loyalist Britons, who echoed his characterization of the Patriots as engaging in a particularly childish sort of rebellion. Samuel Johnson, for instance, gibed even well ahead of Dunmore's Proclamation, that if Britain freed enslaved American, as free people under the British aegis they were bound to "be more grateful and honest than their masters."[89]

Patriots therefore denounced Dunmore and his proclamation in part in context of the politics of rebellion. An early flashpoint came in spring 1775, when Dunmore removed the colony's stores of gunpowder from the capital. Dunmore's own report of the incident to Dartmouth captured the essence of the controversy well: the Patriots railed against this act because "they are apprehensive of Insurrections amongst their Slaves," while his leading justification was "the defenceless state in which I find myself." In the aftermath as well as in that moment, both sides jockeyed for position as the true guarantors of order and "internal security": Dunmore in removing the gunpowder from the reach of white rebels, Patriots in decrying how that left them vulnerable to Black rebels.[90] In June 1775, for instance, Virginia's Patriot-dominated House of Burgesses addressed Dunmore "with equal concern and amazement" at his provocative, "severe and cruel" course. "When everything was perfectly quiet, your lordship sent a message into" Williamsburg threatening to "declare freedom to the slaves and lay the town in ashes." Although they granted that "some irregularities were committed" by Patriots in response to Gunpowder-gate and the news of war from Massachusetts, the ultimate point was that Dunmore had begun the conflict when "everything was perfectly quiet" in Virginia. Thus, they laid all the disorder at the feet of Dunmore's and his superiors' "extraordinary attempts to stretch the powers of government so much beyond their ancient and constitutional limits."[91] Dunmore retorted that this was all revisionist history, "an awkward endeavour to change the effect into the Cause."[92]

An impassioned Patriot letter published in multiple Williamsburg newspapers recoiled from how the Proclamation gave the Patriots "the appellation of *rebel*," and with it "a guilt which, by all good men, is justly abhorred." That was outrageous especially in light of "the many attempts which have been made to enslave us. Nature gave us equal privileges with the people of Great Britain," and because the ministry had threatened that status, "*they are the rebels, rebels to their country, and to the rights of human nature.*"[93] This missive captured well the sting of the term "rebel," especially for white colonists still eager to preserve and proclaim a privileged status within the empire.

Dunmore had compounded the offense, of course, by quite consciously conjuring up slave rebellion, the worst nightmare in the category of rebellion for whites in the slave societies of North America. As historian Robert G. Parkinson has insightfully argued, the very concept of Britain stirring up slave insurrections proved politically useful for the Patriots, allowing them to shift terms like "rebel," which were "fundamental" to the whole crisis, from themselves onto the crown's forces. Moreover, he shows that while Dunmore became the face of arming slaves, Patriot propagandists painted a broad portrait of multiple governors and commanders "encouraging slaves to rebel against their masters." "The aggregate effect" of this assault on British commanders and policymakers, Parkinson rightly concludes, "was powerful."[94] While many historians have correctly emphasized Dunmore's conservatism and the desperation—rather than emancipatory zeal—that prompted his proclamation, Dunmore biographer James Corbett David usefully reminds us that that document in reality "channeled, emboldened, and legitimized" unrest among enslaved Americans. As such it represented "'the nuclear option' of its day," and American Patriots responded in that light.[95]

They wielded this rejoinder even before the proclamation became official. In May 1775, upon learning simultaneously of the April battles in

Massachusetts and rumors of a British-instigated slave plot in their own colony, a South Carolina Patriot committee resolved that "the Dread of Instigated Insurrections at Home" was among the "Causes sufficient to drive an oppressed People to the Use of Arms." White colonists had a history of racializing concepts like loyalty and rebellion, and the British recruitment of fugitive slaves provided both further complication of already fluctuating concepts and a political opportunity for white Patriots. As Edward B. Rugemer has written, in this critical time South Carolina's Patriots "created a new apparatus of government that replaced British authority" but in the name not of disorder but of enhancing their "capacity to maintain order over a restive population of slaves" in this moment of imperial crisis.[96]

Dunmore's Proclamation of November 1775, by officially carrying through on his threat to arm fugitive slaves, only heightened Patriots' outraged determination to fix on him the label of instigator of insurrection. There is good evidence that Dunmore's Proclamation converted some undecided slaveholders to the Patriot cause, convincing them that Dunmore, who threatened both their property in slaves and potentially their lives, could not be the true cause of conservatism.[97] In December 1775, from his position as a Virginia delegate to Congress, Francis Lightfoot Lee urged that "that Devil's" proclamation should be "burnt by the hangman," the traditional British legal response to seditious publications.[98] At the Fifth Virginia Convention in mid-1776, Patrick Henry thundered that George III's representatives' "encouraging insurrection among our slaves, many of whom are now actually in arms against us," unmasked him as a "tyrant instead of the protector of his people." Independence was the only available response for Americans, Henry insisted.[99] An anonymous Williamsburg Patriot aptly summed up this Patriot response to Dunmore's Proclamation. "Whoever considers well the meaning of the word *Rebel*," they penned, will conclude that "the author of the proclamation is now himself in *actual rebellion*, having armed our slaves against us, and having excited them to an insurrection." "*Even Kings* have lost their heads" for such "*treason against the state.*" Any other conclusion would deny essential principles of the British constitution, such as "that the *king* and his *governour's* are *bound by the laws*" rather than their own "*arbitrary mandates.*"[100]

Patriot propagandists also took full advantage of Dunmore's Scottish and Jacobite ancestry to associate him with rebellion against English liberties. In an October 1775 report of Dunmore receiving reinforcements "to complete his corps of *banditti*," a Virginia editor gibed that with such a force, "he expects to perform deeds *worthy of his noble ancestors.*"[101] Immediately upon reading his proclamation, a Patriot in Philadelphia groused that such work was to be expected from "this Jacobite Scotch fortunist."[102] In 1778, "Americanus" in a newspaper letter repelled ongoing British efforts to "brand" Patriots "with the name of rebels" in part by pointing out that the British government had enlisted "the rebellious Scot" as well as "our faithless domestics" in its war effort.[103]

The imperative to brand Dunmore's Black troops as insurgents manifested in policy as well as in rhetoric. In December 1775, when he captured several such troops at the Patriot victory of Great Bridge, commander William Woodford queried Virginia's legislators whether they should be treated as prisoners of war under the king's protection, or under the colony's laws governing slave rebels. When Virginia's Patriot convention took up the question the next month, it legislated based in part on a 1748 act dealing with slaves who committed capital crimes. Under this new statute, flight to Dunmore constituted conspiracy, and bearing arms for the British troops constituted insurrection. Both meant that Virginia's new Patriot legislators claimed the power of life and death over Black British combatants. They did not hesitate to wield that power, although it usually came in the form of what passed for clemency—sale to the West Indies or to work for Virginia's benefit in lead mines—rather than death.[104] A runaway slave advertisement placed by Patriot leader Landon Carter in 1777 also revealed how Dunmore's Proclamation had more fully rendered enslaved people's flight a matter of state. Carter issued this ad not only on his authority as a slaveholder but also "in the name of this Common Wealth, to order" the enslaved man "forthwith to return to his said master," on pain of being proclaimed an outlaw.[105] Patriots' laws, then, embodied their self-image as combating, not committing, insurrection. This was but one of many pressing issues connecting slavery to the imperative of consistency.

5

Humanity

THE CONCEPT of humanity played a central role in both the imperial crisis and the Revolutionary War. Widely treasured because of its deep roots in eighteenth-century British understandings of religion and philosophy, it was politically useful in part because it touched on multiple other values that combatants saw as key to establishing the superiority of their cause. Samuel Johnson's 1755 dictionary defined humanity as synonymous with "benevolence" and "tenderness," but for eighteenth-century writers this was just a baseline. They seemed to know it when they saw it, and its variegated instrumental purposes meant that a precise definition would have analytical value but limit its political usefulness.[1]

Humanity's most politicized manifestations in the imperial crisis and war included ideals connected to civilization, moderation, and the proper locus of sovereignty throughout these conflicts, and to military discipline during the war. To lay successful claim to it was to be safely within all the right categories in the eighteenth-century British Atlantic, including proper religiosity as well as the cult of sensibility. Of all people, the Jamaican planter Edward Long spelled this out quite plainly in a defense of Britain's claim to this value during the war. His 1778 pamphlet led with the idea that Britons highly valued a reputation for humanity among the civilized powers of Enlightenment Europe. Part of why the reputation for humanity was so central to this image and self-image, Long argued, was that it was an expansive virtue encompassing many others, such as true patriotism, a well-regulated love of freedom, "a natural, open, and generous valour" that comprised "true courage," and the sort of "genuine sincerity, and true benevolence" that made an individual and a nation "a stranger to Hypocrisy."[2] In a way it was appropriate that Long would have been the one to articulate all this so well, given that the likes of West

Indian planters had to fight for inclusion in these ideals in the British Atlantic world in this era. For in its usual often unpredictable way, slavery attached itself to the concept of humanity, and all its associated concepts, throughout this period.

Part of why slavery became implicated went beyond its obvious inhumanity as an institution, for claims to humanity were bounded by status and race in this world. Adam Smith, in his influential 1759 treatise on moral philosophy, posited that "the amiable virtue of humanity requires, surely, a sensibility, much beyond what is possessed by the rude vulgar of mankind."[3] Such a conceptualization, as this chapter should make clear, normally left out people of color as well as white people of the lower sorts. Humanity seems to have been less gendered than racialized and assigned by rank. Elite men were used to hearing it preached to them, and yet the British poet William Hamilton contrasted the masculine "God of War, / Roiling in his iron car" with the "Fairest daughter of the sky, / Dove-ey'd, soft HUMANITY!"[4] That men waged war, including potentially on noncombatants, may well be why this at least partially feminine virtue got prescribed to them so often in the name of civilization. In the normal typecasting, true British gentlemen were the ones to enact humanity, with vulnerable inferiors the main recipients.

Metropolitans' expressions of scorn for colonials and fear of what their cultural influence would do to Britain increased in volume (in both senses of that word) during the imperial crisis and war. Those expressions both revealed what fell under the umbrella of the politics of humanity and fundamentally shaped those politics throughout this era. North America had such an image problem that in 1774, when Nicholas Cresswell, a twenty-four-year-old from a family of some means, decided to emigrate there, he knew he would "meet with every possible obstruction from my Parents and Friends," who "think me mad." His family and friends were far from alone in that attitude.[5] Stephen Conway has rightly cautioned that "there was no single British perspective" on the foreignness of North America or other parts of the empire. Neither did his study of British attitudes discern a clear, easily traceable trajectory from dismissing North Americans as mere provincials to complete alienation from them—at least until the Revolutionary War broke out.[6] It is a point well-taken given the number of Britons who talked about their "American brethren" deep into the imperial conflict. But the loudest voices derided colonists—whether in India, the West Indies, or North America—as culturally alien from Britons in a way that residents of, say, Cornwall were not from Londoners.

The imperial crisis increased the tendency of some metropolitans to disparage colonists so much that some even questioned the utility of empire. As Jack P. Greene has written, after the Seven Years' War, when the nature and future of the British Empire was on the political agenda, a critique of "British behavior in India, America, Africa, and Ireland" reached a crescendo. Newly insistent voices questioned whether empire could "be reconciled with the languages of liberty, commerce, and humanity." This new debate appeared rather abruptly, "but it was deeply rooted in a ubiquitous language of alterity or otherness that metropolitans had used" for generations to describe colonists.[7] North American political turbulence put a particular question mark over its colonies in some British minds. In 1772, a London newspaper editor averred that America had revealed itself to be "a very problematick Benefit to England."[8] The political predilections of British lady Janet Schaw, who traveled to the West Indies and North America in 1774 and 1775, shaped her reaction to seeing those places. She excused as marginal the abuses she witnessed in the loyal West Indies, where slavery overall was a scene of "joyful troops" of Blacks "cheerfully" serving "kind and beneficent" masters. But she found the Carolinas to be a "very poor" "strange land," and "the idea of being" lost at night "in the wilds of America was not a pleasing circumstance to an European female." There was, she recorded in her journal, "a most disgusting equality" among the people of North America, and British emigrants had taken a step backward in civilization. "How dearly" Britain had "purchased this habitation for bears and wolves," she regretted. "Dearly has it been purchased, and at a price far dearer still will it be kept." But if Britain decided to keep it, she found that her travels had taught her that "gentle methods will not do with these rusticks." Their slaves were "brutal," and they themselves were "ungrateful" both to God and king.[9]

Even some Britons who sympathized with the political principles of the North American Patriots evinced at best a condescension toward them. Jonathan Shipley, the bishop of Asaph, advocated "treating the Americans as your friends and fellow-citizens" but also pictured North America as sufficiently backward to offer a promising field for the preaching of the gospel.[10] That attitude helped keep Edward Cave, editor of the massively influential London journal the *Gentleman's Magazine*, from joining the ranks of their British supporters. He was friendly in principle to the American cause, but he found Boston's nonimportation resolutions an unacceptable species of effrontery. In response to this provocation, he urged readers to "enquire whether it might not be effectual for shewing these people their insignificancy" to shut them out from trade to Britain or its other colonies, or access to the fisheries.[11]

At the same time, the depredations of the East India Company (EIC) and the character of its officials also formed an increasingly urgent part of metropolitans' hand-wringing about the moral state and impact of the empire. As the EIC decisively expanded its political control over the Indian subcontinent, a growing chorus of Britons at home fretted over the exploitative means and ends of that control and what that said about their empire as a whole. Many elite Britons in particular also evinced serious unease over the growing phenomenon of the EIC's rapacious functionaries returning to Britain with their spoils to live luxuriously and even run for Parliament. In these critics' minds, this class of imperial careerists, derisively known as "nabobs," threatened to break down the moral wall between the free metropole and this particularly savage periphery. For all these reasons, the concern about nabobs touched on multiple fears about the British Empire and constitution after the Seven Years' War. Beginning in the 1760s, this disquiet about Britons who had abandoned their nation's moral norms for India's Oriental despotic code manifested itself from the stage to parliamentary investigations of the EIC. Most participants in this discussion understood that both the EIC and the eighteenth-century British state lacked the capability to govern these vast and truly foreign provinces by themselves, so reform of the status quo rather than revolution was on offer. This was to be a long-term pattern. The shorter-term result was that in 1773 Parliament passed both the Judicature Act and the Regulating Act, which gave the British government more rights to oversee the EIC's workings in the name of securing justice.[12]

This controversy set up the language of humanity as the criteria for judging the entire British Empire's record and gauging its future. It was certainly possible and even common for observers to see in the EIC individual abuses rather than a systemic problem of empire, but a growing number said otherwise.[13] In 1769, "Creon" wrote to the *Gentleman's Magazine* to complain that, "though born in a free country," the money-grubbers of the EIC "were guilty of tyrannies seldom practiced by the most abject slaves of Eastern despotism." By attaching the word "slaves" to the perpetrators rather than the victims of EIC crimes, "Creon" showed, as so many others would in all the imperial controversies of this era, how malleable the s-word was. He also echoed many other observers' obsession with national honor in these debates when he urged that the government in

London must make it abundantly clear that such actions did not enjoy "the sanction of the *People of England*."¹⁴ In 1772, erstwhile EIC employee turned whistleblower William Bolts warned in a pamphlet that the very future as well as the good name of the British Empire was at stake. "There is scarcely any public spirit apparent among" the EIC's venal chieftains, he charged, "either in England or India." Their obsession with extraction pursued by means of "despotism, supported by military violence" had not only oppressed Indians but also sunk subordinate EIC officials and other Britons in India—"even the boasted free subjects of Great Britain"—to "a low degree of eastern servile obedience." And as if this degeneracy abroad were not enough, Bolts complained, the most successful EIC officials, after enacting "such scenes of barbarity" abroad, had returned to Britain where they likewise "have set justice at defiance" by protecting the EIC's untrammeled power. "Humanity," he concluded, "must revolt" at such scenes. Moreover, both the judgment of posterity and "the Honour of this country cannot consent" to their continuation.¹⁵ In 1773, Richard Clarke in his extended poem *The Nabob; or, Asiatic Plunderers*, railed against EIC officials for having "stained the very Name and Annals of our Country with Crimes scarce inferior to the Conquerors of *Mexico* and *Peru*." The sheer "Magnitude of their Cruelties" and "Extortions" had marked them as the "Enemies of Mankind."¹⁶ In such reckonings, Britons were morally responsible for everything done in their name around the globe, and for the empire to be truly beneficial or even stable, it must be selfless and moral.¹⁷

Jack Greene has posited that it was in the context of such writings and parliamentary investigations of the EIC in the 1760s and 1770s that the language of humanity first gained purchase in British politics. It was the process of imperial expansion in India, he has argued, that first raised the broad questions of "how to react to the evident violation of national norms by overseas Britons and the widespread complicity of metropolitans in the larger British imperial world." It was in this controversy that "considerations of humanity became a standard for evaluating overseas empire." Thereafter metropolitans were much more likely to evaluate the plight of the Catholics in Ireland and Quebec, or the slaves in the West Indies and North America, by that standard.¹⁸

Whether or not India affairs initiated this process, metropolitans did scrutinize colonial slavery more intensely in this era and found it a key to the peripheries' dangerous other-ness. North American planters certainly did not escape this image. For instance, John Wesley's important abolitionist tract of 1774 drew on evidence from both North American and West Indian sources to adjudge "all slave-holding" as inconsistent with "even natural justice," let alone Christianity. Glasgow thinker John Millar regarded all slavery everywhere as a dangerous anachronism in the enlightened eighteenth century. And in 1782, an English newspaper editor used an example from South Carolina to argue that only minds "rendered absolutely callous to the impressions of humanity by local habits" could accept the horrors accompanying slavery. But slaveholders' poor image applied with special force to West Indian slaveholders.[19] Even the famed friend of American rights Edmund Burke lumped together the EIC's "set of stockjobbers" exercising "real tyranny" over India with others "among the several kindred Tribes" profiting from the empire. West Indian planters in particular had distinguished themselves for their "head-long Violence," however.[20] Richard Cumberland's play *The West Indian*, which was a West End smash in the 1770s, described its main character, Belcour, in stereotypes including that he was "hot as the Soil, the Clime which gave him Birth," and contrasted this "Creolian" with a true "Christian Englishman." Belcour causes various disturbances when he arrives in London because, "accustomed to a land of slaves," he has no patience to submit to impertinences from customs house officials, workers at the dock, or a young lady he is courting. Cumberland meant his audience to warm to Belcour but repeatedly nodded to strong metropolitan stereotypes of West Indian planters in his attempts to subvert them.[21] Seeing slavery and the slave trade up close for the first time in Barbados, Nicholas Cresswell found them "horrid" and "unjust," and declared the planters "a set of dissipating, abandoned, and cruel people." Alas, "the British nation famed for humanity suffers it to be tarnished by their Creolian Subjects—the Cruelty exercised upon the Negro is at once shocking to humanity and a disgrace to human nature."[22] An essay in the *Gentleman's Magazine* put it succinctly: Black slavery in the New World proved that "that morality, which balances" men's selfish passions "in Europe, remains on this side the tropics."[23]

No one applied the full force of such critiques of empire and its personnel better than Samuel Johnson. This polymath embodiment of the English Enlightenment partook fully in the growing trend among philosophes to question the very "idea that Europeans had any right to subjugate, colonize, and 'civilize' the rest of the world."[24] To be sure, Johnson's biographer James Boswell documented the full range of Johnson's prejudices of "a 'true-born Englishman,' not only against foreign countries, but against

Ireland and Scotland." His was all the snobbery of a provincial turned proud metropolitan. Throughout their famous journey to the remote islands of Scotland, Johnson made it clear that to his mind, the Union with superior England was the source of any civilizational advances the Scottish had made since 1707. And the deeply opinionated high-church Tory Johnson could be just as dismissive of English political opponents, such as when he declared that there was "no room for *Whiggism*" in heaven.²⁵

But Johnson did not perceive Britain's empire as having a similar effect on colonials as the Union had on Scotland. Scholar Nicholas Hudson makes a persuasive case that Johnson's overall stance was not anti-imperial per se, for colonization could have been justifiable if it could have been "a proper and 'English' kind of colonialism based on trade, civilization, and religion." But Johnson saw little evidence of those motives driving the British Empire in reality.²⁶ He took a dim view of India as a barbarous land where Britons were trading English civilization for moneymaking. Both he and Boswell associated nabobs with "*scoundrelism.*"²⁷ As for the West Indies, Johnson declared Jamaica "a place of great wealth and dreadful wickedness, a den of tyrants, and a dungeon of slaves." Wars with France over such prizes were the equivalent of "the quarrel of two robbers for the spoils of a passenger," proving yet again the adage "that no people can be great who have ceased to be virtuous."²⁸ Johnson thus seems to have meant more than mere provocation when he offered his famous toast at an Oxford dinner: "Here's to the next insurrection of the negroes in the West Indies." That toast was of a piece with his long-running argument that the subjugated people of color in the New World had every right to resist their oppressors by force in order to regain "their natural right to liberty and independence."²⁹

Johnson seems to have reserved the fullness of his capacious contempt, however, for North American colonists. As Johnson scholar Thomas M. Curley has put it, "Johnson's dislike of America is legendary," and he was rightly known in his day as "the staunchest foe of America in English literature."³⁰ Boswell certainly compiled plenty of evidence for this dislike, including a conversation in which Johnson declared North Americans "a race of convicts" who "ought to be thankful for any thing we allow them short of hanging." He feared North America's power as a magnet for emigration would lead to the depopulation of the home isle and thus the diminution of British power. The emigration even of the worst of Britons, he declared, would fail to benefit the British Empire, "since, if they have been hitherto undutiful subjects, they will not much mend their principles by American conversation." This utterance captured perhaps the key reason that Johnson found North Americans even more unsavory than other colonials, a reason drawn directly drawn from the imperial crisis: their insubordination.³¹ The principle of "protective subordination," he believed, was highly "conducive to the happiness of society" because it alone could ameliorate humankind's worst tendencies. By challenging their subordination to Parliament, the North Americans—who were already deeply suspect in his mind as emblematic of those worst oppressive tendencies—had put themselves beyond the pale.³²

Colonists throughout the empire were painfully aware of the contempt in which the cultural and political leaders of their world held them. They aspired to full acceptance by these elites and its denial stung bitterly. Multiple white colonists and absentees from the British West Indies protested across the eighteenth century that, "far from" truly "settling in the islands," they thought of those islands "as a land of exile." "It is to Great Britain alone," they emphasized, "that our West India planters consider themselves as belonging."³³ Even worse than ongoing cultural condescension, however, was the threat they perceived in the 1772 *Somerset* decision. That threat was cultural even more than it was political and constitutional because of the stridently antislavery rhetoric employed in lawyers' arguments, Lord Mansfield's decision itself, and the metropolitan press both before and after the ruling. West Indians in particular took deep offense at both the ruling and all this stridently antislavery rhetoric, perceiving it all as a threat to their privileged status within the empire.³⁴

West Indians thus repeatedly protested that Britons had misjudged them. Their life was "no Nabobship," in the words of one defender, and they were not barbarians. Rage at being treated as unequal to Britons at home leaped from practically every page of Nicholas Bourke's 1766 defense of the constitutional rights of Jamaica's legislature. Dismissing those rights, he thundered, was tantamount to "degrading us from the rank of Englishmen, and reducing us to a condition of slavery."³⁵ Multiple passages in Edward Long's massive 1774 *History of Jamaica* bristled with resentment against the disrespect planters felt from the metropole and its corrupt and tyrannical representatives, the colonial governors. Jamaican planters, he protested, abounded in all the noble virtues their age valued including moderation and sensibility; in fact, "there are no men, nor orders of men, in Great-Britain, possessed of more disinterested charity, philanthropy, and clemency, than the Creole gentlemen of this island." More specifically, "the planters of this island have been very unjustly stigmatized with an accusation of treating their Negroes with barbarity." In fact, Long wondered whether the term "slavery" should even apply to people whose servitude in Jamaica "has neither horrors nor hardship." Somewhat incongruously, he also pled that "such men must be managed at first as if they were beasts; they must be tamed, before they can be treated like men." But the critics "so fond of depreciating" planters did them a disservice by focusing inordinately on that taming process.[36] In the same spirit, an anonymous writer claiming to be from Pennsylvania penned a lengthy pamphlet in 1773 with the avowed purpose of dismantling British and North American abolitionists' "scandalous and audacious libel on *every* individual inhabitant of *every* island in the West-Indies." While they had "represented the West-India Planters as a set of hardened monsters," in fact their regime was so mild that if the poor of the British Isles properly understood it, they would flock to "this terrestrial elysium."[37]

North Americans likewise pled that metropolitans had mischaracterized them in nothing more than on the grounds of race and slavery. Planters and merchants and other local elites in North America were far less likely than West Indian planters to be permanent absentees, but as many as could afford it traveled to Britain or sent their sons to get their education in the Enlightenment centers of London and Edinburgh. Desperate to be seen as "respectable" in "his Majesty's civilized Dominions," when they encountered Britain firsthand their predominant recorded reactions were a mix of awe at the grandeur of the imperial seat and vexation at being dismissed as provincials.[38] New Englanders protested that they were "of good stock" and resented Londoners who dismissed them as uneducated provincials. For their part, North American slaveholders claimed their slave laws were actually humane despite their surface appearance.[39] Virginian planter Landon Carter felt such defensiveness that it crept into his diary, where he affirmed that "I in no sort eat the bread of idleness."[40] James Otis groused in a 1764 pamphlet that too many "great men and writers" in Britain considered all the American colonies "rather as a parcel of *little insignificant islands.*" But he wanted them to know that many of the colonies were large and "well settled, not as the common people of *England* foolishly imagine, with a compound mongrel mixture of *English, Indian,* and *Negro,* but with freeborn *British white* subjects."[41]

The question of colonists' cultural and political legitimacy within the British Empire linked naturally to massively consequential issues surrounding how power and sovereignty should work in that empire. This problem emerged within the burgeoning debate about the East India

Company's doings, for instance. After diagnosing the political and moral maladies of India, William Bolts prescribed intervention by London to check the absolute power that EIC governors currently abused. It was only "the wisdom and power of" Parliament shown in passing laws extending British justice throughout India, he warned, "that can prevent the total impoverishment or loss of the Bengal provinces." After all, "the wisdom of the legislature has guarded the subject against this kind of power in every part of the British dominions, except the East Indies."[42] Many others begged to differ, articulating instead a vision of continued decentralized sovereignty that would empower not only the EIC but colonies throughout the empire. Writing to refute the "virtuous zealot" Bolts, the former governor of Bengal Harry Verelst wrote a pamphlet whose central thrust was that "many favourite positions, drawn from the laws and manners of Great Britain, are mere words, when applied to a very different situation of things in Bengal." As West Indian legislators had done before him, he pled that British notions of freedom simply did not translate "amidst a nation of slaves." Native Indian mores were so fundamentally alien that to impose Britons' standards by law was quite simply an "Impossibility."[43] In 1772, a governing committee in Bengal proposed truly draconian measures against bandits, including executing them and selling their families into slavery. The committee granted that "the means we propose can in no wise be reconciled to the spirit of our own constitution" but at present "no conclusion can be drawn from the English law that can be properly applied to the manners or state of this country."[44] Another entrant into this controversy likewise echoed Verelst, cautioning that imposing British laws and morality on India would be "absurd and contradictory to the clearest and most evident principles of human nature." Emissaries might be sent from London to observe Indian affairs, but any laws framed in the metropole must be very few, very targeted, and most importantly "adapted to the meridian of the country."[45] It was a sweeping argument for the empire to pursue a federal legal scheme in recognition of the heterogeneity of moral states it now encompassed across the globe.

The pamphlet war over the sovereignty of the EIC took place in 1772, the same year as the *Somerset* decision. As scholar William M. Wiecek has phrased it, this case "raised portentous questions" about "the 'imperial constitution,' a set of arrangements" that had previously been "inchoate" and "fluid." That was because, as George William Van Cleve has put it, "arguments over slavery in England were often also arguments about imperial governance"—and this was the mother of all arguments over slavery in England. Questions included whether there was a conflict of laws between metropolitan ones in favor of freedom and colonial ones in favor of slavery, and if so whether that conflict could be maintained or would be resolved in favor of either slavery or freedom. Scholars today disagree over whether Mansfield's ruling struck down or preserved the decentralized imperial constitution that could avoid such a resolution.[46] West Indians writing in anguished response to the ruling were more certain that Mansfield had resolved it, and in a way that threatened slavery. But interestingly and revealingly, North Americans who were alarmed at Mansfield's doctrines focused less on this ruling than on his stance over issues of taxation.[47]

Indeed, nothing encapsulated the issues of the locus and distribution of power within the empire like the headliner controversy of this era, Parliament's right to tax the colonies. In that context, and as a function of their sense of metropolitan superiority in all things, some centralizers adopted rather dogmatic positions. Samuel Johnson, for instance, pronounced it as a maxim that "as government advances towards perfection, provincial judicature is perhaps in every empire gradually abolished."[48] In the 1766 House of Lords debate over repealing the Stamp Act, Mansfield unequivocally sided with metropolitan power. "As to the power of making laws," he intoned, Parliament's authority extended to "the whole British empire" and could "bind every part and every subject without the least distinction."[49] As Eliga H. Gould has pointed out, the pressure of the imperial crisis led the likes of Johnson and Mansfield to try to impose certainty on what had previously been flexible and uncertain, "to defend Parliament's imperial sovereignty in stark and unyielding terms" for the first time.[50]

North American Patriots responded in their own stark and unyielding ways, for cultural as well as political reasons. As Rhys Isaac put it so well, they reacted with all "the bitterness of rejection and betrayal" when imperial trade and tax policies reminded them of their "dependent and subordinate status." Everyone concerned knew, as Michal Jan Rozbicki's scholarship has illustrated, that "the question of the political legitimacy of the American elites in the late colonial and Revolutionary periods was closely linked with their cultural legitimacy."[51] American Patriots and some Britons sympathetic to their cause ascribed Parliament's disregard of colonial rights to a disregard of colonists' opinions. "A fixed prejudice against our North American colonies is universal" in London, and the policies followed. As Virginia gentry Arthur Lee phrased it in 1767, "the load of prejudice" against North America he had encountered during his many sojourns in Britain "pours despair on all our attempts to bring this country to reason."[52] They remonstrated even in official documents, such as a 1763 resolution by Virginia's House of Burgesses, that their "Dependence upon *Great Britain*" should be understood as not that of a subjugated people "but of Sons sent out to explore and settle a new World, for the mutual benefit of themselves and their common Parent." Various resolutions of the first Continental Congress in 1774 complained in similar language of the "invidious distinction between his majesty's subjects in Great-Britain and America." All American Patriots thus gloried in William Pitt's dramatic speech attacking the Stamp Act by insisting that "Americans are the sons, not the bastards of Englishmen." During his tour of the House of Commons in 1768, Benjamin Rush "rose up from my seat and began to repeat part of his speech," feeling "ready to kiss the very walls that had re-echoed to his voice" on that occasion.[53]

Perhaps no one channeled North American Patriots' sense of powerlessness and insult into protest literature better than Benjamin Franklin. As something of "the American press-agent-in-chief" in London for well over a decade, Franklin protested against both a series of parliamentary measures abridging North Americans' rights and the prejudice that he was sure made them possible. He found it repeatedly necessary to protest, both in print and in his correspondence, against metropolitan abuse and suspicion of Americans, and to vindicate the latter's good sense, civilization level, loyalty, and overall claim to respect. Franklin, for instance, bristled at the imperial practice of transporting convicts to North America over the repeated objections of colonial legislators. He satirized this insulting practice in print by suggesting that Americans send rattlesnakes to England in return, and by wondering aloud how Parliament would react to the colonies' proposing to transport their convicts to Scotland. More generally, he groused that government officials manifestly thought Americans "unworthy the name of Englishmen, and fit only to be snubb'd, curb'd, shackled and plundered." But "the people of England and America are the same," he pled, under "one King, and one law." "Those who endeavour to promote" the idea of cultural and legal distinctions, he pronounced, "are truly the enemies of both." The passion and sheer volume of these writings suggest that Franklin was not just doing his job; he himself was highly sensitive to the pejorative view of the colonists.[54]

When the political conflict over such issues erupted into war, the politics of humanity became more rather than less consequential to all concerned. In addition to all the considerations to which it attached in the imperial crisis, humanity during the war linked to key elements of the law of nations.[55] Those laws were rooted not only in Enlightenment-era attempts to civilize warfare but also in the ancient Christian imperative for wars to be just. The tight connection of the laws of war to nation-states helped shift the center of gravity of the wartime debate to being less between metropole and colonies and much more between two rival nations. While still linked to universal Enlightenment claims to humanity, it had begun to take on the flavor of rival notions of national character.

Modern scholars have illuminated why this politics was of particular concern to the American Patriots. Their Declaration of Independence, David Armitage has demonstrated, was actually "a declaration of interdependence," with all its appeals to "the Opinions of Mankind" and "a candid World," for their natural audience by inclination as well as by the particular logic of the document was "the collective public opinion of the powers of the earth." The United States could become neither independent nor truly sovereign even in the North American context, Eliga Gould has written, "without the consent of other nations and people" both in North America and in Europe. The pursuit of treaties with other powers that followed the Declaration was preconditioned on the United States's having declared itself not internal rebels but a sovereign state within the international system in keeping with contemporary understandings of international law. "The wider world imagined in the Declaration," Armitage continues, "was populated mostly by mutually recognizing sovereign states, but it was threatened by outlaw powers who acted more like pirates." A key consideration that made the difference between piratical and legitimate powers in this international order was their willingness to abide by "the 'known Rules of Warfare' and cultural standards like civility and barbarism."[56] Especially after the Declaration, therefore, laying claim to humanity within the framework of this international order was of existential importance to the United States in its quest to join that order "as sovereign equals."[57]

The reverse side of this coin was that they saw enormous political usefulness (as well as psychological satisfaction, presumably) in describing British troops and their ministerial masters as "Sons of Depredation" implementing "Diabolical Designs"; the "Sons of Tyranny"; and "sons of Darkness" whose "Barbarity" had not exceeded "even the grand enemy to mankind" and who had "disgraced the Name of Britain, and added to the Character of the Ministry, another indelible Mark of Infamy." This worked politically well beyond lobbing insults; as Thomas Paine put it in his usual pithy way, "a bad cause will ever be supported by bad means and bad men."[58] The bitterness of the war caused Benjamin Rush, for one, to see the entire British Empire in a much harsher light. "Virtue, justice, and humanity have exhausted their tears," he wrote in 1781, "in weeping over her depredations upon human nature" in both hemispheres.[59] The theme of British inhumanity demonstrably worked as an internal argument, unifying and energizing the Patriot movement.[60] But the political work Patriots made this theme perform went well beyond that.

The political usefulness of associating the Patriot cause with eighteenth-century civilizational norms also extended to the diplomatic sphere. John Jay as minister to Spain, for example, found it useful to impress on Spanish rulers' minds Americans' resentment against "the inhuman and very barbarous manner" in which Britain waged the war. This was necessary, he judged, because as late as 1780 the Spanish officials still worried that Americans' "former attachment to Britain" would weaken their resolve. For this reason, as well as his more general solicitude for "the honour of my country," Jay from his European vantage point recoiled at states' draconian laws punishing Loyalists. "We should be careful," he admonished, "not to sully the glory of the revolution by licentiousness and cruelty."[61] And in 1778 Arthur Lee wrote to a Prussian minister arguing that since Britain had initiated the cycle of retribution in this war, its government should be "abhorred throughout all Europe." A corollary was that "we are *now* fighting the battles of humanity and of nations against the avowed and bitter enemies of both."[62] Leading New York Patriot Robert R. Livingston advised Francis Dana, the United States's unrecognized representative in St. Petersburg, Russia, that he should work carefully to undermine Great Britain's broad reputation for humanity in "most of the northern courts" of Europe. Given Britain's literary influence throughout Europe, "they have taught the world to believe that they really possess a superior degree of courage and humanity." Dana should speak often, "with as much coolness as your human feelings will allow, of their" atrocities in America.[63] Connecticut Patriot Jonathan Trumbull Sr. summed it up well when he declared his wish to "Shew to the World, that American humanity rises Superior to that of our Enemys, which does not deserve even the Name."[64]

Another strong evidence of the Patriots' high valuation of humanity was the amount and fervor of the pep talks Patriot leaders gave to raise and/or maintain their people's attachment to it in practice.[65] In them they demonstrated their firm conviction that the reputation, and even the success, of their cause depended on them embracing humanity. "Providence favors Humanity," John Dickinson urged Congress in December 1775. The Patriots should never "stain our Counsels" by proclaiming "dishonorable" severity "to be our Creed to the World." "I wish," General Nathanael Greene put it succinctly even as late as 1782 and even in the inordinately vicious southern theater of the war, "the cause of liberty may never be tarnished with inhumanity."[66] George Washington's orders to his troops produced such appeals in abundance. In March 1778, for instance, he urged his miserable band at Valley Forge that "we who are free Citizens in arms" for such a worthy cause should be ashamed if "mercenary hirelings fighting in the cause of lawless ambition, rapine & devastation" were even close to equal to the Patriot army "in every qualification that dignifies the man or the soldier." The discipline necessary to be humane, of course, was one key qualification of this sort.[67] A curious link to the politics of slavery that underscored Patriots' high valuation of humanity came within the politics of command in the Continental Army. In 1778, Washington's critics spread insinuations against his private character as part of their assault on his command, including "great Cruelty to his Slaves in Virginia" in their indictments.[68] While upbraiding Washington as a slaveholder would likely not have worked in the national coalition that was the Continental Army, these backbiters showed their understanding that officers across the board treasured humanity.

While defenders of the established British Empire and nation operated under none of these imperatives, they had plenty of other reasons to see claiming humanity for their cause as essential. For one thing, associating the United States with international illegality rather than humanity would be terribly useful to the vital purpose of denying it the very status of a legitimate state. Furthermore, charges of Patriot inhumanity helped the transatlantic Loyalist persuasion cohere.[69] On an even more practical level, they hoped that would speed reconciliation with North America once conquered. In 1776, Lord North declared categorically that the ministry's whole policy was to follow up military victory "with prudence and moderation, . . . as a means of cementing a lasting unity and amity." A British informant mixed his slavery metaphors but otherwise made this point clear when he wrote his expectation that the rebels would be "subdued by the Clemency & Moderation of Britain," and thereby "Throw off their Chains."[70] Loyal Britons likewise firmly believed that if their soldiers failed to observe "the rules observed by civilized nations," this would operate "to the disgrace of humanity, and the reproach of a people, heretofore famed throughout the world for their generosity to" their enemies.[71] Their opponents within Britain repeatedly charged that the government's prosecution of the war failed this test of national virtue. John Wilkes, for example, lambasted the government's "cruel persecuting" approach to the war, and lectured that "universal benevolence, and a generous spirit of humanity" had been and should still be the distinguishing "characteristics of the inhabitants of" England.[72] In 1776, in the House of Lords, the Earl of Dartmouth said it all when he described "uniting with" an opponent on "the principle of humanity" but fiercely "differing on the means."[73]

One major arena of conflict was the treatment of prisoners of war. The widespread assumption on both sides was that generosity in victory, just like bravery in battle, was strong evidence not only of individual virtue but also of the rightness of one's cause.[74] This issue therefore led to almost innumerable, often testy exchanges between commanders and diplomats on both sides.[75] It also sparked debates in Parliament, for as the Duke of Richmond put it in 1781, Britain's "humanity was deeply interested" in this question. "All our victories weighed nothing in the scale of consideration, in the eyes of foreign powers," he averred, "compared to the tenderness, the humanity, and the kind manner in which we treated those of our enemies whom the fortune of war had put into our power."[76] Widespread newspaper coverage of these exchanges demonstrated that the prisoner issue was for civilians likewise a preoccupation bordering on an obsession.[77] Robert Livingston, in a 1778 letter to George Washington, offered a window into why this was so especially on the American side. Livingston gushed that reading Washington's correspondence with British commanders "can not fail to impress Europe with the most favorable ideas of the humanity, politeness, & literary address" not only of the commander himself but also "of a people whom they have hitherto taught to consider as but just emerging from barbarism."[78]

The correspondence between British and American military commanders on the issue of prisoners was particularly charged with the rhetoric of civilization and humanity. Given the longstanding metropolitan assumptions of degeneration among Americans, it came quite naturally to British commanders to lecture their American counterparts on "the benevolent maxims" accepted in "the present civilized state of Europe." The subsequent points in all such lectures were how Britain upheld such values, and how American practices were falling well short of that standard.[79] The direct reflection American cruelty to POWs made on the Patriot cause was never far from the surface. For instance, a Virginia Loyalist, after a catalogue of various Patriot cruelties, concluded his letter to Washington by pronouncing, "with your cause I renounce you."[80] Patriot commanders responded within the same terms. Washington assured British commander Thomas Gage in August 1775, for instance, not only that charges of abuse of British POWs had no "Foundation in Truth" but also that this did not surprise him because the American cause had attracted throngs of men "animated with the purest Principles of Virtue." The charge that it was the British who abused POWs followed these assertions as the night followed the day.[81]

Both sides repeatedly used the rhetoric and specter of slavery to dramatize the significance of the POW issue. The theme of bondage proved an effective way to touch on the issues of civilization and liberty at the heart of this issue. In an August 1775 letter to Washington, Gage passed along the report that some "of the King's faithful subjects, taken some time since by the rebels," were "labouring like negro slaves, to gain their daily subsistence, or reduced to the wretched alternative, to perish by famine, or take arms against their king and country." This was "barbarity," and he hoped Washington's "sentiments of liberality" would induce him to correct it.[82] Later that year, in a letter printed in the London press, a white Loyalist raged that the "rebellious Savages" treated their prisoners "with the greatest cruelty." In this case, rather than make them work like slaves, they made a practice of "chaining them to Negroes, &c."[83]

Meanwhile, Patriots spread the charge that British commanders intended to ship captured Americans to far-flung places—variously rumored to include Africa, India, Gibraltar, and the West Indies—in the capacity of enslaved laborers.[84] And a Boston Patriot held as a British POW lashed out at his captors in a June 1776 letter, philosophizing that "slaves envy the freedom of others, and take a malicious pleasure in contributing to destroy it."[85] The American commissioners in Paris in 1777 protested to Lord Stormont that compelling American POWs to fight for the British armed forces "is a new Mode of Barbarity, which your Nation alone has the Honour of inventing." It was "a Manner of treating Captives that you can justify by no Precedent or Custom, except that of the black Savages of Guinea" who fed the slave trade at its source.[86]

A related issue was the treatment of noncombatants. This perhaps even more than these other sub-issues was a running concern for commanders given how it was a function of military discipline. In multiple passages of his published military diary, British officer Alexander Campbell, who had himself suffered as a POW, took enormous pride in contrasting the "Humanity" and discipline of his troops in Georgia with the "shameful and unprecedented Barbarity" of unruly Patriot troops.[87] Washington was particularly conscious that living up to this reputation for indiscipline would bring "Shame & Disgrace" upon the Patriot cause. So he was prolific in exhortations to his troops that they "pride themselves (as Men contending in the glorious Cause of Liberty ought to do) in an orderly, decent and regular deportment" toward noncombatants. "Soldiers fighting in the cause of innocence, humanity and justice" should realize, he cautioned, that "the eyes of all America, and of Europe are turned upon us."[88]

But many more people than commanders cared about and politicized the treatment of noncombatants. A British observer lambasted Patriot persecution of Loyalists as evidence that they were "dead to the feelings of humanity." The Earl of Sandwich introduced Patriots' persecution of Loyalists of all colors into a heated debate in the House of Lords as evidence of "the cruel and cowardly disposition of the Americans." Similarly, a New York Loyalist upbraided the Patriots' "inhuman, unfeeling conduct" toward Loyalists the war put under their power: "And yet these were the people who during the whole war boasted of their humane, generous, behaviour and taxed the British and Loyalists as butchers, cut-throats, and barbarians."[89] On the other side, in 1781 Edmund Burke sparked multiple parliamentary fracases over the politics of inhumanity when he condemned plundering by British troops when taking various West Indian islands. Instead of "instituting a scheme of inhuman plunder and unjust oppression, to make more enemies," he chided, Britain "ought, instead of pushing war to its extremes, to endeavour, by every means in our power, to moderate its horrors." For their part, the Continental Congress on multiple occasions made the direct case that British atrocities constituted evidence that this was a "just and necessary war" on the part of the Patriots.[90]

The related facts that the North administration recruited German mercenaries and that Native Americans overwhelmingly sided with Great Britain also drove the politics of humanity. The lower-class origins of the Germans connected them to ideas of how rank was linked to humanity, while of course Indigenous allies connected to the longstanding racialization of the virtue.[91] Opposition figures John Wilkes and Edmund Burke both made themselves conspicuous in Parliament for their bitter diatribes against the inhumane use of such allies. Wilkes, for instance, pronounced this policy "shocking to a civilized and generous nation" and "unworthy the general[s] of any Christian king." Burke expressed particular revulsion at the use of Indigenous allies, insisting that this was not due to their race but to their methods of warfare. He spoke of their atrocities in terms of British national guilt. "To employ them," he railed, "was merely to be cruel ourselves in their persons; and to become chargeable with all the odious and impotent barbarities, which they would certainly commit whenever they were called into action." Another MP branded the government's alliances and methods "inconsistent with the humanity and generous courage which in all times have distinguished the British nation," and warned that by these means, "the generous spirit of the nation would be perverted, and barbarity called forth to reign over the ruins of civilization and society." The Earl of Shelburne savaged the government's reliance on brutal tactics and allies as "diabolical, horrid, impious, and inhuman.... It could not be men, but monsters that devised it." But that was consistent with the entire program of this administration, which was such "a system of injustice, impolicy, and inhumanity, as was unparalleled in history, and would eternally disgrace the annals of Great Britain." By late 1777, this whole theme had become a byword for opposition, as they referred offhand to the "scalping, tomahawking" defenders "of the present bloody-minded men in office."[92] Whites on both sides debated Britain's Indigenous alliances not as evidence of racial egalitarianism by the British but rather as a symptom of escalation in the war's violence.

This was entirely consistent with the thorough racialization of applications of humanity in contemporary conceptions of warfare. As Elizabeth A. Fenn has pointed out, eighteenth-century Europeans and white Americans believed that the norms governing warfare "did not apply" in situations including "wars against enemies who themselves violated the laws of war"—hence the importance of framing the other side as having first violated those laws—and "wars against 'savage' or 'heathen' people."[93] Indeed, both Patriots and British apologists granted that employing Native American allies was inhumane, based on the assumption that their form of warfare fell outside the bounds of humanity. An early tactic was to insist that no "man bearing the commission of a Christian Prince" could ever be guilty of employing Native Americans against white colonists.[94] When that became untenable, another approach was to describe these alliances as necessary but deflect blame by shifting the focus to Patriot atrocities.[95]

Others, however, advocated hard war, including harsh tactics and allies. George Johnstone, a progovernment MP and former governor of West Florida, "condemned the American Congress in the strongest terms" in a 1778 debate over war policy. He thundered that "no mercy, no quarter, ought to be shewn to them; and if the infernals could be let loose against them, he should approve of the measure." Lord Lyttelton, also in 1778, offered that the Americans, as "men who were fighting for republicanism, joining with the slaves of an arbitrary monarch" after their alliance with France, were beyond the pale.[96] These, however, were exceptions to the rule of participants who squirmed when accused of inhumanity.

Indeed, these exceptions proved the rule, arguing repeatedly that their enemies' inhumanity was what compelled them reluctantly to respond in kind. Even those who became notorious to their enemies for harshness in the war seem to have truly believed in the concept of humanity with all that it entailed. And regardless of their sincerity, they certainly said over and over that only the grim need for retaliation forced them to mimic their enemy's harshness.[97] As historian T. Cole Jones's research on the POW issue has shown, an upward cycle of abuse was in fact the unforeseen consequence of adhering to the politics of humanity in this way.[98] Advocates of hard war, however, applied this logic across all relevant sub-issues. Massachusetts Loyalist Peter Oliver, for instance, shrugged off Britain's use of Indigenous allies because "savage is a convertible term." Its common use, he pointed out, was for "a Person who acts contrary to the Principles of Humanity," which the Patriots had certainly done.[99] On the other side, in 1779 the pseudonymous "A Whig" pronounced that few American errors had proven more damaging than their "lenity to the Tories" in allowing Tories to remain in areas controlled by the Patriots. "At first it might have been right, or perhaps political," but they had proven to be dangerous "internal enemies." Not only had they provoked the war by their political machinations but they had also "persuaded the tyrant of Britain to prosecute it in a manner before unknown to civilized nations and shocking even to barbarians." Therefore, "do you ever expect any grateful return for your humanity, if it deserves that name? Believe me, not a spark of that or any other virtue is to be found in a Tory's breast." So, Patriots, "A Whig" prescribed, should "send them where they may enjoy their beloved slavery in perfection. Send them to the island of Britain, there let them drink the cup of slavery and eat the bread of bitterness all the days of their existence."[100] Likewise, in 1782 Edward Rutledge advocated that the captured Lord Cornwallis "should have been held a Prisoner for Life," not so much for revenge's sake but so that "the World should have known that he was precluded from the Benefits of Freedom, because he was a Monster & an Enemy to Humanity."[101]

North American Patriots' most effective employment of the politics of humanity in direct connection to slavery was their legislative bans on the trafficking of Africans into their colonies. The first resolutions for such a ban came from local Virginia Patriot committees in 1769 and 1770. Their nonimportation resolutions included slaves among other articles they would boycott, and failed to capitalize on the inhumanity of the trade. In 1769, the Virginia legislature saved its rhetorical flourishes for a preamble to their own nonimportation resolutions, vowing to avert the threat Parliament presented of "reducing us from a free and happy People to a wretched and miserable State of Slavery," but did not connect that preamble to the item banning slave imports. And as late as 1774, it was possible for Virginians to pass resolutions against slave importation without any moral or political commentary.[102] But it did not take long for other Patriots to learn the political benefits of linking their drive to stop this human trafficking with the high-flying principles in which the imperial crisis itself trafficked. In 1772, the Virginia legislature passed a remonstrance to George III branding the transatlantic slave trade "a Trade of great Inhumanity" that also endangered the safety of the colonies. County meetings thereafter echoed these twin themes, that the trade in slaves (and sometimes convicts) was "injurious to this Colony" and "a Wicked, Cruel & unnatural Trade." At least one local committee was serious enough about enforcing this branch of the nonimportation resolutions that in 1775 they recommended a sort of secular excommunication for a merchant who had purchased slaves brought to him from Jamaica.[103]

While Virginians took the lead on this issue, others followed suit. In 1771, Massachusetts's assembly voted to ban the noxious traffic, but the royal governor Thomas Hutchinson vetoed it. That veto—and a similar royal veto of Virginia's 1772 legislation—failed to deter Massachusetts's legislature from again voting for a ban in 1774. They responded in part to popular pressure, such as constituents who instructed a representative to enact their "highest regard for (so as even to revere the name of) liberty" by passing another ban. The crown also vetoed that bill, which served to keep the issue alive as part of the imperial crisis in Massachusetts.[104] Rhode Island likewise passed a prohibition on the importation of slaves in 1774, with a "whereas" clause that threatened slavery, not just the slave trade. "Those who are desirous of enjoying all the advantages of liberty themselves," it read, "should be willing to extend personal liberty to others."[105] That same year, the Continental Congress included the slave trade in their nonimportation resolutions. Although it included no moral condemnation of the trade, it was perhaps significant that Congress listed slaves as separate from the inanimate goods not to be imported. Benjamin Rush found immense gratification in Congress's 1774 prohibition, gushing to Granville Sharp that "this resolution does our Congress the more honor as it was proposed and defended entirely upon *moral* and not political principles."[106] He knew better; in fact, he had himself played the politics of the era sufficiently well that he should have taken great satisfaction at the intersection of morality and politics represented by these resolutions.

These royal negatives played right into the Patriots' hands. Imperial officials had strong imperial crisis logic on their side: earlier in the eighteenth century, Massachusetts legislators had essentially won a standoff with the Board of Trade over a prohibitive tax on slave imports, and the whole point of the imperial crisis from the ministry's point of view was to ensure that never happened again.[107] But the apparently cold mercantile logic of the imperial executive branch, candidly privileging the interests of British merchants over colonial considerations, made for a bad look both morally and in terms of American concerns about arbitrary imperial governance.[108] As Donald L. Robinson noted decades ago, "one side effect" of royal governors' vetoing the legislatures' bans "was to identify the slave trade with British supervision and intrusion, and its prohibition with patriotism." He asserted this was "especially significant in Virginia." That was surely true in large part because, as Winthrop D. Jordan noted in another classic historical work, southerners from this early age were far less prone than northerners (especially New Englanders) to internalize the guilt of slavery and the slave trade. These royal vetoes only furthered the growing argument "that responsibility for slavery rested not with themselves but with the British." And as Bruce A. Ragsdale has noted, these vetoes confirmed to anxious planters' minds that the imperial government would forever privilege the interests of slaving merchants in Bristol and Liverpool over those of the colonists. As T. H. Breen demonstrated, the power of those merchants spoke to concerns beyond the idea of economic independence, connecting to the whole ideological complex that convinced Virginian Patriots that they were slaves to all-powerful British merchants.[109]

In his 1774 essay summarizing North American grievances, Thomas Jefferson hammered on all these themes, complaining that George III and his governors had arbitrarily vetoed "laws of the most salutary tendency. The abolition of domestic slavery," he extravagantly extrapolated from importation bans, "is the great object of desire in those colonies where it was unhappily introduced in their infant state." The first step in that emancipation was to abolish the slave trade to those colonies. But the royal representatives chose to prefer "the immediate advantages of a few British corsairs to the lasting interests of the American states, and to the rights of human nature deeply wounded by this infamous practice."[110] In passages such as these, Jefferson announced himself as someone willing to play rough—and smart—in the imperial crisis's politics of slavery. The picture of malevolent British control of the colonies merged seamlessly with that of Britons rather than colonists as the great abusers of human rights (the "British corsairs" phrase for slaving vessels was especially barbed). Henry Laurens, also in 1774, echoed such themes when he complained to a correspondent that when the importers of convict laborers chose to ignore Virginia's law quarantining those convicts, the profit margins of the convict trade had superseded "the health and natural Liberty of a whole Colony of Americans. How many such Instances of Arbitrary power over the Americans might be produced." In a letter to a newspaper, "Landon Carter" likewise raged that the British government had clearly determined to shield from even the least "Inconvenience" the perpetrators of "the Convict and African Trade, those two *glorious* Importations of Corruption and Slavery to every civilized People."[111] Edmund Burke, in a remarkable speech in the Commons in March 1775, warned that these vetoes would also undermine the government's rumored plan to recruit American slaves in the event of war. Would not enslaved Americans "suspect the offer of freedom from that very nation which has sold them to their present masters? From that nation, one of whose causes of quarrel with those masters, is their refusal to deal any more in that inhuman traffic?"[112]

This particular issue likewise helped in the Patriots' drive toward the Declaration of Independence. Jefferson's June 1776 draft of a constitution for a would-be independent Virginia included grievances against George III, including "putting his negative on laws the most wholesome & necessary for the public good." This constituted "an inhuman use of his negative," Jefferson pressed. In this he echoed the Cumberland, Virginia,

County Committee, who in April 1776 resolved that these vetoes by a royal governor constituted "a wanton Abuse of his Negative," by which the crown "has forced the Slave Trade on us for several Years."[113] Likewise, Jefferson's June draft versions of the Declaration of Independence included the charge that George III had "refused his assent to laws the most wholesome and necessary for the public good," and the clearly not-unconnected idea that "he has waged cruel War against human Nature itself" by having "prostituted his Negative for Suppressing every legislative Attempt to prohibit or to restrain an execrable Commerce, determined to keep open a Markett where Men should be bought and sold." Carolinian delegates objected to this explicit repudiation of the slave trade, which they wished to continue. But Congress preserved in the final version the core charge that George III "has refused his Assent to Laws the most wholesome and necessary for the public good" and "forbidden his Governors to pass Laws of immediate and pressing importance" without his own assent, by that means "abolishing our most valuable Laws."[114] As with other slick evasions of slavery in this era, no participant in the imperial crisis doubted as to what the preserved phraseology referred. Jefferson himself found the history of slave trade bans foiled under British rule but enacted upon independence to be so useful for a transatlantic audience that in 1782 he recounted it in a passage of his *Notes on the State of Virginia*.[115]

Imperial officials faltered in defending their vetoes. In 1771, embattled Massachusetts governor Thomas Hutchinson tried to play reverse politics in his explanation of his veto of that colony's prohibitory law. One of his motives, he told his boss the Earl of Hillsborough, was a strong doubt about "whether the chief motive to this bill" was "merely moral" scruples as the legislators had claimed, for their own "provincial laws" gave "no right to the life of" slaves.[116] He had a point about the limits and mixed nature of the Patriots' motives, but protests like this could not undo the political damage done by these negatives. Even Lord Dunmore, the endlessly provocative royal governor of Virginia, expressed unpleasant surprise at the counterproductive vetoes of such beneficial laws.[117] And in his 1776 pamphlet rebutting the Declaration of Independence point by point, all Hutchinson could muster for the clause reproving vetoes such as his was a weak and rather disingenuous claim that "I remember no laws which any Colony has been restrained from passing, so as to cause any complaint of grievance" of this sort.[118]

Defenders of the British regime found more solid ground in shifting the debate to the overall point that the empire as a whole had a much more humane policy and effect than did North American slaveholders. This idea was key to the idea that Britain had been a benevolent parental figure to the ungrateful colonies.[119] In pursuing this theme, of course, they had to reject the multiple critics of the British Empire as rapacious and corrupt. "An Englishman," for instance, published in the *Gentleman's Magazine* in 1781, posited that "the grand idea of British commerce" was "to spread the bounties and blessings of Heaven over all the nations upon earth." This writer did grant that the slave trade was a shameful exception to that rule but pointed out that so was colonial slavery.[120] The savagery of American slavery was always ready to hand in sustaining this argument. Royal governor Lord William Campbell, for instance, seems to have been both genuinely horrified by the lynch law that hanged Thomas Jeremiah in Charleston in 1775 and eager to denounce the Patriots responsible, as a "set of barbarians who are worse than the most cruel savages any history has described."[121] Proadministration British writer John Lind railed against Richard Price for crying against the government as tyrannical while winking at actual tyranny among the faux Sons of Liberty "in America, where *men* and *cattle* are offered to *sale* in the same advertisement."[122]

The British emancipatory policy inaugurated by Lord Dunmore gave Britons a particularly wide opening to make such points, and many burst through it. Even before the war began, Dunmore observed acidly that white Virginians, "with great reason, tremble" at any possible war, for the people they enslaved were "attached by no tye to their masters or to the Country." He would have found that strong sense of moral superiority only further confirmed when he received intelligence from spies. "No Crime is too black and dismal" for these "Sons of murder and devastation" to commit, they reported. For instance, "they shot a Negro going ashore in a Canoe with a Bottle of Rum, which they drank to his health as he was expireing."[123] When Price objected to the military use of freed slaves as inhumane, Lind retorted by demanding which were the true friends of liberty and humanity, the planters or Dunmore? "The planter tells his slaves:—'You are my *property*; I *bought* you; stay with me; be faithful to me; fight for the honour of being my beasts of burthen?' What says the governor? 'See, my brethren, see your *masters* under arms against the authority of the state,'" for doubtful cause. By contrast, Lind's governor continued, "the loads which crush your limbs, the whip which harrows up your back, are present, real, evils. Rise, then, assist us to reduce your tyrants to a due obedience to the laws, and raise yourselves to an equality with them." Lind thus found it perverse in Price to even question whether Britain had humanity and liberty on its side in this instance.[124] In 1775, some British newspapers echoed this assessment that any contest for the loyalty of Black Americans would surely go to British officials. "If Lord Dunmore declares them free," an Englishman who claimed to have traveled extensively in America confidently asserted, "they will fight against their masters. The Negroes are cow-skin'd too much to like their masters."[125] An English newspaper ran a report skewering white Virginians for their panic in response to Dunmore's threats to free their slaves. Their "apprehension of the rising of the negroes" had good cause, for those enslaved Africans were "almost naked, and are like to be still worse on account of the resolution of the congress to shut up the ports." In this reckoning, the futile policies of the Patriots had piled cruelty onto the cruelty that was American slavery, so white southerners' insurrection anxiety was an indictment on themselves, not Dunmore.[126]

British military commanders likewise showed that they understood the full value of playing the politics of humanity even amid the exigencies of a brutal war. In 1776, for instance, Sir Henry Clinton instructed his troops to not only free enslaved Americans who ran to their lines but also treat them "with tenderness & humanity." Four years later, he and at least some of his subordinates had not lost sight of this imperative, for they confined a British soldier for five days "for beating a Neigro in the street," shamelessly in full view of his officers and other onlookers.[127] In the summer of 1781, Brigadier General Charles O'Hara begged his superior Lord Cornwallis not to abandon "the hundreds of wretched Negroes" following his forces in Virginia. "The people of this country are more inclined to fire upon than receive and protect a Negroe whose complaint is the small pox," he argued, and British troops must maintain their moral superiority over such vicious white Patriots. "The abandoning these unfortunate beings to disease, to famine, and what is worse than either, the resentment of their enraged masters" should be avoided to the degree possible, O'Hara urged.[128] Commanders like this understood that a reputation for humanity was worth paying for in this eminently political war.[129]

Given the general association between slavery and inhumanity pervading the culture of the British Atlantic, it might seem that the liberation policy beginning with Dunmore would have sewn up the politics of slavery-cum-humanity for the Loyalist side. But Patriots could never accept that reading in light of the imperial crisis and war that had made them Patriots in the first place. They could neither accept nor admit publicly that the servants of the crown and ministry could act in a truly humane manner. Neither could they accept nor admit publicly the bare possibility that the servants of the crown and ministry could wield their power in any way that proved truly beneficent.[130]

It was therefore neither a coincidence nor unhelpful to the Patriot politics that royal governors, and in particular Lord Dunmore, became so directly associated with the emancipation policy. In the acutest times of crisis, whether in 1765 or 1775, white southerners spread panicked rumors of slave insurrection aided by a shadowy consortium of British civilian and military officials. These whisper campaigns cast royal governors, who both represented forms of British authority and were as a rule at odds with Patriot legislators, in a starring role.[131] Dunmore himself was far from alone in this, but it was fortunate for the Patriots that this royal governor, who had since his appointment in 1771 made it clear that he never wanted to serve in Virginia and thought of himself as a metropolitan representative to rather than a member of its society, became the face of British emancipation. This "accursed enimy to mankind" could do no good to anyone.[132] Indeed, the gunpowder incident and then his notorious proclamation surprised no Patriot observers of Dunmore's time in office. And then in the weeks between when he fled from Williamsburg and issued his November proclamation, Dunmore attracted a who's-who of groups Virginia Patriots perceived as threats: Scottish merchants, army and navy Regulars, and enslaved and indentured Virginians. This was a visual representation of why they could neither believe nor grant that this Scottish-born tool of ministerial power could do or mean anything good for anyone. As Dunmore's biographer has put it, Patriots' reaction to Dunmore's Proclamation "was tempered and informed by the broader struggle for moral capital." And this went for more than Virginia's Patriots; indeed, even before his proclamation, Congress entertained an earnest debate over the wisdom and efficacy of seizing Dunmore as a prisoner. George Washington went beyond that in the aftermath of the proclamation, arguing that only "depriving him of life or liberty will secure peace to Virginia."[133]

The first prong of the Patriot attack on the British emancipation policy was the powerful charge that it represented the height of inhumanity, not humanity. In May 1776, for instance, the Virginia Convention, which called for American independence, argued that "tempting our slaves by every artifice to resort to" British lines to then attack "their masters" was proof positive that Britain "is carrying on a piratical and savage war against us." Jefferson's draft constitution for an independent Virginia followed suit, juxtaposing George III's "inhuman use of his negative" to foist enslaved Africans on North America with the "cruelty and perfidy" of using those slaves as a weapon against America.[134] In Patriot accounts, not only was recruiting American slaves a species of "piratical war" but also the British Army's new Black allies themselves committed atrocities. A commander in North Carolina in 1781, for instance, reported lurid details of American POWs "inhumanly butchered" by "Negroes" fighting "with the brittish." In this way, Patriots repeatedly associated British atrocities, in all their guises, with freedmen in their ranks.[135] Benjamin Franklin and the Marquis de Lafayette thought this theme was so useful for multiple audiences that in 1779 they collaborated on a "List of Prints to Illustrate British Cruelties." One print would depict "Dunmore's hiring the Negroes to murder their Masters Families," and a white family slain by these Black marauders.[136] "Is it possible," Francis Lightfoot Lee demanded of Landon Carter in 1776, "that any one can expect anything good from such abandoned Villains" as Dunmore? "From them & all their hellish plots Good Lord deliver us."[137]

British sympathizers with the Patriot cause also assailed the arming of enslaved Americans as an inordinately bloodthirsty measure. An anonymous response to Johnson's *Taxation No Tyranny* recoiled at his proposal to arm American slaves, as that "would establish a Saturnalia of cruelty" and expose white colonists "to the brutality of their own slaves, enflamed and irritated to retaliate" against the admittedly many "wrongs" of slavery. This was but more evidence that Johnson had sought to "degrade" the Patriots "below the rank of humanity," and he would make Britons who followed his lead into "murderers of our fellow-subjects."[138] In October 1775 in the House of Commons, George Johnstone castigated a proadministration MP's proposed scheme "of calling forth the slaves." Johnstone railed, this plan "is too black and horrid to be adopted." The next day, James Grenville added that the war would prove futile no matter what extreme measures the government pursued. "Let administration," he taunted, "call the Pope from Rome, the Musti from Constantinople, the High Priest from the Synagogue to their aid, let them put the assassinating knife into the hands of slaves, and teach them to butcher their masters, yet still the event must be ruinous to this nation." For such opposition figures, it was axiomatic that arming slaves was tantamount to stirring up murderous insurrection, and thus it was so extreme as to be ridiculous and desperate.[139] In February 1778, in a long speech denouncing the administration's waging of the war as inhumane, Edmund Burke likewise framed the government's policy as barbarity rather than liberation. "Lord Dunmore's attempt to incite an insurrection of negroes," he insisted, went contrary to both British and international law, and consisted in reality of "setting a crew of fierce, foreign barbarians and slaves" loose to do their worst. Lamenting that other royal governors had followed Dunmore's lead, Burke insisted that it was thus up to Parliament "to shew their disapprobation of practices as contrary to all true policy, as to the dictates of feeling and humanity."[140]

White Patriots who valued humanity had to work to reconcile that virtue to the white-hot rage the British emancipation policy fired in their breasts. One wondered whether the biblical "precept, 'if thine enemy thirst give him drink'" ought to be "observed toward such a fiend" as Dunmore. In this rendering of the Bible, Dunmore was the very opposite of a humane liberator and thus might be outside the pale of Christian action. Also, in such depictions, Britons by their very inhumanity had dehumanized themselves.[141] As for the formerly enslaved in the British armed forces, commander Stephen Bull channeled Patriot fury when he recommended that a band of sick men left behind when the British forces deserted Tybee Island in Georgia "be shot if they cannot be taken." Patriots must not be "timid" in this necessary action, he urged. Carolinian Henry Laurens, however, responded that "the prospect is horrible" of executing "the awful business" Bull proposed. But if it proved necessary, Laurens wanted the world to know that the "Royal Miscreants who are carrying on an inglorious picaroon Warr" were the ones responsible for "every inglorious unavoidable act" to which Patriots had to resort "for our self preservation."[142] The Virginia Convention in December 1775 followed much the same line as Laurens when they unanimously resolved that Dunmore's "encouragement to a general insurrection" would force upon the colony's reluctant whites the "necessity of inflicting the several punishments upon these unhappy people" prescribed in their insurrection laws. That logic made Dunmore the truly inhumane party, which the convention reinforced by entreating runaways to "return in safety to their duty" with promise of a pardon. The resolution called on "all humane and benevolent persons in this colony to explain and make known this our offer of mercy to those unfortunate people."[143] One curious manifestation of this impulse was when American diplomat Silas Deane proposed that Americans retaliate by arming Black insurgents in St. Vincent's. That would inevitably wrest that island from Britain's control, but Deane reasoned "they have no title" to it "but what rests on violence and cruelty."[144] This formulation cast Americans as liberators even while they complained of the inhumanity of British liberation of American slaves.

The denunciation of the inhumanity of Britain and its Native, European, and Black allies led to varying assessments of who constituted the worst savages. Opposition MPs fixated on the Native American alliance above all, and the debates in Parliament followed in that track.[145] Most American Patriots, however, found it the most useful and satisfying to define the British as the most barbarous of their gang. It was "the sceptered savage of Great-Britain,""the Royal Brute of England," albeit with his "savage allies," who had broken "through every tie of honor and Humanity." British outrages and alliances, John Wilkes cried in the Commons, had rendered Britons "the savages of Europe." The British government and armed forces were the ultimate target of such tellings, and this was a way to decivilize Americans' erstwhile metropolitan overlords.[146] White Loyalists could also fall under such descriptions, as in the Patriot song from 1780 reproaching the British for including Africans and Native Americans in their pay, plus "Tories worse, by half, than they."[147] A particularly pointed version of this narrative of enemy declension appeared late in the war, when Patriot leader Anthony Wayne spread the word of how "a British Governor attended by British Officers, should be so lost to every feeling of humanity as to parade the streets of Savannah with the scalp" of a slain Patriot officer. "Nor did their barbarity rest there," Wayne breathlessly continued. They ordered the officer's corpse "to remain unburied mangled and disfigured in so horid a manner as to beggar all discription," until some Black troops—who, he pointedly noted, were "more humanized" than the Britons—secretly buried it in "violation of the Savage mandate."[148] In such formulations, white Britons by their wartime atrocities had descended not only well below the civilizational level they had long assigned to white colonists but also below even Africans.

While the charge of inhumane treatment of white Patriots was the most fruitful branch of this particular rhetorical tree, the Patriots hardly left a nearby branch uncultivated: that British officials and soldiers were also in reality cruel to their supposed beneficiaries, fugitive Black Americans. As he did with so many other Patriot arguments in his blockbuster *Common Sense*, Thomas Paine showed how these charges could run together when he raged against "that barbarous and hellish power" which had "stirred up the Indians and the Negroes to destroy us." In this instance, Britain's "cruelty hath a double guilt, it is dealing brutally by us, and treacherously by them."¹⁴⁹ Patriot newspaper editors therefore had a massive appetite for accounts of disillusioned African American recruits deserting or otherwise repudiating the British armed forces.¹⁵⁰ To this end, one Patriot account put an Orwellian spin on an episode in which Virginia forces encountered about a thousand gravely ill Black troops abandoned by Dunmore on Gwynn Island when he was forced to retreat. Vindictive white Patriots set fire to their huts, burning them to death. But in a Patriot telling printed in newspapers, the white Virginians "found the enemy had evacuated the place with the greatest precipitation, and were struck with horrour" at the dead and sick Dunmore had abandoned. "Many were burnt alive in brush huts," the author continued in a classic use of the passive voice, before apostrophizing that "such a scene of misery, distress, and cruelty, my eyes never beheld; for which the authors, one may reasonably conclude, never can make atonement in this world." There was of course meant to be no doubt that Dunmore and his troops were those "authors."¹⁵¹ And this was but the most striking of many gleeful Patriot reports of Dunmore offering his Black recruits "the most cruel and inhuman treatment."¹⁵² This running Patriot argument led to the outlandish conclusion by Nathanael Greene late in the war that the storied tyrants of the ancient world "were never more detested, than the british Army in this Country," meaning South Carolina specifically. "Even the Slaves rejoice," he averred, "and feel a kind of freedom from oppression" whenever "their masters" the Patriots retook an area from British occupation.¹⁵³ And it took pointed political and monetary form during the long, slow evacuation of the British from American ports. In August 1783, in a letter to his state's congressional delegation, Virginia governor Benjamin Harrison expounded his view that the peace treaty should only "be strictly adhered to" by Americans if the British returned or paid for those enslaved Americans who "were spirited away" by their troops. He held that this would apply "even tho' they should be dead, as their deaths in a great measure proceeded from a camp fever got in the british army and their being totally neglected when ill."¹⁵⁴

Another remarkable instance of this theme came from Josiah Atkins, a Connecticut man in the Continental Army, who in June 1781 recoiled at marching past Washington's and other leading Patriots' plantations and reflecting on how many horribly mistreated people they enslaved. But he also reported marching past the corpses of "18 or 20 Negroes" left "by the way-side, putrifying with the *small pox*." This atrocity was "a piece of Cornwallisean cruelty," he explained. For the "artful general" Lord Cornwallis had easily recruited "great numbers" of enslaved Americans, given how "disaffected" they were by "their harsh treatment." But rather than proving their benefactor, he "inoculates them, & just as they all are growing sick, he sends them out in to the country where our troops had to pass & repass." That this candid, antislavery Patriot could have bought into a tale of Cornwallis using African American bodies as biological weapons rather than truly liberating them showed how eager he was to believe the worst of British forces.[155]

The ultimate, and thus most prolific, version of this allegation of British hypocrisy and inhumanity was that they never meant to honor their promises of freedom to enslaved Americans. This theme produced multiple subthemes. One was that the British had stolen these people rather than that they had fled to British lines of their own accord. This allegation was important not only amid the battle over which side was waging a just war but also given how racialized the virtue of humanity had long been; it pictured Black people as pawns and their white manipulators as the ultimate in inhumanity. British raids on American plantations by this reckoning constituted not acts of liberation but pure "acts of violence." This became so commonplace that Dunmore's character in John Leacock's Patriot play *The Fall of British Tyranny* went by the shorthand of "The Kidnapper."[156] A softer version of this interpretation of slave flight was that Britain was "tempting our slaves by every artifice," "tampering with the Slaves," had "inveigled them from their proprietors," and the like. The language of seduction was common in this strand.[157] Even that milder version helped Patriots to police the boundary that grouped themselves as the true friends of liberty and their enemies as the opposite. As a North Carolina Patriot phrased it in 1776, that colony's royal governor "has coaxed a number of Slaves to leave their Masters." This encapsulated in his mind how "everything base and wicked are practised by him," clarifying the core issues for "the Inhabitants that are Friends to liberty."[158] In this context, even a few runaway slave advertisements—usually a genre noted for being straightforward recitals of necessary facts—became politicized. In the aftermath of Dunmore's Proclamation, Virginia slaveholder Robert Brent found it necessary to assert that a man named Charles's "elopement was from no cause of complaint" with his treatment—"for he has always been remarkably indulged"—but instead "from a determined resolution to get liberty, as he conceived, by flying to lord Dunmore."[159]

In whichever guise, it should be noted, this political imperative created the unanticipated consequence of politicizing African Americans' agency. That it was unintended is underscored by the heavy dose of condescension toward Black Americans in these expressions, whom the authors broadly assumed to be easily duped. Edmund Pendleton typified the resulting scrutiny of fugitives' actions when he commented that two escapees were "believed to be willing captives."[160] Francis Lightfoot Lee, for his part, waxed philosophical when consoling fellow Virginia planter Landon Carter on some of his enslaved people having "joined the Arch Devil" Dunmore. "Slavery plants a Vice," he sighed, "where a Virtue might be expected." In this reading, slavery was an evil but seeking freedom with America's archenemy represented vice in those whose choices in this context were inescapably political.[161] In June 1781, Virginia's legislature wrestled with the limits of the agency of the enslaved in response to the petition of a slaveholder. "Will, a Negro man slave belonging to" the petitioner, had been "condemned to suffer death for treason" by a county court. But the petitioner argued that this sentence was "illegal, because a slave cannot commit treason." Whatever crime Will had committed against the revolutionary state, by this logic, could not have been of his own devising. In a triumph of such slaveholding Patriot reasoning rather than humanitarian sentiment, the legislative committee charged with this petition recommended that the legislature pardon Will.[162]

For their part, British commanders both trumpeted and codified Black agency, manifestly for the purpose of neutralizing the "slave stealing" charge. In late 1775, South Carolina Patriot Fenwick Bull confronted British naval captain John Tollemache, demanding the return of enslaved people whom Tollemache and his crew had "inticed" on board. Tollemache readily retorted that they "came as freemen" and that "he could have had near 500" join him because of the allure of freedom.[163] In 1776, British general Henry Clinton instituted an oath of allegiance that would be necessary for any African Americans enlisted in his forces, promising in return that he would do his utmost to assure their freedom "at the expiration of the present Rebellion." The oath required the enlistee to "swear that I enter freely & voluntarily into His Majesty's Service, and I do enlist myself without the least compulsion or persuasion." The repetition was telling of the need to make the consent absolutely clear.[164]

The most explosive subtheme was that British officials and military men had sold these fugitive slaves into slavery in the West Indies. Within days of Dunmore's Proclamation, Pendleton retailed to Thomas Jefferson the public rumor "that he has sent off a sloop load to the West Indies." Pendleton gloated that this would surely mean that his "slave scheme is . . .

at an end." Another slaveholder, Robert Carter, also sought to spin the proclamation immediately upon hearing it—but his immediate audience was his enslaved laborers, whom he called together to warn them that Dunmore would sell them to the West Indies if they joined him.[165] In Virginia's newspapers, the issue that printed Dunmore's Proclamation followed it immediately with an essay condemning it on multiple grounds, including the falseness of the governor's offer of freedom. The English in general, the essayist admonished, were not to be trusted. "Long have the Americans, moved by compassion, and actuated by sound policy, endeavoured to stop the progress of slavery," such as by banning the slave trade. But these "humane intentions" of multiple state legislatures had been "frustrated by the cruelty and covetousness of" English merchants and the government they controlled. "Can it then be supposed," the author pursued, "that the negroes will be better used by the English, who have always encouraged and upheld this slavery, than by their present masters, who pity their condition?" The likely outcomes were that Dunmore, after having used these slaves for his foul purposes, would "either give up the offending negroes to the rigour of the laws they have broken, or sell them in the West Indies, where every year they sell many thousands of their miserable brethren."[166]

In the summer of 1776, South Carolina Patriot Henry Laurens wrote a remarkable letter to his son John that showed how helpful this charge could be on multiple levels both psychological and political. He reported that hundreds of American slaves had already "been stolen & decoyed by the Servants of King George the third," who now "steal those Negroes from the Americans to whom they had sold them." Worse than that complicated hypocrisy, while "pretending to set the poor wretches free," George's military minions "basely trepan & sell them into ten fold worse Slavery in the West Indies, where probably they will become the property of English Men again & of some who sit in Parliament." Knowing from his own earlier experience that John, still resident in London, was swimming in the metropolis's decidedly antislavery waters, Henry paused to assure him that "I abhor Slavery," and that he was "devising means for manumitting many of" the people he had inherited as slaves. Thus, it was his benevolent, essentially antislavery self—not some grasping desire to preserve his human property—that was so horrified by the British forces' "meanness" and "complicated wickedness" in treating Black Americans in this way. A letter from a father to a son might not normally seem political, but this letter clearly had political purposes including preserving the good name of the Patriot cause while Britons posed as emancipators, and preserving his son's high regard for him in Carolina while John drank deep from London's antislavery well.[167]

This charge was so potentially damning that British officials took it deadly seriously. They certainly took it more seriously than strict necessity required, given that Patriots themselves had publicly sold African Americans into West Indian bondage during the war. The Virginia Convention, for instance, made no secret of selling recaptured slaves—including Black POWs taken after the defeat of Dunmore's forces at the Battle of Great Bridge—to the West Indies as well as to lead mines within Virginia.[168] Not content to settle for "what-about-ism" on this serious issue, British officials acted to deny the Patriots any opening based on fact. In 1779, Sir Henry Clinton, British general-in-chief, issued an order not only offering freedom to all slaves who "shall desert the Rebel Standard" but also forbidding "any person to sell or claim right over any Negro the property of a Rebel who may take refuge with any part of this army."[169] Less than two years later, royal governor Sir James Wright, amid all the other challenges and demands on his time during the British occupation of Savannah late in the war, made diligent inquiry about rumors of African Americans "brought into this province with a view to sell or ship off." He was greatly relieved that he "could not discover that any were." Similarly, in 1783 government officials in Jamaica cracked down on the sale of African American slaves by refugee American planters on the island. Even in the chaos at war's end, imperial authorities could not brook a whisper of truth to the American allegations.[170] Such was the power of the political need to be seen as the true benefactor to African Americans.

A variant of these strands going right to the heart of the imperial crisis was the running Patriot argument that Britain's inhumane slave policy fit neatly into the government's pattern of abuse of power. Patriots considered "the present Ministry" and all its representatives and tools "as enemies to the freedom of the human race," two members of Congress warned some London associates, "like so many Devils in the infernal regions, sending out their servants, furies, to torment where-ever they choose their infernal vengeance should fall." The flip side of this same coin was the Patriot logic that "we are fighting for the Dignity and Happiness of Human Nature," so "cursed and Detested will everyone be that deserts or betrays" that cause. These firm convictions could not help but filter how white Patriots viewed fugitive slaves and other allies of the crown—they had betrayed rather than advanced liberty.[171] In an anonymous piece published in Boston in 1782, *A Dialogue between the Devil, and George III*, the running depiction of George as an inordinately dedicated, if often bumbling, servant of the devil's tyrannical schemes against humankind precluded by definition any idea that George and his servants were humane liberators. At one point in this conversation "between the vilest being in the other world, and the worst in this," when George boasted that he would refuse to "stoop so low" as the French king did when he allied with the rebels, the devil responded, "George, you lie like hell, for you've employ'd Indians, Negroes, Tories, thieves, robbers, counterfeiters of money, and the off-scouring, scum, and sweepings of the world" against the Americans. An American hero introduced to speechify at the end of this pamphlet thundered that George, in his scheme "to enslave" the Americans, "formed the horrid design, and have pursued it by means too infernal to be named; you have violated all the sacred laws of heaven and earth, and sported with human misery."[172] Congressman Gouverneur Morris put it rather more succinctly. Many Americans had been quite slow to perceive the ministry's "design to enslave us," but "the conduct of Lord Dunmore, in tendering freedom to all the slaves who should butcher their masters and repair to his standard, was sufficient to have opened our eyes."[173]

Washington therefore meant nary a hint of irony when he urged his troops to "show the whole world, that a Freeman contending for Liberty on his own ground is superior to any slavish mercenary on earth," despite the fact that he meant the epithet to encompass African Americans freed by the British. One of Washington's subordinate commanders was also in deadly earnest when he referred to British and Loyalist forces—including Black Loyalists—as "the Friends of Slavery."[174] White Virginian Samuel Kemp likewise combined obtuseness with clarity by Patriot lights when he defended himself against charges "that I had endeavoured to exasperate the Negroes to rise and carry into Execution the ministerial Measures against the Rights and Liberties of America." Aiding slave insurrection, he insisted in this open letter to the public, would be "repugnant to that Spirit of Liberty which circulates with the Blood in my Veins."[175] The true spirit of liberty could only be on one side in this contest, and by these formulations it was not and never could be with the emancipating British.

Even American Patriots observing all this from Europe, and who were themselves not fully friendly to slavery, joined in linking British emancipation to British abuse of power. In 1777, Benjamin Franklin lectured the American-friendly British politician David Hartley that Britain's "numberless Barbarities, in the Prosecution of the War"—including "bribing

Slaves, to murder their Masters"—had convinced Americans that "you are no longer the magnanimous and enlightened Nation we once esteemed you" and "that you are unfit and unworthy to govern us, as not being able to govern your own Passions."[176] John Adams in the Netherlands, who saw the southern states as "unfortunate" as well as vulnerable to invasion due to slavery, raged that "Great Britain has been moving Earth and Hell to obtain Allies against us." Those included "many States of Germany, many Tribes of Indians, and many Negroes their Allies." In this rendering, slavery made southerners unfortunate, but using those slaves to further their hellish purpose made Britons dastardly.[177]

As with other Patriot themes, Dunmore embodied the idea that British emancipation proceeded from the most ignoble of motives. "Lord Dunmores Negroe Soldiers," Lund Washington jabbed in a letter to his distant cousin George, were largely commanded by Scottish officers— "proper Officers for Slaves, for they themselves Possess Slavish Principles." While such private expressions may not have been playing politics per se, they help explain the politics in which the likes of Dunmore—whom Washington dubbed "that Arch Traitor to the Rights of Humanity"— could do and mean nothing good.[178] Thus, George Washington argued, were a Patriot bullet to kill Dunmore, "the World would be happily rid of a Monster without any person sustaining a loss." That categorization obviously included Dunmore's Black recruits.[179] From the gunpowder crisis to his proclamation and beyond, Dunmore's policies both relative to and unrelated to slavery combined to convince Virginia Patriots "of his fixed determination to do this unhappy country every injury in his power." And he was but the most prominent personification of how the politics of emancipation could never be disentangled from those of the imperial crisis itself.[180]

British opposition figures chimed in that the ministry's foul means of waging the war were commensurate with its foul purposes in waging the war. Britons at home, Edmund Burke wrote, might well become "the Victims" of the cruel tyrannical war waged in America if the ministry succeeded. Among "the improper modes of carrying on this unnatural and ruinous war," he pursued, North's administration had, by means of Dunmore's Proclamation, sought to stir up "an universal insurrection of Negro Slaves." They and Native Americans, Burke chided, "are not fit instruments of an English Government"—at least when it was acting on English principles.[181] In the House of Lords in late 1777, the Duke of Richmond thundered that "to arm negro slaves against their masters, to arm savages, who we know will put their prisoners to death in the most cruel tortures, and literally eat them, is not, in my opinion, a fair war against fellow subjects." But it was the fruit of the ministry's boundless, politically motivated disdain for American subjects, which had spread to British troops fighting there.[182] The common idea that the means and ends of policy in this war were connected led Dissenting minister Joshua Toulmin to preach that the government's brutality in waging it—including "that Negro slaves have been excited to take up arms against their masters"—had rendered "some doubtful of the goodness of our cause."[183]

Toulmin spoke accurately for supporters of government; policies like the Native American alliances and arming of former slaves divided them. While some certainly advocated hard war, others found such policies distasteful as clear signs that Britain had embraced the eighteenth-century version of the nuclear option. Some denied arming Indigenous and African American allies for as long as possible. North Carolina's royal governor Josiah Martin, for instance, denied recruiting fugitive slaves in 1775 in a letter to his superiors even as he made military arguments in favor of doing so. In the fall of that year, William Henry Lyttelton shocked the sensibilities of the House of Commons when he spoke approvingly of how, if even a small British force invaded the southern colonies, "the negroes would rise, and embrue their hands in the blood of their masters." Seeking to distance the administration from such talk in an ensuing debate, Lord North "declared that there never was any idea of raising or employing the negroes or the Indians, until the Americans themselves had first applied to them." The prime minister prevaricated with this statement, but it is telling that he sought to fix on the Patriots the guilt of having escalated the war in this way. Lord Cornwallis likewise followed in this track five years later when he complained that "the infamous falsehoods so industriously circulated by our enemys"—specifically, that Britons were willy-nilly confiscators and emancipators of enslaved Americans—"have done us infinite mischief." Such impressions must be counteracted by policies better suited to assuage the fears of slaveholders in the Carolina theater, he suggested.[184]

Once these alliances could no longer be denied, many proponents of the war shrunk from them. An editorial in the *Gentleman's Magazine*, for instance, contrasted Dunmore's "provocation" with his proclamation with the "benevolent and conciliating disposition" of royal governors who had not embraced such a drastic policy.[185] Jamaican slaveholder Edward Long had his own reasons to bemoan that stark military "*necessity*" had led to

Britain's "engaging *negroe servants* to butcher their masters" and enlisting "Cannibal Indians." He could only pray that the use of such allies, in addition to German mercenaries, would not lead to "*wanton*" actions that went "beyond what are fatally common in all wars," and that even if so "the odium will not be found to press against our *national forces*." For in past empires, "the wickedness of committing such barbarous havock" called down "the judgment of God and man." Whereas abolitionists saw slavery itself as calling down such divine and political judgments, he worried that military emancipation would do so.[186] Well beyond this absentee planter, justifications for these alliances often took on a pronounced defensive tone. One British officer protested that "I am persuaded that I am by no means destitute of the feelings of humanity" and assured that he "can restrain" his nonwhite subordinates "from acts of savage cruelty."[187] Still others lamented the popular connection between Black troops and unrestrained marauding, believing it to reflect reality and therefore to be damaging to the political and military cause of the king. A British officer complained that African American troops "distress and maltreat the inhabitants infinitely more than the whole army," and such ravages led to the "alienation of every thinking mind from the Royal Cause."[188] As a result, some in their writings went out of their way to associate Black recruits with the Patriots rather than their own forces. For instance, Sir Henry Clinton's postwar memoir only directly mentioned the American rebels as having benefited militarily from enslaved labor.[189]

For his part, the German officer Johann Ewald regretted an incident that seemed to confirm that royal troops were no more humane than slaveholding Patriots. He wished he did not have "to record a cruel happening" at the siege of Yorktown, one diary entry read. When the American and French forces assaulted the depleted garrison, "we drove back to the enemy all of our black friends, whom we had taken along toe despoil the countryside. We had used them to good advantage and set them free, and now, with fear and trembling, they had to face the reward of their cruel masters." While scarcity of food meant "this harsh act had to be carried out," he did note that "we should have thought more about their deliverance at this time."[190]

Against what seems to us to be insurmountable odds, then, Patriots contested the politics of humanity in connection with race and American slavery on roughly equal terms with Loyalists. Possibly the most telling example of white Patriots' confidence that they could win the label of humanity for themselves even when connected to slavery came with some fake news they spread in late 1775. Virginia Patriots pushed the rumor that Lord Dunmore's Black troops had fought in the Battle of Great Bridge with "Liberty to Slaves" emblazoned on their uniforms. In reality, as Cassandra Pybus's research has shown, far from being able to inscribe uniforms with slogans, Dunmore was scrambling to find any clothing possible for his underequipped men.[191] It is worth contemplating why Patriots thought it would be politically useful to spread this particular falsehood. Amid the twists and turns of what constituted political high ground, the Patriots, at least in a place like Virginia, seem to have felt it safe to assume that no whites would think Dunmore had seized that high ground as a true liberator. It seems the most likely that this was meant to both leverage white insurrection anxiety and poke fun at British pretensions to stand for liberty.

6

Honor

ᛒᛒ

Honor constituted yet another virtue that contestants eagerly claimed for their cause and wove together with slavery and race in multiple ways. Given the importance of honor in military culture, it was of special importance during the war, but it also ran throughout the whole period of crisis, and political as well as military combatants eagerly claimed it. Ironically, the people white folk throughout the British Atlantic thought least honorable—the enslaved—ended up pushing British officials unexpectedly to take principled antislavery positions in the name of honor. As such, the value whites on both sides placed on this concept powerfully shaped the history of slavery in this era as well as of the conflict itself.

The culture of the British Atlantic in the late eighteenth century placed a high premium not only on personal honor but also on national honor. Nothing was more central to the latter than what a parliamentary resolution described as "the maintenance of an inviolable character for moderation, good faith, and scrupulous regard to treaty."[1] George III touched on both personal and national honor when he told his lord chancellor after Parliament had turned against the American war that to accept opposition leaders as his new cabinet would be to "give up my principles and my honour, which I value above my crown." He also combined both concepts when he tried to be philosophical about losing the thirteen colonies. "Knavery seems to be so much the striking feature of" Americans' character, he mused in late 1782, "that it may not in the end be an evil that they become Aliens to this Kingdom."[2]

American Patriots, of course, rejected the imputation of knavery and committed themselves to demonstrating to their enlightened Atlantic audience that theirs was an honorable cause and then new nation. "Scarcely anything is so important to an individual as a good Name," Massachusetts Patriot Joseph Ward wrote in 1775, "and it is vastly more interesting to a Community." Therefore, he believed, if American Patriots could "maintain the Character of humane, generous, and brave" men, "we shall be invincible to all the tyrants in the world, and even our Enemies will at once fear and reverence the guardians of Liberty."[3] Even after they had declared their independence, Americans felt the need to defend their honor as former provincials in their former metropolis. In 1777, Virginia newspaper editors eagerly ran an account of a "fracas which lately happened in a coffee-house" in London. A man returned from service in the East India Company sparked the fray by waxing "profuse in the abuse of the Americans, whom he repeatedly stiled a cowardly, illiterate, and treacherous set of people, and among whom he had never found one that was worthy of the trust and confidence of a Gentleman." A Virginia planter promptly identified himself as "an American" and retorted that his friends there were "as much above the illiberal epithets thrown out against them, as a Gentleman was the superior of a kidnapper." That the Virginian triumphed in this verbal and physical altercation, and by extension vindicated the character of Americans for honor as well as humanity against this EIC "kidnapper," was surely what made this the paper's lead story.[4]

Keeping national promises was central to national character in leading Patriots' minds, just as it was in those of European diplomats and thinkers. As Craig Bruce Smith has written, elite would-be Founders in particular "carefully and continuously reflected on the ethics of their deeds" and the consequences thereof "for the fledgling nation. They wanted to win, but win well." Thus, in Smith's interpretation, ideas surrounding honor "were a driver of personal and political thought and action, not a tool for the rationalization of material interest or simply an overly dramatic metaphor." "Ethical choices" made a man (and by extension collectives of men, including nations) honorable, they insisted, more than "external rank and reputation" as in aristocratic European notions of honor. That said, as leaders of a fledgling nation, they were if possible more obsessed with national reputation than were the British or any other European power. As Smith has put it, "The emerging nation viewed the opinions of the world as just as vital as those of the country's citizens."[5] Benjamin Franklin certainly asserted that Americans cared more, at least in a purported letter to the Earl of Shelburne published in newspapers. Spurning any idea of the United States's making peace separate from their French ally, Franklin jabbed that such "treachery and ingratitude" might well "be British policy—but I trust it will never by adopted by America." Americans, his sarcasm continued, must reach the same "intoxication of glory and power" as Britain had achieved before it could "fall into those atrocious errors." "You may be certain," he lectured Shelburne, that "we shall preserve our honour." For as a nation just emerging on the world stage, "we cannot exist but by the preservation of our honour."[6] As with George III vilifying American rebels, seeing their enemies as radically dishonorable became a sustaining motive for Patriots like Franklin throughout the war.

Contrary to Franklin's quips, Britons also treasured national honor, which they connected to Britain's imperial glory as well as to its reputation for collective attributes. In 1775, Charles Fox thus aimed to hit the North administration where it hurt when he sneered that it had spent "nearly as large a sum to acquire national disgrace as" previous prime minister William Pitt had spent during the last war "in gaining that glorious lustre with which he had encircled the British name." And North responded in kind when he urged that defending the "insulted honour of the British nation" against American rebels was a key motive for war. These were just opening salvos in a running series of parliamentary battles over whether the administration's war policy upheld or ruined Britain's glory. In a 1777 debate over the king's speech declaring that upholding the national honor against Americans' mortal insults was a key cause for continuing the war, the Earl of Sandwich pronounced that he "could not endure the thought" of admitting American independence, for that would be insupportably "derogatory to the honour" and "disgraceful to the character" of Great Britain. Opposition MPs retorted that it was the ministry's pigheaded war policy that had "precipitated this nation from the highest pinnacle of fame and happiness, to the lowest abyss of wretchedness and disgrace." And on it went—but this debate was about the ethical conduct (never far removed from the questions of humanity dealt with in the last chapter) as well as the military outcome of the war.[7]

One lens through which to see both sides' valuation of keeping promises was the fate of Loyalists following American victory. British negotiator Henry Strachey implored the American commissioners at peace talks in Paris in late 1782 to protect the United States's reputation for "Honour and Humanity" by agreeing to generous terms for Loyalists, but most leading Britons seemed to think the condition of the Loyalists reflected more on their own nation's honor.[8] For the North ministry and George III, protecting these loyal subjects, as we have seen, rose in order of priority as the war progressed. Others followed suit. Parliamentary debates about the draft peace treaty in early 1783 turned on questions of keeping national faith, especially to Loyalists and Native American allies. Lord Walsingham cried that "the cruelty and perfidy" of what he saw as breaches of faith, especially to Indians, were beyond his "powers of description." But he certainly tried: "It was a most impolitic as well as a most dishonourable conduct. Faith, truth, justice, all that was sacred amongst men and nations must disdain and reprobate it; it would be a stain on our character as a people to the latest posterity." Even Josiah Tucker, who thought fighting the war was futile but did not go into opposition to the government, agreed that "in rendering *them* happy, (who were made miserable on our Account) we should consult our own national Honour in the most effectual manner."[9] Loyalists of all ethnic backgrounds pushed British officials hard to keep their promises, including by leveraging slavery rhetoric. "The character as well as interest of the British nation," warned a writer claiming to be a Loyalist in New York, "is materially concerned in" protecting Loyalists in the peace treaty. "What must the world think of a nation" that would sacrifice its friends? "Or what confidence can ever be placed in it hereafter?" Hearing of their betrayal in the treaty of 1783, Creek leaders remonstrated to British officials that "the King and his Warriors have told us they would never forsake us." But in fact, "does he mean to abandon us? Or does he intend to sell his friends as Slaves?"[10] Americans were divided on the postwar fate of Loyalists. As Robert M. Calhoon has shown, at the local and nonelite levels, victorious but war-weary Patriots vacillated between the urges to end this bitter civil war and to nurture grudges. But many leaders of the new nation believed that "strict compliance" with the clauses in the Treaty of Paris protecting Loyalists "was an essential precondition to establishment of a national reputation for justice and civility."[11]

One way in which the combined solicitude for personal and collective honor shaped the entire imperial crisis was that Patriots feared not only slavery but slavishness—the attributes they associated with bondage. Part of why slavery was such a powerful political tool was that so many Patriots, especially but not only in the South, had almost boundless disdain for the submissive characteristics they demanded from and thus observed among their own slaves. But it was far from only American planters who held this view. Josiah Quincy's commonplace book drew on multiple British and ancient sources expressing horror at "the prostitute tameness of slaves." And Adam Smith, in one of his works of moral philosophy, posited that it was "human nature" that "a person becomes contemptible who tamely sits still, and submits to insults, without attempting either to repel or to revenge them." "We are really provoked" when we encounter such "mean-spiritedness," Smith continued.[12] In 1766, an anonymous compiler prefaced his compendium of the laws that comprised the British constitution by reflecting that whenever true men encountered "a *tyrannical and despotic state*," they quite naturally "rise when opportunity offers, and throw off the yoke." He pointedly left "the indolent *Asiatics* out of the question; I write of Northern states, whose subjects are MEN." This was the quintessence of the British fear of and disdain for slavishness: for this writer, standing up for liberty defined not only "civilized states" but also humanity itself.[13]

Patriots drew liberally on this idiom. As one Patriot summed it up, slavery "in one word comprehends Poverty Misery Infamy and every Species of Ruin & Distruction."[14] For instance, singers of a widely influential Patriot song, written in 1768 by luminaries John Dickinson and Arthur Lee, chanted that "to DIE we can *bear*—but to SERVE we *disdain*—/ For SHAME is to *Freemen* more dreadful than PAIN." And its chorus (repeated eight times) was, "In FREEDOM we're BORN, and in FREEDOM we'll LIVE / Our Purses are ready, / Steady, Friends, Steady, / Not as SLAVES, but as FREEMEN our Money we'll give."[15] In this formulation shame was the very essence of slavery, the sort of shame to which these singers vowed never to submit. Indeed, the fear of free white colonists sinking "from the rank of freemen into the class of slaves, overwhelmed with all the miseries and vices, proved by the history of mankind to be inseparably annexed to that deplorable condition," thundered forth from many a Patriot throat and pen.[16] A New York Patriot essayist contended that "*Tyrants* and *Slaves* are the weakest creatures of the human race," and that those who submitted to slavery were "vile and miserable."[17] A Massachusetts pastor in a 1771 election sermon worried that any hearer who acquiesced in Parliament's usurpation would become "wholly dependent on their pleasure, having nothing that he can call his own; and what is he then but a perfect slave." Thus, for all the duties of obedience enjoined on Christians, they must not, "from a mean, timorous, and slavish temper, to resign up their just rights, . . . remembering they are freemen and not slaves."[18] All of this was background for Josiah Quincy's famous outburst in his 1774 Boston Massacre sermon: "I speak it with grief—I speak it with anguish—Britons are our oppressors:—I speak it with shame—'I speak it with indignation—WE ARE SLAVES.'"[19] Patriots like this did not speak of some pseudo-slavery; they dreaded being "degraded from the Rank of free

Subjects, to the despicable Condition of Slaves," with all the character traits they found so despicable in those slaves.[20]

The most politically pointed invocation of slavishness the Patriots made was their multiple accusations that Loyalists manifested an abject servility to parliamentary tyranny.[21] John Adams's frustration with Loyalists boiled over in part because he believed that "the settlement of America" was meant, in the "Design of Providence," to effect "the Emancipation of the slavish Part of Mankind all over the Earth"—and Loyalists were seeking to thwart that divine design.[22] Josiah Quincy approvingly quoted in his commonplace book an English lord's parliamentary statement that if North Americans "submitted to such unjust, such cruel, such degrading slavery" the ministry intended for them, "I should think they were made for slaves." In a similar vein, an MP thundered in 1774 that any Americans who were "such *mean abject Wretches,* such *tame willing Slaves,* to submit to" the Coercive Acts "deserved every Act of Injustice, Administration had hitherto devised to inflict on them."[23]

North American Patriots singled out specific groups within the Loyalist coalition for special abuse as epitomizing slavishness. On such group, in a fascinating example of one faction of provincials rather conspicuously looking down on another, were the Scottish. William Lee urged his brothers in London that they could never be too vigilant against "introducing Scotticism's into your writing," for "not only the principles, but the phraseology of that accursed Country is prevalent everywhere."[24] In 1774, Landon Carter "took notice" to a group of fellow Virginians "of the Part the Gent[lemen] of the Scotch Nation were acting" in the imperial crisis. Most of them in Virginia, he noted, "seem active in endeavouring to Persuade a Submission to this Arbitrary taxation." This should not surprise anyone, Carter continued, for having been raised "under strange feudal tenets, they were strangers to Liberty themselves and wanted the rest of Mankind to live under the same slavish notions, that they had ever done."[25] Especially in the aftermath of the Boston Massacre, it also became common for Patriots to depict soldiers in the standing imperial army as being in "a state of slavery in the midst of a free nation." That was bound to lead to disaster, "for slaves envy the freedom of others, and take a malicious pleasure in contributing to destroy it."[26] Three years of brutal war did not convince the likes of Samuel Adams to look with understanding on any Americans who so much as fraternized with captured Redcoats. "'These people," Adams simmered, clearly possessed "a Degree of Servility shocking to sober Humanity." They "are formd to be Asses & Slaves; Let them remain so."²⁷

A variation on this theme was that Loyalists deserved slavery as their punishment. One of the toasts at a public meeting in Boston offered the choice of "Repentance or Slavery to the *infamous few* who were willing to accept the Stamp-Act."²⁸ In 1765, "Americanus" lampooned defenders of the Stamp Act in the *Boston Gazette*. They loved to quote powerful Britons to the effect "that *a respectful submission is your interest as well as your duty*. And so it is with your brother Americans, the black inhabitants of the West India islands." Their duty was to support their masters "in luxury and grandeur, and it is as plainly their INTEREST, to bear fifty lashes without muttering, for fear of having a hundred."²⁹ A Patriot in London raged that "the Savage Minestry" should be the ones "drove in to Slavry at Barbry or Algirs," and fantasized that his spelling issues notwithstanding, he would gain the power to decide how long they would "remain their."³⁰ Another North American Patriot thundered that anyone who resisted Congress's authority evinced such slavishness that he "should be sold 'at a public Vendue' and sent 'to plant sugar with his fellow slaves in Jamaica.'"³¹

West Indian colonies' reluctance to join the Patriot ranks led to a proliferation of this sort of linkage between Loyalism and West Indian slavery, slavish West Indian politicians, and their slaves. The West Indian lobby's interests very often led them to take policy stands directly in opposition to North Americans', such as supporting the Sugar Act of 1764 and opposing the proposed slave trade bans of the 1770s. Similarly, while North American Patriots regarded the British Army as the avatar of military despotism, white West Indians and their lobby constantly called for more imperial troops in the islands, and in fact increasingly so in the 1760s in light of multiple West Indian slave insurrections and plots. North Americans' resentment only rose seeing how much more powerful the West Indian lobby was than any representation they had in London, but the power of that lobby also led Patriots to scrutinize West Indians' positions during the imperial crisis.³² Keeping their heads down was also good metropolitan politics. William Beckford, who made himself conspicuous in the late 1760s as an opponent of the ministries' American policies, made an easy target as an absentee West Indian slaveholder, and the ministerial party fired away: "To see a slave he could not bear," went one typical squib, "unless it were his own." Beckford's biographer concludes that he and his kind in London backed down from the agitation of West

Indian rights that would have provoked further attacks of this kind.[33] In this they provide a fascinating contrast to the North American Patriots who refused to be cowed by the constant charges of inconsistency.

For many North American Patriots, especially but not only in New England, the prevalence and objective horrors of slavery in the sugar islands of the West Indies, together with white West Indians' perceived backwardness in the Patriot cause, led to some revealing outbursts against the West Indians. In 1766, Portsmouth, New Hampshire, Patriots greeted an arriving sea captain bearing a "let-pass" he had received from Barbados's royal governor under the Stamp Act as one bearing "the Ignominous Ensigns of CREOLE SLAVERY." These Sons of Liberty seized this document so as "to show Posterity their Abhorrence of a People who can so tamely submit themselves to the Yoke of Servitude." All North Americans, they thundered, should withdraw "our Connection with such SLAVES, and let them want the comfortable Enjoyment of every delicious Dainty from us, till they are brought to a State of Despondency, without Cash, without any Thing but stinking Fish and false Doctrines." Just days later these Sons of Liberty consigned the let-pass to a bonfire, together with an effigy of George Grenville to which they affixed some lines of doggerel grousing that "his fav'rite ACT Barbadian Slaves / Adopted have, such menial Knaves / Slavery may suit, but not these Climes, / Where Freedom reigns and Honor shines."[34] A North American visiting Barbados sent an epistle to Patriot newspapers pleading that it was stark necessity rather than lack of spirit that induced West Indian whites "to admit the full Execution of an Act which denominated them rather the Slaves, than the Subjects of Great Britain." Their sugar monoculture, he pled, rendered them dependent on the British Empire for necessities, and in the case of hunger their slaves would resort "to downright Insurrection and Rebellion." Accordingly, they should be pitied rather than despised. "A True North American" was having none of this, retorting that the West Indians' course of classifying the resistance of the North Americans as rebellion "sinks these slavish Islanders below Contempt. If they were content to become Slaves, (which they richly deserve for their Inhumanity to those whom *they* have made so) yet methinks common Decency might have restrained them from bestowing the very pretty Epithet of Rebels" on North Americans. Unlike West Indians, North Americans "are the Fellow Subjects of Freemen, not the Fellow Subjects of Slaves."[35] The Barbadians' and Jamaicans' failure to emulate North Americans' united stand against the Stamp Act, John Adams thundered in his diary, constituted a "base Desertion of the

Cause of Liberty" worthy of "Punishment." He prescribed that they "be made Slaves to their own Negroes," whose frequent insurrections showed that the enslaved people possessed "more of the Spirit of Liberty" than their masters.[36] John Dickinson likewise fumed that West Indians who had admitted the Stamp Act to be oppressive but nevertheless submitted to it presented the unusual spectacle "of a people *chusing* to be *slaves*."[37]

Many metropolitan critics of the ministry and Parliament joined the Patriot refrain by asserting that they acted as if the colonists were their slaves. Possibly worse, the Loyalists' overweening metropolitan pride and excessive disdain for the Americans seemed to have convinced them that they had a right to be the harshest of slave masters. Caleb Evans offered the most vivid of such depictions in his indignant response to the dean of Gloucester's argument "that the Americans have as effectual a check upon the *abuse* of power of taxation as the non-represented here" because MPs would only injure themselves by injuring American trade. A "simple illustration" of this argument would be that "a negro *slave* has a check upon the abuse of his master's absolute power over him, because if his master *kills him*, he can be no longer useful to him. Such, O ye Americans, is the consolation offered you by the Dean of Gloucester! Such the check you have upon the *abuse* of the power of taxation!"[38] Edmund Burke, in his noted 1775 speech warning the ministry against pursuing war, candidly argued that the "vast multitude of slaves" in the southern colonies rendered "the spirit of liberty still more high and haughty than in those to the northward." For them, freedom was "not only an enjoyment, but a kind of rank and privilege." Burke declined to "commend" the "morality of" this racialized "pride" among white southerners but cautioned that the ministry ignored it at its peril.[39] After the outbreak of war, opposition MPs blamed the conflict on, and predicted disaster because of, the ministry's perverse determination to enslave freemen. In the Lords in 1775, the Earl of Effingham cried that although the Americans "know they ought to be free, you tell them they shall be slaves. Is it then a wonder, if they say in despair, 'for the short remainder of our lives, we will be free!'" He challenged any of his peers to say he "would not resolve the same" in such a situation.[40] Although they naturally did not adopt this line of attack from the same sense of personal pique that American Patriots did—allying with rather than being the intended targets of such treatment—they surely found this a useful way to turn back on Loyalists their constant jabs against hypocritical slaveholding Patriots.

During the war, Patriots continued and extended this theme in part by arguing that the British ministry was using slavish allies to enslave white North Americans. A Pennsylvania Patriot demonstrated this logic of slaves seeking to enslave when he asked concerning British brutality: "Have not our Negro slaves been enticed to rebel against their masters, and arms put into their hands to murder them? Have not the King of England's own slaves, the Hanoverians, been employed? And were not the poor Canadians made slaves, that they might be made fit instruments, with other slaves and savages, to make slaves and more wretched beings than savages of us?"[41] Early in the war, a New York Patriot under the pseudonym "An English American" appealed to Redcoats, arguing that while soldiers' profession was normally "highly useful, necessary, and honourable," they had now become the instruments of tyranny. The brutal beginning of the war had put "out of dispute" the fact that "the wicked contrivers" of the conflict would pursue their "hostile intentions" at any cost, "unless we would tamely surrender our dearest rights and liberties, and consent to become slaves." He thus hoped they would desert "such a dishonourable, inhuman, and villainous service" and be "received as brothers and friends" rather than "as enemies."[42]

Indeed, the ways many Patriots deployed race revealed the severity of the perceived threat as well as their pejorative views of African Americans. Over and over again, Patriots from every part of North America expressed the full force of their objections to imperial policy by insisting that the ministry was treating them not only like slaves but very specifically like Blacks. Some few Patriots protested this employment of race, but it became the dominant strain.[43] One bold writer even suggested, in light of the *Somerset* decision, that the ministry (supported by the likes of Mansfield) were treating white colonists worse than Blacks.[44] The most obvious implication of these usages, even if the users did not consciously intend to say as much, was that slavery was natural for Blacks and unnatural for themselves as white Britons. John Adams, perhaps freed up by writing in his pseudonymous guise as the semi-literate farmer "Humphrey Ploughjogger," offered a particularly vulgar version of what he had said in a more genteel fashion when writing as himself. "Ploughjogger" thundered not only that "we won't be their negroes" but also that "Providence never designed us for negroes." If God had "intended us for slaves," God would have "given us black hides, and thick lips, and flat noses, and short woolly hair."[45]

Some of the leading names in the Patriot ranks employed this maneuver in multiple settings, across the entire period of crisis and conflict. Henry Laurens, in letters home from London in the 1770s, used race to invert the standard presumption of metropolitan superiority by comparing fashionable people, British politicians, and corrupt and inept ministers of government unfavorably to Black slaves.[46] John Adams pointedly informed a London correspondent that the Continental Congress represented "three millions of free white people."[47] Josiah Quincy took advantage of an opening to make this argument in a 1774 conversation with Isaac Barre in London. Barre remarked that when he returned from his service in North America in the Seven Years' War, "more than two thirds of this Island at that time thought the Americans were all negroes." Quincy retorted that he "did not in the least doubt it, for if I was to judge by the late acts of Parliament, I should suppose that a majority of the people of Great Britain still thought so, for I found that their representatives still treated them as such." This led to an awkward pause in the conversation, for Barre had voted for the bill to close Boston's harbor.[48] Benjamin Franklin also at times added this directly racial trope to his running complaint of colonists being treated like slaves. As David Waldstreicher has demonstrated, Franklin had been doing so at least since 1754, seeing this bold move as necessary because the stakes of both intracolonial and imperial conflicts were "to see who was the owner among owners and who could be 'blackened' into submission."[49] That the ministry had failed to treat the colonists like free white Britons should not be seen as too surprising, Franklin jabbed, given the British elite's outright enslavement of Scottish colliers despite the fact that "under the Smut their Skin *is white*."[50] In 1778, John Adams railed to a European acquaintance that by "not only hiring European Mercenaries, but instigating Indians and corrupting Domesticks," the British government had confirmed its view that Americans "were fit for nothing but to be cutt to Pieces by Savages and Negroes." But he vowed that "Americans would not submit to these Things," which seemed to amount to yet another sort of racialization of Americans.[51] In 1782, a widely reprinted newspaper article groused that Britain's willingness to negotiate with maroon leaders in Jamaica should undermine the ministry's inflexibility against negotiating a peace with Americans—who were "*white men*, after all."[52]

Rhetoric of this sort, as Michal Jan Rozbicki has demonstrated, illustrated how traditional many Patriots' understanding of liberty was even in the midst of this crisis. Because liberty in the eighteenth-century British Atlantic was "a metaphor for a cluster of specific immunities and entitlements existing along a continuum, with different portions of this spectrum available to different social ranks," freedom was a zero-sum game. "To be free," Rozbicki continues, "meant there had to be others who were less free." John Adams certainly proclaimed this concept, writing in early 1775 as "Novanglus." "There are but two sorts of men in the world," he decreed, "freemen and slaves."[53] To Patriots who employed this racial analogy, parliamentary policy did not just assault their freedom in the abstract; it threatened to push them to the extreme edge of the unfreedom side of the spectrum.

All of this represented more than paranoia on the Patriots' part, for many Britons did disdain them to the point of reading them out of whiteness. As Dror Wahrman's scholarship has shown, the war increased the psychological and political need for loyalist Britons to racialize American Patriots in this way. As a civil war, "the American war was irreducible to any reliable map of 'us' and 'them' based on a stable criterion of difference" familiar from before the war, so Britons struggled to find "new, more reliable ways of conceptualizing differences between" themselves and the rebels. And then after the Declaration of Independence, the revolutionaries' leveling tendencies threatened to destabilize identity even further. In this context, some Loyalist Britons advanced the idea that Patriots were so fundamentally different that race was an appropriate way to capture it.[54] A Loyalist song from 1775 crassly used race as a sure way to reduce the rebels to mere rabble by singing, "The rebel clowns, oh! what a sight! / Too awkward was their figure. / 'Twas yonder stood a pious wight, / And here and there a nigger."[55] Massachusetts Loyalist Henry Hulton adjudged Patriot troops such a "rude, depraved, degenerate race" that he found it mortifying "that they speak English, and can trace themselves from that stock." While a previous incident in which a Patriot mob had blackened their faces was but one of many examples of how participants in this crisis played around with race in almost endless ways, Hulton would thus probably have found that appropriate.[56] By 1781, a British lieutenant colonel's orders to his troops could casually racialize Patriots by warning against emulating the conduct of "Savages & Undiscippled Rebbels."[57]

Such attitudes only added urgency to Patriots' use of race as shorthand in their ongoing attempts to vindicate their cause as orderly rather than anarchic. In the racial politics of North America, Black people had become the avatars of social, cultural, political, and even sexual disorder, and that made them available for a wide variety of uses in this vein.⁵⁸ As if to prove that race as well as slavery was bound to have endlessly complex uses in this debate, some Patriots racialized themselves when perpetrating key acts of protest. In addition to the better-known Boston Tea Partiers dressing up as Indians, there were the Stamp Act protesters in Charleston who blackened their faces "under the 'thickest disguise of Soot.'"⁵⁹ But the more prevalent usage proved to be both sides seeking to insult the other in racial ways. A New York Loyalist, for instance, lampooned the "Provincial Congress" as being attended by "people of all sizes and of all hues! red-skins, yellow-skins, green-skins, grey-skins, bay-skins, black-skins, blue-skins!" He also directly racialized "the sons of loyalty and order" by having them be "all of one colour—*white* as the unsullied snow!" It followed, naturally, that "their conduct" was also "uniform throughout—firm, steady, peaceable, and decent."⁶⁰

But Boston Patriots became especially deft practitioners of this tactic. In 1765, when they sought to harness the traditional November 5 revelries to protest the Stamp Act, they were keenly aware of the unsavory reputation Pope's Day gatherings had gained thanks to rival neighborhood gangs' violence. Therefore, a Patriot account of the 1765 event stressed that "not a Club was seen among the whole, nor was any Negro allowed to approach the Stages." The deep association of Blacks with disorder clearly made them either untroubled by or oblivious to the irony of a rally against "Slavery" that banned Black people.⁶¹ In 1768, Boston Patriots reacted with conspicuous horror to the spectacle of "Negro drummers" flogging white British Redcoats as part of the Regulars' public staging of military discipline. In late 1768, they accused Redcoats in their town, via multiple legal complaints, of being agents both of tyranny and of disorder. A typical one charged that one John Willson sought "to spirit up, by a Promise of the Reward of Freedom, certain Negroe Slaves in Boston aforesaid, the Property of several of the Town Inhabitants, to cut their Masters Throats, and to beat, insult, and otherwise ill treat their said Masters." "To the great Terror and Danger of the peaceable Inhabitants of" Boston, the complaint continued, Willson declared that "the Negroes shall be free, and the Liberty Boys Slaves."⁶² But as Eric Hinderaker's brilliant analysis has shown, race played perhaps its most consummate role in the aftermath of the Boston Massacre, as Patriots sought to defend Boston's reputation. Loyalists had spoken of it not as a massacre but as a "Riot" led by "Factioneers" leading on "Boys and Negroes," and the Patriots felt the need to respond. In the resulting trial of the British soldiers, John Adams did this in large part by racializing the mob that provoked the shooting in order to distance it from the mainstream of the Patriot movement. Adams pointedly depicted the "thoughtless and inconsiderate" mob as "a motley rabble of saucy boys, negroes and molattoes, Irish teagues and outlandish jack tars." Free Black victim Crispus Attucks was thus especially useful to Adams in distancing this "rabble of Negroes, &c." from "the good people of the town."[63]

American Patriots also sought to turn the tables by racializing their British enemies to signify the depths of their dishonor. Massachusetts Patriot James Warren abused "the Black and White Negroes" enabling the British occupation of Boston, and another branded those willing to reconcile with Britain "Catos" to signify their slavishness by means of "the common name of a Negroo-Slave in Modern Times." Warren used "Negro policy" as shorthand for the stupidity of the ministry.[64] In 1776, Richard Henry Lee contended that the British ruling class had practiced tyranny so long that it had become a part of them. "As well," he surmised, "might a person expect to wash an Ethiopian white, as to remove the taint of despotism from the British Court." Even more pithily, he referred offhand to Dunmore as "our African Hero."[65] In a 1777 essay, another Virginia Patriot sought to rally continued effort by contrasting "the GLORIOUS CAUSE we are engaged in" as freemen with the "mercenary army" they faced. That army was "more venal than a court favourite, more savage than a band of Tartars, and more spiritless than the sooty sons of Afric," so Americans must triumph if they held firm.[66]

The Patriots likewise racialized white Loyalists in multiple ways. A newspaper item from Virginia reprobated a John Willoughby, who, with his son "and between 60 and 70 negroes," went to join Lord Dunmore on his fleet in 1776. The fact that Willoughby went "voluntarily, and without any compulsion" not only damned him as "a vile apostate" but also marked him as a *"black traitor."* The italicized word obviously meant to lump him in with his African American companions in flight.[67] Patriots did so with more than words. A Virginia Loyalist complained bitterly that the Patriots treated their prisoners "with the greatest cruelty, chaining them to Negroes, &c." Virginia Patriot commander William Woodford hardly denied such charges; he proudly admitted to ordering a captured British solider "to be coupled to one of his Black Brother Soldiers." This was the cruelty of humiliation, and was neither accidental nor anything other than political.[68]

In all of these ways, the politics of honor reinforced many American Patriots' racial ideas of African inferiority, and drawing on those ideas added force to Patriots' ongoing charges that British officials' policy of liberating and arming enslaved Americans branded their cause with deep dishonor. All of the issues surrounding the imperial crisis and war had convinced Patriots that, as Arthur Lee phrased it, "there never was a period or a people whose faith was so little to be depended on as that of the present Government of G. Britain." But the arming of enslaved Americans against Patriot Americans served for many as the final confirmation that the ministry was prepared "to break through every tie of honor" as well as of "Humanity."[69]

Many Patriots linked British disrepute directly to the allegedly shady ways in which they recruited enslaved Americans. By stealing these people/property, Britons in these accounts waged a piratical warfare that disgraced their own cause and nation. A Maryland clergyman, repulsed by Dunmore's policy of "tampering with our Negroes" and then "enticing them to cut their masters' throats while they are asleep," exclaimed, "Gracious God! that men noble by birth and fortune should descend to such ignoble base servility."[70] Henry Laurens chimed that Britain's "picaroon inglorious War," including "having taken" so many enslaved Americans from their plantations, led him to be "ashamed of" what he had once seen as "the most puissant Nation in Europe."[71] In 1781, Richard Henry Lee pointedly observed that the British forces raiding the Chesapeake seemed "to carry on the war much more upon views of private plunder & enriching individuals, than upon any plan of national advantage." "This is a curious kind of war to wage," he scribbled with deep sarcasm, "and worthy to be sure of the honor of a great King & a powerful Nation. O Britain how art thou fallen!"[72]

The wartime sermons of a Black man in Philadelphia who clearly had roots in South Carolina offer a remarkable window into the degree to which reacting this way to the British emancipation policy seems to have been something of another shibboleth among Patriots. In a discourse under the pseudonym "A Black Whig," this writer used Dunmore's and other British proclamations as some of the evidence that "humanity seems extinguished in the British breast." "They have armed domestics to fight against their masters," he thundered, "contrary to the laws of civilized nations." In 1782, publishing with the pseudonym "An African American," this same man further showed his loyalty to the Patriot cause by expostulating against those of "my own complexion" who had tested "the veracity of British promises and protection" and found them wanting. "Have ye not been disappointed" by these false allies, he remonstrated. The American Patriots, he jabbed under the name of "An Aethiopian," greatly outdistanced the British government "in humanity, generosity, and valour." These denunciations were all the more revealing of Patriot politics surrounding British emancipation because this Black preacher was undeniably antislavery in principle. He repeatedly urged his fellow Patriots to enact emancipation themselves, presumably in the right way rather than the way Dunmore and other British leaders had done it.[73]

Given the heavily racialized nature of the concepts of honor and dishonor, however, for many white Patriots, even setting aside the allegedly suspect manner of recruiting Blacks, the bare association of the British Redcoats with Black recruits stained the British cause. Well before Dunmore's Proclamation—indeed before the war broke out—one Patriot hoped, given American vulnerability, that "the Spirit of the English" would never "allow them publickly to adopt so slavish a way of Conquering" as arming the enslaved.[74] After the proclamation, the mixed-race nature of Dunmore's force led one Virginia Patriot to brand him "the *king of the blacks,* alias *pirate,* alias Dunmore," and them as "his banditti." By late in the war, Patriot poet Philip Freneau could just use shorthand to insult Cornwallis for "your Negro friends."[75] Charleston Patriot Daniel Stevens offered a particularly outraged and sexually and racially charged version of this protest in 1782. "Wou'd you believe it," he thundered in a letter to a fellow white Patriot, "the British tyrants lost to all sense of honour, have arm'd our Slaves, against us, that have fled to them." He hoped upon storming Charleston to make them "pay dear for" this transgression (despite expending no effort to contest those enslaved people's agency in running), but this was only the beginning of the British troops' violations of the racial order. For the British troops occupying Charleston "are not only lost to every sense of honour, but they are likewise to that of shame." In recent weeks they had hosted what "they called an Ethiopian Ball, at which were present the Officers of the Army, (and our female Slaves, only) who these shameless tyrants had dress'd up in taste," and on whom they lavished their attentions as if they were ladies. Worse still, "many of these wretches were taken out of houses before their mistresses faces, and escorted to the ball, by these British tyrants." After such doings by "these shameless brutes," Stevens hoped all could "see what a state of shame and perfidy the Officers of that once great Nation (Britain) has arriv'd too."[76]

The mirror image of this running charge against Britain was Patriots' ongoing self-scrutiny lest their own cause be similarly dishonored by such disreputable recruits. As early as 1775, Arthur Lee sought to derive enormous political capital from the alleged fact that on the British side, this was a war supported only by "the ministry and their Scotch supporters," together with mercenaries, given Englishmen's reluctance to shed "English blood." Meanwhile, he quoted American commander Horatio Gates's proclamation refusing "to enlist any deserter from the ministerial army, nor any stroller, negroe, or vagabond," minor, or suspected Loyalist. For Lee, the moral of "this very marked difference in the means of getting men to carry on this war" was clear: "On the American side the cause is deemed the best that can engage men of property and principle to take up arms; while on the other side, a general abhorrence of the business" prevailed upon just such first-class subjects.[77] This attitude pervaded the American army, as enlisted men as well as officers complained formally of anything smacking of treating free white men like, or enlisting them alongside, enslaved or even free African Americans.[78]

White Patriots, it must be noted, were no more of the same mind about this than they were about almost anything else, so at times fierce debates on the advisability of recruiting African Americans opened up in their ranks. The best known example of this is John Laurens's failed scheme to convince South Carolina legislators to embody a Black regiment. But there were other lower-level examples. In 1775, John Adams hoped to combat a rumor, spread "by Some" unnamed "Persons" and making "an unfriendly Impression upon Some" unspecified "Minds" in and around Boston, "that in the Massachusetts Regiments, there are great Numbers of Boys, Old Men, and Negroes, Such as are unsuitable for the service, and therefore that the Continent is paying for a much great Number of Men, than are fit for Action or any Service." Others of his comrades, however, did not share his alarm. For instance, John Thomas contested the powerful norms of racialized honor, drawing on his experience in the army camp at Roxbury. "We have Some Negros," he stipulated to Adams, but he hastened to add that "I Look on them in General Equally Servicable with other men." He actually took a dimmer view of white southerners' discipline and effectiveness than of African Americans'. Likewise, in the summer of 1776, Jonathan Dickinson Sergeant not only told Adams that he had "amused myself with the Scheme of a Negro Battalion" but also enclosed an article by "Speculator" refuting the idea that they would be unfit soldiers. "Slaves generally are Cowards," Sergeant granted, "but set Liberty before their

Eyes as the Reward of their Valour and I believe we should find them sufficiently brave. Neither the Hue of their Complexion nor the Blood of Africk" but rather the condition of being enslaved was the real question within the issue of military valor, as witnessed the maroons of Jamaica. Unconvinced, as late as 1777 the likes of Samuel Adams hoped to be able to refute the idea that Massachusetts enlisted "Boys, Negroes & Men too aged to be fit for any Service," because these would all, if true, prove embarrassing to his state.[79]

Those who hesitated to enlist African Americans of any description, however, tended to carry the day at least when it came to official national policy. For instance, upon his arrival in Cambridge, Massachusetts, to take command of the American forces, George Washington used "the Number of Boys, Deserters, & Negroes" as evidence of the indiscipline and ineffectiveness of those forces. But it remained a question in his mind whether race or condition of enslavement was at the root of those problems when it came to African American troops. He posed the question to an October 1775 council of war whether the Continental Army should enact "a Distinction between such as are Slaves and those who are Free" in recruitment. The council "agreed unanimously to reject all Slaves, & by a great Majority to reject Negroes altogether." Washington's subsequent general orders explained in pressing ideological terms why they would enlist "neither Negroes, Boys unable to bare Arms, nor old men." "The Rights of mankind and the freedom of America," he held forth, "will have Numbers sufficient to support them, without resorting to such wretched assistance." The British forces might rely on "such miscreants" as the motley crew of "those who wish to put Shackles upon Freemen," but the American armies must and would remain purer than that.[80] Free men of color continued to enlist, however, so Washington determined to put their case to Congress. In response, in January 1776, Congress sought to clarify the boundaries of American honor by resolving "that the free negroes who have served faithfully in the army" in Massachusetts "may be re-inlisted therein, but no others." Washington sought to follow that distinction in subsequent recruiting orders even as persistent manpower shortages challenged such choosiness.[81] And Virginia's legislature, in the desperation of troop shortages amid invasion in 1781, authorized the use of enslaved Virginians not as recruits themselves but as a recruitment bonus (together with land) for white men who belatedly enlisted.[82]

As the war dragged on, desperate Patriot armies expanded their enlistment of African Americans, but even this bow to reality proved controversial within the Patriot movement.[83] Writing from Philadelphia in August 1777, "Antibiastes" in a remarkable pamphlet offered an antislavery take on how this enlisting of the enslaved was dishonorable. They cheered on every glimmer of antislavery hope in Americans' legislation before the war as evidence of the "liberal spirit" and "the consistent zeal of our rulers in the cause of mankind." "Many Slaves, however, too many perhaps, are incautiously allowed to fight under our banners. They share in the dangers and glory of the efforts made by US, the freeborn members of the United States," for freedom, yet "THEY remain SLAVES!" For the United States, "Antibiastes" cautioned, "to stand indebted for the recovery of the least portion of our rights, to a race of men, whose unhappy lot must be to continue in a state of the most dishonourable degradation, would be too painful, too humiliating." The writer ardently wished that "public faith had been pledged to the Slaves, before they were permitted to fight in our cause, that their own liberty was one of the recompences, which they were to receive, for their courage and fidelity!" "GOD forbid, we should act with less generosity and justice" than the many other states who had done the same "on similar occasions!" Americans should be ashamed that even France and Spain in past conflicts had done so, but they were as yet unwilling to rely only on free people to fight for freedom.[84]

British policymakers shared many of these broad ideas that racialized honor, and most of them made it plain that their own preference would also have been to enlist only free white soldiers.[85] Although the current historiographical trend is to play up the antislavery commitments of the British by way of portraying the Patriot cause as driven by the need to protect slavery and white supremacy, many scholars over the years have rightly noted the severe limits on British policymakers' antislavery priorities. As Donald L. Robinson put it succinctly decades ago, these men were "restrained" in their approach to American slavery during the Revolutionary War because they "were trying, not to institute a revolution, but to end a rebellion."[86]

British policymakers instead found manpower to be their most pressing priority. As Piers Mackesy's penetrating analysis has highlighted, this war was unique in the British experience of wars between the Glorious Revolution and the defeat of Napoleon not only because of Britain's defeat. The "unique characteristics" of this conflict began with the herculean feat of moving and supplying tens of thousands of soldiers from beyond the Atlantic in largely hostile territory. The entrance of an unprecedented alliance of maritime powers against Britain after 1777 only exacerbated the chronic issue of manpower. All of this dictated the assembling of allies headlined by German mercenaries, Native Americans, and African Americans. The fact that the latter two were already on the ground in North America, rather than any racial liberalism, explains their inclusion in this military coalition.[87] In fact, Peter M. Voelz in his encyclopedic study of the widespread use of Black soldiers in the colonial Americas concludes that the British use of African American soldiers made it unusual, as "probably the first military struggle where blacks played roles across the board, engaging in almost every conceivable military occupation and position."[88]

But it bears repeating that this expansion of their roles did not flow from determined antislavery or antiracist sentiments among British policymakers. In the leadup to and early days of the war, the idea that the presence of "numerous slaves in the bowels of" North America would pose a major military vulnerability for the Patriots circulated as a truism among the likes of British politicians, pamphleteers, military men, and travelers, as well as North American Loyalists. American Patriots likewise expected—often in a panic—that the British would stir up American slaves in the event of a war. Granted, Samuel Johnson's immediately controversial passage in *Taxation No Tyranny* approving the idea of freeing and arming American slaves noted that this would be "an act which surely the lovers of liberty cannot but commend." But even his overall point was the military value of such a move. Traveler Andrew Burnaby neatly combined this idea of military thinking followed in priority by moralistic metropolitan judgment when he mused that North America's slaves could only "be a subject of terror to those who so inhumanly tyrannize over them."[89] "Self-preservation" and the considerable consternation his policy created in his Virginia Patriot enemies' minds led among Lord Dunmore's stated reasons for his emancipation policy and for the approval his superiors in London granted that policy.[90] Military calculations likewise and quite naturally dominated the writings of other royal governors on this subject as well as the proclamations of military commanders. The presence of a large and embittered enslaved population nurtured a persistent fantasy among policymakers that the conquest of the colonies south of New England would not require large numbers of Redcoats. Freeing the slaves of rebels was, in its essence, a means to the end of defending against and defeating those fighting under "the Rebel Standard."[91]

So was keeping some enslaved people on hand as movable property with which to reward Loyalists, especially in the southern theater late in the war. Indeed, the people most likely to benefit from British freedom proclamations were those enslaved by Patriots. British commanders and troops quickly realized that widespread and indiscriminate emancipation would be politically and militarily counterproductive in areas—such as the Lower South—where they had a reasonable hope of cultivating the favor of potential slaveholding Loyalists. In such regions, they strove particularly hard to avoid anything that could be construed as "injustice to the friends of His Majesty's government"—the white friends, that is. Their orders and correspondence from the southern theater, which by and large aimed to protect and leverage the human property of would-be white Loyalists, thus demonstrate how intensely local the politics of slavery and emancipation could be. And there as elsewhere, the ultimate goal was not Black loyalty but white loyalty. And white slaveholders, if possible even more than non-slaveholding whites, demanded stability and the protection of their property rights from any government they would call theirs.[92] Indeed, at war's end many a British governor and commander in the southern theater acted on this vision in their efforts to resettle refugee Loyalist slaveholders in East Florida. Yes, such an influx of slaveholders and slaves bid fair to bolster this struggling colony. But also, as the province's governor Patrick Tonyn put it, having rejected "every thought of becoming liable to the wanton caprice of upstarts in power, and the usurped authority of American Congress," these white Loyalists would find shelter and renewed prosperity by moving to Florida "under the auspices and paternal care of our gracious Sovereign, ever sensible of the distresses of His Subjects." Obviously, in this case that vindication of the paternal benevolence of George's regime to whites would come at the expense of African Americans forced to relocate as slaves.[93]

British commanders, on the other hand, readily recognized the massive military advantages they accrued by allying with fugitive African Americans. Those advantages were numerous, headlined by vital intelligence gathering as well as the piloting of British forces by those familiar with local terrain.[94] If any one phrase could capture the range of leading Britons' attitudes toward their Black allies, it would be the ambivalent embrace of Black allies for instrumental purposes.[95]

This ambivalence should not be surprising in light of the depths of most Britons' own condescension to and pejorative views of people of African descent, especially but not only the enslaved among them. For instance, Sir Henry Clinton, a major practical liberator as a British commander for most of the war, tellingly wrote in the same dispatch of "Negroes" interchangeably as effective military allies and as "Effects" subject to capture like other property. On the one hand, this and other recordkeeping of the British Army had a ho-hum quality for eighteenth-century white men who assumed that Black people were property. But on the other hand, that is the point worth stressing—this was hardly the recordkeeping of a deeply principled army of emancipation.[96] Furthermore, in his postwar memoir, Clinton gave grudging recognition to the importance of white Loyalists to British military operations despite his preference to rely on Regulars but only mentioned the Patriots as having benefited from enslaved labor in the fortification of Charleston.[97]

Moreover, white British officers often looked with enormous disdain on their African American allies. In 1779, for instance, Alexander Innes gave Clinton a full report of how he rescued the Queen's Rangers from a dire state of indiscipline that he saw as the result of the previous commander's recruiting the likes of "Negroes, Indians, Mulattos, Sailors and Rebel Prisoners." This, Innes was convinced, had worked to "the disgrace and ruin of the Provincial Service." In such men's minds, after all their abuse of the Patriot forces as embodying the forces of disorder and dishonor, it would not do for the British to follow suit. For men whose dominant image of Blacks was as avatars of disorder and indiscipline, not to mention a logistical burden, the imperative was to discourage their flight to British lines. The Britons' remorseless military logic in dealing with those who had fled to their lines is unsurprising given the thinking behind the green light officials had sent them in the first place. But this was military thinking combined with the politics of respectability.[98] In early 1775, getting ready to embark for the southern colonies, Scottish officer Sir James Murray imagined his group "burning the towns and carrying off old negroes and rusty canon." He was sure "the glory of these exploits" would be low, so he would have preferred "to be with the main army."[99] Other British policymakers revealingly distinguished between Blacks and soldiers, as did the officer in St. Lucia who suggested to Clinton that sending him "a couple of hundred Negroes" would not only "disencumber you" but also "save the Lives of many brave soldiers" struggling to build barracks in the Caribbean heat.[100]

West Indian British colonies like this, and the transatlantic slave trade that nourished them, comprised a major reason British officials did not pursue emancipation widely or as an end in itself. As Trevor Burnard has persuasively argued, contrary to the developing literature that posits that American rebels united against an antislavery British Empire, British officials could not even think about systematically attacking slavery or the transatlantic slave trade. British public opinion obviously leaned antislavery, but from a government point of view antislavery as a broad policy was nowhere in sight for most of the American Revolutionary era. Indeed, it is telling that in the aftermath of an insurrection scare in Jamaica in 1776, a Loyalist clergyman there argued that the licentious principles of the rebels—rather than any policy of the government—was to blame for spreading disorder. This is consistent with what historian Brad A. Jones has argued: that questions like slavery divided rather than unified a transatlantic Loyalist community which stretched from New York to Glasgow to Halifax to Kingston, Jamaica.[101]

African Americans played a pivotal role in converting British officials' caution into antislavery commitment, and did so within the framework of honor.[102] Given the range of attitudes and priorities among those British officials and their white subordinates, actual policy, as we have already seen, took on a situational quality. The situations in which they found themselves making decisions were ones largely created by Black fugitives, so those decisions were a reaction to the fugitives' own decisions in reaction to British offers of freedom.[103] Just as the British Army's Revolutionary War reliance on Native American and African American allies merely expanded on past precedents, similarly Blacks in the British Empire had long tested the idea of turning to imperial officials as protectors against the power of local planter elites but now did so in unprecedented numbers.[104] The African Americans who fled to British lines seemed unfazed by British commanders using them as a means to the end of defeating the Patriots, probably in large part because they themselves were using the British as a means to the end of their own freedom. As scholar Michael E. Groth has put it, African Americans "made decisions and pursued courses of action that best served their personal interests or improved their own positions." Those who ran away from bondage "acted out of motivations that had little to do with either Toryism or Whiggery." Those transactional motives in no way changed the fact that their choices "directly challenged the slave system" in North America. Neither did it make them much different from other Loyalists of multiple ethnicities, for those studying these groups have found that Loyalism comprised a broad persuasion held together much less by Tory political ideology than by hostility to Patriots. As they acted on that hostility they joined what Judith L. Van Buskirk has characterized as "networks of self-interested individuals" who pursued interests including "the best offer of freedom." In hotly contested regions, African Americans deftly "maneuvered among the rival claims of both sides, ever alert for openings that the war's permeable boundaries might furnish for a better life."[105]

No matter British officials' hesitancy, African Americans who cast their lot with them treated them as if they were liberators, holding them to the promises made in Dunmore's and subsequent proclamations. While Black Americans' choices might not have been primarily ideological in nature, that did not stop white combatants from politicizing those choices. As historian Van Gosse has written in an important article, this meant that "from a position of great weakness," African Americans "derived a startling degree of political agency" from the wartime situation and British offers of freedom. The mighty British armed forces were clearly "capable of aiding African people" if they acted "in good faith," even at the moment of British defeat. Those who chose the British route to freedom were determined to hold them to that good faith. In choosing the British offer over the Patriot side, Gosse continues, African Americans "exerted power *on behalf of themselves*" and established what would become a long-running association in the United States between the British and Black freedom.[106]

These great expectations for the British began before Dunmore's Proclamation, indeed even before the war. In January 1775, David Margrett, an African-English protégé of the liberal Englishwoman the Countess of Huntingdon, arrived in South Carolina to preach the gospel especially to slaves. He reportedly preached that "the Jews of old, treated the Gentiles as Dogs & I am informed the People of this Country use those of my Complection as such." But "thank God!" he continued, that "I am come from a better Country than this," from post-*Somerset* England. He also spoke of Israel's deliverance from Egypt and assured his hearers that "God will deliver his own People from Slavery." Surely the response to his preaching among African Americans was mixed given the risks involved with such talk, but Margrett seems to have uniformly established a connection between the British government and slave insurrection, at least in white Carolinians' minds. Governor William Campbell's protests against the resulting lynch law for African Americans, including Thomas Jeremiah, proved impotent in the short run but surely helped cement that connection in the minds of Carolinians of both races.[107]

In 1781, another Black man added a remarkable prophetic voice to this corpus of confidence in the British. Murphy Stiel, an African American soldier with the Black Pioneers unit, reported that at noon about two weeks previous, he "heard a Voice like a man's (but saw no body) which called him by his name" and said that he had a message for Henry Clinton to deliver to George Washington. It was that Washington "must Surrender himself and his Troops to the King's Army, and that if he did not the wrath of God would fall upon them." That divine judgment would come in the form of Clinton raising "all the Blacks in America to fight against him." Although Stiel replied to the voice "that he was afraid to do it," the messenger was insistent that Stiel pass on this prophecy to both Clinton and George III. The parting words of the revelation were that Clinton's forces would "put an end to this Rebellion, for that the Lord would be on their Side."[108] One can imagine guffaws among lordly, secular British officers upon hearing of this prophecy, and there is no evidence that Clinton passed this along to either Washington or anyone else. But Stiel offered moral clarity as to not only the outcome but also the purpose of this war. In that moral framework, it was the British who were fighting God's battles for true liberty, and liberating and arming African Americans was both a means toward and a manifestation of that fact.

In his postwar memoir, Boston King likewise painted a clear picture of good (British) guys against bad (Patriot) guys. Born into slavery in South Carolina, he recalled taking early advantage of the wartime opportunity to flee a cruel master and "throw myself into the hands of the English. They received me readily," so with them he "began to feel the happiness of liberty." Amid the vicissitudes of the war that followed, he dreaded American advances as advances for slavery, and bore all hardship under British arms in the name of freedom. At the end of the war, as he was stationed in the main British stronghold, New York City, throngs of would-be enslavers descended on the city. This, King's narrative testified, "filled us all with inexpressible anguish and terror," for these kidnappers seemed to be everywhere, and "the thoughts of returning home with them embittered life to us." But British officials "had compassion upon us in the day of our distress," proclaiming their determination to preserve the freedom of those "who had taken refuge in the British lines, and claimed the sanction and privileges of the Proclamations respecting the security and protection of Negroes." These Britons' honorable course "dispelled all our fears, and filled us with joy and gratitude" for deliverance. It was from these British people both then and during a subsequent journey to Britain that King learned that "White People, instead of being" necessarily the "enemies and oppressors of us poor Blacks," as white Americans were, could be "our friends, and deliverers from slavery, as far as their ability and circumstances will permit."[109] Rather more laconically but very directly, another man who gained his freedom evacuating with British forces took as his new name "British Freedom."[110] People like these had every reason to cheer on the circumstances that enabled the honorable Britons to foil the shady, tyrannical Americans.

As King's narrative demonstrates, few if any of the African Americans who reached British lines were completely safe from the threat of recapture, given the ebb and flow of war and the determination of their erstwhile slaveholders. In this fluid situation, they pressed British commanders to be their strong arm for freedom. In 1779, for instance, India Moore Heyerd found that her former master, like her living in British-occupied New York City, had bribed her landlord to evict her and thus facilitate her re-enslavement. She appealed straight to the top, to Henry Clinton, for protection. She pressed not for some benevolent favor but for "Some Satisfaction." Were Clinton to protect her, she concluded, "I Shall Be Ever Oblige[d]."[111] Evidence that in some contexts Clinton embraced the role of protector came even after the war, when he learned that many African Americans who had departed from the United States upon British defeat had been cheated out of lands promised them in Nova Scotia. "Can we do any thing" to help these people who had requested his aid, he asked a fellow officer.[112]

In the chaotic days between the signing of the peace treaty and the British evacuation of New York City, terrified African Americans turned with even more earnestness to British officers for protection. Yet again their language was less of supplication than of demanding that the British defend the freedom they had promised and former masters sought to overturn. In September 1783, Judith Jackson recounted to British commander in chief Guy Carleton how she was originally from Virginia but had served "with Lord Dunmore, Washing & Ironing in his Service," and how she had come with him from Charleston to New York. But in recent days, "my master came for me" and when "I told him I would not Go with him," he got the aid of another white man "to stale me Back to Virginia." In the process, they "took all my Cloathes which his Majesty Gave me," plus they "took my money from me & Stole my child from me & Sent" the child "to Virginia." Another Virginia woman in New York, Peggy Gwynn, petitioned to the effect that she had come "to New York with the Kings

Troops under protection of His Excellency Genl. Howe's Proclamation." She wished to join her husband serving with the king's troops, "but there is certain Mr. Crammon who wants to detain me & deprive me of my Liberty that I have had & enjoyed."[113] With such insistent language, these women affirmed their rights to freedom, property, and family, all of which they relied on Carleton to vindicate against these white men's criminal encroachments. As German officer Carl Baumeister neatly summed up the process he witnessed in New York City, the Black refugees "insist on their rights under the proclamation," and in response Carleton protected them. It was as simple as that, despite white Americans' remonstrances.[114]

It is notable that so many of these petitioners were women. Granted, William Paley complained in an influential 1780s treatise that "the Law of Honour is a system of rules constructed by people of fashion" to regulate their conduct with those whom they saw as their social equals. His complaint was that it omitted elite men's duties to God "as well as those which we owe to our inferiors."[115] But Black women in New York at war's end showed that in practice, contemporary notions of honor—as with the ideal of humanity—centered on protecting the vulnerable, at least in the virtue's national and/or military manifestations. As Jacqueline Beatty's scholarship has shown, eighteenth-century North American women found multiple ways to leverage ideas of their dependence as they petitioned the patriarchal state, whether British or American. Women of all classes and racial categories "knew well the terms of their multifaceted dependencies" and expressed a certain "power because of their subordinate status" as they called on men in power to live up to the reciprocal obligations of their hierarchical world. Even as the language of rights increased in women's petitions in the Revolutionary era, "women who employed submissive, deferential language that reinforced tropes of femininity in their petitions often found success," while those who struck "a more belligerent tone" routinely "saw their petitions rejected." Given their extreme vulnerability in the British Atlantic world, "the stakes of Black women's efforts in testing and exploiting the boundaries of patriarchal power" were inevitably "higher than those of white women."[116] The Black women who petitioned Carleton threaded this needle, demonstrating their political and cultural savvy alongside their desperation in appealing to powerful British men to play the role of protectors of the weak. While they phrased their appeals as demands rather than requests for favors, the gender as well as racial dynamics of these interchanges nevertheless leveraged British men's paternalistic ideals. Karen Cook Bell's recent scholarship has illuminated how deeply "Black women's freedom was intertwined with" the imperial crisis and war, and that "African American women followed the military conflict and were powerfully influenced by its outcome."[117] But these Black women refugees' colloquies with Carleton illustrate how they helped influence that outcome, especially as it regarded their freedom.

Indeed, their appeals to honoring commitments seem to have had the desired effect on most British policymakers.[118] In addition to Dunmore's Proclamation, the most significant sources for this idea of binding promises of freedom came from generous readings of emancipation proclamations by the commandant of New York City and by Henry Clinton at his temporary headquarters in Phillipsburg, New York, both in June 1779. Given the importance of New York City as a bastion of British power down to the end of the war, and given that Clinton's proclamation happened on the eve of his invasion of the Lower South beginning in Georgia, these documents greatly expanded the reach of the principles of Dunmore's original promise.[119] But they did so less on their face than as applied by those who took advantage of them. As Sean Gallagher has pointed out, British commanders like Clinton drew on an "existing Atlantic language of imperial protection, rather than explicit freedom, in their proclamations." Dunmore had directly offered manumission, but the Philipsburg Proclamation only offered "refuge" to enslaved people fleeing rebels, granting them "full security to follow within" British lines "any occupation" they wished. Clinton forbade those under his authority from treating them as property, but while the war lasted conceived that "they belong to the public." Given such lack of explicitness, Black runaways to British lines sought documentation such as passes that codified their freedom in this military setting. Then as evacuation neared they sought by testimony and petitions to shore up their refugee status and thus their entitlement to freedom. As Gallagher has argued, this process, initiated by Black Loyalists, "shaped British policy as much as it responded to it."[120]

A 1782 letter from James Moncrief, a commander overseeing engineering work in Charleston, reveals this dynamic especially well because he was no abolitionist. His missive to Clinton dripped with paternalistic pride in "the number of slaves" (not freedmen in his conception) who had joined his unit and thus "look up to me for protection." But that sense of responsibility for them, condescending as it was, led Moncrief to urge Clinton to avoid doing anything that might lead them to "lay aside the confidence which they always placed in us." And there was a level of reciprocity in all of this in that Moncrief had come to understand "the many advantages which His Majesty's service has derived from their labour" in the southern theater.[121] Likewise, General Alexander Leslie, preparing for the evacuation of Charleston in the summer and fall of 1782, posed a series of highly involved questions to his superior General Guy Carleton that revealed the complexity of the logistical and political issues arising from a heterogeneous population within British lines that included white Loyalist slaveholders, enslaved African Americans, and African Americans claiming freedom. But while Leslie begged Carleton for clarity on many matters, he had achieved it himself on one: "Those who have voluntarily come in, under the faith of our protection, cannot in justice be abandoned to the merciless resentment of their former masters."[122]

Meanwhile, American Patriots' own sense of honor worked hand in glove with their constant watchfulness for the barest hint of a threat to their budding sovereignty. This solicitude for true American independence thoroughly influenced relations with the United States's allies, let alone its chief enemy, Britain. John Jay, for instance, ever with a wary eye especially on the dilatory would-be ally Spain, argued that "we should endeavour to be as independent on the charity of our friends as on the mercy of our Enemies." That defensiveness about American sovereignty came from a deep "interest in the dignity of my country," Jay wrote, at least as much in negotiations with its allies as with its enemies. Every little gesture and sub-issue, it seemed to American diplomats, would set a precedent that would impact the new nation's international standing for generations to come. And while there were nuances of opinion among the United States's European delegation on how to approach their allies, they were united behind Jay's insistence on "the utter impossibility of our ever treating with Great Britain on any other than an equal Footing."[123]

The issue of the status of fugitive American slaves made no appearance in the ministry's lengthy proposals for negotiation with the Patriots in 1778.[124] But the fate of African American fugitives in British lines repeatedly arose as a question on the ground throughout the war. In 1777, for instance, a Virginia Patriot reported having gone under a flag of truce "to endeavour a recovery of" a certain group of "Negroes" from a British ship. The British sailors responded with an early version of what would become the standard British line: "They were determined to protect all that came on board."[125] This issue came up more formally amid the battles and surrenders in the southern theater late in the war, and directly featured in capitulation agreements and policy memos during campaigns.

These all sought to balance American (both Patriot and Loyalist) property rights in slaves with British promises of freedom to some fugitives, often by means of vague and evasive language. None of them attempted to lay down any broad principles beyond those specific situations, however, and negotiators often agreed on recommendations rather than binding commands. They seem to have understood that anything binding would have to take place at the level of the international negotiations in Paris.[126]

Despite this history of negotiations on the ground, as British and American representatives began their discussions in Paris in summer 1782 the status of fugitive African Americans appeared on neither the American delegates' list of *"necessary"* issues nor on that of *"advisable* articles" in multiple draft treaties. That held true even late into the fall of 1782 after John Jay had arrived with new demands and a more demanding tone.[127] When American negotiators did bring it up, it was in part to parry British demands for Americans to repay debts to British merchants, and especially for reparations to Loyalists for property from which Patriots had dispossessed them. When Congress made this link in a September 1782 resolution instructing the Paris commissioners to bring up this issue, it did so in a straightforward way of balancing one property claim against another. But such discussions never wandered far from the big issues of principle to which they were connected, including national honor. John Adams, for instance, remarked that "I could not comprehend this doctrine of national honor" Britons used to advance Loyalists' claims. For if Britain really wanted to negotiate on that ground, "there is every argument of national honor, dignity of the State, public and private justice and humanity" on the American Patriots' side given their own losses. Therefore, they must meet the British on this ground and "insist upon a compensation for all the plate, negroes, rice, and tobacco stolen, and houses and substance consumed." "Our sufferers," he added, "were innocent people, and theirs guilty ones."[128] This remarkable set of comments from the normally antislavery Adams—in which American slaveholders were innocent victims only—illustrates the blinders competing claims of national honor and sovereignty put on American negotiators on this issue. As a South Carolina slaveholder, albeit one with complex attitudes toward slavery, Henry Laurens had even less difficulty embracing the idea that true justice and honor lay on the side of reparations for American slaveholders. He had seen some of his own enslaved people escape to the British after all. While Adams had raised this issue in a conversation with a French ally on November 10, 1782, and in a letter to Congress's foreign affairs secretary Robert R. Livingston on November 11, Laurens's arrival in Paris in late November further steeled the delegation's resolve to insist that Britain honor American property rights in people. He reminded his fellow delegates to include enslaved people as they itemized American property losses. Accordingly, in Article 7 of the provisional treaty signed on November 30, Britain pledged to evacuate its posts in the United States as quickly as possible without "carrying away any Negroes or other Property of the American inhabitants."[129]

Sir Guy Carleton, who had recently replaced Clinton as commander-in-chief of British forces in North America, became the key figure on the ground in implementing these evacuations and thus in interpreting this article. It was a matter of interpretation because of the aforementioned tensions between proclamation promises of freedom to African American fugitives and the treaty's pledge not to carry them away. Nor was this issue entirely abstract for Carleton, given that he had a Black man named Pomp serving in his household who had fled American bondage under the British military's promise of freedom.[130] Furthermore, the victorious Patriots' insistent tone on this issue grated on Carleton and other British commanders. General Alexander Leslie, for instance, reported to Carleton that he had sought to manage the winding up of the war "with the utmost moderation and forbearance." But once the Patriots in South Carolina had learned that the treaty stipulated "that no Property should be carried off," they became "insulting" and "insolent" in their demands on him for the return of their human property. This, he averred, hampered his ability (and surely his willingness) to cooperate with these white Patriots.[131] In response to all of this, in April 1783, acting under Carleton's authority, British Adjutant General Oliver De Lancey, a North American Loyalist by origin, set up mechanisms by which Article 7 would be "strictly observed" on the part of British officials. British officials in this scheme would seek to differentiate between African Americans owed freedom under British proclamations and those who had entered British lines in some way that did not entitle them to freedom. And his documentation does suggest a good faith effort to sort out this thorny complex of questions.[132]

The most vocal American Patriots did not share this assessment. To them, British commanders performed nothing but "a most impudent evasion of the Treaty" by not just returning African Americans to bondage wholesale.[133] Thus, the British won precisely no points for upholding their national honor by means of their evacuation, for in this simple moral rendering they had violated their promises—in capitulation agreements culminating with the final Treaty of Paris in 1783—to the United States. This assessment was led by, but far from limited to, the highest American officials and southern slaveholders. A short but hard-hitting news piece in a Vermont newspaper, for instance, skewered the British for extreme dishonor as well as hypocrisy in relation to their treaty obligations. They had repeatedly proclaimed "that *strict nicety*" in relation to their promises "is their ruling principle," including of course their argument that they would live up to their promises to African Americans. But they "have lately in direct contravention of the Provisional Treaty, suffered several persons to carry off negro slaves belonging to the citizens of these States, who were wantonly pilfered by [Benedict] Arnold, and his nefarious banditti."[134]

While newspaper readers had no real influence on negotiations either in Paris or in occupied American cities, Patriot leaders in those locales sought to wield just such an influence, and did so on the same grounds as this letter's. Benjamin Franklin, still in France, was reasonably certain that British officials had other than their stated motives for their policy on American slaves and was very certain that Carleton's course constituted a "Violation" of the treaty.[135] Livingston likewise fumed on reading of Washington's and Carleton's conference and correspondence, seeing Carleton as perpetrating a clear and "direct violation of the 7th Article" and arrogating to himself power over American property that international law could never uphold.[136] George Washington, however, led this charge. Having himself lost enslaved people to the British armed forces, he had seen the powerful allure of the promise of freedom. But he also led the military struggle for American sovereignty and approached the issue of escaped African Americans in that context. On May 6, 1783, in a conference with Carleton, he maintained that freeing any fugitives violated both "the Letter and Spirit" of the treaty, and thus it was beyond debate that it amounted to an "Infraction of the Treaty." Washington also raised practical issues with any scheme wherein the British compensated American slaveholders, but his main emphasis was on this breach of faith. To his mind, this was not about money-grubbing or a drive for vengeance by slaveholders; instead it touched on matters "of considerable national concern." For that reason, and certainly not because he was happy with Carleton's answers, Washington deferred the issue to future negotiations by the two nations' political leaders.[137]

In his responses to the likes of Washington, Carleton began by laying out his procedure for assuring that only those African Americans "who had been declared free previous to my arrival" were allowed to evacuate New York City with British troops. But Carleton continued with a vigorous defense of this stance in light of the key issues that drove this controversy. "I had no right," he told Washington, "to deprive them of that liberty I found them possessed of," and it was illiberal in the extreme for Americans to insinuate that the British negotiators in Paris had such a right. For them to have meant to do that in the treaty, Carleton concluded, would have made them "guilty of the notorious breach of the public faith towards people of any complexion." In short, his decided opinion was that "delivering up the Negroes to their former Masters," and thus likely to "severe Punishment" or even "Execution," would constitute "a dishonorable Violation of the public Faith pledged to the Negroes."[138] "I should show an indifference to the feelings of humanity," Carleton offered to the president of Congress in August 1783, "as well as to the honour and interest of the nation I serve, to leave any of the loyalists that are desirous to quit the country a prey to the violence" of the vindictive rebels.[139] While this letter did not say so explicitly, Carleton's actions made it clear that he would not distinguish the Loyalists to whom he would pay this debt of national honor based on skin tones. Both sides clearly agreed that national reputation for honor lay at the heart of this issue but came to diametrically opposed conclusions about where the path of true honor led.

As such this issue poisoned further an already toxic relationship between Britain and the United States right at the key moment at which that relationship became officially international. James Madison, for instance, repeatedly complained of Carleton's "palpable & scandalous misconstruction of the Treaty" in relation to slaves and mused that this was "an ominous sample of candor & good faith in our New friends!"[140] Edmund Pendleton saw him and raised the stakes in a letter to Madison in June 1783. Carleton, he had learned, had been very careful to represent his interpretation of the competing claims on British honor as "his own private opinion" rather than a policy communicated to him by "his Superiors." But what Carleton thought of as proper care, Pendleton damned as piling chicanery on chicanery. This begging off as private opinion was "a subterfuge of the same Character with the construction" of the treaty by Carleton, "for if he is not authorised to Act in the Execution of the Treaty, to what purpose did he" even agree to discuss the matter with Washington? "Was it to deliver his private opinions how the treaty might be evaded, for amusement, whilst the negroes were carrying away out of his & the owners power?"[141]

These most vocal among the aggrieved had to combat, as a competing priority, deep American war weariness. While Alexander Hamilton had introduced a motion in Congress protesting British evacuation of Black Americans in May 1783, he also confided in a political ally that Americans were just as guilty of their own form of "palpable infraction" of the preliminary treaty as Carleton was. "Is it our interest," Hamilton asked rhetorically, "to advance this doctrine" that the preliminary treaty was now null and void "when there are examples of *years* intervening between the preliminary & definitive treaties?" He hoped both the United States and Great Britain would answer that question in the negative.[142] Also in May, Virginia's John Francis Mercer, seconded by South Carolina's Ralph Izard, introduced a motion into Congress that given Carleton's continued occupation of New York City, and that "the said Sir Guy Carleton has suffered many negroes the property of the citizens of these United States to be carried off, contrary to the 7th article of the Preliminary Treaty, *Resolved*, That it is not expedient at present to disband or furlough the army of the United States." After other members found this motion highly "exceptionable," its authors withdrew it.[143]

Still, even after Congress ratified the peace treaty, it instructed its commissioners in Paris to remonstrate to the British government and demand "that speedy and effectual Measures be taken to render that Justice to the Parties interest which the true Intent and Meaning of" Article 7 "plainly dictates." And it still employed Embarkation Commissioners to monitor and formally protest both the dilatory nature of Carleton's evacuation of New York City and the departures of African Americans when they did occur.[144] Those commissioners' final report, in January 1784, lambasted Carleton for having relied so heavily on "the declarations of the Negroes themselves" in establishing who had a right to freedom. But they also confessed their powerlessness to stop him, given that until the moment of final embarkation Carleton "retained and exercised the authority" to make all determinations of this sort. They thus stopped their remonstrances to him as "not only fruitless but also derogatory to the dignity of the Sovereignty" of Congress that had sent them as commissioners.[145] This relative whimper was not an ending to American efforts on this score, however, so this issue would continue to dog Anglo-American relations in the postwar period. It captured the issues of national honor as well as actual national sovereignty and power that had driven this issue during the war.

7

Impacts on Slavery

༄༅

ALL THESE multifarious political usages of slavery for nearly two full decades did not have a single, straightforward impact on slavery in the short term, either in the United States or in the remaining British Empire. To say this, however, is to run contrary to most recent scholarship. That is especially true for the historical literature on the early American republic.

Recent historians have widely expressed skepticism about the relevance of the crisis's rhetoric of political slavery for chattel slavery in the new United States. The thrust of scholarship in the late twentieth and twenty-first centuries has gone against an older body of literature that posited a strong, if complex, relationship between Patriot ideology and antislavery.[1] Even John Phillip Reid, who took slavery seriously "as a motivating concept" for participants, concluded that "a direct connection ... was seldom drawn" by those participants "between chattel slavery" and political slavery. Multiple historians across historiographical generations have focused on fleshing out explanations for the Patriots' lack of antislavery action. The recurrence of the term "limits" in this literature captures its main point.[2]

Other scholars have gone a step further, emphasizing the ways in which the Revolution hampered rather than advanced freedom for African Americans. Patricia Bradley was an early adopter of this interpretation, declaring not only that "antislavery did not become a patriot cause" but also that Patriot usages of the s-word in their propaganda "encouraged, and even legitimized, white American prejudices toward black Americans" because the denigration of slavishness cemented those prejudices toward slaves in their midst. As a result, this rhetoric "may have served to delay a national solution to the American institution of slavery."[3] More recently, James J. Gigantino II has painted a vivid picture of how "the Revolution's destructive power and disruptive influence" in bitterly contested New Jersey "encouraged lawmakers and white citizens to decline to advance abolition." These white revolutionaries became reactionaries on race, he argues, because of "anxiety over a potential statewide slave revolt" and because "the institution of slavery provided security and control over blacks in the insecurity of war."[4] Still others have argued that the pressing nature of the war drained attention away from issues like the abolition of slavery.[5]

The most influential recent iteration of this stance has been that of Robert G. Parkinson, who posits that a powerful propaganda effort highlighting the need to defend against Britain's African American and Native American allies constituted the core "common cause" of the Patriot movement. In some of his book's more provocative passages, Parkinson contends that the American Revolution "had little to do with taxes and rights," being "a war over slavery." Moreover, "the most important ... words in the Declaration are not about equality or happiness" but rather about the king's dastardly use of barbarous allies. Unsurprisingly, therefore, this way of uniting white Patriots had an "indelible" and uniform impact on American race relations: it "blocked off" and worked to "undermine other possibilities" as "unity trumped natural rights." Parkinson's Revolutionary era "was not an opportunity lost" for antislavery, because that opportunity "was never there in the first place."[6]

This trend has quite naturally provoked a reaction from those dedicated to the proposition of an antislavery American Revolution. As early as 2002, Gordon S. Wood began complaining about the work of a (then largely unnamed, uncited) group of "recent historians critical of the founders" who have unduly blamed the nascent nation's elite for the lack of antislavery action in the revolutionary generation. "It has become fashionable," he has worried, "to deny that anything substantially progressive came out of the Revolution," which is to him rank anachronism. "All the prominent leaders" of the Revolution, he has insisted, "thought that the liberal principles of the Revolution would" and should "destroy the institution of slavery." Their optimism was misplaced, in Wood's account, largely because less elite white Americans clung to slavery in defiance of their leadership. But what was remarkable was less this lack of action and more that the Founders put antislavery on the map in the United States, completely changing a situation in which white people took slavery for granted. Moreover, "the desire to abolish slavery was not an incidental offshoot of the Revolution." Breaking with his friend and mentor Bernard Bailyn, Wood has also posited that antislavery was not even "an unintended consequence of the contagion of liberty. It was part and parcel of the many enlightened reforms that were integral to the republican revolutions taking place in the new states."[7] Similarly, prominent American historian Sean Wilentz has pushed back against "the prevailing academic view" by positing that the really significant development in the American Revolutionary era was "the profound shift in moral perception" that was northern antislavery. That sentiment won real gains for freedom in the form of northern state emancipation, "a decisive blow for freedom" "which no degree of southern manipulation or proslavery resolve could undo." In Wilentz's reading, American slaveholders alarmed by this development, not modern scholars who emphasize the limits of this generation's abolitionism, were right.[8]

The short-term impact of the Revolution on American slavery, however, was more complicated than both of these clashing interpretations suggest. Many debaters deployed language that at the very least had strong antislavery potential. Whether by accident or design, they used sweeping formulations that left the line between political and chattel slavery entirely unclear. Rhode Island's Samuel Ward, in urging that even "the Horrors of a civil War" were "infinitely preferable" to "Slavery," added that "Slavery never produced one single Good since the Creation." A decade previous to that, a Massachusetts scribbler suggested epigrams for all editors to use, including one that flatly declared that "Fair Liberty's Sons ... can't see unmov'd one Colonist a Slave." Another Massachusetts Patriot flailed away that "we abhor slavery, and such as would enslave."[9] Richard Henry Lee earnestly, if rather imprecisely, hoped "that America can find Arms as well as Arts, to remove the Demon Slavery far from its borders."[10] A New Jersey Patriot, in an ardent statement of belief in the cause in 1776, professed to be "fully convinced" that "heaven never designed one part of mankind to be slaves to the other."[11] Of course, such loose statements left wide open for interpretation what sort of slavery the authors had in mind.

Willingness to see and act on the practical applications of such rhetoric varied widely. Certainly many Patriots proved almost incredibly imperceptive (or willful) in compartmentalizing chattel slavery from the forms they claimed to resist. Some slaveholding Patriots, for instance, distinguished their own families' allegedly paternalistic practice of slavery from the British ministry's oppressive practice of political slavery. Richard Henry Lee, for instance, dressed his enslaved people in costumes meant to show his solidarity with Wilkes, seemingly blissfully unaware of any potential contagion of liberty spreading among them. For slaveholders of this persuasion, mastery per se was not the problem of their age but rather Parliament having "usurped powers to which they have no claim."[12] But at the other extreme, elite Virginian William Lee, in an impassioned 1775 letter from London calling for armed watchfulness against the ministry's schemes, communicated to his brother a "plan for emancipating the Negroes and abolishg. every kind of Slavery in America."[13] And so strong could the liberating impulse of the Patriot cause be that in 1766, Bostonians celebrating the repeal of the Stamp Act raised "a Subscription for liberating all the poor Prisoners in Goal for Debt," and "on that joyful Day" freed those prisoners.[14] A group of twenty enslaved men hoped to leverage this connection when petitioning the New Hampshire state legislature for freedom in 1779. "Private or publick Tyranny, and Slavery," they submitted, "are alike detestable to Minds, conscious of the equal Dignity of human Nature." They hoped these legislators possessed such minds.[15]

In short, to assert that slaveholding Patriots across the board brushed aside the implications of their rhetoric, and the multiple interconnections between slavery and the war, would be just as simplistic and inaccurate as to assert that they all turned abolitionist. David Waldstreicher has very helpfully suggested that "humility" best becomes historians who "approach the intertwined stories of the American Revolution and the enslavement of Africans," in large part because that subject is so complex rather than easily reducible. If we take the words and actions of a wide range of actors in the revolutionary generation, he shows in his biography of Phillis Wheatley, we can see not only how deeply "entangled" slavery and the political questions of the imperial crisis were but also that neither Patriots nor Tories were able to take predictably antislavery or proslavery positions. What he nicely calls "the heat lamp of politics" sped up the process by which "both antislavery and proslavery became movements." I agree entirely with Waldstreicher that the American Revolution's political sphere is best conceived of as "a battleground for what the Revolution would mean" regarding slavery and race, and as a result it "led in both proslavery and antislavery directions."[16]

The extended imperial crisis created more favorable conditions in which to make antislavery appeals than much of the recent literature would allow. But there was nothing automatic about the practical response of slaveholders, even of slaveholders who accepted many of the premises on which abolitionists built their arguments. As Alan Taylor has aptly phrased it, much of the recent literature "seems to grant" to the worst (and I might add for the other side, the best) statements and actions of the founding generation "the last word in defining a revolution that preserved slavery by asserting racism." But "no one"—whether individuals, the well-known Founders, or this generation as a whole—"succeeded in defining a contradictory revolution." That Revolution "produced a new dialectic between antislavery and proslavery discourses, both expressed with greater clarity and moral urgency thereafter. Each persuasion became crystallized in contest with the other."[17] Rather than resolving conflict over slavery, the multidimensional political impacts of the American Revolution sharpened it in the new American nation.

This was also true in the reconfigured British Empire, as it had been true in key ways before the American Revolution. Indeed, seeing the political effects of this crisis and war as transnational (rather than isolated to the United States as so much of the aforementioned literature does) adds specificity as well as complexity to our picture of their impacts on slavery in the Anglophone Atlantic world. In both nations in and after 1783, the legacies of the American Revolution were not broad and vague and general but rather very specific. And they cut in either very specifically antislavery or very specifically proslavery directions.

Evidence abounds indicating that the war retarded the drive for antislavery action in the United States in the short term. Perhaps on the most basic level, the advent of the war disrupted the nascent organizational work of North American antislavery societies. Antislavery petitions to legislatures also failed to gain traction. Many otherwise sympathetic Patriots thought, as Samuel Hopkins quoted them in 1776, that it was "not a proper time to attend to" antislavery work "while we are in such a state of war and distress."[18] Some antislavery Patriots temporarily shifted their focus almost entirely to the war effort. The Marquis de Lafayette, for instance, whose antislavery credentials have never been in doubt, rejoiced when the French Navy captured key forts in Senegal from the British. He knew this "Conquest will be pleasing to" many of "the Southern Gentlemen of America" and thus would encourage them to adhere to the

Patriot cause. For such men, antislavery qualms at this moment were as nothing compared to shoring up a fragile military coalition against the British.[19]

Furthermore, many a white Patriot willing to dare and risk for that cause turned timid when confronting slavery. Some joined Arthur Lee in pleading that the evil of slavery was "too deeply rooted in America, to give us hope" of immediate "relief" from it. Bold Patriot Patrick Henry meekly admitted to the Virginia Quaker Robert Pleasants that he "cannot justify" slavery but that he could not free his own slaves due to "the general inconveniency of living without them."[20]

Beyond these manifestations of competing priorities, some contemporaries found ways to cognitively separate slavery and the imperial crisis. Bostonian Charles Chauncy launched himself into this pantheon of the obtuse when he exulted over donations of slave-grown rice flowing into Boston after the ministry shut its port in 1774. South Carolinians had pledged many more such donations, Chauncy continued, as long as Boston remained "firm in our refusal to be made slaves."[21] Rhode Islander Samuel Ward crowded into that pantheon when he urged a relative to "read History" so he could "see the dreadful Miseries of the unhappy People who have lost their Liberty." Ward was sure that after such reading—not after looking around him in American society to see actual slaves—one would sacrifice anything for the cause.[22] A tight focus on political slavery alone accounted for such myopia.

And several slaveholders throughout the colonies, but especially in the South, adopted versions of broad Atlantic principles like humanity and liberty that were thoroughly warped by slavery. Many of them managed to traffic in and enslave people without connecting these practices to those virtues. For instance, for large stretches of the imperial crisis, Henry Laurens found it possible to talk along different tracks of "purchasing plantations and Negroes," of humanity, and of "the oppressive Yoke" of parliamentary taxation. He could even talk of the law of retribution and have it apply only to the treatment of, not the enslavement of, his slaves. Laurens's quotable but temporary pledges to desist from "the African Trade" were drowned by letters blithely expounding the themes of liberty and philanthropy alongside talk of shipments of Africans.[23]

Furthermore, many partisans in the imperial crisis turned antislavery tropes such as exhortations to avert (or halt the spread of) heaven's judgments into hostile taunts to the other side rather than actual calls for antislavery action. Dr. Benjamin Rush diagnosed guilt for slavery as weakening both Britain and its colonies but held out hope that North America's moral health might be revived "after she has been purged of Negro slavery." Britain, on the other hand, "like a body weakned and wasted from the opening of an abscess will languish and expire from her rupture with the colonies." Rush simply could not see Britain and its colonies as morally equivalent like his correspondent Granville Sharp tended to do. "The God of armies," Rush lectured Sharp, "cannot be an indifferent spectator of" the impolicy and injustice of "your country" toward its subjects ranging from the Caribs of the West Indies to North Americans.[24]

Britons loyal to the ministry would have none of this. John Wesley, in a key 1774 antislavery pamphlet, inflected the idea of national guilt for slavery and the slave trade with his Loyalism. While he condemned slave merchants and other "abettors" of this wickedness throughout the empire, most of the guilt that called for "retribution" was that of New World slaveholders. "The innocent blood which is shed in consequence of" American enslavers' "detestable" laws "must call for vengeance," he warned.[25] Likewise, the 1775 edition of Briton Thomas Day's influential poem *The Dying Negro* included a long prose preface that swiftly turned political, picturing North American "avarice" as driving the slave trade despite slaveholders' "clamors" for their own liberty. "Let the wild inconsistent claims of America prevail" in the world and before God, Day wished, only "when they shall be unmixed with the clank of chains, and the groans of anguish." Meanwhile, "it is in Britain alone, that laws are equally favourable to liberty and humanity." So much for his opening statement wishing for Britain to expiate its crimes in the West Indies (where his poem was set) and India.[26] Taken as a whole, then, abolitionists wielding the politics of consistency cut more than one way, often because they wielded these politics in so partisan a way.

Yet another way in which the politics of the crisis and war obscured antislavery vision was how they made North America look to many liberal Europeans. As early as the 1760s, for instance, the republican Briton Sylas Neville fondly hoped that Britain's North American colonies would someday "serve as a retreat to those Free men who may survive the final ruin of Liberty in this Country."[27] Such a vision commonly led European reformers to focus narrowly on political rather than chattel slavery. From this point of view, unreformed Britain and Europe constituted the land of slavery in which the vast disenfranchised populace "are absolutely enslaved to those who have votes," and North America with its assertive Patriots constituted the land of liberty.[28] In 1777, opposition MP Temple Luttrell introduced a bill into the House of Commons to replace impressment with other ways of maintaining the Royal Navy. He repeatedly compared impressment to "bondage" and "servitude," and argued that if his bill were passed, working British men would "be no longer the only slaves under the sanction or connivance of law, at least on this side of the Atlantic." Despite that subtle nod to New World slavery, in Luttrell's rendering the dangerous enslavers were the military authorities of Britain prosecuting this war, certainly not the American slaveholders resisting them.[29] Likewise, an anonymous radical British pamphleteer flatly declared both that "to rule over slaves is the spirit and ambition of Satan" and that the American Patriots were "a bold, free, spirited, ingenious people" who held a special place in God's plan for human liberty.[30] Only an outlook restricted to political freedom and slavery could explain seeing the American Patriots in such simple terms.

Dissenting preacher and political radical Richard Price proved an especially important distributor of this Kool-Aid. The American Revolution prompted his first major foray into politics because it not only touched on political principles Dissenters like him held dear but also jeopardized treasured transatlantic friendships.[31] In his wartime pamphlets, Price portrayed the Americans as a godly bunch fighting for the "sacred blessing of liberty." The war thus created the spectacle of Britain, "once the protector of liberty . . . and the scourge of tyranny, exchanged into an enemy to liberty." "Which side then," he asked only rhetorically, "is Providence likely to favour?" He thought he could discern God marking out America as "a safe retreat" for "the friends of liberty" as "civil and spiritual tyranny" triumphed in fallen Britain.[32] Price developed these ideas in a 1781 fast sermon warning against "the demon of corruption" perverting Britain's "public liberty into slavery." Scanning Britain and North America through this lens pushed him to see Britain's attempted subjugation of the Patriots, not the latter's subjugation of African Americans, as "the worst sort of slavery."[33]

Such sentiments echoed through the chamber of Price's correspondence with other reformers both European and American. In a letter commiserating with a Dutch liberal about how "every thing seems to be degenerating" in Europe, led by the descent of Britain into the embrace of "the most slavish principles," he took consolation from the developing idea of the United States as "an Asylum likely to be provided for the virtuous and oppressed among mankind." He reiterated this concept of independent America as "*now* the hope, and likely *soon* to become the refuge of mankind" in letters turning down, but expressing his deep gratitude for, Congress's invitation to come to the United States as an advisor and citizen.[34] In 1778, although the French philosophe Turgot shared with Price his qualms about persistent religious intolerance in the northern states and slavery in the southern states, the Americans were for Turgot "the *hope* of the world." Indeed, "it is impossible not to wish ardently" that they "may become a *model* to it" and their land an "*Asylum*" to "the oppressed" of Europe. Despite Turgot's longing for better from the Americans, then, he was willing to give them a wartime pass and help lead the cheers for their team in the short term. In this he anticipated an important 1782 speech by fellow philosophe the Marquis de Condorcet rejoicing that Louis XVI's first alliance was with "a people so young and already so celebrated: a people forced by oppression to seek safety in liberty."[35]

In the rough and tumble of parliamentary politics during the war, opposition MPs advanced, if possible, even more extravagantly rosy views of the American Patriots. In these MPs' speeches, the martial spirit and nobility of the Patriots had no bounds, "inspired" as they were "by that genius of liberty" which all true Britons should celebrate. Given their political ascendancy in America and the ministry's domination of British politics, it suited the purposes of radical MPs like Wilkes to depict America in the simplest terms as "a resting place, a sure asylum" for liberty.[36] George Johnstone, in a speech to the Commons in October 1775, offered a variation on this theme that proved especially relevant to the politics of slavery. Government men's proposed scheme "of calling forth the slaves," Johnstone railed, was not only "too black and horrid to be adopted" but would also fail due to the peculiar "state of slavery" in North America. In those colonies, "the slave was seldom or ever unfaithful to his master," because the American Patriots were too noble to be anything other than humane masters. "It is not he who uses the scourge and the whip," Johnstone averred, "that is the first to put the musket on his shoulders in such glorious contests as these. It is not he who tortures and frets his fellow creatures" who rallied to the Patriot cause, he continued. Only one "who feels that universal benevolence which extends his affections to all men in their several stations; who feels the spirit of equality, who knows the principles of liberty," was willing "to seal the truth of" such doctrines "with his blood." Those fortunate enough to be enslaved by such paragons would have no reason to flock to any British standard.[37]

American Patriots quite naturally found this Kool-Aid endlessly palatable and eagerly redistributed it to all takers. In that posture, they saw the task at hand as defending rather than reforming their holy land. While representing the United States in Europe, John Adams eagerly imbibed "the high Eulogiums, that are every where bestowed, by learned and ingenious Men" in Europe on Americans as "Combattants for Liberty." He also happily retailed to other Europeans such depictions of the United States as the great innocent on the world stage. Overlooking such things as colonists' record of violent dispossession of Native Americans, Adams ran with the idea that America was free from the stains of the Old World including "War and the Spirit of Conquest."[38] In 1777, American commissioners in France, headed by Benjamin Franklin, marveled that "all Europe is for us," as "the Prospect of an Asylum in America for those who love Liberty gives general Joy" to the enlightened Europeans with whom they corresponded and conversed. "Our cause is esteem'd the Cause of Mankind" in such circles, they exulted.[39]

This blinding euphoria spread to more than American ambassadors. The fact that David Ramsay addressed his oration marking the second anniversary of the Declaration of Independence to a crowd of South Carolina slaveholders did not keep him from rhapsodizing on the theme of the United States becoming a refuge for "thousands and millions" of European peasants "who now groan beneath tyranny and oppression" under "their arbitrary task-masters." For had not liberal Europeans lauded Americans for their proper understanding of "the nature of civil liberty, and the rights of the people"? This European frame of reference allowed him to keep a straight face as he imagined white Americans' "noble example, like a wide-spreading conflagration," making the "arbitrary treatment" that the "tyrants and landlords of the Old World" visited on their tenants—or "their fellow men in bondage"—untenable.[40]

Yet nothing retarded antislavery action in American politics in the short term more than the close association between British power and forcible emancipation. All the Patriot propaganda tarring British emancipation with inhumanity helped frame this lesson of the war for many white Americans. But it was not always a figment of their political imagination. In 1779, for instance, British commander in New York David Jones declared free all fugitives from "the Enemy's Country" while British forces and Loyalists hatched a plot to murder Patriot slaveholders near Elizabethtown, New Jersey. Local Patriots foiled the plot, but the fear was lasting, given that Loyalist forces both Black and white did carry out multiple assaults on the property and lives of Patriots in the larger New York City region. Suspicions and the reality of Loyalist alliances with enslaved

African Americans to do violence to white Patriots in these and other instances linked wartime antislavery politically to the twin pariahs, Britons and Loyalists.[41]

Similarly, the longstanding association between Quakers and antislavery did not help the reputation of the latter given the massive Patriot distrust of the former during the war. Nowhere was the political impact of this association clearer than in North Carolina. In 1777, the state's "Act to Prevent Insurrections" began by lashing out at "the evil and pernicious Practice of freeing Slaves in this State," which "ought at this alarming and critical Time to be guarded against by every friend and Wellwisher to his country." Under this law manumissions would henceforth require specific authorization by the legislature. Everyone knew what sect this law and rhetoric targeted, and the North Carolina Friends Yearly Meeting protested in response that no "Selfish and Worldly Considerations"—like friendliness for the British cause—had motivated their ongoing manumissions. In 1779, a joint committee of the legislature decried "the conduct" of the Quakers "in setting their slaves free when our open and declared enemies were endeavouring to bring about an insurrection of the Slaves." To persist in manumissions in this setting was more than tone deaf; it was "highly criminal and reprehensible." A law resulting from that committee report defined manumitters as "evil minded persons, intending to disturb the public peace."[42] In the context of the British emancipation policy, manumissions by Friends that may have been an irritant before the war took on a much more sinister connotation. Even peaceful liberation could not escape the political and cultural associations with Lord Dunmore and his ilk. As a result, it seemed un-American and dangerous to many white Patriots.

A related political reality stemmed from many American slaveholders' bitter experiences of powerlessness over their enslaved people during the war. They experienced it when the chaos of the conflict visited their locales. Henry Laurens informed his brother in 1776 from Charleston that "your Negroes in some measure Govern themselves" even early in the war, amid unsettled circumstances and the green light the British had given for flight. In 1779, fellow Carolinian Eliza Pinckney likewise sighed that no one could stop the people she had enslaved from joining the British, "for they all do now as they please everywhere."[43] The loss of his tobacco crop led Virginia planter Landon Carter to inveigh against "the brutes" and "Monsters" who had fled bondage on his plantation and left worms to devour that crop. "Indeed," he impotently raged in his diary, "Slaves are devils and to make them otherwise than slaves will be to set devils free."⁴⁴ Carter died soon thereafter, but planters who shared this embittered opinion would prove stubborn opponents of antislavery action after the war.

This massive problem in the slaveholders' minds became even more acute in and around New York City, Savannah, Charleston, and other places occupied by the British. As the port held longest by British forces, New York City in particular became a nightmare for American slaveholders. George Washington, for one, threw up his hands even as the war wound down given that African American freedom seekers "have so many doors through which they can escape from" that city. In July 1783, James Madison shook his head over how "the sending off the negroes" on British ships "continues to take place under the eyes" and despite the "remonstrances of" American inspectors of the process in New York City.⁴⁵ Robert Parkinson has offered helpful context by noting that "never in the eighteenth century had so high a percentage of the enslaved population run away en masse" in North America as those who sought freedom in the British stronghold of Savannah in 1779. And as Lauren Duval has demonstrated, slaveholders in and around Charleston experienced two years of British occupiers consciously undermining their "dual authority of both master and patriarch."⁴⁶

These men did not need modern theories of race and gender to convince them that the private was political. As Charles Lee observed, "In this Slave Country ... dominion is founded on opinion," specifically the impression that slaveholders were in control of both their own households and the broader society.⁴⁷ Thus it was far more than a private irritant that even when slaveholders managed to learn the whereabouts of their fugitive former slaves, they were often impotent to recapture these people without British aid. It was frustrating and humiliating in the extreme for proud slaveholders of all political stripes to first have to negotiate with their erstwhile enslaved people in these circumstances and then curry favor with British military men when those people refused their blandishments to return to bondage.⁴⁸

But it galled leading Patriots the most. South Carolinian John Mathews summed up both edges of their frustration in fuming that "my affairs are left entirely at the mercy of Negroes. & an insatiable enemy."⁴⁹ In 1780, Rawlins Lowndes saw over seventy of his enslaved people seek freedom with the British and sustained other property losses and insults in a British raid on his plantation. Despite being the Patriot governor of

South Carolina, Lowndes could only open a deferential correspondence with the British commander James Simpson. Lowndes granted that "our present Situation must, necessarily and unavoidably Subject us to many Inconveniences which, in the nature of things, cannot be redressed." But he hoped that "the moderation and Generosity of the General" would lead him to suppress "unnecessary and wanton Acts of Oppression and Severity."[50] As late as 1782, Lowndes was still seeking return of his fugitive bondspeople and received a condescending letter from a British major. Although Lowndes's account of the story of one of his enslaved women was "materially different from" what British officers had understood, this major declared they would return her.[51]

Of course, nothing Lowndes experienced during the war was a worse outcome than this was for the unnamed woman whose re-enslavement was a rank betrayal by British forces. But it would have grated on every last nerve for this proud planter and nominal governor to have to beg favors from his enemies and then to have junior officers point out flaws in Lowndes's story before condescendingly agreeing to his requests. Correspondence and personal interactions among British officers, Black freedom seekers, and desperate American slaveholders might not seem like traditional sources of political history. But if anyone was playing politics, and if anyone understood the real-world stakes of such politics, it was these people.

The prodigious political impact of this dynamic came into full focus at war's end. Agents from multiple states encountered several formerly enslaved people in New York City, who by these agents' lights "ought by the treaty to have been restored to their owners." They remonstrated to Sir Guy Carleton against any "detention or removal" of these fugitives, "but all in vain, they were not restored, they were carried off or detained." This ongoing evidence of American feebleness in New York was bad enough, but the story of a white New Yorker, Jacob Duryee, proved particularly provocative. Duryee took an enslaved man on a sloop to New York City to assist as a navigator, and "the Negro refused to return" with him once they had done their business. "On this, with the help of the Master of the sloop, he tied the Negro, carried him in a cart to the water side, put him on board, and set sail." Before long "a Negro Colonel and company of Hessian soldiers" overtook the sloop and boarded it. Treating the white men "with great insolence," this party "obliged the sloop to go back to New-York, seized her, released the Negro," and arrested the white men to be tried by a court martial. British officials refused the "large bail" offered for Duryee and the captain. "Such is the account we have here of this affair," the reporter concluded, "which occasions great speculation and emotion."[52] It is no wonder that American Patriots felt great emotion reading this narrative. It bore all the hallmarks of British highhandedness and the violation of due process that had helped spark the whole crisis and war. Even antislavery white Patriots would have a hard time seeing through all those irritants to their patriotism to celebrate this one Black man being freed.

From his vantage point in Congress in May 1783, leading South Carolina slaveholder Ralph Izard wrote a letter that revealed his sense of powerlessness. He commiserated with friend Arthur Middleton not only "that so many of your Negroes are still missing" but "the more so, as I fear that it will not be an easy matter to recover them." Izard was certain that Carleton's stance on such fugitives was "a most impudent evasion of the Treaty," but crucially, he was also sure that "we are not in a condition to help ourselves" despite having won the war. This was because the national government so markedly lacked "all Continental Strength, & credit, that no Enemy need be afraid of insulting us." Southern members of Congress "have attempted everything in their power" to convince Congress to assert even its paltry powers to press Carleton by making the peace dependent on his return of fugitive slaves but found themselves defeated by the war-weary majority.[53] The lesson was clear for slaveholders like Izard: to protect their property in restive human beings, they would have to secure and maintain political power in both the international and national spheres.

The experience of John Mathews toward the end of the war cemented the idea that control of state governments would not be enough. In 1782, as South Carolina's Patriot governor, he signed agreements with British general Alexander Leslie meant to protect the rights of both Patriot slaveholders and white Loyalists. But Leslie—at least in Mathews's eyes—violated this agreement by honoring previous promises to fugitive African Americans within British lines. Incapable of coercing a different policy, Mathews in October 1782 ended this episode with a whimper by informing Leslie that he considered their agreement null and void.[54]

David Waldstreicher has offered an especially important argument developing the political moral of such stories. Positing a "Mansfieldian Moment" for American slaveholders, he has argued that Lord Mansfield's 1772 *Somerset* decision inaugurated "the modern constitutional politics of slavery" by alerting slaveholders throughout the empire that "never again could British slaveholders reassure themselves that everybody (who mattered) believed in slavery as a traditional form of property."[55] Waldstreicher's concept of a "Moment" for American slaveholders—the stark realization that they must control the state if they were to preserve control over slavery—carries tremendous explanatory power for the political course of slaveholders in both the United States and the remaining British Empire. But as I have argued in more depth elsewhere, there was a difference between the experiences and reactions of North American and West Indian enslavers. British West Indian slaveholders definitely had their Mansfieldian Moment, in advance of an even bigger Wilberforcian Moment. North American slaveholders by and large did not. Still, the North Americans took very similar lessons from what I have called their "Dunmorean Moment."[56]

While it would be significant for the future that leading South Carolina Patriots were among the most assiduous students of this political tutorial, the impact of this Moment went beyond slaveholders. For many white Patriots across the spectrum of investment in slavery, the wartime experience associated forcible interventions for African American freedom with British abuse of power. From that point of view, patriotism dictated resisting rather than facilitating that model of emancipation.[57]

ALTHOUGH AMERICAN abolitionists faced an uphill climb for all these reasons, they saw multiple potential openings in the zeitgeist of the 1760s to 1780s. Every one of the major political and cultural ideas of the crisis and war that had implicated slavery provided such openings. They exploited them early and often.[58] Because they linked their arguments so effectively to these widely held ideals, they found a wide audience ready to nod in agreement, and a subset of this audience willing to act against slavery.

First and foremost, they constantly leveraged the competing sides' burning desire for consistency.[59] This was true of those for whom abolitionism was such a preeminent priority that they took no side in the imperial crisis, instead seeking to appeal to both sides. Anthony Benezet, for instance, seems to have genuinely had no partisan agenda in the imperial crisis but did appreciate both sides' craving for consistency. He called out the inconsistency of all the loud "advocates of liberty" throughout the empire, on both sides of the imperial crisis, who "remain insensible and inattentive" to the vast and crying evils of slavery and the slave trade. By the 1770s, this head of the transatlantic yet marginal abolitionist network perceived such appeals to nonabolitionists' self-interest as powerful enough that he started to nurture hesitant hopes that abolitionism might well be gaining ground throughout the Atlantic.[60] Other abolitionists likewise castigated both Parliament and colonial legislators, both Loyalists and Patriots, for upholding and perpetuating slavery in blatant contradiction of their proclaimed love of liberty. Granville Sharp, for instance, declared that the slave trade and colonial slavery operated both "to the indelible disgrace of the British name" in general and to that of "our American provincials (though they pretend to be very zealous in the cause of liberty)." The toleration of slavery throughout the empire also threatened the rights of everyone in its domains, Sharp pled.[61]

But other abolitionists more carefully targeted their appeals to this theme. Beginning in 1768, London audiences for the popular play *The Padlock* heard an epilogue celebrating "the free-born British land," but only provisionally; the anonymous author pled directly with Britons to "equalise your laws, / Be all consistent—plead the Negroe's cause; / That all the nations in your code may see the British Negroe, like the Briton, free."[62] Arguing for the freedom of James Somerset in 1772 before the staunchly Loyalist Justice Mansfield, his counsel repeatedly leveraged both Mansfield's desire for consistency amid the imperial crisis and the idea of national honor. Especially since the Scottish and French had already cordoned themselves off from the infection of slavery, they pled, allowing slavery in England "would make *England* a disgrace to all the nations under earth."[63]

Given how many abolitionists lived in North America, it was natural that they sought to convince American Patriots specifically to live up to and thus sanctify their professions. New Jersey abolitionist Samuel Allinson lauded the *Somerset* decision and challenged North Americans to match it. In a broad reading of Mansfield's verdict, Allinson asserted he had ruled "that Slavery is not consistent with the English constitution, nor admissible in Great-Britain." North Americans, who claimed to be "blessed with sentiments as truly noble and free as any of their fellow subjects in the mother country," must surely see that slavery must therefore be repugnant to the spirit of colonial laws. "For the credit of my country," he earnestly hoped "that it might appear, and be known, that *Liberty* in America is not a partial privilege, but extends to every individual in it."[64] "Sophistes" wrote to a Boston paper in 1767 to highlight the spectacle involved when New Englanders prosecuted and defended slaving. "These people make the greatest noise and stir about liberty, reason and the rights of mankind" while "boasting of their ancestors" who crossed the ocean in search of liberty. They should either give up slavery or admit that they and the British ministry they despised acted "upon one and the same plan, namely an increase of wealth and power."[65]

Massachusetts's pioneering Black abolitionists proved to be masters at poking at their colony's Patriots for inconsistency in upholding slavery. In 1773, a group of Black Bay colonists formed what Christopher Cameron has helped us to see as "the first antislavery committee in America" to organize persistent petitions to their legislature for freedom. In the appendix to the published version of their petitions in 1773, "A Lover of Constitutional Liberty" challenged those who claimed to be "the Guardians of our Rights" to show to all that they were in reality "led and influenced by the true Principles of *Liberty*, and a sincere Desire to promote the good of Mankind." Only emancipation would "shew, that, instead of being *pretended* Friends to *Liberty*," Massachusetts's leading statesmen "are *really hearty* for the general and unalienable Rights of Mankind."[66]

It is difficult to tell how committed these petitioners were to the Patriot cause beyond its use as a lever, but the best-known African American from this era, Phillis Wheatley, seems to have eventually reached a place of public (if not wholehearted) commitment to that cause. As Waldstreicher's recent biography shows, for long stretches of the imperial crisis and even into the war she played her cards close to the vest, being a politically savvy actor as well as a poet with friends and potential readers on both sides. Not long into the war she made a bid to become "poet laureate" of the American revolutionaries, but at no point could she "be an uncritical believer in the American cause."[67] Especially when in Patriot mode, she deftly interwove the themes of political and chattel slavery into her poems. A 1772 effort decried "the iron chain, / Which wanton *Tyranny* with lawless hand / Had made, and with it mean t' enslave the land." In the same poem she explained that "my love of *Freedom*" had been "snatch'd" from family and freedom in Africa. "And can I then but pray / Others may never feel tyrannic sway?"[68] As with such poetry, there was a lot going on in a letter Wheatley sent to the Reverend Samson Occom in 1774, thanking him for vindicating Africans' "natural rights." She theorized to this fellow New Englander of color that "civil and religious Liberty" combined were necessary to bring to fruition the "Love of Freedom" that God had placed "in every human Breast." Without that combination, "perhaps, the Israelites had been less solicitous for their Freedom from Egyptian Slavery." And then, in a sly and pregnant seeming aside, she asserted, "By the Leave of our Modern Egyptians . . . , that the same Principle lives in us." She wryly prayed that those American Pharaohs would realize that "it does not require the Penetration of a Philosopher" to see "the strange Absurdity of their Conduct whose Words and Actions are so diametrically opposite."[69] Waldstreicher has offered a rich scholarly reading of this letter, pointing out that "to refer to 'modern Egyptians,' and call them 'ours,' raised the question of American slavery *and* its modernity." As an astute observer of the politics of the imperial crisis, she knew how cutting it would be to raise "the distinct possibility that history was going backwards, not forwards, in America"—and thus that white North Americans might be "ancient in all the wrong ways." This threat to the cultural power of the Patriot movement, from an African American woman, led the likes of Thomas Jefferson to challenge her legitimacy, despite her many poems lauding the Patriot cause.[70]

Another famous antislavery character, Sharp, went to great lengths to stay personally consistent as both an abolitionist and a supporter of the Patriot cause, and to help his allies keep those two causes consistent with each other. From the imperial crisis right through the American Revolutionary War, Sharp was an avowed supporter of American rights.[71] He was and is better known for his pamphleteering and legal work to advance abolitionism in Britain in the 1760s and 1770s. He saw balancing these two in rational ways as of essential importance. So, while in pamphlets in the 1760s he inveighed with equal vigor against both chattel slavery and the "injustice and iniquity" of Parliament's American policies, he carefully distinguished between "domestic" and "political slavery."[72] Other abolitionists less committed to the Patriot cause earned a correction from Sharp. Notably, in 1772 Sharp cheered on Benezet's report that thousands of Marylanders and Virginians supported a petition to Parliament against the continued importation of slaves, but insisted that the honor and consistency of the Patriot cause and the cause of the Africans must be considered here. This petition was welcome because it would help "retrieve" those colonies' "honour," as well as offering "a glorious proof that they are not destitute of Christian and social principles." But, Sharp lectured Benezet, only a petition regarding the transatlantic slave trade was proper to send to Parliament. "*With respect to the toleration of slavery in the colonies*, I apprehend the British Parliament has no right to interfere," so such a petition "should be *addressed only to the King, or to the King in Council.*"[73] In his influential 1769 abolitionist pamphlet, Sharp thus bitterly lamented that far too many American Patriots proved they "have no real regard" for liberty despite their "theatrical bombast and ranting expressions" in its praise. He granted that slave advertisements in London newspapers meant that "the Americans may be able, with too much justice, to retort this severe reflection," but the harm this inconsistency did to the Patriot cause clearly pained him.[74]

Others who were committed roughly equally to the Patriot and antislavery causes also had special cause to ring in changes on this theme of inconsistency. Benjamin Rush was especially notable in this regard. Rush ardently hoped for "some great revolution" both "in behalf of our oppressed Negro brethren" and against "the monster of British tyranny in America." He consistently conceived of those two causes as inextricably intertwined and worked to communicate that mental link to all other Patriots. "The late Infringements on the Civil Rights of the Colonists," he frankly confided to Sharp, "afford an Opportunity (which ought not to be lost) of urging home to the Slaveholders, the horrid Effects and unlawfulness of Arbitrary Power, whether it appears in *Domestic* or *Political Slavery*." The perception of this connection was so vital because, as Rush later told Sharp, "*American liberty cannot be firmly established 'till*" some scheme of emancipating American slaves was adopted. Only by such means could his "native country" fulfill its future role in promoting "the happiness of mankind."[75] Keenly aware that "patriotism and patriots have suffered much" from their counterfeits, in a public letter to Patriots he urged that true patriotism "comprehends not only the love of our neighbors but of millions of our fellow creatures, not only of the present but of future generations." American Patriots must show the world that their opposition to British imperial policy was not "founded upon presentment and party rage" but rather upon "a well-informed zeal in the cause of liberty."[76] "Where is the difference," Rush therefore demanded in a widely read 1773 antislavery pamphlet, "between the British Senator who attempts to enslave his fellow subjects in America, by imposing Taxes upon them contrary to Law and Justice; and the American Patriot who reduces his African Brethren to Slavery, contrary to Justice and Humanity?" For "the same Arguments . . . which establish domestic, likewise establish political Slavery."[77]

This rhetorical and political move to vindicate the Patriots as true rather than faux patriots ranged across the whole chronology of the imperial crisis. The Scottish law professor John Millar opposed the government's American tax and war policies but found it baffling "that the same people who talk in a high strain of political liberty, ... should make no scruple of reducing a great proportion of their fellow-creatures" to real slavery. "Fortune," he groaned, "perhaps never produced a situation more calculated to ridicule a liberal hypothesis."[78] Boston's James Otis, in his stirring Patriot oration in 1764, upbraided both Britain's colonial policy and the slavery of and trafficking in Africans as a threat to the freedom and even the civilization of Europe and America. For "it is a clear truth that those who every day barter away other men's liberty will soon care little for their own." Massachusetts petitioners styling themselves "The Sons of Africa" drove this point home in a brief passage that typified its usage by Black petitioners for freedom in late colonial Massachusetts and Connecticut. The "celebrated" virtue of "Patriotism," they lectured, consisted of a broad sense of "Humanity, or a benevolent Regard to *all* their Fellow Men."[79] Patriot John Allen brought it all together in 1774 when he cried, "Blush ye pretended votaries for freedom! ye trifling patriots! who are making ... a mockery of your profession" to be liberty's advocates "by trampling on the sacred natural rights and privileges of the *Africans*; for while you are fasting, praying, non-importing, non-exporting, remonstrating, resolving, and pleading for a restoration of your charter rights, you at the same time are continuing this lawless, cruel, inhuman, and abominable practice of enslaving your fellow-creatures."[80]

This theme resonated well beyond where we might expect to find it. For instance, it would be difficult to describe Virginian Arthur Lee, who disapproved of slavery in the abstract but defended North American slaveholders' practice of it, as an abolitionist. But in his most decidedly antislavery moment, a 1767 essay published in a Virginia newspaper, he sought to leverage the imperial crisis. Amid the Townshend Acts tumult, Lee called for "the abolition of Slavery" in Virginia by means of colonial (not parliamentary) legislation. He pointedly remarked that Virginia's Africans never did "consent to be our Slaves," and hoped to marshal white colonists' empathy by reminding them that the British Parliament had asserted its authority over them by legalizing the slave trade. Even more remarkably, in 1775, a group of citizens in Darien, Georgia, resolved that "to show the world that we are not influenced by any contracted or interested motives, but a general philanthropy for all mankind, ... we hereby declare our disapprobation and abhorrence of the unnatural practice of Slavery in *America*."[81] And on and on it went; as repetitive and seemingly obvious as the inconsistency theme was, abolitionists who also loved the Patriot cause found it too important to neglect.[82]

And while the prewar imperial crisis saw a mountain of such antislavery appeals to consistency, the war years only saw that mountain grow. The prewar antislavery hall of fame, such as Benezet, Wheatley, and Black petitioners in Connecticut and Massachusetts, kept up this drumbeat during the war. Sharp published three antislavery pamphlets in 1776, and in one quoted the American editor of the work as earnestly wishing, "for the credit of my country, ... that *Liberty* in America, is not a partial privilege, but extends to every individual in it." In another Sharp again showed how well he knew his audience's predilections by urging readers to show that theirs was "true PATRIOTISM" by acting out of "UNIVERSAL BENEVOLENCE" toward the enslaved. In 1779, Prime and Prince, enslaved petitioners to Connecticut's Patriot legislature, reminded their audience of the need to be "Consistent" on a global stage, preserving their good name among "all the great Empires of the World."[83]

New converts joined old stalwarts in making antislavery appeals to Patriot consistency during the war. Just days before the first battles, a group of abolitionists met in Philadelphia to found the Society for the Relief of Free Negroes Unlawfully Held in Bondage. Far from conceding that this was no time to agitate abolition, in their founding document, they argued that this moment, "when justice, liberty, and the laws of the land are the general topics among most ranks and stations of men," was just the right time to act. While this was their only meeting for nine years, antislavery Pennsylvanians did echo this idea in their 1780 gradual emancipation act, in passages about extending that liberty to others that they sought for themselves. In a 1783 pamphlet that Benezet distributed far and wide, New Jersey's David Cooper asserted that "now is the time to demonstrate to Europe, to the whole world, that America was in earnest, and meant what she said" when the new nation rested its struggle on universal natural rights. "Let not the world have an opportunity," he pled, "to charge her conduct with a contradiction to her solemn and often repeated declarations; or to say that her sons are not real friends to freedom." Moving to free slaves was the best way to defend against the impression of faux patriotism.[84]

New Black voices added to this torrent. Freedom petitioners to the New Hampshire legislature played on the concept "that private or public tyranny and slavery" were all one "detestable" thing, given that they rested on "coertion" rather than consent. A group of enslaved people in Connecticut argued that they as loyal "Whigs ought to be *free*; and the *Tories* should be sold." Alas, this twin appeal to consistency and the racialization of slavish Loyalists failed.[85] While in Pennsylvania this trope was powerful enough to be inscribed in the very lawbook, nonetheless appeals to it did not always succeed.[86]

A strikingly successful appeal to consistency came during the wartime public debates over a proposed state constitution in Massachusetts. That document had directly excluded "Negroes, Indian and molattoes" from the franchise. One town meeting objected to this clause as not only wearing "a very gross complexion of Slavery" but also being "diametrically repugnant to" the cherished doctrine that citizens must consent to laws. Essex County's detailed response granted that enslaved people by definition lacked the independent will to render consent to laws, but their conclusion was not to support the franchise clause but to advocate for the day when "the slave-holder could not be found in the land." Another protest contended that "no power on Earth has a Just Right" to deprive any "part of the humane race of their Natural Rights." As a result of such bodies of citizens taking the key concepts of their Revolution deadly seriously and applying them to antiracist ends, the provision for suffrage in the state constitution ratified in 1780 was race-neutral. Historian Van Gosse has written that "it is difficult to overstate the significance" of this outcome to this debate. It not only constituted "the only instance of 'white' suffrage overturned by popular revulsion prior to the Civil War" but also set a key precedent for Black voting rights that characterized New England north of Rhode Island in the coming decades.[87]

Late in the war, when American independence seemed assured, antislavery Americans added a powerful new branch to this endlessly fruitful theme: Americans must purify their new nation by pruning slavery and the slave trade as the rank growth of British colonial corruption. A young Joel Barlow's poetic vision of the return of peace with the triumph of "Freedom's cause" envisaged an America in which "no grasping lord shall grind the neighbouring poor" and "no cringing slave shall at his presence bend." In this regenerated land, "Africa's unhappy children, now no more / Shall feel the cruel chains they felt before, / But every State in this just mean agree, / To bless mankind, and set th' oppressed free."[88] Pennsylvania's legislature, looking ahead in 1780 to the prospect of liberation from Britain, passed a gradual emancipation act professedly in part "to extend a portion of that freedom to others which has been extended to us." They also stated that this law seized the opportunity to free "those who have lived in undeserved bondage, and from which, by the assumed authority of the kings of Great Britain, no effectual legal relief could be attained." They did grant that white Pennsylvanians in the colonial era had acted on "narrow prejudices" against Africans, but the Revolution had "weaned" them from such poison. By this law, they would therefore not only "manifest the sincerity of our profession" of liberty but also render Pennsylvania's effective independence a new dawn of freedom after the darkness of colonial days.[89] "Let Great Britain stand alone as the author of the American trade to Africa," Benjamin Rush urged South Carolinians via Nathanael Greene in 1782, by keeping "our new republics" from being "stained with the importation of a single African slave into America."[90]

Massachusetts seems to have become unusually fertile soil for this specific idea. Belinda, an enslaved woman in Massachusetts, brilliantly leveraged these ideas in 1782 when she petitioned her state legislature for freedom and an allowance to be taken from her Loyalist ex-master's confiscated estate. He had fled, Belinda jabbed, from Patriots "armed in the cause of freedom" to England—"a land, where lawless dominion sits enthroned, pouring blood and vengeance on all who dare to be free." She urged the legislature to mark Massachusetts as superior to Britain by playing the part of "a body of men, formed for the extirpation of vassalage," ready to grant her "the just returns of honest industry" by reparations for fifty years of "ignoble servitude for the benefit of" that disgraced slaver. She and/or her representatives played the politics of American liberating virtue versus corrupt British slavery perfectly, and the legislature responded with payment.[91]

In 1783, the Commonwealth's chief justice William Cushing followed suit in his key ruling in the case of *The Commonwealth of Massachusetts v. Jennison*. Slavery, he opined, rather than an institution with full legal standing, had been a mere "usage which took its origin from the practice of some European nations, and the regulations of the British government respecting the then Colonies." But whatever proslavery sentiments might have "formerly prevailed" in Massachusetts after having "slid in upon us by the example of others, a different idea has taken place with the people of America" amid the imperial crisis and war. That different idea was "more favorable to the natural rights of mankind" than backward colonial-era notions. In Cushing's reading, the "Idea of Slavery is in consistent with our own conduct & Constitution" as illuminated by the Revolution.[92]

The power of these ideas also manifested in the exasperation of John Marsham, a New Englander who argued that slavery was fully consistent with God's law. In a long and widely read letter to an editor in 1772, Marsham warned that "we have been carried into Extremes" by the contemporary exaltation of "Freedom, Liberty, and the Rights of Mankind." "What I particularly refer to is the Sentiment many among us entertain of the African Trade, so called. We have it perpetually thundered in our Ears," including by legal decisions such as Mansfield's, "That it is a Disgrace for a People who make such Pretensions to Liberty, to permit such a Species of Slavery." "Our general Notions of Freedom and the Rights of Mankind," however, "only tend to confuse and mislead weak Minds" from the real question, which was whether Africans were descendants of Ham and thus subject to the Bible's perpetual curse of servitude.[93] Both the *Somerset* decision and the constant attempts of abolitionists to harness the power of the imperial crisis's demand for consistency seem to have convinced Marsham to pick up his pen. By his own admission, he was playing defense while abolitionists throughout the British Atlantic were on the offensive culturally and even legally. And he in fact brought on himself a weeks-long newspaper war pitting him alone against multiple refuters, including one who jabbed that Marsham might as well have argued that the Boston Massacre was ordained of God as that slavery was. Marsham's only real retort, other than point-by-point biblical responses, was to complain repeatedly that he was the victim of his age's prejudices.[94]

Another measure of the power of the appeal to consistency was the often-grudging assent these appeals gained among Patriots who did not start out (or even end up) as abolitionists. Josiah Atkins, a Connecticut man in the Continental Army, reflected in this vein on the enslavement he saw while marching past Washington's and other leading Patriots' plantations in summer 1781. "Alas! That persons who pretend to stand for the *rights of mankind* for the *liberties of society*, can delight in oppression, & that even of the worst kind!" He could see this as nothing other than "strikingly inconsistent" behavior.[95] In 1776, in a debate with his school friend and Loyalist Francis Kinloch, young Patriot John Laurens granted that "we Americans at least in the Southern Colonies, cannot contend with *a good Grace*, for liberty, until we have enfranchised our Slaves." This candid admission helped fuel this Carolina scion's earnest wartime antislavery career.[96] In late 1780, learning while in Philadelphia that his home state was debating a law offering enslaved people as recruitment bounties for white Patriot troops, James Madison was troubled. He thought it would be better "to liberate and make soldiers at once of the blacks themselves," because "it wd. certainly be more consonant to the principles of liberty which ought never to be lost sight of in a contest for liberty."

Three years later, still in Philadelphia, he declined to punish his enslaved man Billey for seeking his liberty. Madison professed to his father that he could not contemplate selling Billey abroad "merely for coveting that liberty for which we had paid the price of so much blood, and have proclaimed so often to be the right, & worthy the pursuit, of every human being."[97] Assenting to the basic logic of the antislavery consistency appeal did not equal antislavery action, of course, but it in no way impeded such action and was evidence of an antislavery zeitgeist.

Abolitionists found it especially promising that hatred of slavery and love of liberty constituted the moral high ground for which both sides fought, and that these views connected to broadly shared religious ideals. Abolitionists repeatedly connected the triangle of the imperative for moral superiority for one's cause, the earnest wish for divine aid instead of divine punishments, and doing the right thing relative to chattel slavery. The enormous stakes most participants perceived in the crisis and war also gave abolitionists an opening for this sort of existential, even apocalyptic sort of appeal.

This idea that antislavery action could avert divine punishment had been a running theme in transatlantic abolitionism since the 1750s but took greater strength from its salience to the imperial crisis.[98] Benezet issued this warning of divine judgment for slavery in private as well as public. Whereas his antislavery writings in the 1750s and early 1760s appealed most directly to the Golden Rule and the philanthropy of his readers, in a 1766 pamphlet he pointedly demanded, "Must we not tremble to think what a load of guilt lies upon our nation generally and individually" for encouraging the slave trade?[99] Black abolitionists in Massachusetts also, as Christopher Cameron has demonstrated, "worked to tie slavery to the ethical and religious values Americans held dear." For instance, in 1773, "the sons of Africa" invoked the specter of divine judgment on Massachusetts for the "black and enormous Crimes" involved with slavery. "To avert those deserved Judgments, it is hoped the patriotic Legislature of this Province, will in their present Session" ban the slave trade and adopt an emancipation scheme.[100] In a 1771 case pleading for a slave's freedom, Sharp summed up much of the thrust of these interlocking arguments when he urged that "the publick would be materially injured" by the legal toleration of slavery in Britain—"as well in honour as in Morals and National safety." He had already gone on record pleading for universal liberty and warning that slaves' "cries ... will certainly reach to Heaven," but this was a politically charged add-on in the context of the imperial crisis.[101]

Connecticut Congregationalist minister Levi Hart, in a 1775 sermon, likewise appealed both to Patriots' self-interest and their Christian humanity. "We are accountable to God for all the sufferings which we bring upon the unhappy Negroes," he stated flatly. Thus, if Americans perpetuated slavery, who could suppose that their "liberties will be established on a lasting foundation"?[102]

Other abolitionists asserted that God had already visited the British Atlantic for the sin of slavery in the form of the vexing and painful imperial crisis itself. Quaker Samuel Allinson demurred in a letter to Patrick Henry that it was "not for a Mortal to determine" whether "the present troubles" were a divine visitation, even as he suggested they were just that.[103] Other mortals proved less coy on this point. Sharp shared with Rush his conviction that the imperial crisis, which presaged "the destruction of both" the colonies and Britain, "may, with great probability of Truth, be looked upon as a just punishment from God, for the enormous Wickednesses which are openly avowed and practised throughout the British Empire, amongst which the public Encouragement given to the Slave Trade by the Legislature at home, and the open Toleration of Slavery and Oppression in the Colonies abroad, are far from being the least!"[104] Rush echoed that judgment in a 1773 pamphlet, urging preachers to put their parishioners "in mind of the Rod which was held over them a few years ago in the Stamp and Revenue Acts. Remember that national crimes require national punishments," and that in the absence of antislavery reformation the imperial crisis was likely to persist. Rush also hinted that slave insurrectionists should be classified alongside the British ministry as human agents of divine retribution for slavery.[105] Rush had much company in warning that the imperial crisis was a partial judgment up to that point which could only get worse without repentance. Among others, evangelical preacher Elhanan Winchester, although only a visitor to Virginia, bravely warned that the slave trade and slavery constituted one "national sin." In words deeply tinged with the political setting in late 1774 when he preached, Winchester warned that "if you refuse and rebel" against Christ's determination to free the people white Virginians had enslaved, "you will be enslaved, or devoured by the sword." Indeed, "should a war break out," God would likely use the enslaved people to turn the tables on their enslavers just as the ancient Israelites had done to the Egyptians.[106]

And then it did get worse with the outbreak of war. Multiple wartime speakers and authors pursued the providential punishment theme from a variety of angles. One of the most prolific of these was that the war itself, and whether it was going well or ill for the Patriot cause, was evidence of God's attitude toward America. Late in 1775, New England Congregationalist divine Samuel Hopkins began with a positive spin on this idea, suggesting that Congress's recommendation of a ban on the slave trade "has been one means of obtaining the remarkable, and almost miraculous protection and success, which heaven has hitherto granted to the united Colonies" in their armed "struggle for *liberty*." He pursued this thought by urging Americans to emancipate their slaves to stay in God's good graces.[107] This concept of abolition as gratitude for God's deliverance of Patriots found wide purchase as the sunny version of this theme. Indeed, the idea of paying forward to African Americans the "blessings" of freedom that had "been extended to us" ran through the preamble to Pennsylvania's 1780 emancipation law.[108] In a 1776 pamphlet, however, Hopkins pressed the negative version by insisting that slavery was "a sin which God is now testifying against in the calamities he has brought upon us" in the ongoing destructiveness of the war. That abomination "must be reformed before we can reasonably expect deliverance, or even sincerely ask for it."[109]

While Hopkins was a leading light of this idea that the war was divine judgment for American slavery, other exponents were not few. The Presbyterian Jacob Green of New Jersey balanced his antislavery and Patriot principles in a 1778 fast day sermon, declaring that "God corrects us by Britain," but that this did not mean Britain was in the right. In fact, "God often makes use of the worst of instruments to correct his own people." Still, slavery was America's "most crying sin" and jeopardized the new nation's hold on the moral high ground, Green continued. While the British ministry was only "attempting to violate" God-given liberty, "we in America have a long time been in the actual violation of it."[110] Lemuel Haynes, a Black New Englander, exhorted his fellow Patriots to "candidly" admit that "*the practise of Slave-keeping, which so much abounds in this Land,*" called down God's judgments on that land. If Britain were able to conquer North America, he posited, this very sin "may be the procuring cause of this very Judgement."[111] The pseudonymous, and clearly (at least grammatically) nonelite, "Humanity" wrote an impassioned letter to John Adams in 1776. "Is thar not a caus," the missive began, for these "trubelsom times" for both Britain and America? "Among the many sins that might be named" as that cause, this writer singled out "slave keepen" as bringing down this curse. "Reform" should begin at the top given that

George Washington, the commander of the Patriot armies, "holds 700 of them in bondeg. Thenk ye god will prosper the wor in his hand"? This was a rhetorical question.[112]

As the very pseudonym of this letter writer attests, antislavery advocates did seek to leverage the wartime watchword of humanity in American politics.[113] An interesting carryover of the deep connections between that ideal and prisoners of war was that one of the most vigorous uses of this concept came in the service of freeing individual Black prisoners. In early 1783, "T.G." wrote to appeal for clemency for five men held in jail in Pennsylvania facing execution for a robbery, some of whom were African American slaves. The writer argued that these men had every right to resist the "barbarous laws" that held them in bondage, laws to which they had given no consent. But "T.G's" clinching appeal was that "the people of Pennsylvania have long been considered as possessing great tenderness and compassion," so hopefully "the pious and the humane will at least consider the case."[114]

But the most striking thing about abolitionists' use of the ideal of humanity to appeal to white Americans is that it was vanishingly thin. Certainly when contrasted with the vast evidence of their use of concepts like consistency and divine judgment, it appears they did not place great faith in the appeal to humanity. That suggests the sheer political power of Patriots' railing on the inhumanity of Britons' stirring up slave insurrections. It might have been that this Patriot rallying cry had crowded abolitionists out of the ideal of humanity and/or tainted that ideal in Patriot political circles.

Some antislavery Americans also connected that other great wartime buzzword, the concept of collective honor, to slavery. In a 1776 pamphlet, "Demophilus" exulted that "to the honor of Pennsylvania," that state had "but very few slaves." In 1780, a group of recently freed Black people petitioning Massachusetts's legislature for tax relief called on the notion of loyalty. Given that "many of our colour (as is well known) have cheerfully Entered the field of Battle in the defence of the common cause," they hoped that Patriot legislators would feel some obligation to them.[115] But yet again, the main story of this abolitionist appeal to Americans' honor was one of scarcity. The relative lack of this tactic aimed at white Americans is glaring when contrasted not only with other themes aimed at that audience but also with the purchase the politics of honor found in the British politics of slavery surrounding the war years. Yet again this seems to be a tale of another stance toward slavery claiming the ground: American Patriots deployed the concept of honor so much in relation to reclaiming enslaved Americans that this attitude dominated that particular ideological territory in American slavery politics.

In this complex political environment, then, neither the defenders nor the enemies of North American chattel slavery could declare anything resembling victory. The imperial crisis and war provided powerful political arguments to both sides. This portended ongoing contestation over the legacy of the Revolution for slavery within American politics.

The regional compartmentalization that many American Patriots practiced provided yet another indicator of the divided impact of the Revolution on the new nation's politics of slavery. Even as they sought common cause against the British ministry, they very often thought and spoke of the concept and reality of slavery in sectional terms. As can be said about so many other themes, at times this regional variegation encouraged antislavery thought and action, and at other times it hampered it.

Patriots, for instance, often resorted to very specific geographical analogies when decrying the ministry's threat of political slavery. Many seemed quite logically uncomfortable using the analogy available to them via the enslaved Black people among them. European political bondage and serfdom proved appealing to many of these Patriots. A speaker at a Rhode Island rally, for instance, cried that Americans taxed without consent would be "as compleat slaves to their landlords, as the common people of *Poland* are to their lords."[116] Parallels to the "Egyptian bondage" the Israelites suffered in the Bible, and to the slavery inflicted by Muslims in contemporary Turkey, abounded. In one rendering, subjugation to the British ministry would lead to "a miserable life of slavery in chains, under a pack of worse than Egyptian tyrants" whose "master" was the devil itself.[117] Boston's celebrants of Guy Fawkes Day in 1766 made another religiously freighted likening: to seventeenth-century Catholic conspirators against English liberty. The revelers added to "the Pope's Retinue" of effigies by including those of "a Number of the Friends of slavery and arbitrary Power, and in particular some of the Advocates for the late Stamp Act."[118] An oft-repeated and rather more contemporary parallel was France's 1768 reduction of the previously independent island republic of Corsica to what English people termed political slavery.[119] From all of the above evidence it would seem that these Patriots were desperate to turn a blind eye to the analogy right under their own noses. In addition to keeping the focus on political bondage, there were obvious political advantages to diverting the debate away from the spectacle of Patriots inflicting rather than suffering from slavery.

Other Patriots inched toward that connection to slavery in their own society. In 1773, Boston's town clerk charged newly elected town officials to resist the "infernal Plan of enslaving America" laid by British officials, who were so many "subordinate Tyrants, intrusted with a Rod to scourge us, and suppress that Spirit of Freedom which is the glorious Characteristick of America." The ministry and their lackeys, seeking to exercise "extravagant Powers, are to be held in the same Contempt and Detestation with a *Banditti of Slave Makers on the Coast of Africa.*" Thus, he expected these new town officials to protest all such acts vigorously, in concert with other colonies led by Virginia.[120] This comparison to the transatlantic slave traders fell short of implicating American slavers, especially since he enjoined cooperation with slaving Patriots in Virginia.

But others traversed that moral distance, and as such found white southerners wanting. Josiah Quincy adjudged it illiberal to perceive slavery only from afar. "The Briton says—see France, Spain and Italy—the Calamities of slavery," he noted in his diary in 1774. But "the liberal minded who use a larger scale will think it not needfull to go so far." He made clear how near he was willing to adjust his focus when, in his journal of a 1773 journey to the southern colonies, he registered distaste for "those Zealots for Liberty, who are the Enslavers of Negroes." Southern colonies' laws, he wrote, "savor more of the policy of Pandemonium than the English constitution," and might well have debarred southern whites from being true patriots in the best sense.[121] Abigail Adams confided to her husband, John, that it seemed "a most iniquitous Scheme" to be willing to "fight ourselfs for what we are daily robbing and plundering from those who have as good a right to freedom as we have." During the war years, Abigail's opinions about the advisability of the Patriot alliance with white southerners fluctuated. But in her correspondence with John, she led with doubts about whether slaveholders could adequately defend against British invasion, and whether they could feel the same "passion for Liberty" as non-slaveholding Patriots. White southerners seemed to her uncomfortably "like the uncivilized Natives Brittain represents us to be."[122]

Even some of the targets of such remarks did not shy away from the parallel. In 1769, South Carolina Patriot Christopher Gadsden, in a letter to a newspaper, warned that if Americans failed to resist the Townshend Acts, "we are as real Slaves as those we are permitted to command, and differ only in degree."¹²³ In early 1775, his compatriot Henry Laurens wrote to a London acquaintance that "the terms of Submission required from American Subjects to Parliamentary Authority are more unjust more intolerable than the Laws by which I govern my Plantation Negroes."¹²⁴ In 1774, George Washington echoed Laurens and Gadsden. "The Crisis is arrived," he hectored his hesitant friend Bryan Fairfax, "when we must assert our Rights, or Submit to every Imposition that can be heap'd upon us; till custom and use, will make us as tame, & abject Slaves, as the Blacks we Rule over with such arbitrary Sway."¹²⁵ Clearly, abolitionists and other writers amid the imperial crisis had so effectively battered the wall of cognitive dissonance that it proved impossible for all Patriots to write and think about chattel slavery as happening elsewhere.

However, debaters widely practiced another form of geographical distancing in which they contained the political and moral liabilities of slavery to particular regions within the British Empire. The political advantages of cordoning off the guilt and inconsistency associated with slavery, together with Patriots' anger at white West Indians for their political hesitancy, encouraged Patriots to single out those West Indians. New Englanders, who seem to have been in advance of others in their sense of regional identity, practiced this tactic in particular.¹²⁶ Such reflections and deflections abounded amid the bitterness of 1764, when the West Indian lobby supported the Sugar Act at North Americans' expense. Slaveholding's tendency to create petty tyrants, James Otis thundered in this context, was the cause of "that ferocity, cruelty, and brutal barbarity that has long marked the general character of the sugar islanders." Stephen Hopkins similarly groused that the West Indians' selfish stance encouraged the "untoward conclusion, that as these people are used to an arbitrary and cruel government over slaves, and have so long tasted the *sweets* of oppressing their fellow creatures, they can hardly forbear esteeming two millions of free and loyal British subjects, inhabitants of the northern colonies, in the same light."¹²⁷ And on it went; for instance, surely the Rhode Islander Henry Marchant's enthusiasm for the play *The West Indian* in 1771 had to do with relief that it was West Indians in Londoners' crosshairs when they celebrated British liberty by contrast.¹²⁸ This sort of differentiation allowed North American Patriots to imagine, or at least present, their "great Continent" as "the seat of freedom" imperiled by the imperial crisis, and the West Indies as the seat of slavery.¹²⁹

Other Patriots, however, less certain that *all* of North America was the seat of freedom, had no problem loading some of slavery's guilt and inconsistency onto the southern colonies. Amid the Stamp Act debate, a British friend to the Patriot cause lamented that too many Britons failed to distinguish among North Americans. Those in the northern colonies, in this telling, were peopled by hardy, freeborn English settlers similar to English yeoman farmers. It was, however, all too true that "the Inhabitants of the Southern [colonies] approach nearer to the *West Indians*" than did those from the northern colonies, due to climate and slavery. As slaveholders, "they are habituated by Precept and Example, to Sensuality, Selfishness, and Despotism."[130] Although in 1774 Benjamin Rush talked warmly with Arthur Lee of a "general union among the colonies," the year before he had thrown the southern colonies under the bus in a letter to a French philosophe. While his antislavery writings had been well received in New York City and Boston, he reported, he had turned down a lucrative medical position in Charleston because he was too attached to Pennsylvania, "where one owes one's ease only to free and honest toil, to be tempted to exchange it for a country where wealth has been accumulated only by the sweat and blood of Negro slaves."[131] While Rush dedicated himself to antislavery activity, one likely outcome of all such regional differentiation was to encourage self-satisfied complacency among northern North Americans.

Nor were they alone in this. Thomas Jefferson, for instance, recorded the congressional debates over his slavery-related clauses in the Declaration of Independence with an air of bemused Virginian superiority. The proposed clause "reprobating the enslaving the inhabitants of Africa" went down to defeat "in complaisance to S. Carolina and Georgia, who had never attempted to restrain the importation of slaves, and who on the contrary still wished to continue it." But many in the northern colonies, Jefferson surmised, also "felt a little tender under those censures; for tho' their people have very few slaves themselves, yet they have been pretty considerable carriers of them to others."[132]

Still other Patriots distrusted their comrades in arms not because they were insufficiently antislavery but because they leaned too much against African American bondage. By 1782, the ongoing and continent-wide debate about freeing some enslaved men and putting them in the Patriot ranks convinced South Carolinian Aedanus Burke for one that northern Patriots "regard the condition in which we hold our slaves in a light different from us." He worried that at the end of "the present struggle," they would fully reveal how much they "*wish* for a general Emancipation." And he had a point given some of the high-flying antislavery principles on which some advocates of this scheme based their case.[133] Burke was not unique among white southern Patriots in wondering what sort of allies they had hitched themselves to and how that would impact them, and slavery, in the postwar period.[134] But as they should have known from John Laurens's heading the charge for Black troops, they had more to worry about than antislavery northerners. White Carolinian Christopher Gadsden, for instance, objected to the negotiated evacuation of the British from Charleston in 1782 in part because the agreement "seems so particularly careful of the great negro owners." He hoped "the country at large" would not get the impression that "their honor and safety" would be "sacrificed to that particular species of property" in future agreements of this sort.[135] Far from working for some sort of proslavery national policy, Gadsden recoiled from such a policy forming a part of the nascent nation's reputation.

Given the deep-seated localism of most Americans' identities in this era, none of this should be particularly surprising. Still, it is worth highlighting the spectacle of Patriots scrambling to cordon off the moral and political stain of slavery because it fits so very ill with the dominant historiographical portrait of white men united in the common cause of preserving slavery and white supremacy. Nor would this be a short-term phenomenon: large numbers of Americans in coming decades would find that engaging with Britons on the panoply of issues surrounding slavery led less to the circling of American nationalist wagons than to the exacerbation of American divisions on those issues.

The American Revolution also had many major impacts on the politics of slavery in Great Britain. But as with the United States, that impact was so complicated and contested that making pronouncements about some unitary impact would be misleading. Only many years of continued debate would clarify the influence the imperial crisis and American war would ultimately have on the empire's stance toward the slave trade and slavery.

Historian Christopher Leslie Brown has influentially posited that the era of the American Revolution proved a crucial shift in many Britons' thinking about slavery and empire. Beyond protesting the evil of slavery, they came to entertain "an alternative concept of Empire" freed from slavery. Brown stresses in particular the British wartime emancipation policy as advancing new ideas of the power of the imperial state and the inclusion of its subjects. Political allegiance to the crown, rather than religion or ethnicity, would structure such an iteration of the empire, and an expanded imperial infrastructure would police such social institutions as colonial slavery. A flurry of emancipation schemes in the 1770s and especially 1780s further developed such ideas, but Brown argues that ultimately war had a bigger impact than pamphlets.[136]

For much of the period since Brown published his excellent book, his interpretation has gone largely uncontested. Indeed, after reviewing prominent journal literature between 2012 and 2021, the late Trevor Burnard posited that the debate over the origins of British abolitionism needs a "restart," being dormant.[137] The late David Richardson, however, revived some debate about the importance of the American Revolution's impact on British abolitionism in his final book. He laid great emphasis, consciously contra Brown, on how "antislavery impulses in Britain relating to Africans had a protracted, century-long gestation period" before abolitionists organized those impulses in the 1780s. These antislavery impulses "were not, moreover, utterances of isolated moralists. Rather, they were interwoven into seventeenth-century defenses of English liberties," much as they were in the eighteenth century. Richardson did see the American Revolutionary era as significant but only within "an evolving intergenerational process." "The American Revolution arguably accelerated political interest in" a vision of a moral British empire and society; "it did not give birth to it, however." The sheer scale of the political movement against the slave trade once it got organized "was testament to the breadth of the long-standing growth in public nervousness about the trade's compatibility with British values ... over the previous century."[138]

Other historians have likewise discerned great significance in the British government's wartime policies. Maya Jasanoff, for instance, has judged that the British government's record of honoring promises to Black Loyalists was better than it was to white Loyalists. She depicts Guy Carleton as especially important among the wide cast of imperial officials whose stances indicated "an emerging contrast between certain American and British attitudes toward slavery." Carleton was no abolitionist, and many other key British officials both in the Paris negotiations and on the ground in North America had every interest in preserving property rights in humans (beginning with but well beyond white Loyalists' claims). But the dedication to honoring British promises to Patriots' erstwhile human property reflected a commitment among these men "to a concept of national honor—and the paternalistic government's responsibility to uphold it—that would rapidly gain momentum among the rulers of the postwar

British Empire."[139] As scholar Eliga Gould has aptly phrased it, the decision by Carleton and his superiors in London "to place Britain's obligations to the Black Loyalists above its obligations to the United States heralded a new government-level commitment to emancipation."[140]

While I am in broad agreement with these interpretations, the aim of the past several chapters has been to flesh out the ideological and political contexts for these policies. In other words, the British emancipation policy mattered enormously but so did the pamphlets and other political documents and debates that set the political context for, and thus helped determine the political impact of, that policy. Politics as well as wartime logistics dominated at every stage of the development and confirmation of that policy, so it is best to see it as essentially political both in its origins and in its impact. As such, it divided rather than united Britons, both during the war and in its aftermath.

During the American Revolutionary years, abolitionists targeting a British audience echoed those targeting Americans in leveraging the concepts and debates dominating those years' headlines. They appealed to those who feared for the future of the empire, for instance. In an anonymous 1777 poem, an abolitionist celebrated the freedom of the island of Britain, as confirmed by Mansfield's *Somerset* decision. But they also warned that Rome, the enslaver of nations ranging from India to Britain, "now stands an empty name!" To avoid such a fate, the British Empire should make "Mercy" its predominant quality "Till slav'ry cease, and bondage be no more!"[141]

The concept of divine punishment on Britain and its empire proved a powerful adjunct of this secular vision of imperial decline and fall. This offered an efficacious indictment of the North ministry by those who held it accountable for that national ruin, but it also allowed for an indictment of the nation that supported the government. In a 1782 tract, Thomas Parker told a lamentable tale of national declension from the height of national security and glory in 1763. "The evils we have suffered" as a result of the lamentable "civil war" in America, he insisted, had led every sensible man to "cry out, What have we done to call down such a judgment as this upon ourselves!" His answer arraigned British exploitation and oppression of peoples around the world, headlined by the utter failure to enact "any reformation" of the "criminal" transatlantic slave trade, "which at once produces and tolerates all the ill-treatment which the Africans receive at our hands." Moreover, in Parker's judgment, "the whole country" shared this guilt, the government in particular, given its use of military might to protect slavers and defend Britain's slave colonies. Worse, when American legislatures attempted to withdraw from this human trafficking, George III's government vetoed those bans, despite the *Somerset* decision that "had solemnly declared, that slave-holding in this nation was against our laws, because against natural justice and humanity." No wonder God had punished the nation "in whose name all these crimes have been committed against every principle of justice, humanity, and whatever is allowed to be right among mankind."[142] The likes of Parker invited fellow Britons to see the war as an opportunity to right the ship of empire in a moral sense, lest it shipwreck on God's wrath.

This sort of appeal came readily to the pen of Granville Sharp, not only because of his longstanding abolitionism and deep religiosity but also because he opposed the war. In 1776 alone he published three tracts hammering home the idea that the whole slave system constituted an "abominable 'NATIONAL SIN'" of which both Great Britain as a nation and (the capacious category of) "British American slaveholders" must repent "before it is too late!" Neither the would-be United States nor the British Empire, he aptly cautioned, could claim to be a pure paragon of antislavery, for both of their "reformation is but half compleat." "THE COLONIES *protest* against the Iniquity of the SLAVE-TRADE; but continue to hold the poor wretched *Slaves* in a most *detestable Bondage!*" Britain, at least after 1772, "keeps *no Slaves,* but publicly encourages the *Slave-trade,* and contemptuously neglects or rejects every petition or attempt the *Colonists* against that notorious wickedness!" Still, because the British Empire had for generations sanctioned both slavery and the slave trade "by *national* Authority," Sharp did seem to believe it the prime candidate for retribution. "Alas!" he cried, "the WHOLE BRITISH EMPIRE is involved" in all this "horrible Guilt" and the resulting "tremendous *National* Punishment." "Our present Civil Dissentions and horrid *mutual* Slaughters of *National Brethren*" were present proof of the "severe *National Retribution,* which" was clearly "ready to burst upon us!" The only escape hatch, Sharp concluded, was not victory in such a war but rather "a speedy Reformation." It would not be a limited one: national repentance "is absolutely necessary" both "with respect to the *African Slave-trade*" and "the *Toleration of Slavery* in the British American Dominions."[143]

This theme proved trickier for those not in the opposition, for they wanted no truck with those who denounced the ministry's policies, and the war, as a provocation or means of divine wrath. Britons of multiple denominations and even races walked this tightrope. Church of Scotland divine Alexander Carlyle, in a December 1776 fast sermon, disclaimed that "we cannot be accused of any guilt in respect of the immediate occasion or grounds of this war." But he did believe the war was a punishment for "the murders, and rapines, and enormities that have been committed in various places of the British Empire, and still remain unaccounted for." While he was keen to bring white North Americans into their share of guilt for the violent dispossession of Native Americans and the enslavement of Africans, Carlyle argued that such deeds perpetrated abroad by people of British descent would "stain the British annals to the latest posterity." He hoped, therefore, not only that Britain's "righteous cause" would prevail in the war but also that such crimes would no longer happen "with impunity" under the British banner.[144] Methodist luminary John Wesley, also in 1776, lamented the calamity of civil war and thought it plain that "we are punished with the sword" for Britain's sinful state. "One principal sin of our nation," he exhorted, was "the blood that we have shed in Asia, Africa, and America." The transatlantic slave trade in particular "has stained our land with blood!" He was a leading Loyalist, so he was careful to include white Americans among the guilty, but his clarion call was that there could be no peace "while these evils continue."[145] African-Briton Ignatius Sancho was also a decided Loyalist and cheered for British victory in the American war. But he was under no illusions about Great Britain's role in the enslavement "of my brother Negroes" and urged Britons to repent of the atrocities they fostered "in the East-West Indies—and even on the coast of Guinea." "War in all its horrid arrangements," Sancho warned in 1777, was "the bitterest curse that can fall upon a people," and this one had proven to be "one of the very worst—of worst things," a "just judgement" on the empire's rulers and an imperative call for national repentance.[146]

Still others appealed to Loyalist Britons' deep psychological and political need to play the role of the true lovers of liberty. In 1776, pamphleteer Josiah Tucker rebuked his fellow Britons for their inhumanity to trafficked Africans. And instead of ceasing and repairing such harms, "we make Slaves of these poor Wretches" in the West Indies, "contrary to every Principle, not only of Humanity and Justice, but also of" any true understanding of the nature of "national Profit and Advantage." "We," he continued, "the boasted Patrons of Liberty, and the professed Advocates for the natural Rights of Mankind, engage deeper in" the transatlantic slave trade "than any Nation whatever:—And to shew our Consistence, we glory in it!"[147]

In December 1775, opposition MP David Hartley offered a motion in the Commons that, for all its political obtuseness, was grounded in part on the need for consistency. His proposed bill would give every enslaved subject of the empire the right to trial by jury. He claimed to believe that American colonists' acceptance of this imperial reform could be the basis of a reconciliation with Parliament. In a classic understatement, historian Colin Bonwick has suggested that a "hint of unreality" flavored this daydream of imperial reconciliation. But in reference to the politics of slavery, it was significant that Hartley also offered it as a first step toward rooting out "a vice, which has spread through the continent of North America, contrary to the laws of God and man, and to the fundamental principles of the British constitution. That vice is slavery." Hartley's vision was of freedom-loving Britons and Americans "re-united in this, as a foundation to extirpate slavery from the face of the earth. Let those who seek justice and liberty for themselves, give that justice and liberty to their fellow-creatures."[148] For all of Hartley's apparent naivete about the toxicity of the crisis-turned-war, he did seek to harness one of the most pressing ideological and political desiderata of both of those sides to an antislavery vehicle, and at the same time harness antislavery to the wagons of imperial reform and reconciliation.

From October 1780 to September 1781, the *Gentleman's Magazine* published an occasional series of articles damning slavery in the British West Indies specifically, for reasons including its glaring contradiction to Britons' self-image as epitomizing modern civilization. "Publicus," for one, cried that slavery comprised "violences so very disgraceful to our country, so unworthy of our boasted constitution; but, above all, so utterly inconsistent with our truly Divine Religion, founded on the wide basis of universal Love and Charity," that his feelings were "agitated" by the initial essay in this series condemning it. "A.Z." wondered "how compassionate persons" in the West Indies could possibly "enjoy life" there. Modern Europeans prided themselves on their superiority to "those barbarous days when the feudal system prevailed, and . . . deservedly (at least in some respects) extol the humanity of the present age." But chattel slavery in the New World exceeded the savagery of the dark ages in the Old. "An Englishman" chimed in that the slave trade was "most unworthy of the grand idea of British commerce, delighting to spread the bounties and blessings of Heaven over all the nations upon earth." So they offered a plan to ameliorate the treatment of West Indian slaves, promising that these reforms, "if practised, would add much to the welfare and riches of those colonies, as well as to the glory of the British empire."[149]

The most significant development among nonabolitionist Britons was when governmental officials, during and especially at the end of the war, publicly committed to an antislavery policy built on the twin pillars of national honor and humanity. The power of these ideas, which had only expanded as a result of wartime politics, meant that retreating from this position would be very difficult, if not downright politically impossible. It also tied those concepts, as inflected by an antislavery stance, to the sacred concepts of national faith and reputation. The British negotiators of the agreement when British forces evacuated Charleston in 1782, for instance, secured a clause that was essentially toothless but revealingly face-saving. It stipulated "that no Slaves restored to their former Owners, by virtue of this agreement shall be punished by authority of the State" for their desertion to the British forces. Also, "it will be particularly recommended to their Respective Owners to forgive them for the same."[150] The operative word "recommended" did not bode well for these people, but such a clause allowed the British to salvage a semblance of honor while betraying the enslaved. British officials could also thereby retain their pose as the advocates of humanity in the inhumane South.

Carleton himself planted one foot each on humanity and honor in the summer of 1783 when retorting to American complainants about his approach to evacuating freed African Americans. "He should shew an Indifference to the feelings of humanity," he insisted to a group of aggrieved Virginians, "as well as to the honor and Interest of the Nation he serves," were he to abandon Loyalists to persecution. While the complaining Patriots saw his evacuation of Black Loyalists as evidence that he was no honorable man, he clearly meant his statement to apply to Loyalists of whatever skin tone. And it is telling that he framed humanity and honor not as ethereal concepts but as concrete elements of national interest.[151]

Carleton received plaudits for this stance up and down the British political and military chains. No less a personage than Foreign Secretary Charles James Fox heartily endorsed Carleton's ripostes to Washington's complaints as both "solid & founded in Equity." For the government "to have restored Negroes, whom we had invited, *seduced* if you will, under a Promise of Liberty, to the tyranny and possibly to the Vengeance of their former masters," would have offended any "Man of Honour," let alone a great and honorable imperial nation.¹⁵² For Fox, American Patriots' ongoing protests against Britain's seducing slaves were beside the point, as were American slaveholders' property claims. The real "tyranny" in this situation would be faithlessly delivering allies back to their inhuman former enslavers. Such attitudes about what true humanity and honor dictated also obtained among the rank and file of those loyal to Britain. One New York City Loyalist, for instance, described Carleton's "altercation" with the "rancorous and malignant" rebels "about Negroes." He agreed entirely that "no minister can by a Treaty disannul" the proclamations that had offered freedom, "and indeed it would be inhuman to the last Degree and a base Violation of Public Faith to send those Negroes back to their Masters who would beat them with the utmost Cruelty."¹⁵³ What this commitment would translate to in practice for the reconfigured postwar British Empire remained unclear, but the commitment itself was very clear and would prove consequential.

Despite the antislavery zeitgeist in Britain in which such decision-makers and writers operated, what the practical application of antislavery ideas should be was just as contested in Britain as it was in America. In the Revolutionary era, Britons who wished to deflect antislavery demands had multiple tactics available. One impulse within the Loyalist political culture was a pride that Britain was by definition the home of freedom and the British Empire its avatar in the world. Such pride could easily nurture complacency regarding slavery and the slave trade.¹⁵⁴ Temple Luttrell's 1777 House of Commons motion linking impressment to "bondage" and "servitude," discussed above, illustrated one means of deflecting true antislavery. In a subsequent debate, Luttrell granted that many Britons "indeed object to the slave trade as inhumane and impious." But he argued that it was better for British sugar islands to be supplied with enslaved laborers by British ships rather than those of its enemies. Moreover, he built on his impressment campaign by submitting that, "hard as the case of a negroe-slave may appear to a free born Briton at first view, I conceive him to be far less an object of commiseration . . . than a poor, impressed" British sailor. The African's "confinement is not so strict; his discipline not so severe, his sustenance full as good, and his labour, upon the whole, less harsh and burdensome."¹⁵⁵ This maneuver proved to be more than a diversion from nascent assaults on British slaving. In Luttrell's scenario, the real—indeed, the worst—slavers were ultimately the ministry that had launched and continued the war.

Arguably the most significant drag on governmental movement in an antislavery direction was the prominence and profitability of the British West Indies. Preserving them for the empire, as discussed previously, became a, if not the, top priority in the later stages of the war, and that would require a political as well as a military effort. Despite their deep-seated loyalty to the empire during crisis and war, planters and their representatives looked with great suspicion and hostility even on the limited and utilitarian emancipation policy imperial officials adopted after Dunmore's Proclamation. By 1782, Jamaica's assembly felt the need to officially protest "that arming slaves was 'an expedient too dangerous' to imagine," even though the imperial government had for seven years gone well beyond imagining it.[156] One MP demonstrated the chilling effect of the West Indian interest even as he dipped a toe into antislavery waters. In a Commons debate on protecting the West Indies in 1781, Earl Nugent wished "to God" that the commodity "sugar had never existed. It is a luxury which is procured to the Europeans, and their descendants, by the blood and sweat of thousands of their fellow creatures." However, "while we pity the poor negroes," Nugent backtracked, "we must own that sugar, though not absolutely a necessity of life, is yet now become so common among all ranks that" Britons could not easily do without it. The upshot: Britain should exert itself to protect its West Indian colonies.[157]

For the British Empire, then, just as much as for the infant United States, the impact of the American Revolution on the practice and future of slavery was contested and murky rather than uniform and obvious. It would actually have been a comfort to many in these divided nations had they been as unified on these issues as much recent historiography suggests they were. But as contemporaries knew all too well, the political and ideological legacies of the imperial crisis and war offered powerful and specific supports for both proslavery and antislavery positions.

Epilogue

A LONG LETTER published in a provincial British newspaper in September 1783 reveals that Britons had hardly laid aside the buzzwords of the painful revolutionary struggle just concluded. Indeed, its author sharpened its appeal to general eighteenth-century European values by deploying specific Revolutionary-era buzzwords. "W.T.," under the headline "Remarks on the Slave Trade," told the dramatic tale of a newly enslaved African in Virginia saving the life of a captured runaway from their "Barbarian" enslaver. This brute was determined to give the fugitive three hundred lashes as a conspicuous exercise of "the absolute Power he pretended over" these enslaved people. Among the morals of this story for "W.T." was that "what in an European would be called glorious struggling for Liberty, we call in them Rebellion, Treachery, &c." But "in a Breast sensible of the least Touches of Humanity, Compassion must arise to see our fellow Creatures" oppressed in so "barbarous" a way.[1] Perhaps luring in the audience by comfortably casting a white Virginian as the villain, this writer moved to general denunciations of the whole slave system rather than that of American Patriots specifically. And the letter did that by touching many of the era's political hot buttons, including the question of who constituted rebels, the fear of absolute power, and the premium on humanity.

The author's casting of a Virginia planter in the role of villain also nicely illustrated how neither Britons nor Americans were done with each other after the finalization of their wrenching imperial divorce. The British government's recognition of the sovereignty of the United States fundamentally reordered the Anglo-American relationship. As such, 1783 is the natural end date for this volume. But as the postwar political debates helped work out the American Revolution's legacies for slavery, the answers in one nation would have multiple impacts on the other nation in this changed but still intense relationship.

Moreover, many historians of the early national period treat the drafting and ratification of the US Constitution as a continuation of the American Revolutionary era. For some this new Constitution has seemed a sort of counterrevolution, betraying the high promises and ideals of the early days of the Revolution. For others it fulfilled those promises in key ways. In both narratives, 1787–89 puts a period to 1776.[2] So a brief, suggestive word on what light this book sheds on the US Constitution's relationship to slavery, as a proximate legacy of the American Revolution, seems in order here.

Because of this historiographical relationship between the American Revolution and the US Constitution, it should surprise no one that the literature diverges on slavery and the Constitution just as sharply as it does on slavery and the Revolution. For some, the Constitution, like the Revolution, is essentially proslavery; for others, antislavery.[3] It should also come as no surprise to those who have read to this point that I differ with this bifurcation as a false choice. Americans were bitterly divided over the Constitution on multiple issues including the stances its framers had taken on issues related to slavery. And that Constitution's framers had to manage the politics of slavery not only because it intertwined with core issues like taxation and representation but also because Americans were so divided on the issue. In other words, there would have been nothing to manage politically had the American Revolution not intensified rather than resolved conflict in this arena.[4] They formulated and advocated their respective positions both in the shadow of the Revolution's multiple legacies and within an international as well as national and state frames of reference.

The "Dunmorean Moment," for instance, powerfully shaped the stances American slaveholders would take not only in the founding era but also across the entire remaining history of their embattled institution in the United States. The master class's searing experiences of debility when out of political power during the chaos of war and in the face of British occupation remained firmly in mind when they joined with others in Philadelphia in 1787 and debated the proposed Constitution thereafter. It motivated enslavers to confirm slavery's legitimacy at the national level and contain the new national state's potential threat to the institution.[5]

But they had to face down more than shadows from the wartime past. Many framers and debaters of the Constitution pushed for more power to abolish the transatlantic slave trade and sooner, and for less weight for slaveholders in the branches of the new government that represented population. Especially in relation to the slave trade clause, they rarely hesitated to appeal to international opinion. Indeed, the contemporary growth of the British abolitionist movement, in conjunction with the revival of abolitionist societies in the United States, meant that many Americans were attuned to the movement against the transatlantic slave trade as being itself inherently transatlantic.

In turn, as scholarship kicked off by Christopher Leslie Brown has shown, the successful secession of thirteen North American colonies gave a major boost to British antislavery.[6] But the legacy of the American Revolution also divided Britons. Abolitionists and their allies, for instance, could and did appeal to the notion that the British Empire was in crisis after 1783, in need of reconceptualization. They drew on and amplified previous arguments that the empire would need a strong moral foundation if it were to endure and be worth defending. But their opponents, headed by but not inclusive of the West India lobby, also drew on and amplified older arguments. In their telling, the truncated British Empire would need to be more sober and realistic than ever about its economic interests. Statesmanlike wisdom, not the starry-eyed humanitarian zeal of the abolitionists, should distinguish British governments in the face of the republican threat of the United States. All such arguments, for both sides, took on even greater urgency with the advent of the wars with the French revolutionary republic in the 1790s, but they had begun in the political culture of the mid-1780s in reference to the United States and what that nation represented.

And on it would go for decades after American independence. White (let alone Black) Americans could never achieve the sort of consensus that many contemporary scholars attribute to them. That was true in part because of, rather than despite, the ongoing engagement of British voices in the American debates. Neither could white (let alone Black) Britons themselves find consensus. So, while the mountains of paper historians have produced in explaining the parliamentary triumph of slave trade abolition in 1807 and of emancipation in 1833 have been well worth it, it is also worth understanding why it took so long in both cases. The debaters on both sides, in both donnybrooks, found multiple ways to use the Americans and the nationalist rivalry with the United States. These and many other complexities built on the endless complexities of the Anglo-American politics of slavery in the colonial and Revolutionary eras.

NOTES

Abbreviations

Adams	*The Papers of John Adams.*
APW	Charles S. Hyneman and Donald S. Lutz, eds., *American Political Writing during the Founding Era, 1760–1805.*
BG	*Boston Gazette.*
BP	Harry T. Dickinson, ed., *British Pamphlets on the American Revolution, 1763–1785.*
Bruns	Roger Bruns, ed., *Am I Not a Man and a Brother.*
Carleton	Sir Guy Carleton (British Headquarters) Papers, 1747–1783.
Clinton	Henry Clinton Papers.
Dunmore	Lord Dunmore Correspondence.
Franklin	Papers of Benjamin Franklin.
G3	J. W. Fortescue, ed., *The Correspondence of King George the Third from 1760 to December 1783.*
GM	*The Gentleman's Magazine* (London).
Greene	Nathanel Greene, *The Papers of General Nathanael Greene.*
JCC	Worthington C. Ford, ed., *Journals of the Continental Congress, 1774–1789.*
Laurens	Henry Laurens, *The Papers of Henry Laurens.*
LD	Paul H. Smith et al., eds., *Letters of Delegates to Congress, 1774–1789.*
Lee	*The Letters of Richard Henry Lee.*
Letters	Margaret Wheeler Willard, ed., *Letters on the American Revolution, 1774–1776.*
MG	*Massachusetts Gazette and Boston News-Letter.*
Middleton	"Correspondence of Hon. Arthur Middleton, Signer of the Declaration of Independence."
PGW	*The Papers of George Washington: Revolutionary War Series.*
PR	*The Parliamentary Register.*
Price	*The Correspondence of Richard Price.*
RV	William J. Van Schreeven and Robert L. Scribner, eds., *Revolutionary Virginia: The Road to Independence.*
Simmons	R. C. Simmons and P. D. G. Thomas, eds., *Proceedings and Debates of the British Parliaments Respecting North America, 1754–1783.*

Spirit   Henry Steele Commager and Richard B. Morris, eds., *The Spirit of 'Seventy Six: The Story of the American Revolution as Told by Participants*.

Stock   Leo Francis Stock, ed., *Proceedings and Debates of the British Parliaments Respecting North America*.

Introduction

1. Sandoz, ed., *Political Sermons*, 1:595–603, quotations on 595, 603. For other such sweeping religious characterizations of the Patriot cause, see *GM* 45 (June 1775): 295–96, and Ramsay, *History of South Carolina*, 1:150–51.
2. *BP,* 1:340.
3. Gabriele and Perry, *Bright Ages*, 252.
4. Gosse, "Patchwork Nation," 46, 78. Gosse's *First Reconstruction* is a book-length assault on the idea of hegemonic white supremacy and Black disenfranchisement in the decades between the American Revolution and the Civil War. For another excellent example of attention to debate rather than consensus, in this case in the long run in the British Empire, see Blanton, "This Species of Property."
5. Kendi, *Stamped from the Beginning*, 2, 4.
6. Wood, *Radicalism of the American Revolution*, 7, 42, 54–55, quotations on 7, 54; Wood, *American Revolution*, 126–27; Wood, *Revolutionary Characters*, 38; Wood, *Power and Liberty*, 100–105. For five decades now, this idea has certainly been most readers' takeaway from David Brion Davis's massively influential duet, *Problem of Slavery in Western Culture*, esp. 83–112, and *Problem of Slavery in the Age of Revolution*. For more of the relevant historiography, see my discussion of this point in chapter 2.
7. Burnard, *Writing Early America*, 173–93, quotations on 174.
8. Sword, "Remembering Dinah Nevil," quotations on 315, 316, 318. For another excellent exploration of the contested nature of slavery in the empire throughout the colonial period, see Blanton, "This Species of Property." Indeed, the sheer length of this exhaustive study of political and legal conflict underscores this point.
9. Again, I engage with these works more intensively below, but representative historians include Robert G. Parkinson and Woody Holton on one side, and Gordon Wood and Sean Wilentz on the other. I do not mean to inflate my claim to originality here; what I mean very specifically is that the currently booming literature, and the older historiography on which it builds, analyzing the American Revolution's impact on slavery in the new United States tends to be narrowly national in focus. Much of the literature on the impact of the American Revolution on slavery in the British Empire, and on the rise of especially (if not only) British abolitionism in

the late eighteenth century, is transatlantic by design and definition. For especially good examples, see Oldfield, *Transatlantic Abolitionism*; Brown, *Moral Capital*; Sinha, *Slave's Cause*; Rael, *Eighty-Eight Years*; Pybus, *Epic Journeys*; Schama, *Rough Crossings*; and Blackburn, *Overthrow of Colonial Slavery*. Also much of the literature on the American Revolution itself, especially when focused on Loyalists, is explicitly transatlantic in scope; for especially good examples, see Jones, *Resisting Independence*; Jasanoff, *Liberty's Exiles*; Bannister and Riordan, eds., *Loyal Atlantic*; Gould, *Among the Powers of the Earth*; Griffin, *Townshend Moment*; and Lockwood, *To Begin the World*.

1. The Politics of Servitude in the Seventeenth-Century English Empire

1. Christopher Leslie Brown, "The Politics of Slavery," in Armitage and Braddick, eds., *British Atlantic World*, 232–50, quotations on 234, 237. For much more evidence of the political struggles over slavery throughout the colonial period than I provide in this and the next chapter, see Blanton, "'This Species of Property." It is worth noting that his focus is more on how "questions raised in the colonies . . . reflected back to imperial planners in London" (5), whereas my focus is more vice versa. Thus, I consider that these two studies complement rather than compete with or negate each other.
2. Stamatov, *Origins of Global Humanitarianism*; Kupperman, ed., *America in European Consciousness*, esp. 33–75.
3. Douglas Bradburn, "The Eschatological Origins of the English Empire," in Bradburn and Coombs, eds., *Early Modern Virginia*, 15–56; Anthony Padgen, "The Struggle for Legitimacy and the Image of Empire in the Atlantic to 1700," in Canny, ed., *Oxford History*, 34–54; Loren E. Pennington, "The Amerindian in English Promotional Literature, 1575–1625," in Andrews, Canny, and Hair, eds., *Westward Enterprise*, 175–94; Working, *Making of an Imperial Polity*; Mancall, ed., *Envisioning America*. Nicholas Canny has made a vigorous case for how the average English person paid more attention to colonization in Ireland than in North America; see Canny, "England's New World and the Old, 1480s–1630s," in Canny, ed., *Oxford History*, 148–69. I find Misha Ewen's and Lauren Working's counterarguments to be persuasive, given the sheer weight of evidence they adduce of English people's engagement with North American empire in the seventeenth century, in spheres ranging from formal politics to print and material culture. See Ewen, *Virginia Venture*, and Working, *Making of an Imperial Polity*.
4. Nicholas Canny, "The Permissive Frontier: The Problem of Social Control in English Settlements in Ireland and Virginia, 1550–1650," in Andrews,

Canny, and Hair, eds., *Westward Enterprise*, 17–44, quotation on 21; Stock, 1:46, 52–53, 67, 269; Lauren Working, "'The Savages of Virginia Our Project': The Powhatans in Jacobean Political Thought," in Musselwhite, Mancall, and Horn, eds., *Virginia 1619*, 42–59; Musselwhite, *Urban Dreams*, esp. 18, 56; Karen Ordahl Kupperman, "Introduction: The Changing Definition of America," in Kupperman, ed., *America in European Consciousness*, 22–23.
5. Orr, *Empire on the English Stage*, 3, 9.
6. Kelly, *Marooned*; Bailyn, *Barbarous Years*, xv, 31.
7. Hall, ed., *Narratives of Early Maryland*, 106–8, 115–44, 163–308, 337–87, quotations on 107; Working, *Making of an Imperial Polity*, esp. 33–34; Andrews, ed., *Narratives of the Insurrections*, 110–41, 101–354.
8. For some of my previous thoughts on this theme for both the seventeenth and especially eighteenth centuries, and some other evidence not included here, see Mason, "Slavery, Servitude," and Mason and Mason, eds., *History of the Life*, esp. 26–34, 212–25.
9. Chakravarty, *Fictions of Consent*, 15. See also Tomlins, *Freedom Bound*; Steinfeld, *Invention of Free Labor*; Shannon, "A 'Wicked Commerce'"; and Donoghue and Jennings, eds., *Building the Atlantic Empires*, passim and esp. 2.
10. Guasco, *Slaves and Englishmen*, 4, 25, 33, 206.
11. Pestana, *English Atlantic*, is an excellent treatment of this whole history.
12. Donoghue, *Fire under the Ashes*, quotations on 7, 8; John Donoghue, "The Unfree Origins of English Empire-Building in the Seventeenth Century Atlantic," in Donoghue and Jennings, eds., *Building the Atlantic Empires*, 109–31, quotations on 131.
13. Stock, 1:302–4, 357–61, 366, 375, 382, 397, 400, 417–19, quotation on 1:256; Swingen, *Competing Visions of Empire*, quotation on 41; Anna Suranyi, "Indenture, Transportation, and Spiriting: Seventeenth Century English Penal Policy and 'Superfluous' Populations," in Donoghue and Jennings, eds., *Building the Atlantic Empires*, 132–59; Beckles, *White Servitude*; Drescher, *Abolition*, 13–14.
14. *Englands Slavery*, 5–7.
15. Stock, 1:247–63. Interestingly, this debate "ended in no result" (1:263). For more on the issue of prisoners of war and servitude and how it worked in practice, see Tycko, "Legality of Prisoner of War Labour."
16. Stock, 1:250, 256. See also Hilary McD. Beckles, "The 'Hub of Empire': The Caribbean and Britain in the Seventeenth Century," in Canny, ed., *Oxford History*, 231; Rodgers, *Ireland, Slavery*, 33–54, esp. 38. For some of the more perceptive among the many studies of the history of race, see Hudson, "From 'Nation' to 'Race,'" and Fredrickson, *Racism*.
17. Rose, ed., *Documentary History*, 17.

18. Newman, *New World of Labor*, 35; Newman, "'In Great Slavery and Bondage': White Labor and the Development of Plantation Slavery in British America," in Gallup-Diaz, Shankman, and Silverman, eds., *Anglicizing America*, 59–82, quotation on 69; Rugemer, *Slave Law*, 25, 32.
19. Amussen, *Caribbean Exchanges*, quotations on 43, 91, 129; Rugemer, *Slave Law*, 20–51. For an excellent discussion of the shifting metropolitan bodies exercising colonial oversight, and especially the later rise of the Board of Trade, see Brewer, "Slavery, Sovereignty," esp. 1040, 1060–73. Susan Dwyer Amussen, Edward B. Rugemer, and Holly Brewer thus dissent (as do I) from Simon P. Newman's assertion that Barbadian planters developed their labor system "all but completely free of English oversight" (Newman, *New World of Labor*, 14), and from Lee B. Wilson's emphasis on "how seamless this process was as a practical and theoretical matter" (Wilson, *Bonds of Empire*, 38). For a similar process involving Virginia later in the century, see Blanton, "This Species of Property," 359–67. For yet another treatment of this growing differentiation, see Suranyi, *Indentured Servitude*.
20. Kupperman, *Providence Island*, 165–80, quotation on 172. For more linking this imperative to slavery, see Amussen, *Caribbean Exchanges*, 107–44, and Greene, "Liberty, Slavery, and the Transformation."
21. Ligon, *True and Exact History*, 20, 44.
22. Hall, ed., *Narratives of Early Maryland*, 337–87, esp. 357.
23. Hampton, ed., *Radical Reader*, 50–70, 112, 121, quotations on 70, 112; Stock, 1:42–43. For a nice concise discussion of the longstanding use of slavery as an analogy for "any overwhelming human experience" in Irish culture, see Rodgers, *Ireland, Slavery*, 25.
24. Brewer, "Creating a Common Law," quotation on 772; Brewer, "Slavery, Sovereignty"; Blanton, "This Species of Property."
25. Pestana, *English Atlantic*, 170. For other scholars who have made this point about New World slavery's impact on English rhetoric, see Ferguson, *Subject to Others*, 18–26; Walvin, *England, Slaves, and Freedom*, 17–18, 26–67, esp. 27; and Donoghue, *Fire under the Ashes*.
26. Pepys, *Diary*, 59.
27. Nyquist, *Arbitrary Rule*, 2.
28. Hampton, ed., *Radical Reader*, 177–78, 186, 188–90, 192, 194–95, 197, 201, 207, 224–26, 228–29, 232, 235–36, 243, 251–53.
29. Donnan, ed., *Documents Illustrative*, 3:108.
30. Andrews, ed., *Narratives of the Insurrections*, 341.
31. Hudson, "'Britons Never Will Be Slaves,'" 563, 565.
32. Greenblatt, ed., *Norton Anthology*, 3019–22; see also 2427.
33. For examples other than those cited below, see Greenblatt, ed., *Norton Anthology*, 2475, 2477. This was also not a uniquely British attitude; see Drescher, *Abolition*, 71.

34. Hampton, ed., *Radical Reader*, 266–68.
35. Locke, *Two Treatises*, 3–5. See also Brewer, "Slavery, Sovereignty," esp. 1054.
36. Locke, *Two Treatises*, 89–90, 115, 126–27, 141, 156–57, 204, 212, quotations on 126, 204. For especially useful readings of Locke on slavery, see Armitage, "John Locke, Carolina," and Brewer, "Slavery, Sovereignty."
37. Brown, *Moral Capital*, 33–101, quotation on 40. All such interpretations emphasizing the severe limits on antislavery expression and action until the very late eighteenth century build on the work of David Brion Davis, especially in *Problem of Slavery in Western Culture* and *Problem of Slavery in the Age of Revolution*. However, it is worth highlighting—as my conversations with David Waldstreicher have helped clarify in my mind—that there is tension in these two volumes between Davis's treating slavery as always a "problem" and as only a pressing political problem beginning in the era of the American Revolution.

2. Slavery and Politics in the British Atlantic, 1680s–1764

1. Nicholas Canny, "The Origins of Empire," in Canny, ed., *Oxford History*, 30–32; Beckles, "The 'Hub of Empire,'" 218–40. This passage also avoids reference to the "sugar revolution," thanks to the valuable cautions in Menard, *Sweet Negotiations*, and Higman, "Sugar Revolution."
2. Gallay, ed., *Indian Slavery*, 119, 134–35, quotation on 127; Gallay, *Indian Slave Trade*, 62, 67–68; Lauber, *Indian Slavery in Colonial Times*, 130–52, 165–95, 253–59; Lepore, *Name of War*, 150–70; Pulsipher, *Subjects unto the Same King*, 125, 130, 147, 152, 204, 223–26, 241; Pulsipher, *Swindler Sachem*, 41, 45, 174, 295n19; Hardesty, *Black Lives, Native Lands*, 13–16, 41.
3. See, e.g., Annesley, *Memoirs of an Unfortunate*, and Beckles, *White Servitude*.
4. Stock, 4:851–57, quotations on 853, 855, 856. As late as 1771, the Earl of Hillsborough asked Virginia's governor Lord Dunmore to help free a young Briton from a cruel Virginia master. He lamented that "unguarded youths are too often seduced" into "all the Miseries of a Servitude or rather Slavery in the Colonies." Hillsborough to Dunmore, 4 Dec. 1771, Dunmore, vol. 1, p. 88. See also Mason, "Slavery, Servitude."
5. Philip D. Morgan, "The Black Experience in the British Empire, 1680–1810," in Marshall, ed., *Oxford History*, 465–86; Walvin, *Black and White*, 46–73, 159–74.
6. Wilson, *Island Race*, quotation on 6; Wilson, *Sense of the People*, passim, esp. 22–25, quotation on 24. See also Mandler, *English National Character*, and Colley, *Britons*.
7. Armitage, *Ideological Origins*, 5, 8. For another excellent consideration of this discussion as a debate, see Pincus, "Rethinking Mercantilism." For

some seventeenth-century examples of these conceptions of British Empire, see Basker, ed., *Amazing Grace*, 14, 48–49.
8. Marshall, "Free though Conquering People," quotations on x; P. J. Marshall, "The British in Asia: Trade to Dominion, 1700–1765," in Marshall, ed., *Oxford History*, 487–507; Glyndwr Williams, "The Pacific: Exploration and Exploitation," in Marshall, ed., *Oxford History*, 552–75.
9. Hall and Rose, eds., *At Home with the Empire*, esp. 1–52, quotation on 2.
10. Richard Drayton, "Knowledge and Empire," in Marshall, ed., *Oxford History*, 231–52.
11. Wilson, *Sense of the People*, esp. 38–40, 137–205.
12. Langford, *Polite and Commercial People*, 2–3.
13. Stock, 4:460; Monod, *Imperial Island*, 190; Simmons, 1:195.
14. Sirota, *Christian Monitors*, quotations on 6, 7; Mandeville, *Fable of the Bees*, 1:xxi–xxii, xxxiv, xxxix, cxiv–cxvii, 13–16, 26–28, 381–412; 2:401–17; Blanton, "This Species of Property," 272–375.
15. Simmons, 1:29–40, quotation on 31; [Burke and Burke], *Account of the European Settlements*, 1:31–32, 47; 2:145–54, 231–32, 292–95, 106–10; quotations on 1:31, 2:106. Similarly, historian Fred Anderson has demonstrated that the Seven Years' War's unusually long and intense contact between North American colonists and British officials convinced most of the latter that the former were wholly degenerate; see Anderson, *Crucible of War*, 146–49, 182–83, 221–31, 286–90, 324, 371, 584–87.
16. Greenblatt, ed., *Norton Anthology*, 2487–636, quotations on 2631, 2634.
17. Glasson, *Mastering Christianity*, quotations on 41; Glasson, "'Baptism Doth Not Bestow Freedom,'" quotation on 311; Klingberg, ed., *Codrington Chronicle*. For a compelling (if slightly overstated) argument that conservative Anglicans have been underrated as antislavery pioneers, see Hudson, "'Britons Never Will Be Slaves.'" For other historians who have seen the SPG controversy as a key chapter in the history of slavery in the British Atlantic, see Jordan, *White over Black*, 208–10, and Young, ed., *Proslavery and Sectional Thought*, ix, 1–52, 68–133.
18. Godwyn, *Negro's and Indians Advocate*, 7, 40, 41. For a valuable reading of how Godwyn's anti-Stuart politics also informed his critiques in this and other works, see Blanton, "This Species of Property," 20–21, 218–23, 267–70.
19. Brokesby, *Some Proposals*, quotation on 3; Paley, Malcolmson, and Hunter, eds., "Parliament and Slavery," 265, 272–75, quotations on 273, 274. Morgan Godwyn before them had tried the tactic of shame vis-à-vis the Catholics; see Godwyn, *Negro's and Indians Advocate*, unpaginated dedication, 161–62.
20. Van Horne, ed., *Religious Philanthropy*, 99–100; see also 105, 112, 115–19, 127–32, 138–39, 165, 185–86, 195, 212, 220–21, 226, 239–40, 248, 261, 267,

271, 281–84, 289–90. And for echoes of these aggrieved observations from another Chesapeake Anglican divine in the 1760s and 1770s, see Boucher, *View of the Causes*, 38–42, 185–89.
21. For an international example of this mix of high-flying rhetoric and narrow focus on baptism as the outcome, see the reply of Spanish Florida's governor to South Carolinian complaints of runaway slaves in Ramsay, *History of South Carolina*, 1:76–77.
22. Whitefield, *Three Letters*, 13, 14, 16.
23. [Tryon], *Friendly Advice*, 75, 77, 175, 188.
24. Krise, ed., *Caribbeana*, 16–30, 51–146; Orr, *Empire on the English Stage*, 227–31.
25. Leslie, *New History of Jamaica*, 14, 39, 288, 305.
26. GM 5 (Jan. 1735): 21–23.
27. GM 10 (Jan. 1740): 341.
28. [Burke and Burke], *Account of the European Settlements*, 2:86, 116–33, quotation on 124.
29. Smith, *Theory of Moral Sentiments*, 398–405, quotations on 402.
30. Montesquieu, *Spirit of the Laws*, 231–84, quotation on 246. For good discussions of Montesquieu's influence in British thought, see Fletcher, "Montesquieu's Influence," and Walvin, *England, Slaves, and Freedom*, 98–99.
31. Wallace, *System of the Principles*, 1:88–98, quotations on 89–91.
32. Jack P. Greene, "Liberty and Slavery: The Transfer of British Liberty to the West Indies, 1627–1865," in Greene, ed., *Exclusionary Empire*, 50–76, quotation on 60. See also Greene, "Liberty, Slavery, and the Transformation." For similar passages from scholarly luminaries downplaying the political significance of antislavery sentiment before the American Revolution, see Davis, *Problem of Slavery in the Age of Revolution*, 83–112; Wilentz, *No Property in Man*, 112–13; and Walvin, *Zong*, esp. 106. Then there is also what now seems to me to be my own overstatement in Mason, *Slavery and Politics*, 9.
33. Blackburn, *American Crucible*, 3–4, 88. Interestingly, large swaths of this synthetic book that treat the history before the Age of Revolutions acknowledge pressing issues surrounding Atlantic slavery that certainly seem political; see Blackburn, *American Crucible*, 49–96, 145–69. For an earlier version of this idea, see Blackburn, *Overthrow of Colonial Slavery*, 35–104.
34. Burnard, *Creole Gentlemen*, 2–3, 15–16, 205–58, quotation on 15; Kilbride, *Being American in Europe*, 9–44; Gragg, *Englishmen Transplanted*; Brown, *Good Wives*, esp. 3, 319–66; Parent, *Foul Means*, 194–235; Sachse, *Colonial American in Britain*; Canny and Pagden, eds., *Colonial Identity*.
35. Moore, *Slavery and the Making*, xi.
36. Sachse, *Colonial American in Britain*, 47–69, 93–115. For a fascinating set of documents capturing the essential ambivalence of colonial Americans in Britain, see Colbourn and Peters, eds., "Pennsylvania Farmer."

37. Lockridge, *Diary, and Life*, 17–48, 78–122, 154–66.
38. Isaac, *Landon Carter's Uneasy Kingdom*, 55–120.
39. Gauci, *William Beckford*, 66, 67, 90, 114.
40. *GM* 32 (July 1762): 317–19.
41. Jordan, *White over Black*, 208–10.
42. Carter, *Letters*, 79–85, quotations on 81–82.
43. *GM* 11 (March 1741): 145–47.
44. Natalie Zacek, "A Death in the Morning: The Murder of Daniel Parke," in Olwell and Tully, eds., *Cultures and Identities*, 223–43, quotation on 226.
45. Burnard, *Creole Gentlemen*, 222.
46. Jones, *Present State of Virginia*, 47–50, 75–76, 93, 102, 130, quotation on 45; Beverley, *History and Present State*, xi–xxxviii, 37, 216–18.
47. Tinling, ed., *Correspondence of the Three*, 2:443–45, 448, 464.
48. Amussen, *Caribbean Exchanges*, 133, 139.
49. Oldmixon, *British Empire*, 1:290; 2:14, 38, 47, 60–61, 113–27, 343–44, quotation on 2:119. See also Stock, 2:129; Walvin, *England, Slaves, and Freedom*, 17–18, 26–67, 78–79; Hardesty, *Unfreedom*, 47; and Gary Nash, "Social Change and the Growth of Prerevolutionary Urban Radicalism," in Young, ed., *American Revolution*, 20.
50. Rugemer, *Slave Law*, 1–170.
51. Quoted in James, *Rise and Fall*, 22.
52. *GM* 5 (Feb. 1735): 91–93.
53. Donnan, ed., *Documents Illustrative*, 1:51, 57, 125–36, 156; 3:433–34.
54. Simmons, 1:418–21, 491, 500–501, 510–11; Donnan, ed., *Documents Illustrative*, 1:164–65, 173–74, 178, 194–95, 267–71, 377–80, 411–12, 418, 421; 2:44–45, 67–68, 82, 96–99, 107–9, 132–34, 139–41, 146, 171–73, 209–10, 291–92, 393–94, 468, 474, 487–88, 513–24; 3:436–38; Christopher Leslie Brown, "1763 and the Genesis of British Africa," in Olwell and Vaughn, eds., *Envisioning Empire*, 109–28. For a forceful discussion of "the primacy of national interest" in most Europeans' thought about slavery and the slave trade, see Blackburn, *American Crucible*, 329–89, quotation on 331.
55. Molineux, *Faces of Perfect Ebony*, quotations on 11; Molineux, "Pleasures of the Smoke."
56. Roberts, *Slavery and the Enlightenment*, 1.
57. Keith, *History of the British Plantations*, 3–15, 177–87, quotations on 6.
58. Oldmixon, *British Empire*, 1:iv, vii, xxxvii; 2:60. For another work from roughly that same era making similar points, see Thomas, *Historical Account*. For another characterization of planters as "some of the most useful Subjects in the King's Dominions," see *GM* 11 (March 1741): 145.
59. Pettigrew, *Freedom's Debt*, quotations on 2, 105; Swingen, *Competing Visions of Empire*, quotations on 74, 82, 113; William A. Pettigrew, "Transatlantic Politics and the Africanization of Virginia's Labor Force, 1688–1712," in

Bradburn and Coombs, eds., *Early Modern Virginia*, 279–99, quotation on 295. For a similar debate featuring some of these arguments from 1667, see Stock, 1:342–50.
60. Stock, 3:191.
61. Gee, *Trade and Navigation*, 37.
62. Burnard and Garrigus, *Plantation Machine*, 88–89, 96–97, 179.
63. GM 11 (April 1741): 186–88.
64. "British Merchant," *African Trade*, 2, 6, 17, 44.
65. [Postlethwayt], *National and Private Advantages*, 1, 5, 81–82, 104.
66. Swingen, *Competing Visions of Empire*, 173.
67. Trenchard and Gordon, *Cato's Letters*, 747–53; [Wilkes], *North Briton*, 149–50.
68. Hammon, *Narrative*, 13–14.
69. Langford, *Polite and Commercial People*, 145–49, 235–87, 461–518, quotations on 145.
70. GM 10 (Jan. 1740): 341.
71. Wallace, *System of the Principles*, 1:96.
72. Indeed, Manisha Sinha's point that "the history of abolition begins with those who resisted slavery at its inception" is well-taken; see Sinha, *Slave's Cause*, 9–20, quotation on 9.
73. Rugemer, *Slave Law*, 130, 140–70, quotations on 140, 141, 155; [Trelawny], *Essay Concerning Slavery*, quotations from unpaginated introduction. For more on this essay, see Robertson, "*Essay Concerning Slavery.*"
74. Brown, *Tacky's Revolt*, esp. 228–29; Burnard and Garrigus, *Plantation Machine*, 101–36. For more on the scale and impact of slave resistance and maroons in Jamaica and other British West Indian islands, see Craton, *Testing the Chains*, 61–139, and Rugemer, *Slave Law*.
75. Greene, "'Plain and Natural Right,'" 805–8.
76. Woolman, *Journal and Major Essays*, 203.
77. Bruns, "Anthony Benezet's Assertion"; Benezet, *Short Account*, 28–50, quotations on 31, 32.
78. For good discussions of this idea, see Pestana, *Protestant Empire*, 90, 131–33, 137–39, and Walvin, *England, Slaves, and Freedom*, 99–100.
79. Carey, *From Peace to Freedom*, 25, 35, 36.
80. *Epistle of Caution and Advice*, 2.
81. Sword, "Remembering Dinah Nevil," 323–31, quotation on 323; David Waldstreicher, "The Origins of Antislavery in Pennsylvania: Early Abolitionists and Benjamin Franklin's Road Not Taken," in Newman and Mueller, eds., *Antislavery and Abolition*, 45–65, quotations on 45, 48. For similar readings, see also Crosby, "Anthony Benezet's Transformation," and Blanton, "This Species of Property," 420–23. On the other hand, for recent

examples of this particular brand of hagiography that takes the Quaker abolitionists outside the realm of politics, see Jackson, *Let This Voice Be Heard*, and Slaughter, *Beautiful Soul of John Woolman*.
82. Benezet, *Observations*, quotations on 4, 9; Benezet, *Short Account*, 28.
83. Woolman, *Journal and Major Essays*, 93, 210–37, quotations on 93, 213; Woolman, *Considerations*, 31–85, quotations on 64.
84. Le Jau, *Carolina Chronicle*, 48, 108, 130.
85. Greene, ed., "'Plain and Natural Right,'" 803.
86. Bruns, 65; *GM* 11 (Jan. 1741): 30.
87. Gerbner, "'We Are against the Traffik,'" 158–59, 168–69; Bruns, 3–4.
88. Bruns, 6–8, 21–22, 26, 36.
89. Lay, *All Slave-Keepers*, 29, 18.
90. Woolman, *Considerations*, 53.
91. Benezet, *Short Account*, 3–56, quotations on 55, 40, 45.
92. Bruns, 12.
93. Taylor, *American Colonies*, 217.
94. Greene, ed., "'Plain and Natural Right,'" 807, quotations on 801.
95. Colbourn and Peters, eds., "Pennsylvania Farmer," 268–69, 274–75, 277–78, 421–22, 429, quotations on 275, 277–78.
96. Important historians have depicted South Carolina as significantly different from other North American colonies, politically and socially a sort of branch of the Caribbean on the continent. See Beeman, *Varieties of Political Experience*, 127–48, and Wood, *Black Majority*. But I have found no significant political distancing between other North Americans and Carolinians, or vice versa, in the context of the themes in this passage. For a suggestive piece on how slowly regional differentiation took place in eighteenth-century America, see Gough, "Myth of the 'Middle Colonies.'"
97. Richard S. Dunn, "The Glorious Revolution and America," in Canny, ed., *Oxford History*, 445–66; Rugemer, *Slave Law*, 1–170; Burnard and Garrigus, *Plantation Machine*, 101–36, 180–81.
98. Nuala Zahedieh, "Economy," in Armitage and Braddick, eds., *British Atlantic World*, 58–67; Stephen Foster and Evan Haefeli, "British North America in the Empire: An Overview," in Foster, ed., *British North America*, 18–66; Donnan, ed., *Documents Illustrative*, 3:24–25, 102–17, 122–47, 281–90, 454, 456; 4:9–10, 21, 91–94, 250, 274–76, 303, 315, 415, 587–611.
99. Stock, 4:123–44, 159–70, 179–215, quotations on 136, 189, 206.
100. Flavell, *When London Was Capital*, esp. 23; Weimer, *Constitutional Culture*, passim, including 8, 275, where Weimer wisely avoids overstating New England's exceptionalism and unity.
101. Washington, *Barbados Diary*. His lone entry on Barbadian society was a rather laconic one written on the last day of his visit. My reading thus

differs from that of the editors, who stress that the nineteen-year-old "became acquainted with a slave-based economy very different from that of his home colony" (59).
102. Jones, *Present State of Virginia*, 83; see also 104–5.
103. William Byrd II to John Perceval, Earl of Egmont, 12 July 1736, in Tinling, ed., *Correspondence of the Three*, 2:487–89, quotations on 488.
104. Newman, *Freedom Seekers*, esp. xxvi–xxix, 66–67, 146–49, 155–65, 185–92, 209–15, quotation on 185. For more scholarship of this sort, see Wilson, *Bonds of Empire*, and Blanton, "This Species of Property," as well as the works of Holly Brewer cited in the next note.
105. Brewer, "Creating a Common Law," quotations on 824, 831; Brewer, "Slavery, Sovereignty," esp. 1043, 1048–52, 1060, 1073.
106. This was true beyond Britain. In France, for instance, leading Enlightenment thinkers formulated their "critique of monarchy via the metaphor of slavery." Peabody, "There Are No Slaves in France," 96–103.
107. Addison, *Works*, 1:386–446, quotations on 390, 409, 411, 448, 450, 451. For this play's influence, see Addison, *Works*, 1:lvii–lix, 14–15, 375–85; Shaffer, *Performing Patriotism*; Litto, "Addison's Cato"; and Wiencek, *Imperfect God*, 35–36.
108. The same of course was true of the term "liberty" with its own multifarious uses; see, e.g., Montesquieu, *Spirit of the Laws*, 154–227.
109. [Mather], *Declaration*, 2. See also Warren, *New England Bound*, 231, 322n33.
110. Molyneux, *Case of Ireland Stated*, 129. This precise line of argument became very common among Irish radicals; see York, *Neither Kingdom nor Nation*, 47, 55, 62, 81, 252–53.
111. Bolingbroke, *Political Writings*, 127, 217–94, quotations on 127, 217.
112. Gadsden, *Writings*, 17–50, quotations on 30.
113. Hampton, ed., *Radical Reader*, 227; see also 121, 138.
114. Hampton, ed., *Radical Reader*, 297–98.
115. Hair, ed., "Slavery and Liberty," 140, 146.
116. Trenchard and Gordon, *Cato's Letters*, 11, 54, 117, 123–24, 168–69, 171, 265, 323, 332–38, 430–31, 441–42, 501–2, 508, 510, 518–21, 531–32, 543, 553–55, 611, 613, 631, 664–66, 669, 677–78, 682, 702, 706, 711, 729, 803, 823, 867, 877, 889, 897, 952, quotations on 11, 171, 669.
117. Paley, Malcolmson, and Hunter, eds., "Parliament and Slavery," 273. For an important American sermon decrying these Tory ideas in the same way, see Bailyn, ed., *Pamphlets of the American Revolution*, 204–47, esp. 213.
118. Hampton, ed., *Radical Reader*, 295, 312, 316–17, quotation on 319.
119. [Wilkes], *North Briton*, 10.
120. Peter S. Onuf, "Federalism, Democracy, and Liberty in the New American Nation," in Greene, ed., *Exclusionary Empire*, 132–59, quotation on 134; Bilder, *Transatlantic Constitution*, quotations on 1, 7; Greene, *Peripheries*

and Center; Olson, *Making the Empire Work*, esp. 134–73; Shankman, "Toward a Social History"; Marshall, *Making and Unmaking*; Butler, *Becoming America*, 125–30; LaCroix, *Ideological Origins*; Bowen, Mancke, and Reid, eds., *Britain's Oceanic Empire*, part 2, esp. chap. 4; Hulsebosch, *Constituting Empire*.

121. Thomas Bartlett, "'This Famous Island Set in a Virginia Sea': Ireland in the British Empire, 1690–1801," in Marshall, ed., *Oxford History*, 253–75, quotation on 254; Karl S. Bottigheimer, "Kingdom and Colony: Ireland in the Westward Enterprise, 1536–1660," in Andrews, Canny, and Hair, eds., *Westward Enterprise*, 45–64; Ned C. Landsman, "British Union and American Revolution: Imperial Authority and the Multinational State," in Spero and Zuckerman, eds., *American Revolution Reborn*, 107–31; York, *Neither Kingdom nor Nation*; James, *Ireland in the Empire*; Campbell, *Ireland's History*, 56–60, 65–69, 80, 84–87, 94, 97–111, 114, 151–53.

122. Gould, "Zones of Law," 474, 476. See also Brown, *Moral Capital*, 101. Dana Rabin has, it should be noted, offered an important qualification to this interpretation by highlighting just how contested and complex notions of law and rights were in the metropole as well as throughout the empire; see Rabin, *Britain and Its Internal Others*.

123. Steinfeld, *Invention of Free Labor*, 90; Leslie, *New History of Jamaica*, 162.

124. Peabody and Grinberg, eds., *Slavery, Freedom, and the Law*, passim, quotations on 46, 48, 49; Peabody, "There Are No Slaves in France," quotation on 14; Peabody, "Alternative Genealogy"; Weiss, "Infidels at the Oar." For an especially virulent example of the exclusionist attitude toward Africans in Britain, see Walvin, ed., *Black Presence*, 66.

125. Drescher, *Abolition*, 9–11, 61–66, 75–79, quotations on 75–76.

126. Swingen, *Competing Visions of Empire*; Jerry Banister, "The Oriental Atlantic: Governance and Regulatory Frameworks in the British Atlantic World," in Bowen, Mancke, and Reid, eds., *Britain's Oceanic Empire*, 151–76.

127. Clark, *Language of Liberty*, 7–8; Stanwood, *Empire Reformed*.

128. [Burke and Burke], *Account of the European Settlements*, 1:preface; Marshall, *Making and Unmaking*, quotation on 113; Beaumont, *Colonial America*; Brown, "1763 and the Genesis"; Anderson, *Crucible of War*, 146–49, 182–83, 221–31, 286–90, 324, 371, 584–87.

PART TWO. IMPERIAL CRISIS AND WAR

1. Rush, *Letters*, 1:54, 62–64, 67–69, quotations on 54, 68. I have chosen to capitalize the term "Patriots" to describe the adherents (both in North America and in Britain) of resistance to British ministries' American policies from 1764 to 1783, rather than "patriots." I do so not in deference to their own claims to the term but instead because, as will become obvious

later in this book, both sides claimed to be true patriots. I mostly use "Loyalists" for both North Americans and Britons in Britain who were loyal to the crown and ministries' policies.
2. James Otis Jr., for instance, had already resorted to such language in 1761, well before his famous 1764 tract discussed below; see Larson, *American Inheritance*, 38–40.
3. This sketch of course refers to a vast literature, but it is instructive to consider the role of slavery in classic accounts such as Bailyn, *Ideological Origins*, in which the Revolution and slavery make up 15 pages (pp. 232–46) out of 379 total. For an excellent discussion of the recent battle, especially in the popular sphere, over the issue of slavery's and race's role in the causation of the American Revolution, and the stakes of that controversy, see Waldstreicher, "Hidden Stakes."
4. Wood, *American Revolution*, xxiv. For a similar lament, see Wood, *Idea of America*, 19–22.
5. Holton, *Liberty Is Sweet*, 199–206, quotations on 204. See also Parkinson, *Common Cause*. It might be noted that such bold phrases fit uncomfortably with other more nuanced passages from Holton regarding the complexity of slavery's relationship to the causes of the Revolution; see Holton, *Liberty Is Sweet*, 468–70, 487–88.
6. Hannah-Jones et al., eds., *1619 Project*, xxv–xxviii, 11–21.
7. Zelnik, "Self-Evident Walls," 1, 3, 8, 15.
8. Sharples, *World That Fear Made*, 207–41, quotations on 208, 211.
9. Fisher, "Fit Instruments," 648–50, 652. For other especially good examples of historians who have shown how interwoven slavery was with all the major issues of this era, see Lynd and Waldstreicher, "Free Trade, Sovereignty, and Slavery," and Waldstreicher, *Slavery's Constitution*. And for an especially nice turn of phrase along these lines, see Edward J. Larson: "With liberty as its objective, *slavery* became the activating metaphor invoked to inspire a revolution that carried mixed meaning for chattel slavery." Larson, *American Inheritance*, 30.
10. Mason, "A Loyalist's Journey," 151–57, quotation on 157.
11. Sword, *Wives Not Slaves*, 210–11.

3. Stakes

1. *GM* 38 (Dec. 1768): 564. For other similarly high estimates of the stakes involved, see *GM* 37 (Oct. 1767): 491–93, and Seabury, *Letters of a Westchester Farmer*, 43. For a case that the Townshend Acts comprised their own "Moment," and an excellent discussion of that concept and contemporary awareness of it, see Griffin, *Townshend Moment*, esp. 7–10, 83, 117, 131–32,

142–65, 213–16, 226–27. For a useful discussion of the novelty of at least the intensity of these debates about sovereignty, see LaCroix, *Ideological Origins*, esp. 1–104.
2. Nelson, "Patriot Royalism."
3. Simmons, 3:73, 223; 5:368.
4. Donoughue, *British Politics*, passim, quotation on 35; Stephen Conway, "Britain and the Revolutionary Crisis, 1763–1791," in Marshall, ed., *Oxford History*, 325–37.
5. Silas Deane to Elizabeth Deane, 8 Sept. 1774, in *LD*, 1:50.
6. Wahrman, "English Problem of Identity," quotations on 1238, 1257; Armitage, *Civil Wars*, 134–47.
7. Davidson, *Propaganda and the American Revolution*; Berger, *Broadsides and Bayonets*; Hoock, *Scars of Independence*, 18–19, 36–37; Conway, *War of American Independence*, esp. 34, 247. That the Revolutionary War was one of propaganda as well as of bullets is also demonstrated exhaustively in Parkinson, *Common Cause*. I differ from his analysis chiefly in seeing wartime rhetoric in key areas as a continuation, if in refined and intensified form, of rhetoric and issues from the prewar imperial crisis. Parkinson, at least at times, suggests the political issues and rhetoric of the imperial crisis were submerged by new wartime issues and an emphasis on race rather than on previous appeals. For examples of this argument and of passages that seem to contradict or qualify it, see Parkinson, *Common Cause*, 109, 184, 192, 226, 248, 254, 368. For another example of his argument that the war changed the issues at hand, see Parkinson, "War and the Imperative of Union."
8. Gould, *Persistence of Empire*, 148–80, quotations on 155, 159; Berger, *Broadsides and Bayonets*, 106.
9. See, e.g., *PGW*, 23:373–74; 25:60–61; 26:3–4, 221–23, 399–400, 636; 27:565–67; 28:6, and Washington, *Writings*, 24:62–63, 228, 275, 471–72; 25:151, 166, 194–95, 272–75, 280, 343, 435; 26:25–26, 28–29, 37, 50–51, 77–78, 99–100, 103–4, 118, 183.
10. Mackesy, *War for America*, 155–59, 189, 219–20, 463, 491.
11. Huston, *American and British Debate*; Wahrman, "English Problem of Identity," 1249–57.
12. Boswell, *Life of Johnson*, 880. For other similarly vehement statements by Johnson, see Boswell, *Life of Johnson*, 965, 1128–29.
13. G3, 5:376–421, 425; 6:316–17.
14. Mackesy, *War for America*, 181–86, 190–212, 263–66, 306–18, 323–24, 367–518.
15. Burke, *Writings and Speeches*, 2:375.
16. *PR*, 14th Parliament, 9:34, 94; *PR*, 15th Parliament, 1:58–60, 69; 5:107, 119–20.

17. G3, 4:54–90, 119, 122, 132, 134–35, 152, 186–87, 213–17, quotations on 77, 122. For other Loyalist Britons' realistic assessment of the crisis late in the war, see BP, 7:146.
18. G3, 4:220–21, 351, 358 360, 379, quotation on 208; PR, 14th Parliament, 9:64–76, 246, 255, quotation on 16:4; [Chalmers], Plain Truth, 104–7; Wahrman, "English Problem of Identity," 1262.
19. For more on the heightened stakes upon the entry of France and her allies, see Mackesy, War for America, 172–74, 281–93, 301, 433–36, 516–17.
20. Muller, "Bonds of Belonging," 31, 46. For similar discussions, see Conway, British Isles, 166–202.
21. York, Neither Kingdom nor Nation, 1–194.
22. Young, Political Essays, 19–22.
23. GM 44 (June 1774): 258. For a few of the many other invocations of posterity, see JCC, 1:32; MG, 28 May 1772; BG, 6 Jan. 1766; Virginia Gazette (Purdie and Dixon), 11 Nov. 1773; Farmer's and Monitor's Letters, 78; APW, 1:97–108; Robert Wormeley Carter Diary, entry for 20 June 1774, American Antiquarian Society; New York Packet, 21 March 1776; Mayhew, Snare Broken, 13–14; Bolts, Considerations on India Affairs, 148; and Verelst, View of the Rise, 148. For useful scholarly discussions helping to explain the Patriots' intergenerational frame of reference, see Glover, Founders as Fathers, esp. 4, 52–56, 164–91, and Hattem, Past and Prologue, esp. 56–94.
24. Bickham, Making Headlines, 7. For a similar assessment of the divisiveness of this era, see Conway, British Isles, 129–65, 203–66, 315–45.
25. Bowen, "British Conceptions," 14–15.
26. Simmons, 3:11.
27. G3, 5:30, 304. For more on this point of view among Loyalists, see PR, 15th Parliament, 5:2, 107, 114, 119–20, 166, 175–76; 8:26, 45, 60, and Mackesy, War for America, 37–38, 263, 460–61.
28. Nicholls, Recollections and Reflections, 1:93; du Rivage, Revolution against Empire, passim, quotation on 5.
29. GM 36 (April 1766): 155; 37 (July 1767): 353. For similar rhetoric, see Hutchinson, Diary and Letters, 1:282.
30. Wilson, Sense of the People, 237–84, 433–35, quotations on 237–38, 433.
31. GM 47 (April 1777): 167–68. For similar expressions against the British friends of America, see Simmons, 6:119; PR, 14th Parliament, 6:248; 8:1–2, 23, 29–30; and Caledonian Mercury (Edinburgh), 21 July 1779.
32. PR, 14th Parliament, 15:163, 166–67, 359–60, 379, 384, 397, quotations on 167, 359, 379, 397; PR, 15th Parliament, 2:1–48, 297; 3:212–76; 4:70; Lockwood, To Begin the World, 11–124, quotation on 66. For yet other expressions from George III and his cabinet that their cause was the preservation of the Constitution, see George Germain to Lord Cornwallis, 9 Nov. 1780, Earl of Shelburne Papers, William L. Clements Library; Lord Dartmouth to Lord

Dunmore, 5 July 1775, Dunmore, vol. 2, pp. 586–88; and G3, 3:256–57, 263, 273, 449; 5:27, 30, 42–44, 61, 96–97, 135–36, 145, 243, 247, 256, 297, 304–5, 312–14, 326, 334–35, 374, 425. For a useful portrait of the importance of constitutional order in George III's thinking, see Black, *George III*. For another example of the wartime pamphleteering expressions of this idea, see *Short Appeal*, 18–19.

33. Wilson, *Sense of the People*, 206–36, quotation on 67; Brewer, *Party Ideology*, esp. 18–19; Thomas, *House of Commons*, 68–71; Bonwick, *English Radicals*, xi–xxii, 3–80; James M. Vaughn, "The Ideological Origins of Illiberal Imperialism: Metropolitan Politics and the Post-1763 Transformation of the British Empire," in Olwell and Vaughn, eds., *Envisioning Empire*, 27–56; Vaughn, *Politics of Empire*; Harlow, *Founding of the Second British Empire*, 1:146–56.

34. *Resistance No Rebellion* (1775), in *BP*, 4:1–69, quotations on 12, 37, 52.

35. *Address to the Right Honourable*, 21, 15, 29. For other similar accusations against the government and its supporters, see *GM* 44 (June 1774): 258; 46 (Jan. 1776): 32; Simmons, 5:346–47; *PR*, 15th Parliament, 1:182; Burke, *Writings and Speeches*, ed. Langford, 2:43–57, 102; and *Pamphlet, Entitled "Taxation No Tyranny,"* 7, 68.

36. Simmons, 5:368. For a modest sampling of other examples of threats/fantasies of such capital punishment for one's enemies in Britain during the war, see Simmons, 5:579; *Bath Chronicle*, 9 Jan. 1783; and *Pennsylvania Packet* (Philadelphia), 20 March 1783.

37. Simmons, 5:368.

38. Simmons, 6:73, 102, 462, 491.

39. *PR*, 15th Parliament, 1:163–83; 2:1–48, 297; 3:212–76; 4:7, 175–76, quotations on 1:167, 168.

40. "Independent Whig," *Revolution in MDCCLXXXII*, 5, 6, 8.

41. Washington, *Writings*, 21:158–59; Nathanael Greene to the Officers Commanding the Militia in the Salisbury District of North Carolina, 31 Jan. 1781, in *Greene*, 7:227–28.

42. Morgan, ed., *Prologue to Revolution*, 8–17, 46–69, 92–93, 114, 117, 163.

43. As David Waldstreicher has illustrated, this was the least surprising outcome, for "the metaphor of slavery was far too entrenched in British politics to be separated out from the colonial controversy, because it was more than a metaphor. The comparison of political liberties to bondage did not have to be discovered; it had been there from the start." Waldstreicher, *Slavery's Constitution*, 30–38, quotation on 33.

44. *BG*, 18 Nov. 1765.

45. Dorsey, *Common Bondage*, 4. Dorsey's whole book gives sustained attention to the rhetoric of slavery; for another thoughtful exploration of the nature of this rhetoric, see Griffin, *Townshend Moment*, 232–40.

46. Enfield, *Language vs. Reality*, 2, 3, 15, 175.
47. *MG*, 25 Aug. 1768.
48. Gadsden, *Writings*, 76.
49. Washington, *Papers: Colonial Series*, 10:109–10, 114–18, 128–31, 143–50, 154–56, 368, quotations on 131, 368. For other examples of Washington's correspondence framing the issue this way, see Washington, *Papers: Colonial Series*, 8:178, 182; 10:96–97.
50. *LD*, 1:269. For other expressions of these as Americans' only alternatives, see *LD*, 1:271, 524, 536, 703; 3:210–11; 4:318; Haynes, *Black Preacher to White America*, 9–15; and *GM* 45 (Aug. 1775): 359–60.
51. *Spirit*, 108–9.
52. *RV*, 1:12; see also 1:1–14, 139, 249.
53. McDonald, ed., *Empire and Nation*, 44. For the origins and vast influence of these letters, see Flower, *John Dickinson*, 62–70; McDonald, ed., *Empire and Nation*, x–xiii; and Adams, *American Independence*, xi–xii.
54. Lovell, *Oration*, 11.
55. For the centrality of property rights to Whig political thought in Britain and the colonies, across a wide range of opinions on other matters, see Marshall, "Free though Conquering People," 530–44. For other connections between slavery and being forcibly deprived of property in addition to the ones quoted below, see *APW*, 1:55, 111–12; *MG*, 28 May 1772; and Thomas Cushing to [Dennis De Berdt], 15 Oct. 1767, Arthur Lee Papers, Houghton Library.
56. *MG*, 2 Jan. (supplement), 16 Jan. 1766; *BG*, 22 Feb. 1768.
57. [Lee], *Appeal*, 15, 23.
58. Warren, *Oration Delivered March 5th, 1772*, 10–11.
59. *New York Packet*, 4 Jan. 1776. For other striking wartime examples, see *GM* 46 (Feb. 1776): 61, and Simmons, 6:37.
60. Kearsley, ed., *American Gazette*, 172.
61. *Franklin*, 21:183–86. For a similar satire, see *Franklin*, 21:220–22.
62. Breen, *Will of the People*, 32, 49–50, 83, 224, quotation on 50.
63. *JCC*, 2:68.
64. *JCC*, 2:153. See also Morison, ed., *Sources and Documents*, 144–45, and *GM* 45 (Aug. 1775): 357–60.
65. Paine, *Writings*, 1:162; see also 1:178, 200, 232. For other examples of such dramatizations of the stakes early in the war, see *Spirit*, 92, and *Lee*, 1:140–41.
66. Rhodehamel, ed., *American Revolution*, 71.
67. *PGW*, 9:493–94, 14:576. For other similar usages of this rhetoric, see *PGW*, 9:178; 10:12, 456–57; 11:165; 14:573–79, 667; 15:72; 19:201; 25:83, 551; 26:398; *Virginia Gazette* (Dixon and Hunter), 24 Jan. 1777; and *Virginia Gazette* (Purdie), 1 Aug. 1777.

68. Pendleton, *Letters and Papers*, 1:255–56.
69. *Spirit*, 650.
70. *PR*, 14th Parliament, 6:62. For other opposition expressions of the threats posed by this new war, many of them via the rhetoric of slavery, see *PR*, 14th Parliament, 6:19; Simmons, 6:6–9, 36–37, 54–56, 61–62, 68, 73–74, 85–87, 97–98, 101–11, 113–18, 136–39, 174–76, 181–83, 211, 267–68, 274, 284, 294–98, 318–20, 332, 344, 348–50, 354–55, 414, 462, 491; and *Virginia Gazette* (Purdie), 28 March 1777 (supplement).
71. *PR*, 14th Parliament, 15:163. For similar expressions from still later in the war, see *PR*, 15th Parliament, 3:546–48, 8:20–21.
72. Rodgers, *Ireland, Slavery*, 187–96; Griffin, *Townshend Moment*, 247–48, 263.
73. *Spirit*, 265–66, quotations on 265; *Price*, 1:261–67. For other examples from continental Europe and the British Isles of such rhetoric used for such purposes, see *Franklin*, 25:534; Wilson, *Sense of the People*, 240; and Rodgers, *Ireland, Slavery*, 87–96.
74. *Spirit*, 331.
75. *MG*, 16 May 1771.
76. *BP*, 1:121, 126.
77. Zachary McLeod Hutchins, "The Slave Narrative and the Stamp Act; or, Letters from Two American Farmers in Pennsylvania," in Hutchins, ed., *Community without Consent*, 115–47, quotations on 133.
78. Wesley, *Calm Address to Our American Colonies*, 6, 21. For another, even more extended argument that Patriot claims were factious because most Britons at home were virtually rather than directly represented, see Young, *Political Essays*, 19–73.
79. Wesley, *Political Writings*, 73–74; see also 82.
80. Fletcher, *Vindication*, 8, 20, 22.
81. *Patriots of North-America*, 15, 18.
82. *BP*, 2:93. For other such retorts, see *BP*, 2:88, 93–95, 113–14, 121–44; Simmons, 4:343; *Letters*, 29; and Lee, *Life of Arthur Lee*, 1:272–73.
83. [Johnson], *Taxation No Tyranny*, 15, 60, 75, 79, 89.
84. Simmons, 6:127; *PR*, 14th Parliament, 6:36.
85. *BP*, 4:282.
86. [Tucker], *Series of Answers*, ix–xiv.
87. *PR*, 15th Parliament, 3:523.
88. *PR*, 14th Parliament, 8:58–59.

4. Consistency

1. Davis, *Problem of Slavery in the Age of Revolution*, 273–84, quotations on 273, 281; Runciman, *Political Hypocrisy*, 1–15, 74–115, quotation on 1. For

more on the Patriots' burning desire to ground their cause in "right sentiment," see also Knott, *Sensibility and the American Revolution*, 17.
2. *APW*, 1:38; Robert Wormeley Carter Diary, entry for 20 June 1774, American Antiquarian Society. For one good discussion of the growing influence of providential theology in the eighteenth-century British Atlantic, see Anstey, *Atlantic Slave Trade*, 126–41.
3. *BP,* 4:295–325, quotations on 300, 301, 317.
4. *BP,* 4:327–52, quotations on 348. For other samples of providential rhetoric from opposition figures of varying religiosity, see *PR*, 14th Parliament, 9:34, 237; *PR*, 15th Parliament, 1:69, 3:546–48, 5:62.
5. *BP,* 7:135–60, quotations on 146, 148, 149.
6. *BP,* 2:365–66.
7. *MG*, 18 Aug. 1768. For the full (long) speech of which this quote is a part, see Goldsmith, *Vicar of Wakefield*, 95–98.
8. *MG*, 8 Dec. 1774.
9. Wheatley, *Complete Writings*, xxii.
10. *BP,* 1:253. For similar, if less irresistibly quotable, metropolitan disdain channeled through the picture of the slaveholder crying for liberty, see Philbrick, ed., *Trumpets Sounding,* 29–38, especially 36, and *GM* 45 (April 1775): 181; 46 (June 1776): 279.
11. Burnaby, *Travels,* 4–50, quotations on 22, 24.
12. [Tucker], *Series of Answers,* 101–6, quotations on 102, 103. He was so fond of this argument that he repeated it multiple times in his writings; see [Tucker], *Series of Answers,* 22, and Macleod, *British Visions of America,* 65.
13. [Serle], *Americans against Liberty,* 33.
14. Hutchinson, *Diary and Letters,* 2:274–77. Interestingly, however, it was in this context that Mansfield issued one of his clearest disclaimers against a broad reading of his judgment. "His L'dship remarked" to Hutchinson "that there had been no determination that they were free, the judgment (meaning the case of Somerset) went no further than to determine the Master had no right to compel the slave to go into a foreign country, &c." Hutchinson was tempted to press this point but desisted because he could sense that Mansfield had no stomach "for such an altercation." Hutchinson, *Diary and Letters,* 2:277. For more on the case set in Bristol, involving the enslaved and then freed men Little Ephraim Robin John and Ancona Robin Robin John, see Sparks, *Two Princes of Calabar,* esp. 90–104.
15. Simmons, 3:219–21; Hinderaker, *Boston's Massacre,* 152–54.
16. [Johnson], *Taxation No Tyranny,* 82, 69, 78, 88, 89. For a useful reading of Johnson's 1770s political tracts as a function not only of scoring debating points against rivals like Burke but also of sincere anticolonial and antislavery commitments, see Bate, *Samuel Johnson,* 412–17, 443–47.
17. Cresswell, *Journal,* 43–46, quotations on 44.

18. MG, 4 Aug. 1774. For another warning about the tyranny of pretend Patriots, see Fletcher, *Vindication*, 57.
19. Chopra, *Unnatural Rebellion*, 2.
20. Simmons, 6:202–9, quotations on 204, 203.
21. Tucker, *Tract V*, iv–vi.
22. GM 46 (Sept. 1776): 403–4.
23. [Lind and Bentham], *Answer to the Declaration*, 106–10, quotations on 107. For similar sorties against the Patriots in this vein, see [Lind], *Three Letters to Dr. Price*, 45–47, and [Hutchinson], *Strictures upon the Declaration*, 9–10.
24. "Lucius," in *Virginia Gazette* (Purdie and Dixon), 23 Dec. 1773; "Letters of Hon. James Habersham," 80–81. For other contemporary assertions and candid expressions of the need to cultivate this image, see "The Earl of Clarendon," in BG, 20 Jan. 1766; *Laurens*, 5:338–41, 391–464; 6:386–87, 400–401; and Thomas Cushing to [Dennis De Berdt], 15 Oct. 1767, Arthur Lee Papers, Houghton Library.
25. MacLeod, *Slavery, Race*, 27. For headliners in this debate, on the side of Patriots' sincerity, see Bailyn, *Ideological Origins*, and Smith, *American Honor*; and on the other side, see Dorsey, *Common Bondage*; Burstein, *Sentimental Democracy*; and Nelson, "Patriot Royalism."
26. Trenchard and Gordon, *Cato's Letters*, 250–51; Bolingbroke, *Political Writings*, 193–294. For the seventeenth-century examples, see Greenblatt, ed., *Norton Anthology*, 2218, and Hampton, ed., *Radical Reader*, 243. For the tight connection between benevolence and a true love of liberty in eighteenth-century British culture, see Anstey, *Atlantic Slave Trade*, 96–125, 142–53.
27. Bailyn, *Ideological Origins*, 64–65, 79–159, quotations on 95, 150–51, 153. For more on the contested idea of patriotism in eighteenth-century England, see Armitage, "A Patriot for Whom?" and Brewer, *Party Ideology*, 96–111.
28. Carey, *British Abolitionism*, 38.
29. *Virginia Gazette* (Purdie and Dixon), 11 Feb. 1773; *Virginia Gazette*, 18 June 1772.
30. [Morgann], *Plan for the Abolition*, 32; GM 50 (Sept. 1780): 406.
31. Boswell, *Life of Johnson*, 568; Johnson, *Yale Edition*, 10:387–400, quotation on 396; see also 10:313–45.
32. *Patriots of North-America*, 6; Henry Hulton to Charles Steuart, 9 Aug. 1769, Charles Steuart Papers, National Library of Scotland. Future Patriot Henry Laurens, when victimized by a Stamp Act mob in Charleston, said much the same thing about mob tyranny; see *Laurens*, 5:26–40, 78.
33. Reprinted in *MG*, 25 April 1771.
34. *MG*, 13 Feb. 1772.
35. *Letters*, 266–68. For other Loyalists warning against Patriot wolves in sheep's clothing, see *Virginia Gazette* (Purdie and Dixon), 25 Nov. 1773; *MG*, 4 Aug. 1774; 19 Dec. 1771; Seabury, *Letters of a Westchester Farmer*, esp.

45–46, 73, 76; Hutchinson, *Diary and Letters*, 1:167; and [Tucker], *Series of Answers*, passim.
36. John Cunningham, Intelligence, 26 Feb. 1780, Clinton.
37. D. Dulany Jr. to Arthur Lee, 1774, in Lee, *Life of Arthur Lee*, 2:319. Alan Taylor has shown that Benedict Arnold's defection to the British Army in 1780 prompted a particularly acute bout of self-doubt among Patriots. But as I suggest in this passage, that was hardly new. See Taylor, *American Revolutions*, 206–8.
38. Robert Beverley to Landon Carter, 28 Aug. 1774, Landon Carter Papers, Virginia Historical Society. Carter had his own worries on this score; see Carter, *Diary*, 1:418, 2:847–48. For yet another leading Patriot earnestly studying what constituted genuine patriotism, see Quincy, *Portrait of a Patriot*, 1:149–51, 163.
39. [Wells], *A Few Political Reflections*, 4–5, 24, 28, 70–74, quotations on 5, 28. For other Patriots' private worries and public warnings on this score, see *Virginia Gazette* (Purdie and Dixon), 11 Nov. 1773; *Adams*, 1:184–87; *Virginia Gazette* (Dixon and Hunter), 11 April 1777; *Laurens*, 9:434–38; *APW*, 1:390–91; and Waldstreicher, *Odyssey of Phillis Wheatley*, 324.
40. *MG*, 7 Aug. 1766; 18 Aug. 1768; 19 Dec. 1771; 27 Oct. 1774.
41. Seabury, *Letters of a Westchester Farmer*, 60–62, 66, 87, 109–10, 156, quotations on 60, 61.
42. *BP*, 1:251–52, 257–58.
43. "African Merchant," *Treatise upon the Trade*, 5, 13, 29, appendix 33. For a similar warning, from a South Carolina Loyalist, that Patriot rhetoric would lead to the calamities of "general Manumission of Negroes," see *Some Fugitive Thoughts*, 25.
44. *GM* 46 (Nov. 1776): 509–11, quotation on 511; Jasanoff, *Liberty's Exiles*, 7, 21–56, 107, 113, 178, 222, 275–76, quotation on 23. For other wartime rhetoric fulminating over the Patriots' actions against Loyalists as coercive in the extreme, see Hutchinson, *Diary and Letters*, 1:147, 557; 2:46–53, 82–84, 110, 220, 271, 276; *Letters*, 179–83, 252–54; Ewald, *Diary*, 341; and Taylor, *American Revolutions*, 128, 213, 216. For another scholar who emphasizes the coerciveness of Patriot committees, see Canale, "'When a State Abounds in Rascals.'" Meanwhile, in a suggestive essay Peter Thompson has argued that Patriots meant to treat white Loyalists in ways reminiscent of nothing more than of slavery, both chattel and political; see Thompson, "Social Death and Slavery: The Logic of Political Association and the Logic of Chattel Slavery in Revolutionary America," in Griffin et al., eds., *Between Sovereignty and Anarchy*, 139–64.
45. *Royal Gazette* (New York), 8 Dec. 1779, in *PGW*, 23:616–17. For more Loyalist rhetoric comparing their treatment to slavery, see Oliver, *Peter Oliver's*

Origin and Progress, 98, and Serle, *American Journal*, 40, 46–47, 58–60, 64, 71–72, 88, 90, 94, 98–99, 106, 135, 167–68, 188, 249, 256, 259.

46. *BP,* 5:1–64, quotations on 39, 43. For a widely circulated echo of this argument, see Wesley, *Calm Address to the Inhabitants of England*, 15–17.
47. *PR*, 14th Parliament, 6:36, 6. For yet other statements of liberating Loyalists as a war aim, see *PR*, 14th Parliament, 6:26, 57–58, 62, 248; 7:1, 9, 15–16, 99, 109; 8:1–2, 23, 29–30, 111, 264, 317–20; *PR*, 15th Parliament, 1:32, 35; *BP,* 5:167; and George Germain to Lord Cornwallis, 9 Nov. 1780; Germain to Henry Clinton, 3 Jan. 1781, Earl of Shelburne Papers, William L. Clements Library.
48. *G3,* 4:245, 291. For similar estimations of the loyalties of North Americans under Patriot bondage, see Peter Dubois to James Robertson, 10 May 1780, Clinton.
49. Campbell, *Journal of an Expedition,* 35.
50. [Chalmers], *Plain Truth,* 73–74; Crary, ed., *Price of Loyalty,* 220–24, quotations on 222–23.
51. *GM* 46 (June 1776): 279.
52. Davies, ed., *Documents,* 11:115; see also 11:144.
53. Davies, ed., *Documents,* 11:93–98, quotations on 97. For an excellent narrative of this complex and revealing affair, see Harris, *Hanging of Thomas Jeremiah.*
54. Hutchinson, *Diary and Letters,* 1:543.
55. Simmons, 6:365, 370.
56. Sainsbury, *Disaffected Patriots,* offers a useful portrait of this network. Smith, comp., *English Defenders,* 4–5, 11, 16, makes the respectability point. For a good analysis of the political-cum-religious ideology of leading dissenters in this group such as Richard Price and Joseph Priestley, see Fruchtman, *Apocalyptic Politics.*
57. *Pamphlet, Entitled "Taxation No Tyranny,"* quotation on 86; *An Answer to a Pamphlet; Tyranny Unmasked; GM* 45 (March 1775): 134–36. This was an attack on Johnson among English political dissenters that stretched back to the early 1760s; see [Wilkes], *North Briton,* 65–68. The skill with which these responders played politics helped to make *Taxation No Tyranny* the start of a decline of Johnson's towering reputation, as large parts of the English reading public found it too heavily seasoned with Toryism and gross prejudice toward Americans to be palatable. See Boswell, *Life of Johnson,* 590–92, and Clark, *Samuel Johnson,* 225–33, 238–51.
58. *Franklin,* 13:355, 366; 15:132–35; 19:7, 71–72; 20:155–56, 296, 314. See also Franklin, *Benjamin Franklin's Letters,* 186–92. For a fuller analysis of the complex intersection between the politics of slavery and Franklin's work in London in this era, see Waldstreicher, *Runaway America,* 175–209.

59. Franklin, *Benjamin Franklin's Letters*, 222–23. See also *Franklin*, 19:112–16, 187–88, 269.
60. *Virginia Gazette* (Rind), 9 Dec. 1775; *Pennsylvania Packet*, 25 Dec. 1775.
61. *Pennsylvania Packet*, 24 Jan. 1776.
62. Rushton and Morgan, *Treason and Rebellion*, 3, 4.
63. Wilson, *Sense of the People*, 246. For more on the seventeenth-century framing of this debate, see Hattem, *Past and Prologue*, 95–125, and Fisher, "Fit Instruments."
64. Simmons, 2:4, 7–8. For Beckford's key role in opposition circles in London, see Royle and Walvin, *English Radicals*, 16–19.
65. *Address to the Right Honourable*, 21, 18, 29.
66. Priestley, *Address to Protestant Dissenters*, 14. This 1774 speech continued themes from Priestley's 1769 pamphlet, including very strong usages of the s-word; see Priestley, *Political Writings*, 129–44. For other examples of this sort of rhetoric from opposition figures before the war, see Burke, *Writings and Speeches*, 2:17–18, 73–75, 169–70; Burke, *Writings and Speeches*, ed. Langford, 2:65, 3:59; Simmons, 2:12–18, 80, 86, 88–89, 92, 150, 322–23, 484; 3:166; 4:226, 231, 260, 366, 422, 491–92, 499; 5:78, 143, 158, 229, 270, 283, 346–47, 374–75, 543, 607, 611, 613, 630; and Evans, *Reply to the Rev. Mr. Fletcher's*, esp. 34–35.
67. Davies, ed., *Documents*, 11:152, 198–200, quotations on 199.
68. Hutchinson, *Diary and Letters*, 2:46, 52.
69. Simmons, 6:5, 69, 79, 119, 364, 458, quotations on 5, 79, 69, 119.
70. Lee, *Lee Papers*, 1:180–85, 188–93, 216, quotations on 190.
71. Marston, *King and Congress*, esp. 35–63, quotation on 36; Jones, *Captives of Liberty*. For good explorations of how such terminology as "rebellion" and "treason" interacted with the formative laws of war in the early modern period, see Rushton and Morgan, *Treason and Rebellion*; and Fenn, "Biological Warfare," esp. 1573–74. Virginia Patriots labeled Loyalist military activities as "the late insurrection in Somerset and Worcester Counties"; see *Virginia Gazette* (Purdie), 4 April 1777. For other Patriot offerings along this line, see Jefferson, *Notes*, 189, and Trumbull, *Poetical Works*, 1:4–6, 23–24.
72. Laurens, 11:180–81, 192, 581, quotation on 181.
73. *JCC*, 3:410–11, 5:690–91, 7:279. This design of the seal seems to have been Franklin's idea; see *Franklin*, 22:303–4, 562–63.
74. [Sewall], *Gen. Washington*.
75. London writer reprinted in *Virginia Gazette* (Dixon and Hunter), 29 Aug. 1777.
76. *BP*, 4:12–18, 52, quotations on 12.
77. York, ed., *Crisis*, 100; see also 39–47, 75–82, 91–96, 123–28, 135–36, 261–72, 307–8, 333–38, 461–75, 713–30.
78. Price, *Political Writings*, 14–100, quotations on 17, 20, 33, 66.

79. *BP,* 6:60–69, quotations on 62, 65, 66. For another British pamphlet making a similar point, see Smith, comp., *English Defenders,* 219.
80. Simmons, 6:5, 7, 86, 111, 319–20, 361, 364, 366, 458, quotations on 86, 111, 320.
81. *PR,* 14th Parliament, 6:44, 60–62; 7:23–24, quotations on 6:61–62; *PR,* 15th Parliament, 1:182, 5:107, 176.
82. Lockwood, *To Begin the World,* 85; *JCC,* 2:215–16.
83. Price, 1:262.
84. Davies, ed., *Documents,* 9:107–10, 132, 200–205, quotations on 109, 132, 204.
85. *Letters,* 106–7.
86. Frey, *Water from the Rock,* 64.
87. Dunmore's Proclamation was published, among other places, in *Virginia Gazette* (Rind), 23 Nov. 1775; *Virginia Gazette* (Purdie), 24 Nov. 1775; and *Virginia Gazette* (Dixon and Hunter), 25 Nov. 1775. Peter Rushton and Gwenda Morgan offer a nice discussion of how "martial law on the British side was often the first resort of the authorities in the face of colonial resistance," precisely because it was "a way of avoiding the difficulties" and uncertainties surrounding terms like "rebel" and "traitor" in the common law; see Rushton and Morgan, *Treason and Rebellion,* 7–8.
88. Lord Dunmore to Richard Corbin, 27 Jan. 1776, Papers of John Murray, Library of Congress. For other similar writings, see Lord Dartmouth to Dunmore, 1 June, 8 Sept. 1774; 3 March 1775; Dunmore to Dartmouth, 24 Dec. 1774, 14 March 1775, Dunmore, vol. 2, pp. 420–57, 491–92; Dunmore to "Dear Sir," 23 Oct. 1775, John Murray, 4th Earl of Dunmore Papers, Swem Library.
89. [Johnson], *Taxation No Tyranny,* 85. For examples of Dunmore as hero, see *Edinburgh Advertiser,* 27 June 1775, and *Caledonian Mercury* (Edinburgh), 28 June, 1 July 1775.
90. Lord Dunmore to Lord Dartmouth, 1 May 1775, Dunmore, vol. 2, pp. 527–31; *RV,* 3:54–55. For more on this pivotal incident and examples of such rhetoric from both sides, see *RV,* 3:62–63, 70–71, 77–78, 80–82, 84–85, 89–90, 107–13, 172, 500–502; McDonnell, *Politics of War,* 49–102; Dartmouth to Dunmore, 5, 12 July 1775, Dunmore; and *GM* 45 (July 1775): 344–45.
91. Davies, ed., *Documents,* 9:179–91, quotations on 179, 185, 186.
92. Lord Dunmore to Lord Dartmouth, 25 June 1775, Dunmore, vol. 2, pp. 559–72.
93. *Virginia Gazette* (Rind), 23 Nov. 1775; *Virginia Gazette* (Purdie), 24 Nov. 1775; *Virginia Gazette* (Dixon and Hunter), 25 Nov. 1775. This letter is also available in modern published collections; see Rhodehamel, ed., *American Revolution,* 82–85, and *RV,* 3:459–62.
94. Parkinson, *Common Cause,* esp. 20, 143, 197–212, quotations on 197, 143.

95. David, *Dunmore's New World*, 104, 6.
96. Harris, *Hanging of Thomas Jeremiah*, 76–91, quotation on 87; Rugemer, *Slave Law*, 171–212, quotation on 189; Rushton and Morgan, *Treason and Rebellion*, passim, esp. 15–16. For other Carolinian expressions of their need to be vigilant against the real threat of "insurrection," see John Lewis Gervais to Alexander Cameron, 27 June 1775, Charleston, Clinton.
97. Wineman, *Landon Carter Papers*, 39–74; Tinling, ed., *Correspondence of the Three*, 2:613. Michael A. McDonnell, on the other hand, has stressed that while it energized the patriotism of many Virginia planters, it demoralized and made Loyalists out of others; see McDonnell, *Politics of War*, 135–74.
98. *LD*, 2:426.
99. Quoted in Pybus, *Epic Journeys*, 15.
100. *Virginia Gazette* (Purdie), 8 Dec. 1775. For other examples of Patriots classifying the proclamation as insurrectionary treason against the British constitution, see *RV*, 5:60, 125, 139.
101. *Virginia Gazette* (Purdie), 13 Oct. 1775.
102. *Letters*, 232. For other examples of Patriot anti-Scottish slurs against Dunmore and his kind, see *Lee*, 1:148, and *Virginia Gazette* (Purdie), 8 Dec. 1775.
103. *Virginia Gazette* (Dixon and Hunter), 30 Oct. 1778; *Virginia Gazette* (Purdie), 30 Oct. 1778.
104. *RV*, 5:57, 64n20, 139, 140, 240n6, 277, 423–24.
105. Landon Carter, "Notice Concerning a Runaway Slave," 1777, Carter Family Papers, Swem Library.

5. Humanity

1. "Humanity," Samuel Johnson's Dictionary, https://johnsonsdictionaryonline.com/views/search.php?term=humanity. For a good, concise exploration of the mid-eighteenth century as the origin point for humanitarian discourse in the Atlantic world, see Klose, *In the Cause of Humanity*, 39–45. "Humanity" is thus analogous to as well as a companion of the similarly amorphous value "mercy," which was also rooted in eighteenth-century British religion and philosophy; see Gregory, *Mercy and British Culture*.
2. [Long], *English Humanity No Paradox*, 1–3, 9–11, quotations on 9.
3. Smith, *Theory of Moral Sentiments*, 44.
4. *GM* 56 (July 1786): 603–4.
5. Cresswell, *Journal*, 1–7, quotations on 1, 3. For another vivid example, see Iredell, *Papers*, 1:1, 6–7, 29–30, 32–33, 53–54.
6. Conway, "From Fellow-Nationals," 66.
7. Greene, *Evaluating Empire*, xi, 200, xii.
8. Reprinted in *Virginia Gazette*, 31 Dec. 1772.

9. Schaw, *Journal of a Lady*, 107, 104, 145, 146, 153, 141, 157.
10. Smith, comp., *English Defenders*, 35–36; see also 17–27.
11. *GM* 38 (Oct. 1768): 467–68. For the identity of Cave, who edited this journal under the pseudonym "Sylvanus Urban," see Boswell, *Life of Johnson*, 81.
12. Lawson and Phillips, "'Our Execrable Banditti'"; Edwardes, *Nabobs at Home*; H. V. Bowen, "British India, 1765–1813: The Metropolitan Context," in Marshall, ed., *Oxford History*, 530–51; G3, 2:483, 491, 500–501; James, *Raj*, 34, 45–52. Nechtman, *Nabobs*, offers an especially well-documented case in regards to the intensity of these concerns.
13. Even Thomas Paine, the soon-to-be systemic critic of the entire order of British monarchy and empire, as late as 1775 used Robert Clive, the conqueror of much of India in the mid-eighteenth century, as an individual morality tale in his essay "Reflections on the Life and Death of Lord Clive"; see Paine, *Thomas Paine Reader*, 57–62. For similar broad attacks on the British Empire, see Freneau, *Prose*, 47–48, 83–84.
14. *GM* 39 (Aug. 1769): 374–75. For another letter very similar in tone, see *GM* 42 (Feb. 1772): 69.
15. Bolts, *Considerations on India Affairs*, vi–viii, 87, 228.
16. [Clarke], *The Nabob*, iii.
17. For other iterations of this idea, see *GM* 37 (April 1767): 152, and Wilson, *Sense of the People*, 275.
18. Greene, *Evaluating Empire*, 1–19, 120–55, 244–95, quotations on 121, 154.
19. Wesley, *Thoughts upon Slavery*, quotations on 34–35; Millar, *Origin of the Distinction*, esp. 249–54, 272; *Ipswich [Eng.] Journal*, 10 Aug. 1782. For a contrary case emphasizing that "West Indians received metropolitan respect" and only felt threatened by the growing British antislavery movement in the 1780s, see Burnard and Garrigus, *Plantation Machine*, passim, quotation on 99. The exact timeline and causation of these planters' perceiving a growing cultural and political threat to their power is confused in this book, however. And that confusion is compounded by Burnard's argument elsewhere that West Indian planters found both the *Somerset* decision of 1772 and "the general trend of British thinking about the empire" in this era "disturbing"; see Burnard, "Powerless Masters," 193. For clearer recountings of the many depictions of West Indians as deviants, see Rozbicki, *Complete Colonial Gentleman*, 111–24; Greene, *Evaluating Empire*, 156–99; and O'Shaughnessy, *Empire Divided*, 9–14.
20. Burke, *Writings and Speeches*, ed. Langford, 2:67, 76, 373.
21. Cumberland, *West Indian*, 3–4, 13–17, 34–37, 51–52, 82, quotations on 13, 16, 52; for the prologue, see *GM* 41 (Feb. 1771): 87.
22. Cresswell, *Journal*, 16–20, 35–40, quotations on 36, 39.
23. *GM* 45 (April 1775): 167.
24. Muthu, *Enlightenment against Empire*, 1.

25. Boswell, *Life of Johnson*, 135, 160, 301–2, 391–92, 439, 527, 581, 585, 774–75, 914, 1021, 1038, 1143, 1197–98, 1209–13, quotation on 93; Johnson and Boswell, *Journey to the Western Islands*, 38, 40–41, 51–52, 60, 69, 72–74, 97–99, 114–18, 134, 143, 151, 163–66, 176–77, 185, 193–95, 225, 228, 282, 293, 310–11, 324, 348, 351, 368–69, 392, 397, 400–401, quotation on 399. For a good discussion of the arc of Johnson's life that led him to his pride as a Londoner, see Bate, *Samuel Johnson*, esp. 5–168.
26. Hudson, *Samuel Johnson*, 8–9, 170–220, quotation on 181.
27. Boswell, *Life of Johnson*, 984–85, 1031, 1117–20, 1230; Johnson and Boswell, *Journey to the Western Islands*, quotation on 215.
28. Johnson, *Yale Edition*, 10:134–50, 184–96, quotations on 137, 188, 150.
29. Basker, "'The Next Insurrection,'" 37, 44.
30. Curley, "Johnson and America," 32.
31. Boswell, *Life of Johnson*, 260–61, 374, 470, 521, 590–92, 767, 912, quotation on 590; Johnson and Boswell, *Journey to the Western Islands*, 58–59, 75, 78, 80, 101–3, 128–29, 169, 198, 234, 327–28, 355, quotation on 103; Johnson, *Yale Edition*, 2:19, 29, 63, 252–54, 257, 270; 10:167–76, 206–12, 276–77; Curley, "Johnson and America," 38–40.
32. Bate, *Samuel Johnson*, quotation on 195; Boswell, *Life of Johnson*, 316–17, 360, 464–65, 924, 1017–18, 1133, quotation on 289.
33. O'Shaughnessy, *Empire Divided*, 3.
34. For this argument fleshed out, see Mason, "North American Calm."
35. Iredell, *Papers*, 1:109–10, quotation on 109; [Bourke], *Privileges of the Island of Jamaica*, passim, quotation on 47.
36. Long, *History of Jamaica*, 1:3–7, 9–31, 38–43, 88–122, 156–59, 433–35; 2:261–71, 351–505; 3:921–49, quotations on 2:269, 267, 401, 441. Long is a good example of Candace Ward's important point that the cult of sensibility could be and was marshaled for both antislavery and proslavery ends; see Ward, "Sensibility, Tropical Disease, and the Eighteenth-Century Sentimental Novel," in Carey, Ellis, and Salih, eds., *Discourses of Slavery and Abolition*, 63–77. Samuel Martin wrote a similarly defensive passage about the upgrade Africans received by being transferred from "absolute slavery" to something far better in Britain's colonies. This fit poorly with the overall thrust of his pamphlet, which was to persuade planters to stop abusing their slaves. See Martin, *Essay upon Plantership*, 2–3.
37. *Personal Slavery Established*, 10, 14, 24.
38. Robert Carter to Frances Wilkes, 30 June 1770, Letterbooks of Robert Carter of Nomini Hall, Virginia Historical Society. Benjamin Rush's visit to the Palace of Westminster discussed earlier is a good example of this, and his autobiography, written in 1800, retained that ambivalence. In it he claimed political kinship with his ancestor who fought with Oliver Cromwell, and asserted that his republican principles began while he was a

medical student in Edinburgh. He downplayed his reverence for the monarchy in this autobiography, recording only briefly the royal sites he visited in London. But even in that selective history he had to admit that his growing commitment to republicanism had to overcome "the prejudices of my education," which had taught him "to consider them [kings] nearly as essential to political order as the Sun is to the order of our Solar System." Rush, *Autobiography*, 23–24, 39–66, 74–75, 115, quotations on 46. For other American travelers and sojourners whose responses to Britain were ambivalent, see Marchant, *Journell of a Voyage*, and Potts, *Arthur Lee*, 14–35. Michal Jan Rozbicki has produced an insightful book-length treatment of the North American elites' cultural insecurity within the empire and its political impact in *Complete Colonial Gentleman*. For a briefer but similarly insightful discussion, see Harris, *Hanging of Thomas Jeremiah*, 39–47.

39. Davies, ed., *Documents*, 2:272; Peter Livius to his brother in London, 18 Oct. 1768, Arthur Lee Papers, Houghton Library (quotation); *MG*, 15 Apr. 1768 (supplement).
40. Carter, *Diary*, 2:716.
41. Bailyn, ed., *Pamphlets of the American Revolution*, 435.
42. Bolts, *Considerations on India Affairs*, xi, 139.
43. Verelst, *View of the Rise*, 2, 3, 20, 130.
44. Major, *Slavery, Abolitionism and Empire*, 41–43.
45. Keir, *Thoughts on the Affairs of Bengal*, 13, 14, 52–53.
46. Wiecek, "*Somerset*," 112; Van Cleve, "'Somerset's Case' and Its Antecedents," quotation on 603; Hulsebosch, "Nothing but Liberty"; Van Cleve, "Mansfield's Decision"; Waldstreicher, *Slavery's Constitution*, 38–40; Gould, "Zones of Law," esp. 472, 504; Rabin, *Britain and Its Internal Others*, 73–107.
47. For a full discussion of this, see Mason, "North American Calm."
48. Johnson and Boswell, *Journey to the Western Islands*, 65; see also 280. On the other hand, largely for reasons of practicality, Johnson did support the idea of a "despotick governor" for India, unfettered either by London or by local checks on his power. See Hudson, *Samuel Johnson*, 214.
49. Quoted in Greene, *Peripheries and Center*, 101.
50. Eliga H. Gould, "Liberty and Modernity: The American Revolution and the Making of Parliament's Imperial History," in Greene, ed., *Exclusionary Empire*, 112–31, quotation on 128. For more useful scholarly discussions of this shift and the ensuing debate over the imperial constitution, see Olson, *Making the Empire Work*; Morgan and Morgan, *Stamp Act Crisis*; and Bailyn, *Ideological Origins*, 198–229.
51. Isaac, *Landon Carter's Uneasy Kingdom*, 121–84, quotations on 121, 124; Rozbicki, *Complete Colonial Gentleman*, quotation on 8. T. H. Breen's recent interpretation of the American Revolution places great emphasis on North Americans' feelings of rejection from the metropolis as the main

cause of the crisis turning to war. Especially after the Coercive Acts, he argues, all classes of colonists felt attacked by the British ministry; see Breen, *Will of the People*, 19–53. For another depiction of the planters who led Virginia into Revolution as an anxiously defensive rather than a confident ruling class, see Holton, *Forced Founders*.
52. MG, 8 Sept. 1768 (quotation); Lee, *Life of Arthur Lee*, quotation on 1:190; Quincy, *Observations*, 5–6.
53. RV, 1:1–8, quotation on 2; JCC, 1:82–83, quotation on 24; Rush, *Letters*, 1:68.
54. Taylor, *American Colonies*, quotation on 315; Franklin, *Benjamin Franklin's Letters*, xi–liii, 49–52 quotations on xi; Franklin, 12:118–20; 13:4–8, 20–22, 38–39, 44–49, 64–65, 79–81, 240–42; 14:22, 65, 76–87, 101–7, 110–16, 129–34, 229–30, 315–19, 337–39, 349–51; 15:3–14, 17–19, 36–38, 52, 63–67, 110–12, 187–89, 191–95, 206–10, 220–22, 233–44, 272–73; 16:22–26; 18:3; 19:7, 71–72, 295–97, 321–22, 362; 20:96, quotations on 12:120, 13:81.
55. For an excellent discussion of how easily politicized the laws of war could be in this period, and thus how readily accusations of violations by the other side occurred to combatants, see Fenn, "Biological Warfare."
56. Armitage, *Declaration of Independence*, 1–87, quotations on 30, 60, 61; Gould, *Among the Powers of the Earth*, 1–119, quotation on 2.
57. Onuf and Onuf, *Federal Union, Modern World*, esp. 1–26, 93–113, quotation on 7. For other analyses of the American Revolutionaries' respect for the rule of the law of nations and associated values, see Moots and Hamilton, eds., *Justifying Revolution*; Breen, *Will of the People*, esp. 2, 18, 45–46, 52–53, 86–158, 195–222; Janis, *America and the Law of Nations*, 24–33; W. B. Allen, "Happiness the End; Consent the Foundation; Character the Means," in Jordan, ed., "*When in the Course*," 9–20; and Lyons, "Law of Nations."
58. LD, 2:141, 260, 309, 313, 463; Paine, *Writings*, 1:188.
59. Rush, *Letters*, 1:265.
60. Parkinson, in *Common Cause*, has amply demonstrated this. See also Hoock, *Scars of Independence*, 18–19, 36–37; Butterfield et al., eds., *Adams Family Correspondence*, 1:241, 269; Crary, ed., *Price of Loyalty*, 152–55; PGW, 2:73, 227, 235–36, 271, 301–2, 325, 345, 576; 22:216; Laurens, 11:199, 216, 242, 250, 255–56, 271; Paine, *Writings*, 1:86–93, 100–101, 112–13, 131–32, 141–44, 166, 186–88, 220, 233–49, 262–67, 346, 355–59; and Freneau, *Poems of Philip Freneau*, 1:142–52, 185–87; 2:115.
61. Copy of Instructions to William Carmichael, 27 Jan. 1780; John Jay to Count De Florida Blanca, 25 April 1780, John Jay Papers, Library of Congress; Jay, *Life of John Jay*, 1:112–13, 179–80; 2:121, 134, 148–49, quotations on 1:112, 2:134. For other American diplomats who argued that British atrocities precluded reconciliation, see Franklin, 28:420, 461–64, 588; 30:247; 31:436–39; 33:481; 34:315; Wharton, ed., *Revolutionary Diplomatic*

Correspondence, 2:290–91, 858–60, 868–69; and GM 47 (April 1777): 169–70.
62. Arthur Lee to Baron Schulenburg, 25 Dec. 1778, in Lee, Life of Arthur Lee, 2:22–23. For other American diplomats' emphasis on this idea, see Lee, Life of Arthur Lee, 1:63; Adams, Diary and Autobiography, 4:38–39; Adams, 10:203–4, 252, 298–99; 11:63; and Madison, Papers, 3:180–81.
63. Robert Livingston to Francis Dana, 2 March 1782, in Wharton, ed., Revolutionary Diplomatic Correspondence, 5:211.
64. Jonathan Trumbull Sr. to George Washington, 12 Jan. 1777, in PGW, 8:54.
65. T. Cole Jones, in Captives of Liberty, argues throughout that elites were much more likely to adhere for longer to the ideal of humaneness in war than were more quickly embittered nonelites. While the newspaper evidence I cite in this chapter would seem to qualify that argument, this need for repeated preaching from commanders upholds Jones's analysis.
66. LD, 2:502–3; Nathanael Greene to Gov. John Martin, 9 Jan. 1782, in Greene, 10:174. For other examples of such exhortations, see Greene, 8:346, 349–50, 356, 477–79, and Franklin, 34:354–55.
67. PGW, 14:1–2. For other such exhortations from Washington to his own side, see also PGW, 2:50–51, 199.
68. Joseph Reed to Nathanael Greene, 5 Nov. 1778, in Greene, 3:43–44.
69. Gould, Persistence of Empire, 183–98.
70. PR, 14th Parliament, 6:36; Peter Dubois to James Robertson, 10 May 1780, Clinton. See also G3, 3:156, 175.
71. GM 47 (Oct. 1777): 501–2.
72. PR, 14th Parliament, 6:248. For other opposition assaults on the ministry's inhumanity in the war, see PR, 14th Parliament, 6:11–19, 24, 62, 67, 157, 164–71, 233–37, 240–48, 254, 258, 279–80, 287; 7:4, 7–8, 22, 26, 120, and GM 47 (Dec. 1777): 582.
73. Simmons, 6:470. For a similar expression from William Pitt, see PR, 15th Parliament, 10:80.
74. For other associations of humanity in victory with the rightness of the cause, see Middleton, 26:186, 189, 197–98; 27:29, 144. For two good recent historians' discussions of the politics of prisoners, see Jones, Captives of Liberty, and Dzurec, Our Suffering Brethren, chap. 1.
75. For military and diplomatic correspondence dwelling on this issue not cited elsewhere in these notes, see Lord Dunmore to George Germain, 28 Feb. 1777, Dunmore, vol. 3, p. 785; Greene, 10:582–85; Lee, Life of Arthur Lee, 1:102–12, 430–31; PGW, 6:45, 76, 361–62, 378–79; 7:58, 114–15, 117, 124–25, 130, 144, 254, 264–65, 322–23, 351, 375, 405, 499; 8:7–8, 53–54, 58–60, 72, 91–93, 119, 137–38, 141, 242, 247, 472–74, 510–11, 516–18, 548, 591; 9:102–5, 228–30, 496, 591–92, 618; 10:353–56, 408, 420, 625; 11:180, 219, 271–72, 354, 384, 409, 492, 562; 12:135–36, 143–44, 236–37, 255–56, 319–20, 330–31,

363–64, 412–13, 438; 13:1–2, 5–6, 86, 177–78, 280–81, 289–90, 296–97, 412, 455–57, 620–26; 14:39–40, 83–88, 192, 253; 15:194, 202–3; 16:389–90, 533; 17:45–46, 73, 231; 18:31, 585–86; 19:666, 762; 20:29; 21:401, 424–25, 483, 534–39, 545–48, 586, 617, 681; 22:289–90, 406; 23:374–75, 383, 413, 590; 25:166–68, 185, 550; 26:94, 466–67, 539; 27:189–90, 298, 535–36, 617; 28:36, 255–324, 373, 390–92, 441, 569, 605–7, 644–45; Washington, *Writings*, 21:143–44; 23:170, 391, 407–9, 434; 24:144–47, 186–87, 218–21, 226–27, 241–42, 305–8, 315–20, 364–68, 327–73, 467; 24:182; 26:195, 283–84, 304–6, 316, 320; and Davies, ed., *Documents*, 15:104–5.

76. *PR*, 15th Parliament, 4:319–21, 371–78; 5:184–97; 8:81–100, quotations on 4:320, 372.

77. *GM* 47 (Aug. 1777): 355–59; 47 (Sept. 1777): 434–36, 456–57; *Virginia Gazette* (Dixon and Hunter), 7 March, 2, 16 May, 13, 27 June, 4, 25 July, 15, 29 Aug., 12 Sept., 3 Oct., 7 Nov. 1777; 27 Nov. 1778; *Virginia Gazette* (Purdie), 10, 31 Jan., 7, 14, 21, 28 (supplement) Feb., 14 March, 2 (supplement), 16, 23, 30 May, 13 June, 25 July, 15, 22, 29 Aug., 5 Sept., 24, 31 Oct., 12 Dec. 1777; 1 May (supplement), 23 Oct. 1778; *Virginia Gazette* (Dixon and Nicolson), 15, 22 May, 5 June, 4 Sept. 1779; *South-Carolina Gazette; and Country Journal* (Charleston), 31 March 1779; *Pennsylvania Packet*, 27 April, 1, 27 May, 3 June, 11 Nov. 1779; *Spirit*, 81, 88, 96, 123, 183, 188, 223, 298–300, 322, 335–41, 449–50, 524–29, 548–50, 559–61, 736–40, 763, 831, 845–46, 906, 1151; *Letters*, 189–94. Many of these news and polemical items cited here, it should be noted, also included politically charged news surrounding the treatment of noncombatants.

78. Robert Livingston to George Washington, 10 April 1778, in *PGW*, 14:464. For very similar thoughts and even phrasing, see Hamilton, *Papers*, 3:91–93, 118, 326.

79. Davies, ed., *Documents*, 15:31, 49–52, 241–47; 21:106–8, quotation on 21:107; *PGW*, 1:301–2, 5:341–42, 11:72–73.

80. *PGW*, 1:252–55.

81. *PGW*, 1:289–90, 399; 2:47–48, 234, quotation on 1:326–27; Washington, *Writings*, 23:237.

82. Thomas Gage to George Washington, 13 Aug. 1775, in *PGW*, 11:72–73, and also published in *GM* 45 (Sept. 1775): 447. For a milder variant of this charge, alleging that Americans had made indentured servants of POWs, see Brig. Gen. Alured Clarke to Maj. Gen. Benjamin Lincoln, 25 May 1783, Carleton.

83. *Letters*, 244–45.

84. Richard Henry Lee to Patrick Henry, 15 April 1777, in *Lee*, 1:275; *Virginia Gazette* (Dixon and Hunter), 20 June 1777; *Virginia Gazette* (Purdie), 20 June 1777; Lee, *Life of Arthur Lee*, 1:103, 107; *Franklin*, 37:193; Wharton, ed., *Revolutionary Diplomatic Correspondence*, 2:859.

85. James Lovell to Arthur Lee, 25 June 1776, in Lee, *Life of Arthur Lee*, 1:50.

86. American Commissioners to Lord Stormont, 2 April 1777, in *Franklin*, 23:548–49.
87. Campbell, *Journal of an Expedition*, 3, 28–29, 32–33 48, 50, 52, 57–58, quotations on 29. For more on British officers' high valuation of discipline in contrast to the rebels, see Wickwire and Wickwire, *Cornwallis*, 49–78, and Brigade Orders for 8 July 1781, Cornwallis Orderly Book, Rockefeller Library, Colonial Williamsburg.
88. *PGW*, 1:455–59; 2:300; 3:150; 4:59, 75; 5:457; 11:141–42, 148; 12:571, quotations on 1:456, 4:59, 11:148.
89. *GM* 46 (Nov. 1776): 509; Simmons, 6:370, quotation on 365; Crary, ed., *Price of Loyalty*, 15, 19, 30, 57, 102, 197, quotation on 79–80.
90. *PR*, 15th Parliament, 3:299–342; 5:82–97, 301–3, quotations on 3:299; *JCC*, 2:43, 136–37, 151–52, 165; 3:391, 412; 4:33; 5:538; 6:919, 1018–19, 1029; 7:12–13, 276–79, quotation on 3:274. Some of Burke's key speeches on these issues are also available in Burke, *Writings and Speeches*, ed. Langford, 4:103–28. For some recent scholarship that engages the issue of noncombatants via women's history in the war, see Mayer, ed., *Women Waging War*, esp. chaps. 1, 3, 4.
91. It is worth noting that Native Americans reacted to the war in relation to their own politics of humanity, in which the Patriots posed the cruelest and most present threat to their lives and liberties; see Dowd, *Groundless*, 125–43. For a recent history of the German mercenaries, see Baer, *Hessians*.
92. *PR*, 14th Parliament, 8:10–11, 45, 349; 11:106; 14:42, 45. For more Patriot and opposition political assaults on Britain's allies and the debates those assaults generated, see *PR*, 14th Parliament, 8:3, 6–12, 19–20, 24–25, 45, 54, 86, 100, 101, 132–37, 145–49, 263–65, 347–61; 11:19–21, 60, 106–19; 14:15–18, 42–45, 48–101; *PR*, 15th Parliament, 3:523, 528–29, 541, 560, 564; 4:81, 86; 6:394–95; *JCC*, 2:215–16; 4:20–23, 142, 208–9, 229–30; 11:476–78; Ewald, *Diary*, 91; Lockwood, *To Begin the World*, 200; *GM* 45 (Sept. 1775): 446; 47 (April 1777): 169–70; *Virginia Gazette* (Dixon and Hunter), 7 March 1777; Iredell, *Papers*, 1:409, 441; *LD*, 4:39; 7:147; 10:249, 417; Fisher, "Fit Instruments"; and Dowd, *Groundless*, 167–201.
93. Fenn, "Biological Warfare," esp. 1555–57, 1567–75, quotations on 1574.
94. *GM* 45 (Nov. 1775): 543–48, quotation on 548.
95. *PR*, 14th Parliament, 8:17, 22, 30, 352–61; 10:100–101; 11:108; 14:77; [Long], *English Humanity No Paradox*, 81–84; Thomas Taylor to John Wesley, 28 Feb. 1782, Earl of Shelburne Papers, William L. Clements Library.
96. *PR*, 14th Parliament, 11:118, 14:76. For other British advocates of hard war against the American rebels, see *PR*, 15th Parliament, 8:96–97, and [Lind], *Three Letters to Dr. Price*, 156.
97. See, e.g., Wickwire and Wickwire, *Cornwallis*, 171–82; *G3*, 2:245; 3:130–31, 171, 485; Davies, ed., *Documents*, 11:45; *PGW*, 4:427; 5:295, 325, 329,

398–401; 13:402; *Spirit,* 547–48; and Wharton, ed., *Revolutionary Diplomatic Correspondence,* 2:167.
98. Jones, *Captives of Liberty.* Wayne Lee has offered an incisive analysis, with certain logical parallels to what Jones found with the POW issue, of how American Patriots justified brutal warfare against Native Americans, in Lee, *Barbarians and Brothers,* 169–231.
99. Oliver, *Peter Oliver's Origin and Progress,* 123, 132–34, 143–44, quotations on 132.
100. *Pennsylvania Packet,* 5 Aug. 1779, in Rhodehamel, ed., *American Revolution,* 530–33. For a remarkable case of Black petitioners arguing that Tories rather than themselves should not be the ones enslaved, see Basker and Seary, eds., *Black Writers,* 182–83.
101. Edward Rutledge to Arthur Middleton, 23 April 1782, in Middleton, 27:15. For other Americans advocating hard war in similar terms, see *PGW,* 11:403; 14:622, 655; 16:145, 197, 273.
102. Jefferson, *Papers,* 1:27–31, 44, quotation on 28; *RV,* 1:72–84, 232. For a good, concise summary of the legislative history of these bans in both Virginia and Maryland, see MacMaster, "Arthur Lee's 'Address,'" 143–52.
103. *RV,* 1:85–88, 116, 119, 127–33, 140, 151, 162; 2:307–8, quotations on 1:87, 116, 132; Davies, ed., *Documents,* 5:56–57. For more documents illustrating the imperial politics of Virginia's attempted bans, see Donnan, ed., *Documents Illustrative,* 4:150–62.
104. Davis, *Problem of Slavery in the Age of Revolution,* 23–24; Donnan, ed., *Documents Illustrative,* 3:76–77. For the slave trade ban in local politics in 1775, see *Adams,* 2:397.
105. Donnan, ed., *Documents Illustrative,* 3:289.
106. *JCC,* 1:77; Benjamin Rush to Granville Sharp, 1 Nov. 1774, in Woods, ed., "Correspondence of Benjamin Rush," 13.
107. Blanton, "This Species of Property," 446–51.
108. For an example of this candidness, see Lord Hillsborough to Lord Dunmore, 1 July 1772, *Dunmore,* vol. 1, p. 133.
109. Robinson, *Slavery in the Structure,* 469n80; Jordan, *White over Black,* 297–301, quotation on 301; Ragsdale, *Planters' Republic,* 111–36; Breen, *Tobacco Culture.* For an interesting example of how this sense of the politics of this issue resonated beyond the elites, see Basker and Seary, eds., *Black Writers,* 120.
110. Jefferson, *Papers,* 1:121–37, quotations on 130.
111. *Laurens,* 9:348; *Virginia Gazette,* 3 Dec. 1772. For another writer who diagnosed these vetoes as a symptom of the "baleful influence" of colonial rule, see "HUMANITY," in *BG,* 15 June 1772. Even Arthur Lee, who in 1773 cautioned Richard Henry Lee to approach the slave trade carefully, cast that continued trade to North America, and even slavery itself, as an

emblem of "the galling yoke of dependence" that he had been railing against for years within his London radical circles. See Arthur Lee to Richard Henry Lee, 14 Feb. 1773, Arthur Lee Papers, Houghton Library, and Potts, *Arthur Lee*, 25–35, 56–104, quotation on 101.

112. Simmons, 5:611–12.
113. *RV*, 6:433–34; 7:459–66, 594–98, 649–64, quotations on 6:433, 7:459–60.
114. *JCC*, 5:494–98, 511–13; 6:1093, quotations on 5:494, 497, 511, 513.
115. Jefferson, *Notes*, 141.
116. Thomas Hutchinson to Lord Hillsborough, 1 May 1771, in Davies, ed., *Documents*, 3:90.
117. Davies., ed., *Documents*, 5:94–95, 6:182.
118. [Hutchinson], *Strictures upon the Declaration*, 10.
119. Lord Dunmore to Richard Corbin, 27 Jan. 1776, Papers of John Murray, Library of Congress; Lord Dartmouth to Dunmore, 3 March 1775, Dunmore, vol. 1, pp. 476–81; Lord Dunmore, Speech to the General Assembly, Rockefeller Library, Colonial Williamsburg.
120. *GM* 51 (Sept. 1781): 417–18. See also *Short Appeal*, 20–21.
121. Harris, *Hanging of Thomas Jeremiah*, 136–52, quotation on 143. For other similar political usages of this affair, see Simmons, 6:365, 370, and [Lind and Bentham], *Answer to the Declaration*, 95–104.
122. [Lind], *Three Letters to Dr. Price*, 46.
123. Lord Dunmore to Lord Hillsborough, 11 May 1772; "Information of Two Spies Given to Lord Dunmore," 3, 11 May 1776, Dunmore, vol. 3, pp. 751–53. See also Dunmore to Lord Dartmouth, 25 June 1775, Dunmore, vol. 2, pp. 559–72. For other, often subtler digs at American slaveholders in contrast with British liberation policy, see *GM* 46 (Jan. 1776): 39–41; Alexander Leslie to Guy Carleton, 18 Nov. 1782, Earl of Shelburne Papers, William L. Clements Library; and *G3*, 4:542.
124. [Lind], *Three Letters to Dr. Price*, 156–59. Lind, writing with Jeremy Bentham, repeated much of this sort of argument in critiquing the Declaration of Independence; see [Lind and Bentham], *Answer to the Declaration*, 106–10.
125. *Leeds Intelligencer*, 22 Aug. 1775; *Newcastle Weekly Courant*, 26 Aug. 1775.
126. *Leeds Intelligencer*, 8 Aug. 1775.
127. Henry Clinton to George Martin, 10 May 1776; Return of Prisoners, Charleston, 21 May 1780, Clinton.
128. Charles O'Hara to Lord Cornwallis, 5, 9 Aug. 1781, in Saberton, ed., *Cornwallis Papers*, 6:45, 48. For their full exchange, see Saberton, ed., *Cornwallis Papers*, 6:43–52.
129. For another example of this calculus, see Saberton, ed., *Cornwallis Papers*, 6:270, 283.
130. Virginia Patriots who opposed a legislative scheme to recruit white soldiers using slaves as a bounty (in part because it was "inhuman and cruel" to the

enslaved), and those few who publicly supported John Laurens's scheme to raise Black troops by freeing slaves in the name of retaking the moral high ground, came the closest to admitting publicly that Britain had in fact seized that ground. But they comprised a clear minority of white Patriots. See Madison, *Papers*, 2:209–10, 219, 233, quotation on 233; Massey, *John Laurens*, 93–97, 130–31, 143–43, 155–56, 201–3, 207–9, 229; and Jay, *Correspondence and Public Papers*, 1:191–93.

131. Harris, *Hanging of Thomas Jeremiah*, 61–62, 76–91, 113–28; Peter H. Wood, "'Liberty Is Sweet': African-American Freedom Struggles in the Years before White Independence," in Young, ed., *Beyond the American Revolution*, 149–84; *RV*, 3:54–55. Parkinson, *Common Cause*, passim and esp. 143, makes it clear that Dunmore was just the most prominent of many British policymakers Patriots associated with this policy.

132. Carter, *Diary*, 2:981. For more on Dunmore's attitude toward and reputation in Virginia, see Lord Dunmore to Lord Hillsborough and Earl Gower, 9 March, 2 July 1771; Dunmore to Hillsborough, 1 May 1772; Dunmore to Lord Dartmouth, 24 Dec. 1774, Dunmore; and Nelson, *William Tryon*, 87–91.

133. David, *Dunmore's New World*, 94–130, quotation on 108; *JCC*, 3:482–84; George Washington to Richard Henry Lee, 26 Dec. 1775, in *PGW*, 2:611; see also 3:23.

134. Jefferson, *Papers*, 1:290–91, quotation on 290; *RV*, 7:459–66, 487, 594–98, 649–54, quotations on 460.

135. Greene, 9:91; 10:282; 11:106, 581, 639; 12:181, 492–93, quotations on 4:89, 7:457; Lee, 2:242–44, 271, 273; *Virginia Gazette* (Rind), 6 Dec. 1775; *South-Carolina and American General Gazette* (Charleston), 17 Nov. 1775; *Pennsylvania Packet*, 17 Aug. 1779; *Freeman's Journal; or, The North-American Intelligencer* (Philadelphia), 9 Jan. 1782; Middleton, 27:71–72; Laurens, 13:233–34; 14:289–90, 333, 362, 375, 496, 534–35, 545, 551; 15:55–56, 75, 139, 247, 292, 471; *PGW*, 3:136; Madison, *Papers*, 3:52–55, 110–11, 172, 180–81, 215; 5:91.

136. Franklin, 29:590–93.

137. *LD*, 3:238. For a full sense of the wide variety of political contexts and usages of Patriot assaults on the British emancipation policy (often including Indian allies and mercenaries as well as arming fugitive slaves) as inhumane, see *JCC*, 2:215–16; 4:208–9, 229–30; 11:476–78; *LD*, 1:604–7, 613; 2:406; 11:85, 538; *Virginia Gazette* (Dixon and Hunter), 30 Oct. 1778; *Virginia Gazette* (Purdie), 30 Oct. 1778; *South-Carolina and American General Gazette* (Charleston), 12 Nov. 1778; Price, *Political Writings*, 67; Price, 2:51–52; *PGW*, 5:270–71; Franklin, 22:96–98, 196–97, 199–201, 216–17, 323, 392–93, 502–3, 519, 603; 23:117–18, 281–85, 301–11; 37:184–97, 268; *RV*, 3:62–63; 5:362; Nedelhaft, *Disorders of War*, 64; Davies, ed., *Documents*,

NOTES TO PAGES 126–129   255

11:94; Burke, *Writing and Speeches*, ed. Langford, 3:277–86, 288–330, 354–67; [Lee], *Second Appeal*, 66–67; Paine, *Thomas Paine Reader*, 84–85, 93; Paine, *Thomas Paine: Collected Writings*, 334–37; Sandoz, ed., *Political Sermons*, 1:595, 599; *Sermon, on the Present Situation*, 9; John Lewis Gervais to Alexander Cameron, 27 June 1775, Clinton; Moore, ed., *Songs and Ballads*, 334; and Trumbull, *Poetical Works*, 1:50–53, 76–77, 130, 148–50, 160.

138. *An Answer to a Pamphlet*, 60–63. For a favorable review of this pamphlet as a useful warning against extremism, see *GM* 45 (April 1775): 189–92.
139. Simmons, 6:105, 126.
140. *PR*, 14th Parliament, 8:351–52. For more on this theme from British critics, see *PR*, 14th Parliament, 6:263–64, 10:42, and Frey, *Water from the Rock*, 69–70.
141. George Wythe to Thomas Jefferson, 27 July 1776, in Jefferson, *Papers*, 1:476. For others who dehumanized Dunmore, see *PGW*, 2:436, and *RV*, 5:60.
142. Stephen Bull to Henry Laurens, 14 March 1776; Laurens to Bull, 16 March 1776, in *Laurens*, 11:162–64, 172–73.
143. *RV*, 5:139. For another discussion of this resolution, see Quarles, *Negro in the American Revolution*, 25–26.
144. Silas Deane to William Bingham, 17 Oct. 1776, in Wharton, ed., *Revolutionary Diplomatic Correspondence*, 2:173.
145. For a sense of proportion, see *PR*, 14th Parliament, 6:263–64; 8:3, 6–12, 17, 19–20, 22, 24–25, 30, 45, 54, 86, 100, 101, 132–37, 145–49, 263–65, 347–61; 9:87, 218–20, 237; 10:9–10, 24–26, 41–44, 47–49, 60–65, 72–83, 92–106, 252–53, 306; 11:19–21, 60, 106–19; 14:15–18, 42–45, 48–101; 16:56–57; *PR*, 15th Parliament, 6:394. Bickham, *Making Headlines*, 206–33, makes a similar point.
146. Parkinson, *Common Cause*, 20, 258, 288, 341, 410, 454, 543–44, 654, quotations on 288, 454, 341; *PR*, 14th Parliament, 8:12 (Wilkes quotation). Robert G. Parkinson does note in passing that such tales meant "the patriots could malign their enemies and demarcate their cultural cousins as aliens" but does not fully pursue that insight. Parkinson, *Common Cause*, 20. For other examples of this theme, see *Virginia Gazette* (Rind), 6 Dec. 1775; *New York Packet*, 15 Feb. 1776; Sandoz, ed., *Political Sermons*, 1:688–710; Lee, 2:243; Ronald Hoffman, "The 'Disaffected' in the Revolutionary South," in Young, ed., *American Revolution*, 281–82; Franklin, 37:586–88; *PGW*, 3:539; *Laurens*, 13:225, 234; and Jefferson, *Notes*, 126–27. For an exception in which the ranking was "insidious Neighbours, the lawless plundering Soldier, & the more savage Slave," see *RV*, 5:362.
147. Moore, ed., *Songs and Ballads*, 334.
148. Anthony Wayne to Nathanael Greene, 25 March 1782, in Peckham, ed., *Sources of American Independence*, 2:394.
149. Paine, *Writings*, 1:86–93, 100–101, 112–13, quotations on 100.

150. *Virginia Gazette* (Dixon and Hunter), 23 Dec. 1775, 6 Jan. 1776; *South-Carolina and American General Gazette* (Charleston), 26 Jan. 1776; *Virginia Gazette* (Rind), 30 Nov., 13 Dec. 1775; *Pennsylvania Gazette* (Philadelphia), 13, 27 Dec. 1775, 1 Jan. 1776; *Maryland Gazette* (Annapolis), 4 Jan. 1776. For similar expressions in other sources, see Carter, *Diary*, 2:1055, 1057, and *Adams*, 11:63.
151. *Virginia Gazette* (Purdie), 19 July 1776. For the actual facts, see Taylor, *American Revolutions*, 149.
152. *Virginia Gazette* (Rind), 13 Dec. 1775; *Pennsylvania Gazette* (Philadelphia), 27 Dec. 1775; *Maryland Gazette* (Annapolis), 4 Jan. 1776. See also *South-Carolina and American General Gazette* (Charleston), 26 Jan. 1776; *Pennsylvania Gazette*, 13 Dec. 1775; and *Virginia Gazette* (Rind), 30 Nov. 1775.
153. Nathanael Greene to Robert R. Livingston, 13 Dec. 1781, in *Greene*, 10:48. For an example of the circulation of Greene's formulation, see Jay, *Selected Papers*, 2:676.
154. Madison, *Papers*, 7:264.
155. Rhodehamel, ed., *American Revolution*, 689, 694.
156. *RV*, 3:501, 5:60, quotation on 4:269; Philbrick, ed., *Trumpets Sounding*, 106–15; *Laurens*, 11:50, 13:233–34; *Pennsylvania Gazette* (Philadelphia), 3 April 1776; *Hartford [Conn.] Courant*, 9 March 1779; *Vermont Journal* (Windsor), 4 Sept. 1783; Rawlins Lowndes to James Simpson, 20 May 1780, Clinton; Middleton, 27:52; *Greene*, 9:91; *PGW*, 21:349, 22:245; *Franklin*, 34:551. For a good discussion of the influence of Leacock's play, see Parkinson, *Common Cause*, 282–85.
157. Jefferson, *Papers*, quotation on 1:290; Madison, *Papers*, quotation on 1:153; Martin, *Narrative of a Revolutionary Soldier*, quotation on 207; *RV*, 5:60, 139; *Franklin*, 25:65; Jonathan Pafford to Brig. Gen. Samuel Birch, Commandant of New York, July 1781, Carleton; Hoffman, "The 'Disaffected' in the Revolutionary South," 281–82; *New York Packet*, 21 March 1776. For the broad eighteenth-century context of colonial slaveholders' understanding slave flight in these terms, see Mullin, *Flight and Rebellion*, 110–63, esp. 114.
158. John Penn to John Adams, 17 April 1776, in *Adams*, 4:128.
159. *Virginia Gazette* (Rind), 16, 23, 30 Nov. 1775; *Virginia Gazette* (Purdie), 1 Dec. 1775. For similarly politicized ads from other slaveholders, see Landon Carter, "Notice Concerning a Runaway Slave," 1777, Carter Family Papers, Swem Library, and Smith and Wojtowicz, eds., *Blacks Who Stole Themselves*, 129–30.
160. Edmund Pendleton to James Mercer, 19 March 1776, in Pendleton, *Letters and Papers*, 1:160. For a brief discussion of how "the political actions of slaves" were central to British policy, see David, *Dunmore's New World*, 5–6.
161. *LD*, 4:472.
162. *Journal of the House of Delegates*, 14, 16.

163. Frey, *Water from the Rock*, 64.
164. Henry Clinton to George Martin, 10 May 1776, Clinton.
165. Edmund Pendleton to Thomas Jefferson, 16 Nov. 1775, in Jefferson, *Papers*, 1:261; Morton, *Robert Carter*, 55–56. In that orchestrated meeting the audience assured him they had no intent to join Dunmore, but in 1781 thirty enslaved people from Carter's plantation did join the British forces.
166. *Virginia Gazette* (Rind), 23 Nov. 1775; *Virginia Gazette* (Purdie), 24 Nov. 1775; *Virginia Gazette* (Dixon and Hunter), 25 Nov. 1775; also reprinted in Rhodehamel, ed., *American Revolution*, 81–86. For other examples of this allegation, see *Virginia Gazette* (Purdie), 17 Nov. 1775, 2 May 1777 (supplement); *Pennsylvania Gazette* (Philadelphia), 13 Dec. 1775, 1 Jan. 1776; *Virginia Gazette* (Rind), 30 Nov. 1775; Philbrick, ed., *Trumpets Sounding*, 108; Madison, *Papers*, 5:440; Parkinson, *Common Cause*, 277–79, 367, 509, 519–25, 569; Paine, *Thomas Paine Reader*, 93; Adams, 10:298–99; *LD*, 5:30–31; and Taylor, *American Revolutions*, 25. For variations involving accusations of both Britons and Loyalists trafficking to places other than the West Indies, see Mary Butler to Sir Guy Carleton, 16 Sept. 1782; Evert Byvanck to Carleton, 3 April 1783; Representation of Sarah Haviland of Elizabeth Town to the American Commissioners in New York, 23 June 1783; Deposition of William Higgins, 24 June 1783, Carleton; *Greene*, 11:355; and *LD*, 19:586.
167. Henry Laurens to John Laurens, 14 Aug. 1776, in *Laurens*, 11:222–35, quotations on 224. For John's reply, written 26 Oct. 1776, which made plain just how antislavery his feelings had become, see *Laurens*, 11:276–77.
168. *RV*, 5:140, 240n6, 277, 363, 423–24. For the extraordinarily meticulous modern historian Cassandra Pybus's excellent investigation of the truth of this Patriot claim, see Pybus, *Epic Journeys*, 30–31.
169. Sir Henry Clinton, Proclamation, 30 June 1779, Clinton. See also Pybus, *Epic Journeys*, 28.
170. James Wright to Nisbet Balfour, 5 Jan. 1781, in Saberton, ed., *Cornwallis Papers*, 3:433; Richard Oswald to Charles Townshend, 15 Nov. 1782; Benjamin Vaughan to Henry Strachey, 14 Nov. 1782, Earl of Shelburne Papers, William L. Clements Library; Patrick Tonyn to Alexander Leslie, 14 Nov. 1782; John Cruden to George Nibbs, 16 March 1783; Cruden to J. Fahia, president of the Council at Tortola, 24 March 1783; Cruden to Maj. C. Nesbit, 25 March 1783, Carleton; Heerman, "Abolishing Slavery in Motion," 251–56; Giunta et al., eds., *Emerging Nation*, 1:659.
171. Joseph Hewes and Robert Smith to a London mercantile firm, 31 July 1775, in *LD*, 1:685; American Commissioners to the Committee of Secret Correspondence, 12 March–9 April 1777, in *Franklin*, 23:473.
172. Sandoz, ed., *Political Sermons*, 1:688–710.
173. Gouverneur Morris to Sir Henry Clinton, 20 Oct. 1778, in *LD*, 11:85.
174. *PGW*, 4:411–13; 5:180, 207, 235; 21:62, quotations on 5:180, 21:62.

175. *RV*, 4:102–3.
176. *Franklin*, 25:64–68, 650–54, quotations on 2:65–66.
177. John Adams to Benjamin Franklin, 14 Oct. 1780, 16 April 1781, in *Franklin*, 33:418–20, 34:551–52.
178. Lund Washington to George Washington, 17 Dec. 1775; George Washington to Lt. Col. Joseph Reed, 15 Dec. 1775, in *PGW*, 2:553, 571. This despite Lund's admission, in a letter to George two weeks previous, that Dunmore would likely rack up Black recruits because "Liberty is sweet." *PGW*, 2:480. For another jab at Scottish officers in this connection, see *Lee*, 1:148.
179. George Washington to Richard Henry Lee, 27 Nov. 1775, in *PGW*, 2:436.
180. *RV*, 3:54–55, 62–63, 70–71, 84–85, 89–90, 107–13, 172, 500–502; 5:59–61, 124–26; 6:433–34, 447–48; 7:142–43, quotation on 3:501. For yet other examples of these links beyond those cited above, see Philbrick, ed., *Trumpets Sounding*, 106–15; *Virginia Gazette* (Purdie), 6 Oct. 1775; *JCC*, 4:208–9, 229–30; *LD*, 4:39, 7:147; *Laurens*, 16:30–31; *PGW*, 6:220–21; *Adams*, 3:17; *Spirit*, 146–47; Pendleton, *Letters and Papers*, 1:216; Morison, ed., *Sources and Documents*, 162; Sandoz, ed., *Political Sermons*, 1:599; *GM* 45 (Aug. 1775): 357–60; 46 (June 1776): 260–61; 48 (Sept. 1778): 414–17; *Letters*, 165–67, 231–34; Bland, *Papers*, 1:42–45; *Proceedings of the Massachusetts*, 342–43; *Pennsylvania Packet*, 21 May 1782; and Pybus, *Epic Journeys*, 15. For a good discussion of points related to this, including that Dunmore's Proclamation "was evidence that the British would break any compact—including, in the Virginians' view, the sacred one between master and slave," see Bradley, *Slavery, Propaganda*, 132–53, quotation on 135.
181. Burke, *Writings and Speeches*, ed. Langford, 3:258–76, quotations on 260, 268, 269.
182. *PR*, 14th Parliament, 10:42. For others who made such connections, see *PR*, 14th Parliament, 16:56–57.
183. *BP*, 4:327–52, quotations on 347.
184. Berger, *Broadsides and Bayonets*, 103–4; Simmons, 6:96, 281; Lord Cornwallis to James Wemyss, 31 Aug. 1780, in Saberton, ed., *Cornwallis Papers*, 2:210. For other downplaying and denials, see *PR*, 14th Parliament, 8:17, 22, 30, 352–61; *GM* 45 (Nov. 1775): 548; Wesley, *Political Writings*, 78–79; and Rhodehamel, ed., *American Revolution*, 306–7, 314–17. For good discussions from other historians of how divided both Britons and American Loyalists were about these issues, see Frey, *Water from the Rock*, 67–77; Piecuch, *Three Peoples*, 9–11, 38–44, 76–87, 120–24, 158–72, 214–16, 265–70, 308–27; and Chopra, *Unnatural Rebellion*, 112, 114–15, 146–48.
185. *GM* 46 (Jan. 1776): 39–41.
186. [Long], *English Humanity No Paradox*, 78–84.
187. Guy Johnson to George Germain, 12 March 1778, in Davies, ed., *Documents*, 15:69.

188. Patrick Ferguson to Unknown, Nov. 1779, Clinton. See also David Taitt to Sir Henry Clinton, 11 June 1779; William Carson to James Simpson, 1 May 1780, Clinton. For another military man's discomfort with the policy and its effects, see Ewald, *Diary*, 14, 183, 302, 305–6, 339, 350, 359.
189. Clinton, *American Rebellion*, 162. See also Serle, *American Journal*, 88, 159–60.
190. Ewald, *Diary*, 130–31, 335–36.
191. Pybus, *Epic Journeys*, 11.

6. Honor

1. *PR*, 15th Parliament, 7:58. For an interesting discussion of the tight connection between personal and national reputation and honor, see [Long], *English Humanity No Paradox*, 1–3, 9–11.
2. G3, 5:392, 6:54. For other examples of his deep commitment to national-cum-personal honor, see G3, 6:40–45, 210–11.
3. Joseph Ward to John Adams, 3 Dec. 1775, in *Adams*, 3:343. For a similar sentiment, see Holton, ed., *Black Americans*, 52–53.
4. *Virginia Gazette* (Dixon and Hunter), 25 July 1777.
5. Smith, *American Honor*, esp. 22–168, quotations on 7, 8, 12, 199. For more on these themes, see Washington, *Writings*, 27:12–13, and Armitage, *Declaration of Independence*, 1–87. For an interesting example of an American working through what honor would mean for Americans in their post-monarchical state, see Charles Thomson to John Dickinson, 29 July 1776, in *LD*, 4:562.
6. Published in extract form in *Caledonian Mercury* (Edinburgh), 11 Jan. 1783. I have been unable to find this exact letter from Franklin to Shelburne in any of the relevant published sources. But for similar language from Franklin denouncing the mere suggestion of a separate peace that makes this newspaper piece ring true, see Giunta et al., eds., *Emerging Nation*, 1:299–301, and *Franklin*, 36:435–38, 583–84.
7. Simmons, 6:118, 125, 236–37, 334, 503, 518, quotations on 118, 503; *PR*, 14th Parliament, 6:5–7, 26, 36, 57–58, 62, 248; 7:1, 9, 15–16, 99, 109; 8:1–2, 10, 134; 9:34, 64–76, 94–95, 107, 168–69, 236–37, 246, 255; 10:12, 61, 88, 105, 113; 14:45, 65, 90, 100, quotations on 7:15, 16; 9:34; *PR*, 15th Parliament, 5:61–62, 82–97, 184–97, 224–28, 301–3; 6:394–95; 7:69, 144; 8:81–100, 213–17.
8. Henry Strachey to the American Commissioners, 5 Nov. 1782, Earl of Shelburne Papers, William L. Clements Library. For another such sentiment, see Harlow, *Founding of the Second British Empire*, 1:275.
9. *PR*, 15th Parliament, 9:208–10, 265, 305; 11:30–93, quotations on 11:41, 44; [Tucker], *Series of Answers*, 82. See also Mackesy, *War for America*, 461, 490–91.

10. *GM* 52 (Oct. 1782): 496–97; Jasanoff, *Liberty's Exiles*, 100. For a similar rhetorical appeal, see William Franklin to George Germain, 6 Nov. 1781, in Davies, ed., *Documents*, 20:255–57.
11. Robert M. Calhoon, "The Reintegration of the Loyalists and the Disaffected," in Greene, ed., *American Revolution*, 51–74, quotations on 64. For examples of this from leading Patriots, see Middleton, 26:197–98, 27:29.
12. Quincy, *Portrait of a Patriot*, 1:132–33, 137, 159, 164–66, quotation on 133; Smith, *Theory of Moral Sentiments*, 69–70. For unusually good examples of this disdain for slaves and how that got translated into declamation against slavishness in politics, see Lee, *Life of Arthur Lee*, 1:194–95, 201, 216, 220, 239, 252. For a deservedly influential analysis of the impact of such rhetoric on the American revolutionary and subsequent generations, see Furstenberg, "Beyond Slavery and Freedom."
13. *British Liberties*, xliv–lvi, quotations on xliv.
14. Samuel Ward to John Dickinson, 14 Dec. 1774, in *LD*, 1:269. For a similar expression of the supreme calamities of slavery "and its terrible Concomitants," see the resolutions of the New York Sons of Liberty printed in *Virginia Gazette* (Purdie and Dixon), 13 Jan. 1774.
15. *BG*, 18 July 1768. For some few indicators of this song's influence, see Flower, *John Dickinson*, 70–71; Richard Henry Lee to [Landon Carter], 25 April 1774, in *Lee*, 1:109; and *Virginia Gazette* (Purdie and Dixon), 11 Aug. 1774.
16. *RV*, 2:149.
17. *BG*, 24 Aug. 1767.
18. *APW*, 1:163, 171. For similar expressions elsewhere in this collection, see *APW*, 1:171–73, 182, 240–53, 316.
19. Quincy, *Observations*, 69.
20. *MG*, 28 May 1772. For other execrations of slavish submission, see *BG*, 31 Aug. 1767; *Virginia Gazette*, 13 Feb. 1772; *Virginia Gazette* (Purdie and Dixon), 30 June 1774; *New York Packet*, 14 March 1776; *Farmer's and Monitor's Letters*, 64–65, 71–72, 78, 80, 95; Warren, *Oration Delivered March 5th, 1772*, 17; Warren, *Oration; Delivered March Sixth, 1775*, 17; *RV*, 4:102–3, 5:141; Washington, *Papers: Colonial Series*, 10:154–56; Morison, ed., *Sources and Documents*, 105, 110; [Bourke], *Privileges of the Island of Jamaica*, 45, 58–59, 66; Dickinson, *Essay on the Constitutional Power*, 13–14; *Price*, 1:188–91; *JCC*, 2:68–70, 150, 153, 155, 163, 165–66, 205; 4:136–40, 144–46; 6:1018–20; *LD*, 1:536; 2:86; 3:212, 442, 456; 4:144, 469, 531; 7:148; *Letters*, 143; *Lee*, 1:140–41; Moore, ed., *Songs and Ballads*, 88, 90–91; [Sewall], *Gen. Washington*; *Spirit*, 95, 108–9, 297–98; Paine, *Writings*, 1:174; Wharton, ed., *Revolutionary Diplomatic Correspondence*, 3:568, 572–73; Jay, *Life of John Jay*, 1:55; and Breen, *Will of the People*, 32, 49–50, 83, 224.

21. For an excellent discussion of the multiple roles slavery and slavishness played in Patriots' treatment of Loyalists, see Thompson, "Social Death and Slavery."
22. Adams, *Diary and Autobiography*, 1:255–58, 280, 282, 313; 2:62, 86, quotations on 1:257. See also *Adams*, 1:117, 123–24, 126, for Adams's disdain for slavishness in general.
23. Quincy, *Portrait of a Patriot*, 1:252–61, quotation on 258; *Virginia Gazette* (Purdie and Dixon), 9 June 1774.
24. William Lee to Francis Lightfoot Lee, 5 Sept. 1774, Arthur Lee Papers, Houghton Library.
25. Carter, *Diary*, 2:821–22. For other expressions of Carter's fear that fellow colonists—Scottish and otherwise—would slavishly betray the cause, see Carter, *Diary*, 2:912–13, 917, 931–33. For the prominence of anti-Scottish sentiment among Wilkesite and Patriot circles, see Hamilton, *Scotland, the Caribbean*, 19–22, 140–85.
26. Lovell, *Oration*, 9.
27. Samuel Adams to James Warren, 14 July 1778, in *LD*, 10:274–75.
28. *BG*, 11 Aug. 1766 (supplement).
29. *BG*, 21 Oct. 1765.
30. Charles Burg to Ralph Wormeley Jr., 3 Aug. 1775, in *RV*, 4:34–35.
31. Burnard and Garrigus, *Plantation Machine*, 202–3. For other examples of extreme anger at Loyalist slavishness to the point of threatening them with slavery, see *JCC*, 1:32, 86; *BG*, 31 Aug. 1767; 18 Jan., 21 March, 15 Aug. 1768; *Considerations upon the Rights*, 16; *Virginia Gazette*, 13 Feb. 1772; *APW*, 1:421–22, 484, 526; Paine, *Thomas Paine Reader*, 119; Sandoz, ed., *Political Sermons*, 1:700; *GM* 46 (Oct. 1776): 450–51; Rhodehamel, ed., *American Revolution*, 532; and Breen, *Will of the People*, 99–100.
32. O'Shaughnessy, *Empire Divided*, 14–17, 34–57, 62–69; Simmons, 3:498–502, 505. For examples of contemporaries' scrutiny of and complaints about the West Indian lobby, see *GM* 36 (May 1766): 228–31, and *BG*, 9 Dec. 1765.
33. Gauci, *William Beckford*, 164–94, quotation on 177.
34. *BG*, 6, 13 Jan. 1766; also printed in *MG*, 2 Jan. 1766 (supplement), 16 Jan. 1766 (supplement).
35. *BG*, 12, 19 May 1766.
36. Adams, *Diary and Autobiography*, 1:285.
37. [Dickinson], *Address to the Committee*, 8. For other Patriots and British allies who depicted West Indians in similarly pejorative terms, see Smith, comp., *English Defenders*, 151.
38. Evans, *Reply to the Rev. Mr. Fletcher's*, 101. See also *GM* 35 (Dec. 1765): 589–90; 37 (Oct. 1767): 491–93, and Smith, comp., *English Defenders*, 96–98, 137–40.

39. Simmons, 6:606–14, quotations on 607. For similar thoughts from Burke in 1777, see Burke, *Writings and Speeches*, 2:187–245, esp. 227.
40. Simmons, 6:36–37, 97–98, 137, 211, 350, quotation on 61; *PR*, 14th Parliament, 8:14, 98.
41. Parkinson, *Common Cause*, 194. For similar expressions, see *Adams*, 12:89; *Virginia Gazette* (Purdie), 6 Oct. 1775; [Lee], *Second Appeal*, 16, 27, 30, 36–37, 52–54, 66–67; and Lockwood, *To Begin the World*, 200.
42. *GM* 45 (July 1775): 329–31.
43. When John Allen complained in print that white American colonists had become so shorn of their rights that they could even "be confined" and tried "by the accusation of a negro," some of his readers protested and asked for a more antislavery spin. In response, "he revised his argument" in subsequent editions. "No longer were black litigants posing a threat to white colonists; instead, African slavery became the benchmark of imperial despotism." See Sesay, "Revolutionary Black Roots," 111.
44. "BEN SCOTUS," in *Boston Spy*, 17 Sept. 1772. This was also the logic of Dickinson, *Essay on the Constitutional Power*, 51–52. In addition to the examples quoted below of Patriots equating their treatment with that of Black people, see [Lee], *Appeal*, 29; "John Hampden," in *BG*, 9 Dec. 1765; "F.A.," in *BG*, 17 March 1766; "AMERICANUS," in *Boston Spy*, 15 Oct. 1772; Morgan, ed., *Prologue to Revolution*, 86; Iredell, *Papers*, 1:251–67, esp. 264; *BP*, 4:66; *GM* 46 (Feb. 1776): 61; *PGW*, 8:21–22; and *Franklin*, 22:6–7. In 1769, a group of backcountry dissidents headed by Charles Woodmason showed their dexterity in turning just such rhetoric against colonial legislators; see Nedelhaft, *Disorders of War*, 16.
45. *BG*, 14 Oct. 1765. See also *Adams*, 1:124–25, 147. Alexander R. Jablonski offers a thorough reading of the meaning of all these uses of race in this debate in "'Providence Never Designed Us for Negroes': Slavery and British Subjecthood in the Stamp Act Crisis, 1764–1766," in Hutchins, ed., *Community without Consent*, 148–73. It should be reiterated, however, that this generation debated it all, including the justifiability of racial prejudice, and some antiracist voices emerged; see, e.g., *GM* 41 (1771, appendix): 594–96.
46. *Laurens*, 8:38, 67, 239; 9:304, 316–18.
47. *LD*, 1:297.
48. Quincy, *Portrait of a Patriot*, 1:248.
49. Waldstreicher, *Runaway America*, 142–46.
50. Franklin, *Benjamin Franklin's Letters*, quotation on 191; *Franklin*, 12:413–16.
51. Adams, *Diary and Autobiography*, 4:38–39.
52. Parkinson, *Common Cause*, 529. For further Patriot complaints of being treated like Blacks and slaves, see *Price*, 1:203; York, ed., *Crisis*, 535–41; *Laurens*, 11:125; and Philbrick, ed., *Trumpets Sounding*, 76, 89.
53. Rozbicki, *Culture and Liberty*, 11; *Adams*, 2:242.

54. Wahrman, "English Problem of Identity," 1238, 1239. Robert Travers, "Contested Despotism: Problems of Liberty in British India," in Greene, ed., *Exclusionary Empire*, 191–219, is a rich exploration of a similar crisis of identity, racial and otherwise, among Britons in India during the war years.
55. Moore, ed., *Songs and Ballads*, 101; Basker, ed., *Amazing Grace*, 224.
56. Hulton, *Letters of a Loyalist Lady*, 99, 25.
57. Lt. Col. James Abercrombie, Brigade Orders for 8 July 1781, Cornwallis Orderly Book, Rockefeller Library, Colonial Williamsburg. For other racialization of and extreme condescension toward Americans and other colonials, see Foote, *Nabob*, 22, 28; Edward Montagu to [Landon Carter?], 30 Sept. 1772, Carter Family Papers, Swem Library; Murray, *Letters from America*, 15, 29, 36, 38, 40, 47–48, 52, 57, 64–65; *Letters*, 244–45; Cresswell, *Journal*, 251–57, 259–64; and Serle, *American Journal*, 88, 159–60.
58. For examples of the close association of Blacks both free and enslaved with disorder and disrespect, see *MG*, 18 Aug. 1768; Haynes, *Black Preacher to White America*, xxiii; and Sword, *Wives Not Slaves*, 26, 41–45. For an excellent analysis of how Africans as well as others fell into this association throughout the early modern Atlantic world, see Linebaugh and Rediker, *Many-Headed Hydra*.
59. Wood, "'Liberty Is Sweet,'" 157.
60. *Triumph of the Whigs*, 4–8. For similar Loyalist attempts to racialize the Patriots, see *BG*, 9, 30 Dec. 1765; 27 Jan. 1766, and Morgan, ed., *Prologue to Revolution*, 100–102.
61. *BG*, 11 Nov. 1765.
62. Hinderaker, *Boston's Massacre*, 119–20; Kearsley, ed., *American Gazette*, 267–320, quotation on 283.
63. Hinderaker, *Boston's Massacre*, 187–220, quotations on 204, 207; Oliver, *Peter Oliver's Origin and Progress*, 87–90.
64. *Adams*, 3:68; 4:45, 115.
65. Richard Henry Lee to Landon Carter, 1 April 1776; Lee to Thomas Jefferson, 21 July 1776, in *Lee*, 1:173, 210.
66. *Virginia Gazette* (Dixon and Hunter), 24 Jan. 1777.
67. *Virginia Gazette* (Purdie), 10 May 1776; *Pennsylvania Gazette* (Philadelphia), 22 May 1776. For further rhetorical racialization of Britons and white Loyalists, see *RV*, 3:180–82; *Price*, 1:253–55; and *Spirit*, 113. John Jay offered a gendered variation of this abuse in 1783 when he recommended that victorious Patriots not punish those who had joined the British out of "timidity"; severity was inappropriate toward these men "because nature had made them like women." Jay, *Life of John Jay*, 1:180.
68. *Letters*, 245; *RV*, 5:117. Woodford's letter was published in the *New York Packet*, 4 Jan. 1776.

69. Arthur Lee to Richard Henry Lee, 6 Dec. 1777, Custis-Lee Family Papers, Library of Congress; John Henry to Thomas Johnson, 30 Jan. 1779, in *LD*, 11:538. For other linkages of race and British disgrace by Patriots and British opposition figures beyond those cited below, see Middleton, 27:71–72; *PR*, 14th Parliament, 8:54, 134, 351–52; 10:10, 74; *Hartford [Conn.] Courant*, 4 Feb. 1783; Sandoz, ed., *Political Sermons*, 701; *RV*, 4:102, 5:161; *PGW*, 3:539; 19:542; 20:344, 454; Pendleton, *Letters and Papers*, 1:216; and Gibbes, ed., *Documentary History of the American Revolution*, 3:234. This was a trope that dated back at least to the Seven Years' War, during which John Dickinson regretted the British government's policy of relying so much on mercenaries to wage the war in the European theater. Especially when it came to the defense of Britain itself, he wondered very early in the war, "Can one single reason be assignd why that important trust should be committed to slaves & foreigners rather than to freemen & natives?" Colbourn and Peters, eds., "Pennsylvania Farmer," 449.
70. Hoffman, "The 'Disaffected' in the Revolutionary South," 281–82; Hoffman, *Spirit of Dissension*, 148.
71. Henry Laurens to John Laurens, 16 March 1776, in *Laurens*, 11:174; see also 11:224.
72. Richard Henry Lee to William Lee, 15 July 1781, in *Lee*, 2:242–43. For other examples of this charge, see *Hartford [Conn.] Courant*, 9 March 1779; *Franklin*, 31:436–39; and Basker, ed., *Amazing Grace*, 236.
73. Basker and Seary, eds., *Black Writers*, 207–15, 221–31, 233–44, quotations on 212, 213, 226, 227, 236. While James G. Basker and Nicole Seary, the editors of this outstanding volume, cannot be sure that this preacher was Black or that these pseudonyms all covered the same author, their interpretation of the evidence to that effect strikes me as persuasive.
74. William Bradford to James Madison, 4 Jan. 1775, in Madison, *Papers*, 1:132.
75. *Virginia Gazette* (Rind), 16 Nov. 1775; Freneau, *Poems of Philip Freneau*. 2:98. For very similar expressions from others, see *Pennsylvania Gazette* (Philadelphia), 4 Dec. 1775; *Virginia Gazette* (Rind), 6 Dec. 1775; *Pennsylvania Packet*, 25 Dec. 1775; and *Virginia Gazette* (Purdie), 22 March 1776.
76. Daniel Stevens to John Wendell, 20 Feb. 1782, in *Proceedings of the Massachusetts*, 342; also published in the *Pennsylvania Packet*, 21 May 1782. For a milder but still telling Patriot squib against this ball, see *Freeman's Journal; or, The North-American Intelligencer* (Philadelphia), 24 April 1782.
77. [Lee], *Second Appeal*, 52–54.
78. *PGW*, 25:306, 325; 26:535, 594.
79. *Adams*, 3:183–84, 239–40; 4:453–55; *LD*, 7:461. For more on this and related debates, see Quarles, *Negro in the American Revolution*; Robinson, *Slavery in the Structure*, 116; Massey, "Limits of Antislavery Thought"; Middleton, 26:194, 27:4; and Hamilton, *Papers*, 3:120–21.

80. *PGW*, 1:90; 2:125, 354; see also 2:188, 199. For a useful discussion of the ideology behind such ideas, see Murrin, *Rethinking America*, 214–15.
81. *PGW*, 2:620, 623; 6:536–37; 8:44; 10:232, 280, 328; *JCC*, quotations at 4:60. I thus disagree entirely with the emphasis in Gordon Wood's very brief and selective account of Washington's actions in which, after some initial hesitation, he very quickly "began advocating" the arming and liberating of American slaves, and in 1778 somehow "allowed Rhode Islanders to raise an all-black regiment." See Wood, *Revolutionary Characters*, 39.
82. Philyaw, "Slave for Every Soldier."
83. For extended, useful discussions of the controversial politics and manpower desperation involved in all of this, see Smith, *American Honor*, 4, 112–17, and Van Buskirk, *Standing in Their Own Light*, 60–172.
84. "Antibiastes," *Observations on the Slaves*, 1. For a similar argument put more succinctly, see Brig. Gen. Thomas Nelson Jr. to George Washington, 21 Nov. 1777, in *PGW*, 12:342.
85. Thus both sides were part of a tradition, stretching back to the ancient world, of preference for free citizen soldiers that only stark military necessity has tended to challenge; see Brown and Morgan, eds., *Arming Slaves*, 3, 14–39, 136–37.
86. Robinson, *Slavery in the Structure*, 105–6, 110. The most influential recent statements positing British antislavery and Patriot proslavery as dominant is Parkinson, *Common Cause*, but see also Horne, *Counter-Revolution of 1776*, and Horne, *Negro Comrades*. For other historians offering a more nuanced assessment of British policymakers' motives, see Frey, *Water from the Rock*, 45–171; Quarles, *Negro in the American Revolution*, esp. 120; Schama, *Rough Crossings*, esp. 5–6, 105; Piecuch, *Three Peoples*, 9–11, 38–44, 76–87, 120–24, 158–72, 214–26, 265–70, 308–27; Taylor, *Internal Enemy*, 23, 36; Taylor, *American Revolutions*, 228; Heerman, "Abolishing Slavery in Motion," 251–56; Christopher Leslie Brown, "From Slaves to Subjects: Envisioning and Empire without Slavery, 1772–1834," in Morgan and Hawkins, eds., *Black Experience*, 111–39; Asaka, *Tropical Freedom*; Jasanoff, *Liberty's Exiles*, 13, 78; Bell, *Running from Bondage*, 80–105; and Foy, "'Unkle Sommerset's' Freedom." As for the flip side of this coin, Trevor Burnard and John Garrigus in particular have usefully raised the question of whether insurrection anxiety—as important as that was for all planters—actually determined the political stances of any appreciable number of North American or West Indian slaveholders. See Burnard and Garrigus, *Plantation Machine*, 200–201. For similarly nuanced analyses of the political impact of insurrection anxiety for slaveholders in this era, see O'Shaughnessy, *Empire Divided*, 137–248; Rugemer, *Slave Law*, 171–212; Hoffman, "The 'Disaffected' in the Revolutionary South," 273–316; and Craton, *Testing the Chains*, 172–80.

87. Mackesy, *War for America*, 39–40, 61–73, 103, 141, 259, 273, 309, 338, quotation on xxiv. O'Shaughnessy, *Men Who Lost America*, usefully seconds and expands on Piers Mackesy's analysis.
88. Voelz, *Slave and Soldier*, 82. For similar conclusions within a comparative framework, see Philip D. Morgan and Andrew Jackson O'Shaughnessy, "Arming Slaves in the American Revolution," in Brown and Morgan, eds., *Arming Slaves*, 180–208, and Helg, *Slave No More*, 4–5, 77–81, 118–30. And for a sense of how the American Revolutionary War in general represented an expansion of, rather than the invention of, the British Empire's reliance on local allies, see Wayne E. Lee, "Subjects, Clients, Allies, or Mercenaries? The British Use of Irish and Amerindian Military Power, 1500–1800," in Bowen, Mancke, and Reid, eds., *Britain's Oceanic Empire*, 179–217.
89. Thomas Gage to Lord Barrington, 27 Aug. 1774, in Peckham, ed., *Sources of American Independence*, 1:117–18; [Johnson], *Taxation No Tyranny*, 64–69, 85, quotation on 85; Burnaby, *Travels*, 109–15, quotation on 111. See also Jensen, ed., *Tracts of the American Revolution*, 383–87; [Draper], *Thoughts of a Traveller*, 20–21; Schaw, *Journal of a Lady*, 198–200; Lord Dunmore to Lord Hillsborough, 1 May 1772, Dunmore, vol. 1, pp. 115–16; Simmons, 6:96; *Derby [Eng.] Mercury*, 16 June 1775; *Edinburgh Advertiser*, 16 June 1775; *Freeman's Journal* (Dublin), 24 June 1775; *Jackson's Oxford [Eng.] Journal*, 24 June, 5 Aug. 1775; *Ipswich [Eng.] Journal*, 24 June 1775; *Leeds Intelligencer*, 27 June 1775; Murray, *Letters from America*, 16–17; and *BP*, 4:256–57. For some examples of white Americans' apprehensions and a range of resulting political responses, see Madison, *Papers*, 1:129–30, 132; Alden, "John Stuart"; Davies, ed., *Documents*, 11:53–54; *LD*, 11:538; Harris, *Hanging of Thomas Jeremiah*; and Calhoon et al., *Tory Insurgents*, 99–105.
90. Davies, ed., *Documents*, 9:200–205, 11:45, quotation on 9:204; Lord Dunmore to Lord Dartmouth, 1 May, 25 June 1775; Dunmore to Dartmouth, 1 May, 2 Aug. 1775, Dunmore, vol. 2, pp. 527–31, 559–72, 604–5. It is also worth noting that Dunmore, the great emancipator of American nightmare, claimed 48 human beings, valued at over 2,500 pounds sterling, among his losses after the war. See Dunmore to Commissioners on Losses of American Loyalists, 25 Feb. 1784, Dunmore, vol. 3, pp. 815–23.
91. Sir Henry Clinton, Proclamation, 30 June 1779 (quotation); Clinton to George Martin, 10 May 1776; Josiah Martin to the Earl of Dartmouth, 30 June 1775, Clinton; *G3*, 3:224–27, 265–72; 4:542–49; *PR*, 15th Parliament, 3:519–20.
92. Davies, ed., *Documents*, 18:38–39, 264–65; 20:94–95, 101, quotation on 18:264; Edward Fenwick to John Andre, 15 May 1780; James Simpson to John Andre, 6 June 1780; William Carson to Simpson, 1 May 1780; David Taitt to Henry Clinton, 11 June 1779; Allan McDonald to "Captain Gibson," 8 March 1780, Clinton; L. Fuser to James Penman, 29 Sept. 1779; Fuser to

Clinton, 25 Sept., 12 Dec. 1779; Alexander Leslie to Guy Carleton, 11, 27, 28 June, 19 July 1782, Carleton; Saberton, ed., *Cornwallis Papers*, 2:95, 99, 210; Jennifer K. Snyder, "Revolutionary Repercussions: Loyalist Slaves in St. Augustine and Beyond," in Bannister and Riordan, eds., *Loyal Atlantic*, 165–84; Duval, "Mastering Charleston"; Piecuch, *Three Peoples*, esp. 9–11.

93. Patrick Tonyn to Alexander Leslie, 14 Nov. 1782, Carleton.
94. M. Arbuthnot to Henry Clinton, 18 April 1780; "Joe," Deserter's Deposition, 6 Nov. 1780; Joseph Cox, Deserter's Deposition, 5 May 1781; Nehemiah Marks to Oliver De Lancey, 18 Sept. 1781; "Marquard" to De Lancey, 11 July 1781; John Hader, Intelligence, 11 July 1781; George James, Deserter's Deposition, 14 July 1781; Marquard to De Lancey, 24 July 1781; Intelligence, 24 Oct. 1781, Clinton; Campbell, *Journal of an Expedition*, 15, 20–21, 26, 63–64.
95. Lt. Col. Archibald Campbell's reaction to ninety enslaved people reaching his lines gives a fuller sense of the many uses to which British commanders put such people. He approached their Patriot owner offering to return them if the owner and his family provided Campbell with intelligence. When that was forthcoming Campbell kept the enslaved people as hostages for this planter's continued cooperation. See Campbell, *Journal of an Expedition*, 53, 56.
96. Henry Clinton to Commissioners of Captures, July 1779 (quotation); "Return of Captured Negroes and Horses," 17 March 1780; "List of the Names of the Negroes Belonging to Captain Martin's Company," n.d., Clinton; Pybus, *Epic Journeys*, 26.
97. Clinton, *American Rebellion*, 110, 119, 127–28, 154–55, 162, 192, 352–53.
98. William Innes to Henry Clinton, 9 Nov. 1779 (quotations); Inspector's Report, 14 March 1777; Patrick Ferguson to Unknown, Nov. 1779; Charles Morris to Unknown, 22 March 1780; Lord Cornwallis to Clinton, 11 May 1780; Clinton to Cornwallis, 20 May 1780, Clinton; Davies, ed., *Documents*, 17:156–57; Saberton, ed., *Cornwallis Papers*, 1:48, 63; 6:43–52; Todd W. Braisted, "The Black Pioneers and Others: The Military Role of Black Loyalists in the American War for Independence," in Pulis, ed., *Moving On*, 3–7.
99. Murray, *Letters from America*, 21.
100. Maj. Gen. Edward Mathew to Henry Clinton, 26 April 1782, Carleton.
101. Sheridan, "Jamaican Slave Insurrection Scare," esp. 300–301; Burnard, *Jamaica in the Age of Revolution*, 5, 9–11, 15, 36–42, 50–52, 67–69, 103–4, 119–30, 151–213; Jones, *Resisting Independence*, passim, esp. 4–5. I should note that my reading of this source, a letter from Rev. John Lindsay, differs from Sheridan's. For particularly direct wartime examples of the importance for British policymakers of preserving the West Indies and the transatlantic slave trade, see G3, 6:126, and *PR*, 15th Parliament, 3:422. For

yet other examples illustrating the racist views and instrumental uses of African Americans among a wide range of Britons and Loyalists, see *GM* 46 (Jan. 1776): 39–41; *Letters*, 244–45; Clinton, *American Rebellion*, 356; Shields and Teute, "Meschianza," 191; Ewald, *Diary*, 305–6; and Jasanoff, *Liberty's Exiles*, 104–5.

102. Thus, nothing in the previous discussion should be taken to accord with the remarkable conclusion by W. Robert Higgins that "the Negro was not a party to the American Revolution in the South; he was a tool, a means to an end" only. See Higgins, "The Ambivalence of Freedom," in Higgins, ed., *Revolutionary War in the South*, 43–44.

103. For a good discussion of the long-running situational nature of the British Empire's interactions with people of African descent, see Morgan and Hawkins, eds., *Black Experience*, 3–4, 11–20.

104. Morgan and Hawkins, *Black Experience*, 11–20; McConville, *King's Three Faces*, 175–82.

105. Michael E. Groth, "Black Loyalists and African American Allegiance in the Mid-Hudson Valley," in Tiedemann et al., eds., *Other Loyalists*, 81–104, quotations on 93, 94; Van Buskirk, *Generous Enemies*, 4–7, 129–54, 172–76, quotations on 4, 7, 131; Bannister and Riordan, eds., *Loyal Atlantic*, ix–xvii, 3–74; Duval, *Independence Lost*, esp. xix. The pioneering interpretation of African American choices in the Revolution, which accords with mine and that of others cited here, is Quarles, *Negro in the American Revolution*, esp. xxvii.

106. Gosse, "'As a Nation,'" 1006, 1011, 1016. See also Carretta, ed., *Unchained Voices*, 5–10, 45–53. Benjamin Quarles pioneered this insight by arguing that no matter Dunmore's liabilities and inconsistencies as a liberator, "to those who whispered his name in slave quarters" he was a major emancipator; see Quarles, *Negro in the American Revolution*, 19–32, quotation on 32. For a much less nuanced, if well-researched, version of this argument, see Horne, *Negro Comrades*. For a good discussion of how flight to the British was an uncertain but clearly more reliable road to freedom than armed revolt, see Helg, *Slave No More*, 4–5, 77–81, 118–30.

107. Harris, *Hanging of Thomas Jeremiah*, 76–91, 136–49, 152, quotations on 78.
108. Murphy Stiel to Unknown, 16 Aug. 1781, Clinton.
109. Carretta, ed., *Unchained Voices*, 353–66, quotations on 353, 356, 366.
110. Schama, *Rough Crossings*, 5.
111. India Moore Heyerd to Henry Clinton, 10 Feb. 1779, Clinton.
112. Henry Clinton to Oliver De Lancey, n.d., Clinton.
113. Judith Jackson to Sir Guy Carleton, 18 Sept. 1783; Petition of Peggy Gwynn, 19 Nov. 1783, Carleton. According to the notes with these documents, British soldiers investigated Jackson's claim but ruled that Gwynn was not free and must return to slavery.

114. Bauermeister, *Revolution in America*, 569.
115. Paley, *Principles of Moral and Political Philosophy*, 2.
116. Beatty, *In Dependence*, 5, 9, 114, 143. See also Carin Bloom, "A Black Loyalist's Liberty: How Lucy Banbury Took Back Her Freedom," in Mayer, ed., *Women Waging War*, 195–211. Rachel Devlin has unearthed a similarly gendered element to twentieth-century efforts to desegregate US schools in which Black girls and young women led. Rooted in these girls' and women's everyday experiences accommodating while also confronting white Americans in the pre–civil rights movement era, Devlin's narrative is suggestive of fascinating comparisons to as well as contrasts with this eighteenth-century story. See Devlin, *A Girl Stands at the Door*.
117. Bell, *Running from Bondage*, esp. 4, 160–61.
118. My interpretation in this chapter thus diverges from Cassandra Pybus's in a book for which I have the utmost regard. Rather than my emphasis on the culture of honor, she emphasizes "close bonds," forged between freedmen and British soldiers and seamen over the course of years, for Britons' willingness to facilitate African Americans' evacuations with the British Army; see Pybus, *Epic Journeys*, 58.
119. Pybus, *Epic Journeys*, 28, 40. For an interesting suggestion of how at least one previous Black petition may have influenced Clinton, see Basker and Seary, eds., *Black Writers*, 174.
120. Sir Henry Clinton, Proclamation, 30 June 1779, Clinton; Gallagher, "Black Refugees," 144, 145, 142.
121. James Moncrief to Henry Clinton, 13 March 1782, Carleton.
122. Alexander Leslie to Sir Guy Carleton, 27 June, 10 Aug. (quotation), 3, 18 Oct. 1782, Carleton. For British officials' pervasive sense of almost insurmountable difficulty distinguishing African Americans' true legal status, see Lt. Col. Archibald McArthur to Leslie, 15 Nov. 1782; Unknown to the Board of Commissioners for Adjusting Matters, 31 Aug. 1783; John Cruden to James Clitherall, 27 April 1783; Memorial by Charles Johnston et al., 30 May 1783; Clitherall to Cruden, 25, 31 May 1783, Carleton; and Jasanoff, *Liberty's Exiles*, 57–109.
123. "Notes of a Conference between the Count de Florida Blanca and Mr. Jay," 23 Sept. 1780; John Jay to the President of Congress, 20 Sept. 1781; Jay to Robert Livingston, 17 Nov. 1782, John Jay Papers, Library of Congress. See also Jay to Count Montmorin, 27 April 1782; Jay to Robert Livingston, 18 Sept. 1782, John Jay Papers, Library of Congress; Richard Oswald to the Earl of Shelburne, 11 July 1782, Earl of Shelburne Papers, William L. Clements Library; and Jay, *Correspondence and Public Papers*, 2:327–29, 335, 345–452; 3:7–11, 14–19, 26, 55–61. For other similarly vigorous expressions of American sovereignty and independence in the fullest sense as the overriding priorities among American leaders, see Wharton, ed., *Revolutionary*

Diplomatic Correspondence, 5:660–61, 703–7, 743–47, 754–56, 800, 854–56, 863–66; 6:19, 122–24, and Lee, *Life of Arthur Lee*, 2:249. For good discussions in the secondary literature of the centrality of the issue of sovereignty to all diplomacy during the war and the varied impacts that had on the numerous political aspects of this complex negotiations, see Mackesy, *War for America*, 1, 27–28, 33–34, 87–88, 102, 155–59, 189, 219–20, 279, 463, 489, 491, 505–6; Harlow, *Founding of the Second British Empire*, 1:223–311, 408–92; Jones, "'Dreadful Effects'"; Lyons, "Law of Nations"; Stahr, *John Jay*, 136, 152–58; and Potts, *Arthur Lee*, 165–249, 256–57.

124. Morison, ed., *Sources and Documents*, 186–203.
125. *Virginia Gazette* (Dixon and Hunter), 19 Dec. 1777.
126. "Articles of Capitulation at Surrender of Fort Moultrie," 7 May 1780; "Memorandums for the Commandant of Charles Town and Earl Cornwallis," 3 June 1780, Clinton; "Agreement between A. Wright and James Johnston, Commissioners for Lieut. Gen. Leslie, and Edward Rutledge and Ben Geurard, Commissioners for Governor Mathews," 10 Oct. 1782, Carleton; Washington, *Writings*, 23:262, 264–65; Alured Clarke to Lord Cornwallis, 10 July 1780, in Saberton, ed., *Cornwallis Papers*, 1:337–38; Piecuch, *Three Peoples*, 160.
127. Richard Oswald to the Earl of Shelburne, 10 July 1782; Oswald, Minutes, 29 Aug. 1782; Oswald to Charles Townshend, 11 Oct., 8 Nov. 1782, Earl of Shelburne Papers, William L. Clements Library; *Franklin*, 36:390–402; 37:94–95, 167, 170–71, 177–78; 38:190–94, 263–75, 321–25; Adams, *Diary and Autobiography*, 3:61.
128. Wharton, ed., *Revolutionary Diplomatic Correspondence*, 5:715–16, 873, 876, quotations on 873, 876; *Franklin*, 38:350–56. Robert Parkinson has written that South Carolina governor John Matthews was the first to tie return of slaves to debts by threatening nonpayment in case of nonreturn. Parkinson, *Common Cause*, 566.
129. Morris, *Peacemakers*, 378–79, 535n156; *Laurens*, 16:153–54, 363–64, 409. For other discussions that normally slightly overstate Laurens's impact on this clause, see Parkinson, *Common Cause*, 563–65; Bemis, *Diplomacy*, 238; and Stahr, *John Jay*, 170–71. David N. Gellman, on the other hand, emphasizes the delegation's unity behind what he insists was no "mere afterthought" and deemphasizes Laurens's impact; see Gellman, *Liberty's Chain*, 58–66, quotation on 61. Still other historians, it should be noted, have seen this clause as sufficiently low in priority that they have ignored it or treated it only very slightly in their histories of this negotiation; see Hoffman and Albert, eds., *Peace and the Peacemakers*.
130. James Peters to Guy Carleton, 5 Oct. 1783, Carleton.
131. Alexander Leslie to Guy Carleton, 18 Nov. 1782, Earl of Shelburne Papers, William L. Clements Library. See also Davies, ed., *Documents*, 21:140, and Leslie to Carleton, 18 Oct. 1782, Carleton.

132. Oliver De Lancey, Order, 15 April 1783, Carleton.
133. Ralph Izard to Arthur Middleton, 30 May 1783, in both Middleton, 27:79, and *LD*, 20:287–88. For similar assessments, see *Greene*, 12:310.
134. *Vermont Journal* (Windsor), 4 Sept. 1783. For another article similar in tone, see "Americanus," in *Pennsylvania Packet*, 22 July 1783.
135. *Laurens*, 16:231.
136. Robert Livingston to the American Peace Commissioners, 28 May 1783, in *Franklin*, 40:75–77.
137. Washington, *Writings*, 26:403–5, 408–9; 27:27–28, quotations on 26:404, 27:28.
138. Guy Carleton to George Washington, 12 May 1783, in Davies, ed., *Documents*, quotations on 21:165–66; "Substance of a Conference between General Washington and Sir Guy Carleton," 6 May 1783, in Washington, *Writings*, 26:403–5, and Founders Online, https://founders.archives.gov /?q=account%20of%20a%20conference%20Author%3A%22Washington %2C%20George%22&s=1111311111&r=90.
139. Guy Carleton to Elias Boudinot, 17 Aug. 1783, in Davies., ed., *Documents*, 21:208–9.
140. *LD*, 20:247–48; see also 20:582; Jefferson, *Papers*, 6:268–69.
141. Edmund Pendleton to James Madison, 2 June 1783, in Madison, *Papers*, 7:106.
142. Alexander Hamilton to George Clinton, 1 June 1783, in Hamilton, *Papers*, 3:365, 367–72, quotations on 369.
143. *JCC*, 24:861, 25:965–67. For more on that weariness as the driving priority, see *Franklin*, 39:578–80.
144. *Franklin*, 40:315–17; Jefferson, *Papers*, 6:393–400; Giunta et al., eds., *Emerging Nation*, 2:157–58.
145. Commissioners of Embarkation at New York to George Washington, 18 Jan. 1784, in Washington, *Papers: Confederation Series*, 1:50–56, quotations on 50, 51.

7. Impacts on Slavery

1. For representatives of that older strand, see Bailyn, *Ideological Origins*, 232–46, 302; Jordan, *White over Black*, 287–94; and preeminently, Davis, *Problem of Slavery in the Age of Revolution*.
2. Reid, *Concept of Liberty*, 38–122, quotations on 38, 45; Glover, *Founders as Fathers*, esp. 164–91; Mayer, *Son of Thunder*, 166–70; Littlefield, "John Jay"; Massey, "Limits of Antislavery Thought"; Higginbotham, "Some Reflections"; Saillant, "Slavery and Divine Providence"; Lynch, "Limits of Revolutionary Radicalism"; Sword, *Wives Not Slaves*, 15, 207–84; Klooster, *Revolutions in the Atlantic World*, esp. 41–44; Clark, *Thomas*

Paine, 11, 93–97, 212–13; Rozbicki, *Culture and Liberty*, 1–33, 78–162; Young, ed., *Beyond the American Revolution*, 123–48, 333–40; Greene, ed., *American Revolution*, 1–13, 230–52; Sinha, *Slave's Cause*, 34–96; Gilbert, *Black Patriots and Loyalists*; Blackburn, *Overthrow of Colonial Slavery*, 24, 111–28, 267–91, 519; Higgins, ed., *Revolutionary War in the South*, 43–63; Stovall, *White Freedom*, 112–21; Adams, *First American Constitutions*, 164–88; Wiencek, *Imperfect God*.

3. Bradley, *Slavery, Propaganda*, xiii–xxiv, 1–24, 45–65, quotations on xiv. For other examples of this argument, see MacLeod, *Slavery, Race*; Furstenberg, "Beyond Slavery and Freedom"; and Dorsey, *Common Bondage*. For an especially provocative version, see Okoye, "Chattel Slavery."
4. Gigantino, *Ragged Road to Abolition*, 31–63, quotations on 33. For similar interpretations and emphases, see Frey, *Water from the Rock*, esp. 45; Olwell, "'Domestick Enemies'"; Horne, *Counter-Revolution of 1776*, esp. 196–97; and Ruddiman, "'Is This the Land of Liberty?'"
5. Drescher, *Abolition*, 112–13, 119; Richardson, *Principles and Agents*, 184.
6. Parkinson, *Common Cause*, 109, 254, 261, 411, 457, 587, 662. For more nuanced statements that are at least in tension with the above, see Parkinson, *Common Cause*, 184, 192, 226, 248, 350, 368, 373, 626, 639. But the bolder iterations of Parkinson's argument have constituted its impact on fellow historians and the general public. For a small sampling of evidence for this interpretation's influence, see Breen, *Will of the People*, 9–11, 52, 87, 219; Taylor, *American Revolutions*, 146; and Hannah-Jones et al., eds., *1619 Project*, xxv–xxviii, 11–21. Woody Holton's recent argument is reminiscent of Parkinson's in the seeming disconnect between the quotable passages and the deep tracks. He directly states that "the American Revolution cannot be described as a net contributor to Black freedom." And yet his overall discussion of the medium- and long-term impacts of the Revolution on slavery are more nuanced than that would suggest. See Holton, *Liberty Is Sweet*, 549–54, 568, quotation on 554.
7. Wood, *American Revolution*, xxiv–xxv, 56–57, 126–29, quotations on xxiv–xxv; Wood, *Revolutionary Characters*, 8, 26–28, 37–41, 94, 286n8, quotations on 8, 26; Wood, *Power and Liberty*, 8, 100–125, quotation on 112; Wood, *Idea of America*, 19–22, 226–28, 267–69, 288–89; Wood, *Radicalism of the American Revolution*, 179, 186–87. See also Bailyn, *Ideological Origins*, 232–46. For an excellent summary and analysis of this historiographical debate, see Waldstreicher, "Changing Same." For just how stark and unyielding these historiographical sides can be, see "American Revolution from Two Perspectives," pitting Gordon Wood versus Woody Holton. The polarizing nature of this debate would seem to be why Wood might have gone steps beyond the Bailynesque position.
8. Wilentz, *No Property in Man*, 7–12, 25–53, quotations on 12, 26–27, 36.

9. Samuel Ward to Samuel Ward Jr., 15 Aug. 1775, in *LD*, 1:703; "Bostoniensis," in *BG*, 2 Dec. 1765; "A.F.," in *BG*, 31 Aug. 1767. For other Patriot expressions that had strong antislavery potential, see "A.B.," in *BG*, 7 Oct. 1765; "BRITANNUS AMERICANUS," in *BG*, 7 Sept. 1767; anonymous writer in *BG*, 22 Feb. 1768; "Phocion," in *Virginia Gazette*, 13 Feb. 1772; Quincy, *Observations*, 78–79; Warren, *Oration; Delivered March Sixth, 1775*, 21; and Freneau, *Poems of Philip Freneau*, 2:228.
10. Richard Henry Lee to Landon Carter, 15 Aug. 1765, in *Lee*, 1:11.
11. *New York Packet*, 29 Feb. 1776.
12. Sachse, *Colonial American in Britain*, 151; "Philo Patria," in *Virginia Gazette* (Rind), 18 Feb. 1773.
13. William Lee to Francis Lightfoot Lee, 25 Feb. 1775, Arthur Lee Papers, Houghton Library.
14. *BG*, 26 May 1766.
15. Basker and Seary, eds., *Black Writers*, 190–93.
16. Waldstreicher, *Odyssey of Phillis Wheatley*, esp. ix, 8–9, 61–68, 74, 102, 111, 164, 187–88, 248–49, 299–302, 321, 342, quotations on 342, 68, 111, 164, 321, 8.
17. Taylor, "Introduction: Expand or Die," *William and Mary Quarterly*, 623, and *Journal of the Early Republic*, 603–4. For other challenges to the idea of a single white supremacist legacy of the Revolution, and more generally powerful doses of nuance in this historiography, see Polgar, *Standard-Bearers of Equality*, 13–14, 23–44; Waldstreicher, *Runaway America*, passim, esp. xii–xiii; Rael, *Eighty-Eight Years*, 2–3, 29–79; Gordon-Reed and Onuf, *"Most Blessed,"* esp. 81–90; Van Buskirk, *Standing in Their Own Light*, esp. 4–5; Jane E. Calvert, "An Expansive Conception of Rights: The Quakerly Abolitionism of John Dickinson," in Jordan, ed., *"When in the Course,"* 21–54; McDonnell, *Politics of War*, esp. 7–13, 135–74; Oshatz, *Slavery and Sin*, 3–37; Gellman, *Emancipating New York*, esp. 1–5, 26, 48, 76–77, 139; Gellman, *Liberty's Chain*, esp. 3–4, 29, 37–41, 44, 50–51; Blanton, "This Species of Property," esp. 1–4, 478–83; and James Sidbury, "Blacks in the British Colonies," in Klooster, ed., *Cambridge History of the Age*, 398–421. Recently, Edward J. Larson, seemingly writing largely for a popular audience, has characterized the Revolution as creating sectional division rather than uniformity. As suggested in this book, I think that a tale of straight sectional division is a bit simplistic. Also, Larson's engagement with the literature is curiously dated, with his most direct historiographical discussions centering on works from the 1960s and 1970s. That said, this discussion strikes me as more useful than the polarized either/or of the literature cited above. In short, his book-length revivification of Edmund Morgan seems to me to be equal parts welcome and dated. See Larson, *American Inheritance*, esp. vii–x, 5–6, 14–15, 30, 40, 111, 148, 166. See also Morgan, *American Slavery, American Freedom*.

18. Bruns, 384–85, 441–42, 452, 511, quotation on 399. For a secondary account that emphasizes the war's disruptive effects on abolitionist activity, see Sword, "Remembering Dinah Nevil," esp. 316, 333.
19. Marquis de Lafayette to Benjamin Franklin, 20 March 1779, in *Franklin*, 29:172. Lafayette also proposed a scheme to raid the British West Indies and "take a way the negros &c.," with no mention of liberating said people; see Lafayette to Henry Laurens, 14 Dec. 1777, in *Laurens*, 12:150. For other Patriot correspondence suggesting this wartime change in focus and priority, see Rush, *Letters*, 1:110–12, 114, 235, 268, and Jay, *Selected Papers*, 2:84.
20. Arthur Lee to Anthony Benezet, 1773, Granville Sharp Collection, New-York Historical Society; Patrick Henry to Robert Pleasants, 18 Jan. 1773, in Bruns, 222.
21. Charles Chauncy to Richard Price, 18 July 1774, in *Price*, 1:172. This came despite the antislavery turn Chauncy had otherwise taken; see Waldstreicher, *Odyssey of Phillis Wheatley*, 180–81.
22. Samuel Ward to John Ward, 10 Feb. 1776, in *LD*, 3:224.
23. *Laurens*, 4:595–97; 6:90, 134, 149–50, 240–41, 408, 422, 438; 7:172, 297–99, 360, 371, 429; 9:352–55, 360, 389–98, 409–10, 414–15; 10:97–98, quotations on 7:297–99, 9:264. For Virginia versions of these virtues, see Pendleton, *Letters and Papers*, 1:53–56; Robert Wormeley Carter Diary, entries, e.g., for 2 Feb., 20 June, 1, 7 Dec. 1774, American Antiquarian Society; and Robert Carter to Daniel Dulaney, 25 Dec. 1768, Letterbooks of Robert Carter of Nomini Hall, Virginia Historical Society.
24. Benjamin Rush to Granville Sharp, 9 July, 20 Sept. 1774, in Woods, ed., "Correspondence of Benjamin Rush," 6–9, 12.
25. Wesley, *Thoughts upon Slavery*, passim, quotations on 32.
26. Day, *Dying Negro*, viii–ix. For the influence of Day's poem, see Wood, ed., *Poetry of Slavery*, 36.
27. Neville, *Diary*, 3–4; see also 31, 36, 49.
28. Hampton, ed., *Radical Reader*, 330–31.
29. *PR*, 14th Parliament, 7:4–8.
30. *BP*, 6:85–162, quotations on 131, 142.
31. Cone, *Torchbearer of Freedom*, esp. 69–95; Macleod, "Proper Manner"; Bonwick, *English Radicals*, xi–xxii, 3–80. Carl B. Cone also offers a useful discussion of the wide influence of Price's pamphlets, especially in the United States.
32. Price, *Political Writings*, 63–65, 68–69, 72.
33. Price, *Political Writings*, 111–14. For a similar expression that this was the worst slavery, see *Price*, 2:116.
34. *Price*, 2:34–35, 38; see also 2:35–36, 42, 149–50.
35. A. Turgot to Price, 22 March 1778, in *Price*, 2:12–17; Condorcet, *Condorcet: Selected Writings*, 11. For Revolutionary-era ideas of and policies built on

the idea of the thirteen colonies as an asylum for liberty and its Old World lovers, and the colonial origins of such ideas and policies, see Baseler, *"Asylum for Mankind,"* 1–151. For more on European liberals' hopes for the American Revolution, see R. R. Palmer, "The Impact of the American Revolution Abroad," in *Impact of the American Revolution Abroad*, 5–18, and Lloyd Kramer, "Interpreting a Symbol of Progress and Regression: European Views of America's Revolution and Early Republic, 1780–1790," in Klooster, ed., *Cambridge History of the Age*, 519–41. My interpretation here diverges a bit from Kramer's valuable essay in that he posits that "every European advocate for American progress condemned the persistence of" slavery (534), whereas I have found some instances, like Turgot and Condorcet here, of European liberals willing to look the other way in certain contexts.

36. *PR*, 14th Parliament, 6:13–14, 17–18, 24, 42, 245–46; 8:9–10, 14, 18–19, 83, 86, 98–99, 101–2, 109, 122–24, 134–37; 11:20, 26; quotations on 8:98, 11:26; *PR*, 15th Parliament, 3:546–48; 5:185, 187, 189.
37. Simmons, 6:105.
38. Adams, *Diary and Autobiography*, 2:408, 4:154. See also Wharton, ed., *Revolutionary Diplomatic Correspondence*, 3:635–39.
39. American Commissioners to the Committee of Secret Correspondence, 12 March–9 April 1777, in *Franklin*, 23:473. For the full weight of the evidence of this sympathy encountered by Franklin and his comrades, see *Franklin*, 24:6–7, 524–25, 551–52; 25:219, 242–43, 288–90, 463–64, 532; 26:42–46; 27:11–12, 14–19; 28:393; 29:52–56, 423; 30:5–6, 33–36, 589–90; 31:234–35; 32:14–17; 33:502–4; 34:223; 35:412–14; 36:105–7, 222–25; 37:9–10, 704–5; 38:183–85, 303, 318–20, 398–401; 39:27–41, 45–58, 186–87, 227, 240–44, 314–16.
40. Ramsay, *Oration on the Advantages*, 13–16, 21. For other American repetitions of the idea of the United States as European darling and pure asylum, see Lee, *Lee Papers*, 4:4–7; Paine, *Writings*, 1:85–90, 100–101, 118–19, 206–8, 252–54; and *New York Packet*, 14 March 1776.
41. Gigantino, *Ragged Road to Abolition*, 31–63, esp. 40, 48, quotation on 40; *RV*, 6:253.
42. Crawford, *Having of Negroes*, 66–67, 107–38, quotations on 66–67, 112, 121, 127. For an exploration of a very dramatic example of wartime anti-Quakerism among the Patriots, and of the full range of issues that provoked it, see Donoghue, *Prisoners of Congress*.
43. Henry Laurens to James Laurens, 6 Jan. 1776, in *Laurens*, 11:4–7, quotation on 5; Nedelhaft, *Disorders of War*, 64. For more evidence of a sense of helplessness against slave flight, see *Laurens*, 11:39–40, 74, 160, 264–65, 269, 284, 350–51, 410, 482; 13:540; 14:289–90; 15:20, 32, 297, 304–7, 311–12.
44. Carter, *Diary*, 2:1148–49.

45. George Washington to Benjamin Harrison, 30 April 1783, in Washington, *Writings*, 26:370; James Madison to Edmund Randolph, 8 July 1783, in Madison, *Papers*, 7:217, see also 7:265n5. For more on the significance of British power in New York City to American slaves and slaveholders, see Van Buskirk, *Generous Enemies*, 4–7, 129–54, 172–76, esp. 7, 135.
46. Parkinson, *Common Cause*, 453; Duval, "Mastering Charleston," quotation on 599. For other excellent analyses of the patriarchal angle in all of this for Patriot slaveholders, see Glover, *Founders as Fathers*, esp. 4, 52–56, and Isaac, *Landon Carter's Uneasy Kingdom*, 3–36, 184–264, 313–22.
47. Charles Lee to George Washington, 5 April 1776, Williamsburg, in *PGW*, 4:43–44. For a very similar phrasing, see Charles Lee to Richard Henry Lee, 5 April 1776, in Lee, *Lee Papers*, 1:378–80; see also 1:369, 372, 410.
48. William Carson to James Simpson, 1 May 1780; Jane Cadmus to Guy Carleton, 16 July 1782, Clinton; Jonathan Pafford to Brig. Gen. Samuel Birch, July 1781; Mary Butler to Carleton, 16 Sept. 1782; Evert Byvanck to Carleton, 3 April 1783; John Harberk to Carleton, 14 April 1783; "Representation of Sarah Haviland of Elizabeth Town to the American Commissioners in New York," 23 June 1783; Neil Jamieson to Andrew Elliot, 22 April 1783; "Petition of Sundry Inhabitants of Norfolk and Princess Anne Counties, Virginia," 28 April 1783, Carleton; *Laurens*, 15:303–4; *Virginia Gazette* (Dixon and Hunter), 19 Dec. 1777; Egerton, *Death or Liberty*, 199–200; Pybus, *Epic Journeys*, 28, 44, 63, 69.
49. John Mathews to George Washington, 14 Oct. 1780, in *PGW*, 28:553.
50. Rawlins Lowndes to James Simpson, 20 May 1780, Clinton.
51. Maj. Frederick Mackenzie to Rawlins Lowndes, 9 Sept. 1782, Carleton.
52. *Independent Gazetteer* (Philadelphia), 19 July 1783; *Virginia Gazette; or, The American Advertiser* (Richmond), 2 Aug. 1783.
53. Ralph Izard to Arthur Middleton, 30 May 1783, in Middleton, 27:79, and *LD*, 20:287–88.
54. Nedelhaft, *Disorders of War*, 88–91.
55. Waldstreicher, *Slavery's Constitution*, 21–56, quotations on 38, 39, 40.
56. Mason, "North American Calm."
57. For more on this concept, see Mason, "Missed Opportunity?" esp. 204–6.
58. Thus, it is baffling to me that Patricia Bradley would have declared that antislavery activists in the 1770s were marginal in part because they "failed to make the issue integral to national identity" and "did not adapt their religious discourse into political rhetoric." Even their attempts to decry slavery as a national sin, she declares, "flew in the face of revolutionary propaganda that stressed American innocence." See Bradley, *Slavery, Propaganda*, 81–131, quotations on 82, 83. This undervalues the blurriness among religion, politics, and national identity, as well as the ability of Patriots to carry around conflicting ideas concerning national internal guilt and innocence

vis-à-vis Britain. It was certainly possible for abolitionists to make their case straight up, without any reference to the imperial crisis—see, e.g., "J.F.," in *MG*, 2 April 1767, and "MANETHO," in *Boston Spy*, 1 Oct. 1772. But this was infinitely less common than abolitionists who used the political situation. For a valuable exploration of abolitionists in this era as "political men as well as men of ideas" who understood "that the slavery issue could no longer be addressed apart from the American issue," see Waldstreicher, *Runaway America*, 175–209, quotations on 195.

59. These abolitionists, and those who came to agree with them, thus offer a severe qualification to arguments insisting that the eradication of slavery lay beyond the limits of the mental universe of the age. Edward Countryman even argues that white Virginians' particular understanding of the term "liberty" meant that "they had no reason to see the contradiction between freedom and slavery in their lives that is so painfully obvious to us now." See Countryman, "'To Secure the Blessings of Liberty': Language, the Revolution, and American Capitalism," in Young, ed., *Beyond the American Revolution*, 123–48, quotation on 130. For other examples of this line of argument, see Bernard Bailyn, "The Central Themes of the American Revolution: An Interpretation," in Kurtz and Hutson, eds., *Essays*, 28–31, and Rozbicki, *Culture and Liberty*, esp. 1–33.

60. Benezet, *Complete Antislavery Writings*, 87, 202–5, 208–15; see also 106, 118, 146–50; Anthony Benezet to Robert Pleasants, 8 April 1773; Benezet to Samuel Allinson, 14 Dec. 1773; Benezet to Moses Brown, 28 Dec. 1773, 9 May 1774; Anthony Benezet Letters, Haverford College Library; Benezet to Granville Sharp, Nov. 1772, 18 Feb. 1773, Granville Sharp Collection, New-York Historical Society. For good portraits of Benezet's role as the ultimate transatlantic antislavery networker, taking advantage of existing Quaker infrastructure but also willing to collaborate with allies no matter their political persuasion or nationality, see Sassi, "With a Little Help from the Friends," and Brookes, *Friend Anthony Benezet*, 76–109, and multiple letters in the appendix.

61. Sharp, *Representation of the Injustice*, 48, 51n. See also "NO BEAM NO MOTE," in *BG*, 18 Jan. 1768, and Swan, *Dissuasion to Great-Britain and the Colonies*, 12, 27.

62. Basker, ed., *Amazing Grace*, 185–86; for a similar appeal to Britons, see Basker, ed., *Amazing Grace*, 196. For an example of the ongoing influence of this epilogue in the Anglo-American world as late as 1788, see Gellman and Quigley, eds., *Jim Crow New York*, 37–38.

63. Lofft, *Reports of Cases*, 30–35, 41–43, quotation on 43.

64. Samuel Allinson, preface, in Sharp, *Essay on Slavery*, vi–viii.

65. *BG*, 13 July 1767. For other examples, see *APW*, 1:183, and "Lover of Constitutional Liberty," 13–15.

66. Cameron, *To Plead Our Own Cause*, 1–69, quotation on 3; "Lover of Constitutional Liberty," appendix, 6–7; Sinha, "To 'Cast Just Obliquy'"; Porter, ed., *Early Negro Writing*, 254–55; Gosse, *First Reconstruction*, 169. For a useful discussion of the sheer volume and evolving nature of these petitions for freedom in Massachusetts, see Sesay, "Revolutionary Black Roots." For a forceful, sustained argument that this era's Black abolitionists stood in the attitude of critics much more than of deployers of the ideological appeals of the American Revolution, see Sinha, *Slave's Cause*, 41–47, 66–76, 130–59. I personally do not think it necessary to think of their critical stance toward Patriot hypocrisy as mutually exclusive of their willingness to leverage the Patriots' ideals. Sinha does not seem to go as far as to suggest such a mutual exclusion, but her emphasis is almost entirely on the critiques.
67. Waldstreicher, *Odyssey of Phillis Wheatley*, esp. 6–9, 285–304, quotations on 293, 300. For more on her relationship to the politics of the day, see Wheatley, *Complete Writings*, 75–76, 88–90, 90–94, 101–2; Carretta, *Phillis Wheatley* 154–60, 174; and Sinha, *Slave's Cause*, 29–33. For a useful admonition against reading Black authors' antislavery commitments in isolation from their other priorities and their political savvy, see Hanley, *Beyond Slavery and Abolition*, passim, esp. 13.
68. Wheatley, *Complete Writings*, 39–40; see also xxviii, 128–31, 143–44.
69. Wheatley, *Complete Writings*, 152–53.
70. Waldstreicher, "Ancients, Moderns, and Africans," 726, 727, 732.
71. Lascelles, *Granville Sharp*, 35–49; Hoare, *Memoirs of Granville Sharp*, 118–27, 172–202.
72. Sharp, *Declaration of the People's*, 17–18. For a passage where he blurred that line, see Sharp, *Representation of the Injustice*, 15–18.
73. Granville Sharp to Anthony Benezet, 21 Aug. 1772, Granville Sharp Manuscripts, Boston Public Library; also reprinted in Brookes, *Friend Anthony Benezet*, 420–21. Sharp also told Lord North and Benjamin Rush as much; see Hoare, *Memoirs of Granville Sharp*, 78–79, and Sharp to Benjamin Rush, 21 Feb. 1774, in Woods, ed., *Correspondence of Benjamin Rush*, 4.
74. Sharp, *Representation of the Injustice*, 80–90, quotations on 82, 81, 87.
75. Benjamin Rush to Granville Sharp, 29 Oct. 1773, 27 July 1774, 18 July 1775, 1 Nov. 1774, in Woods, ed., "Correspondence of Benjamin Rush," 3, 10, 16, 14. For other letters intertwining these causes, see Woods, ed., "Correspondence of Benjamin Rush," 6–9, and Rush, *Letters*, 1:79, 81–84.
76. Rush, *Letters*, 1:83–84.
77. Bruns, 239, 243. For some similar points from Rush's fellow Philadelphian Richard Wells, see [Wells], *A Few Political Reflections*, 5, 24, 28, 75–86.
78. Millar, *Origin of the Distinction*, 278–79. For Millar's political leanings during the imperial crisis, see 61–68.

79. Bailyn, ed., *Pamphlets of the American Revolution*, 408–82, quotation on 439; Basker and Seary, eds., *Black Writers*, 114–15, 122–25, quotation on 76.
80. Bruns, 335.
81. Davis, *Problem of Slavery in the Age of Revolution*, 280; Bruns, 107–9, quotations on 109. See also MacMaster, "Arthur Lee's 'Address,'" 154–55. MacMaster's article not only includes the full original text of Lee's address but also nicely contextualizes its arguments and reception in Virginia.
82. For more evidence of the sheer size of this chorus, see Bruns, 98, 135–36, 208, 214, 228–32, 239–43, 273–77, 293–302, 326, 335–40, 344–47, 376–79.
83. Sharp, *Just Limitation of Slavery*, appendix 9; Sharp, *Law of Liberty*, 16; Basker and Seary, eds., *Black Writers*, 180. See also Benezet, *Serious Considerations*, 27–28; Benezet, *Short Observations*, 1–5; Benezet, *Complete Antislavery Writings*, 220–34; Brookes, *Friend Anthony Benezet*, 110–37, 497–500; Wheatley, *Complete Writings*, 90–94, 101–2; Basker and Seary, eds., *Black Writers*, 152–53, 179–83; and Cameron, *To Plead Our Own Cause*, 65–69.
84. Bruns, 408–9, 425, 429, 438–40, 446, 453, 456–59, 475–86, quotations on 385, 477. For yet other examples of antislavery usages of the theme of consistency, see *Pennsylvania Packet*, 3 Aug. 1782, 1 Feb. 1783; *Independent Gazetteer* (Philadelphia), 10 Aug. 1782; Donnan, ed., *Documents Illustrative*, 3:77–78; Green, *Observations*, 15; Adams, 3:18–19, 389; and *Sermon, on the Present Situation*, 9.
85. Holton, ed., *Black Americans*, 72–73; Kaplan and Kaplan, *Black Presence*, 27–28. For another African American appeal to white Patriots for consistency, see Haynes, *Black Preacher to White America*, 17–30.
86. Indeed, Pennsylvania's law was itself tremendously controversial and fragile even in the short term; see Larson, *American Inheritance*, 141–44, and Basker and Seary, eds., *Black Writers*, 216–20.
87. Taylor, ed., *Massachusetts, Colony to Commonwealth*, 53, 64–65, 69, 81, 125, 133–36, 154, quotations on 53, 65, 69, 81; Gosse, *First Reconstruction*, 2, 149, 159–60, 170–71, quotations on 170. For a rather different reading, see Willi Paul Adams's classic account of revolutionary state constitutions in which he covers these debates over Black suffrage but waves them away as "surely not typical of the rest of the country." This is in service of his overall argument that "neither the political theory nor the social practice of whites towards blacks changed in any basic way in the years 1764 to 1783." Adams, *First American Constitutions*, 164–88, quotations on 185, 181. For other examples of antiracism in the Revolutionary War era, see Sandoz, ed., *Political Sermons*, 1:456.
88. Barlow, *Works*, 2:6, 10.
89. *Spirit*, 405–6. For another example of this idea beyond those cited below, see Basker, ed., *American Antislavery Writings*, 75.

90. Benjamin Rush to Nathanael Greene, 16 Sept. 1782, in Rush, *Letters*, 1:286.
91. Carretta, ed., *Unchained Voices*, 142–44. The legislature only paid out for one year, so in 1787 Belinda repetitioned for resumption of payments.
92. *Spirit*, 407; William Cushing Judicial Notebook, Massachusetts Historical Society. Gloria McCahon Whiting's recent analysis upholds Cushing in a way, positing that Massachusetts public opinion, as reflected by slaveholders giving up in wartime negotiations with enslaved people, had already abolished slavery, which change such legal decisions ratified. See Whiting, "Emancipation without the Courts." For another illuminating discussion of what was and was not new about this case, see Blanton, "This Species of Property," 566–83.
93. *Boston Evening-Post*, 7 Sept. 1772.
94. *Boston Evening-Post*, 21 Sept.–26 Oct. 1772.
95. Rhodehamel, ed., *American Revolution*, 689.
96. Massey, *John Laurens*, quotation on 63; Massey, "Limits of Antislavery Thought," 501–4, 514, quotation on 504. For other examples of Laurens's accepting American guilt for slavery, see *Laurens*, 12:305, 390–92.
97. *LD*, 16:397, 20:627. For other Virginia slaveholders who opposed at least the most egregious violations of the ideas of liberty, see McDonnell, *Politics of War*, 486–87.
98. For a systematic analysis of this strand in abolitionist discourse, see Coffey, "'Tremble, Britannia!'" His interpretation stresses Providentialism's consistent role in sustaining abolitionists' efforts from the 1750s through the 1800s, but he does allow for (although he does not fully explore) the idea that nonabolitionists' responses to that rhetoric changed over time. For another excellent discussion of such themes accelerating in the 1770s, see Essig, *Bonds of Wickedness*. For examples of how prevalent this belief and rhetoric, in addition to those in the next few notes, see [Wells], *A Few Political Reflections*, 83; Bruns, 97–98, 226, 273, 364, 376–79; *APW*, 1:184, 305–17; "Timothy Pickering," in *BG*, 26 May 1766, supplement; and *Boston Evening-Post*, 2 Nov. 1772.
99. Benezet, *Complete Antislavery Writings*, 6–111, 160, 181, quotation on 106. For his private warnings of this sort, see Brookes, *Friend Anthony Benezet*, 272–74, 284, 292, 294–96, 301, 318–21; Benezet to the "Society for the Propagating the Gospel," [1767], Anthony Benezet Collection, New-York Historical Society; Benezet to Joseph Phipps, 28 May 1763; Benezet to George Dillwyn, 15 Feb. 1774; Anthony Benezet Letters, Haverford College Library; and Benezet to Granville Sharp, 14 May 1772, Granville Sharp Collection, New-York Historical Society. In these private letters in particular, one can observe some of Benezet's mental process in figuring out what would make for good abolitionist activism.

100. Cameron, *To Plead Our Own Cause*, 29–49, quotation on 44; "Lover of Constitutional Liberty," appendix, 12.
101. "Notes on the King agt. Stapleton," 1771, Granville Sharp Collection, New-York Historical Society; Sharp, *Representation of the Injustice*, 72n.
102. *APW*, 1:305–17, quotations on 306, 315.
103. Samuel Allinson to Patrick Henry, 17 Oct. 1774, in Bruns, 349.
104. Granville Sharp to Benjamin Rush, 27 July 1774, in Woods, eds., "Correspondence of Benjamin Rush," 10.
105. Bruns, 237, quotation on 231. Arthur Lee in 1767 also hinted this about slave insurrections; see Bruns, 110–11.
106. Winchester, *Reigning Abominations*, 7, 31. See also "Assecla Majorum," in *MG*, 1 June 1769; Bruns, 316–21, 325–27, 334–36; and Gadsden, *Writings*, 72.
107. Samuel Hopkins to Thomas Cushing, 29 Dec. 1775, in *Adams*, 3:388–90.
108. *Spirit*, 405–6. See also *LD*, 19:358n4; Bruns, 385–86; and Paine, *Writings*, 1:65–66, 188–89.
109. Bruns, 399.
110. Bruns, 434–35.
111. Lemuel Haynes, "Liberty Further Extended; or, Free Thoughts on the Illegality of Slave-keeping," in Haynes, *Black Preacher to White America*, 17–30, quotations 18, 19, 27. For Haynes's devotion to the Patriot cause, see Haynes, "Liberty Further Extended," 9–15.
112. "Humanity" to John Adams, 23 Jan. 1776, in *Adams*, 3:411. For more examples of such arguments, see *Adams*, 414, 424–26, 432–36, 460–65; Benezet, *Serious Considerations*, 27–40; Benezet, *Complete Antislavery Writings*, 220–34; Butterfield et al., eds., *Adams Family Correspondence*, 1:313; Sharp, *Law of Liberty*, esp. 46–49; "Antibiastes," *Observations on the Slaves*, 2; Green, *Observations*, 15; "Brief of Levi Lincoln," 440; *Pennsylvania Packet*, 3 Aug. 1782; *Independent Gazetteer* (Philadelphia), 10 Aug. 1782; Taylor, ed., *Massachusetts, Colony to Commonwealth*, 64–65; Brookes, *Friend Anthony Benezet*, 499; Taylor, *Unity in Christ and Country*, 65–73; Jay, *Correspondence and Public Papers*, 1:407; Jay, *Selected Papers*, 2:253; and Jay, *Life of John Jay*, 230.
113. See, e.g., Benezet, *Short Observations*, 3, 4; *Pennsylvania Packet*, 3 Aug. 1782; and *Independent Gazetteer* (Philadelphia), 10 Aug. 1782.
114. *Pennsylvania Packet*, 1 Feb. 1783.
115. *APW*, 1:349; Holton, ed., *Black Americans*, 76. For another fleeting abolitionist appeal to honor, see Benezet, *Short Observations*, 4.
116. *APW*, 1:105. See also McDonald, ed., *Empire and Nation*, 14, 58, 60; *Virginia Gazette* (Rind), 28 Jan. 1773; Quincy, *Observations*, 69; *RV*, 1:157; and *Adams*, 2:297.

117. Richard Henry Lee to [Arthur Lee], 4 July 1765, in *Lee*, 1:10; *Virginia Gazette* (Rind), 28 Jan. 1773. See also Quincy, *Portrait of a Patriot*, 1:151, 225; Jensen, ed., *Tracts of the American Revolution*, 89; *BG*, 30 Dec. 1765, 18 Jan. 1768, 3 Aug. 1772; Morgan, ed., *Prologue to Revolution*, 160; and Zubly, "A Warm and Zealous Spirit," 125–26.
118. *MG*, 6 Nov. 1766 (supplement).
119. *Franklin*, 16:19–20; *BG*, 24 Aug. 1767.
120. *Virginia Gazette* (Purdie and Dixon), 3 June 1773.
121. Quincy, *Portrait of a Patriot*, 1:225; 3:108–14, 211–24, 248–57, 270–75, quotations on 1:225; 3:114, 221.
122. Abigail Adams to John Adams, 22 Sept. 1774, 31 March 1776, in Butterfield et al., eds., *Adams Family Correspondence*, 1:162, 369; see also 1:357, 381–82.
123. Gadsden, *Writings*, 77.
124. Quoted in Harris, *Hanging of Thomas Jeremiah*, 51.
125. Washington, *Papers: Colonial Series*, 10:155.
126. For New England identity, see, e.g., Blassingame, "American Nationalism." David Brion Davis argued that the strong "temptation to sectionalize a national burden of 'inconsistency' first arose in England" with the drive to label the colonies slave soil and Britain free soil; see *Problem of Slavery in the Age of Revolution*, 386–402, quotation on 386. As the first chapter of the present volume and earlier parts of this chapter demonstrate, that is true in its largest sense. But as a political shield wielded during the imperial crisis, the Patriots were the leading practitioners. For a similar analysis to mine here, see Waldstreicher, *Slavery's Constitution*, 25–29, 31–33.
127. Bailyn, ed., *Pamphlets of the American Revolution*, 439; Jensen, ed., *Tracts of the American Revolution*, 3–18, quotation on 11.
128. Entry for 26 Aug. 1771, in Marchant, *Journell of a Voyage*.
129. *LD*, 1:179. For other examples of this move, see *BG*, 13 Jan., 19 May 1766; *Virginia Gazette* (Dixon and Hunter), 25 July 1777; *GM* 46 (Feb. 1776): 61; and [Lee], *Essay in Vindication*, esp. iv, 30.
130. *BP*, 1:139–88; 3:74, quotations on 1:178, 182.
131. Rush, *Letters*, 1:76–77, 85.
132. *JCC*, 6:1093. For this and other evidence of American sectionalism in Jefferson's notes, see Jefferson, *Papers*, 1:314–15, 320–27.
133. Edmund Burke to Arthur Middleton, 25 Jan. 1782, in Middleton, 26:194. For some examples of such rhetoric among proponents, see Jay, *Correspondence and Public Papers*, 1:191–93, and *Laurens*, 12:305.
134. See, e.g., Edward Rutledge to John Jay, 29 June 1776, in Jay, *Correspondence and Public Papers*, 1:67–68.
135. Christopher Gadsden to Gov. John Mathews, 16 Oct. 1782, in Gadsden, *Writings*, 179–83.

136. Brown, "From Slaves to Subjects," 111–40, quotation on 114. This chapter seems to me to be in some tension with Brown's significant monograph, which characterizes the direct impact of the imperial crisis and war years as being limited. In short, in the monograph's telling, the implications for British antislavery of this imperial crisis remained "unrecognized" until the postwar period. Brown, *Moral Capital*, 105–206, quotation on 134. For a similar downplaying of British antislavery momentum during the war years, see Drescher, *Abolition*, 112–45. I hope that my discussion here makes it clear that while I agree that the full implications of the American Revolution's legacy did come more clearly into view in the postwar years, it had a short-term impact on the British politics of slavery as well, which were not dormant during the war years.
137. Burnard, *Writing Early America*, 74–75.
138. Richardson, *Principles and Agents*, 97–201, quotations on 101, 103, 136–37, 190. For a good review that shows especially well how intensive and vigorous debates over the rise of British abolitionism have been, see Bender, ed., *Antislavery Debate*.
139. Jasanoff, *Liberty's Exiles*, 11–14, 57–109, 215–34, quotations on 91.
140. Gould, *Among the Powers of the Earth*, 147–57, quotation on 153. For a similar idea developed in less depth for the war years, see Brown, *Moral Capital*, 312.
141. Krise, ed., *Caribbeana*, 333–36.
142. Parker, *Evidence of Our Transactions*, quotations on Enquiry, pp. 2, 13, 15, 28, 54.
143. Sharp, *Just Limitation of Slavery*, quotations on 2, appendix 31; Sharp, *Law of Liberty*, quotations on 48, 49; Sharp, *Law of Retribution*, quotations on 3, 148, 305.
144. BP, 5:233–78, quotations on 258, 269, 270, 271.
145. Wesley, *Political Writings*, 186–97. For another Loyalist preacher who adjudged both Americans and Britons to be recipients of divine fury via the war on account of slavery, see Sandoz, ed., *Political Sermons*, 1:567–68.
146. Sancho, *Letters of the Late Ignatius Sancho*, i–iv, 31–32, 71–72, 83, 117–29, 148–51, 197, 213, 225–28, 271–94, quotations on 119, 125, 149.
147. [Tucker], *Series of Answers*, 20–21.
148. Simmons, 6:336–39; Bonwick, *English Radicals*, 105. Hartley tried out these ideas on his frequent correspondent Benjamin Franklin before offering it to Parliament; see Hartley to Franklin, 14 Nov. 1775, in *Franklin*, 22:254–60.
149. GM 50 (Dec. 1780): 564; 51 (March 1781): 122–23; 51 (Sept. 1781): 417–18. This series began with an antislavery essay by "A West Indian," in *GM* 50 (Oct. 1780): 458–59.

150. "Agreement between A. Wright and James Johnston, Commissioners for Lieut. Gen. Leslie, and Edward Rutledge and Ben Geurard, Commissioners for Governor Mathews," 10 Oct. 1782, Carleton.
151. Virginia Delegates to Benjamin Harrison, 23 Aug. 1783, in *LD*, 20:583–84.
152. Charles James Fox to David Hartley, 9 Aug. 1783, in Giunta et al., eds., *Emerging Nation*, 1:916; see also 1:922.
153. Crary, ed., *Price of Loyalty*, 360–62.
154. For an example of this impulse in Loyalist political culture, see Boswell, *Life of Johnson*, 885–86.
155. *PR*, 14th Parliament, 7:3–23, 252–53, quotations on 4, 5, 8, 252–53.
156. Rugemer, *Slave Law*, 171–212, quotation on 207; O'Shaughnessy, *Empire Divided*, 137–248; Burnard, *Jamaica in the Age of Revolution*.
157. *PR*, 15th Parliament, 3:422.

Epilogue

1. *Derby [Eng.] Mercury*, 18 Sept. 1783.
2. The literature is vast, of course. But for an excellent summary of the two sides, as well as a vigorous statement of one of the competing interpretations, see Bailyn, *Faces of Revolution*, 225–78.
3. This brief summary also nods to a venerable and massive literature. For some of the most influential recent entries, see Van Cleve, *Slaveholders' Union*; Waldstreicher, *Slavery's Constitution*; Wilentz, *No Property in Man*; and Wood, *Power and Liberty*.
4. There is no better account of this management than Waldstreicher, *Slavery's Constitution*.
5. As well demonstrated by Waldstreicher, *Slavery's Constitution*, passim.
6. See Brown, *Moral Capital*, as well as other works I discuss at the end of chapter 7.

BIBLIOGRAPHY

Archival Sources
American Antiquarian Society, Worcester, Massachusetts
Robert Wormeley Carter Diary, 1774

Boston Public Library
Granville Sharp Manuscripts

Earl Gregg Swem Library, The College of William and Mary, Williamsburg, Virginia
Carter Family Papers, 1667–1862
Dunmore Family Papers
John Murray, 4th Earl of Dunmore Papers, 1768–1804

Houghton Library, Harvard College, Cambridge, Massachusetts
Arthur Lee Papers, 1741–1882

John D. Rockefeller Jr. Library of the Colonial Williamsburg Foundation, Williamsburg, Virginia
Cornwallis Orderly Book, 1781
Lord Dunmore, Speech to the General Assembly at Williamsburg, 1 June 1775
Lord Dunmore Correspondence, 1771–78
Sir Guy Carleton (British Headquarters) Papers, 1747–1783 (Photocopies of Originals in the National Archives, London)

Manuscripts Division, Library of Congress, Washington, D.C.
Elias Boudinot Papers, 1773–1812
Custis-Lee Family Papers, 1700–circa 1928
John Jay Papers, 1776–1809
Papers of John Murray, Earl of Dunmore

Massachusetts Historical Society, Boston
William Cushing Judicial Notebook, 1783, Cushing Papers, MHS Collections Online

National Library of Scotland, Edinburgh
Charles Steuart Papers

New-York Historical Society
Anthony Benezet Collection, 1768–1783
Granville Sharp Collection, 1768–1803

Quaker and Special Collections, Haverford
College Library, Haverford, Pennsylvania
Anthony Benezet Letters, 1750–1936

Virginia Historical Society, Richmond
Landon Carter Papers, 1763–1774
Letterbooks of Robert Carter of Nomini Hall, 1761–1773

William L. Clements Library, University of Michigan, Ann Arbor
Earl of Shelburne Papers
Henry Clinton Papers

PUBLISHED PRIMARY SOURCES

Adair, Douglass, and John A. Schutz, eds. *Peter Oliver's Origin and Progress of the American Rebellion: A Tory View*. San Marino, Calif.: Huntington Library, 1961.
Adams, John. *Diary and Autobiography of John Adams*. Edited by L. H. Butterfield. 4 vols. Cambridge, Mass.: Belknap Press of Harvard University Press, 1961.
Adams, John. *The Papers of John Adams*. Edited by Robert J. Taylor et al. 22 vols. to date. Cambridge, Mass.: Belknap Press of Harvard University Press, 1977–.
Addison, Joseph. *The Works of Joseph Addison*. Edited by George Washington Greene. 6 vols. Philadelphia: J. B. Lippincott, 1883.
An Address to the Right Honourable L—d M—sf—d; in Which the Measures of Government, Respecting America, Are Considered in a New Light: With a View to His Lordship's Interposition Therein. London: J. Almon, 1775.
"An African Merchant." *A Treatise upon the Trade from Great-Britain to Africa; Humbly Recommended to the Attention of the Government*. London: R. Baldwin, 1772.
[Alleyne, John Gay]. *A Letter to the North American, on Occasion of His Address to the Committee of Correspondence in Barbados. By a Native of the Island*. Barbados: George Esmand, 1766.

Andrews, Charles M., ed. *Narratives of the Insurrections, 1675–1690.* New York: Charles Scribner's Sons, 1915.

Annesley, James. *Memoirs of an Unfortunate Young Nobleman, Return'd from a Thirteen Years Slavery in America Where He Had Been Sent by the Wicked Contrivances of His Cruel Uncle.* 2 vols. London: J. Freeman, 1743.

An Answer to a Pamphlet, Entitled Taxation No Tyranny. Addressed to the Author, and to Persons in Power. London: J. Almon, 1775.

"Antibiastes." *Observations on the Slaves and the Indented Servants, Inlisted in the Army, and in the Navy of the United States.* Philadelphia: Styner and Cist, 1777.

Bailyn, Bernard, ed. *Pamphlets of the American Revolution, 1760–1776.* Cambridge, Mass.: Belknap Press of Harvard University Press, 1965.

Barlow, Joel. *The Works of Joel Barlow.* Edited by William K. Bottorff and Arthur L. Ford. 2 vols. Gainesville, Fla.: Scholars' Facsimiles and Reprints, 1970.

Basker, James G., ed. *Amazing Grace: An Anthology of Poems about Slavery, 1660–1810.* New Haven, Conn.: Yale University Press, 2002.

Basker, James G., ed. *American Antislavery Writings: Colonial Beginnings to Emancipation.* New York: Library of America, 2012.

Basker, James G., with Nicole Seary, eds. *Black Writers of the Founding Era, 1760–1800.* New York: Library of America, 2023.

Baurmeister, Carl Leopold. *Revolution in America: Confidential Letters and Journals 1776–1784 of Adjutant General Major Baurmeister of the Hessian Forces.* Edited and translated by Bernhard A. Uhlendorf. New Brunswick, N.J.: Rutgers University Press, 1957.

Bell, John. *An Epistle to Friends in Maryland, Virginia, Barbadoes, and the Other Colonies, and Islands in the West-Indies, Where Any Friends Are.* London: n.p., 1741.

Benezet, Anthony. *The Complete Antislavery Writings of Anthony Benezet, 1754–1783: An Annotated Critical Edition.* Edited by David E. Crosby. Baton Rouge: Louisiana State University Press, 2013.

Benezet, Anthony. *Observations on the Inslaving, Importing and Purchasing of Negroes.* 2nd ed. Germantown, Penn.: Christopher Sower, 1760.

Benezet, Anthony. *Serious Considerations on Several Important Subjects; viz. On War and Its Inconsistency with the Gospel, Observations on Slavery, and Remarks on the Nature and Bad Effects of Spiritous Liquors.* Philadelphia: Joseph Crukshank, 1778.

Benezet, Anthony. *A Short Account of That Part of Africa, Inhabited by the Negroes; . . . with a Quotation from George Wallis's System of the Laws, &c. and a Large Extract from a Pamphlet, Lately Published in London, on the Subject of the Slave Trade.* Philadelphia: W. Dunlap, 1762.

Benezet, Anthony. *Short Observations on Slavery, Introductory to Some Extracts from the Writing of the Abbe Raynal, on that Important Subject.* [Philadelphia: n.p., 1781.]

Beverley, Robert. *The History and Present State of Virginia*. Edited by Susan Scott Parrish. Chapel Hill: University of North Carolina Press, 2013.

Blackstone, Sir William. *Commentaries on the Laws of England*. Edited by Wilfrid Prest. 4 vols. 1765–69; Oxford: Oxford University Press, 2016.

Bland, Theodorick, Jr. *The Bland Papers: Being a Selection from the Manuscripts of Colonel Thedorick Bland, Jr., of Prince George County, Virginia*. Edited by Charles Campbell. 2 vols. Petersburg, Va.: Edmund and Julian C. Ruffin, 1840–42.

Bolingbroke, Henry St. John, Viscount. *Political Writings*. Edited by David Armitage. Cambridge: Cambridge University Press, 1997.

Bolts, William. *Considerations on India Affairs; Particularly Respecting the Present State of Bengal and Its Dependencies*. London: J. Almon, 1772.

Boswell, James. *Life of Johnson*. 1791; London: Oxford University Press, 1957.

Boucher, Jonathan. *A View of the Causes and Consequences of the American Revolution; in Thirteen Discourses, Preached in North America between the Years 1763 and 1775: With an Historical Preface*. London: G. G. and J. Robinson, 1797; reprint, New York: Russell and Russell, 1967.

[Bourke, Nicholas]. *The Privileges of the Island of Jamaica Vindicated*. London: J. Williams et al., 1766.

"Brief of Levi Lincoln in the Slave Case Tried 1781." *Collections of the Massachusetts Historical Society*, 5th series, 3 (1877): 438–42.

British Liberties; or, The Free-Born Subject's Inheritance; Containing the Laws That Form the Basis of Those Liberties, with Observations Thereon; Also an Introductory Essay on Political Liberty and a Comprehensive View of the Constitution of Great Britain. London: Woodfall and Strahan, 1766.

"A British Merchant." *The African Trade, the Great Pillar and Support of the British Plantation Trade in America*. London: J. Robinson, 1745.

Brokesby, Francis. *Some Proposals towards Promoting the Propagation of the Gospel in Our American Plantations*. London: George Sawbridge, 1708.

Burke, Edmund. *The Writings and Speeches of Edmund Burke*. Edited by Paul Langford. 9 vols. to date. Oxford: Clarendon Press, 1981–.

Burke, Edmund. *The Writings and Speeches of Edmund Burke*. 12 vols. Boston: Little, Brown, 1901.

[Burke, William, and Edmund Burke]. *An Account of the European Settlements in America*. 2nd ed. 2 vols. 1757; London: R. and J. Dodsley, 1758.

Burnaby, Andrew. *Travels through the Middle Settlements in North-America. In the Years 1759 and 1760. With Observations upon the State of the Colonies*. 2nd ed. 1775; reprint, Ithaca, N.Y.: Great Seal Books, 1960.

Butterfield, L. H., et al., eds. *Adams Family Correspondence*. 15 vols. to date. Cambridge, Mass.: Belknap Press of Harvard University Press, 1963–.

Campbell, Archibald. *Journal of an Expedition against the Rebels of Georgia in North America under the Orders of Archibald Campbell Esquire Lieut. Col. of*

His Majesty's 71st Regiment. Edited by Colin Campbell. 1778; Darien, Ga.: Ashantilly Press, 1981.
Carretta, Vincent, ed. *Unchained Voices: An Anthology of Black Authors in the English-Speaking World of the Eighteenth Century.* Lexington: University Press of Kentucky, 1996.
Carter, Landon. *The Diary of Colonel Landon Carter of Sabine Hall, 1752–1778.* Edited by Jack P. Greene. 2 vols. Charlottesville: University Press of Virginia, 1965.
Carter, Robert. *Letters of Robert Carter, 1720–1727.* Edited by Louis B. Wright. San Marino, Calif.: Huntington Library, 1940.
[Chalmers, James]. *Plain Truth; Addressed to the Inhabitants of America, Containing, Remarks on a Late Pamphlet, Entitled Common Sense . . . Written by Candidus.* Philadelphia: R. Bell, 1776.
[Clarke, Richard]. *The Nabob; or, Asiatic Plunderers. A Satyrical Poem, in a Dialogue between a Friend and the Author.* London: J. Townsend, 1773.
Clinton, Henry. *The American Rebellion: Sir Henry Clinton's Narrative of His Campaigns, 1775–1782.* Edited by William B. Willcox. New Haven, Conn.: Yale University Press, 1954.
Colbourn, H. Trevor, and Richard Peters, eds. "A Pennsylvania Farmer at the Court of King George: John Dickinson's London Letters, 1754–1756." *Pennsylvania Magazine of History and Biography* 86 (July, October 1962): 241–86, 417–53.
Commager, Henry Steele, and Richard B. Morris, eds. *The Spirit of 'Seventy Six: The Story of the American Revolution as Told by Participants.* New York: Harper and Row, 1967.
Condorcet, Marquis de. *Condorcet: Selected Writings.* Edited by Keith Michael Baker. Indianapolis: Bobbs-Merrill, 1976.
Considerations upon the Rights of the Colonists to the Privileges of British Subjects. New York: John Holt, 1766.
Crary, Catherine, ed. *The Price of Loyalty: Tory Writings from the Revolutionary Era.* New York: McGraw-Hill, 1973.
Cresswell, Nicholas. *The Journal of Nicholas Cresswell, 1774–1777.* New York: Dial Press, 1928.
Cumberland, Richard. *The West Indian; a Comedy, in Five Acts. As Performed at the Theatres Royal, Drury Lane and Covent Garden . . . with Remarks by Mrs. Inchbald.* London: Longman, Hurst, Rees, and Orme, [1806?].
Davies, K. G., ed. *Documents of the American Revolution, 1770–1783 (Colonial Office Series).* 21 vols. Shannon, Ireland: Irish University Press, 1972–81.
Day, Thomas. *The Dying Negro: A Poem.* 3rd ed. 1773; London: W. Flexney and J. Robson, 1775.
Dickinson, Harry T., ed. *British Pamphlets on the American Revolution, 1763–1785.* 8 vols. to date. London: Pickering and Chatto, 2007–.

[Dickinson, John]. *An Address to the Committee of Correspondence in Barbados. Occasioned by a Late Letter to Their Agent in London. By a North American.* Philadelphia: William Bradford, 1766.

[Dickinson, John]. *An Essay on the Constitutional Power of Great-Britain over the Colonies in America. With the Resolves of the Committee for the Province of Pennsylvania, and Their Instructions to Their Representatives in Assembly.* Philadelphia: William and Thomas Bradford, 1774.

Donnan, Elizabeth, ed. *Documents Illustrative of the History of the Slave Trade to America.* 4 vols. Washington, D.C.: Carnegie Institution of Washington, 1930–35.

[Draper, William]. *The Thoughts of a Traveller upon our American Disputes.* London: J. Ridley, 1774.

Englands Slavery; or, Barbados Merchandize; Represented in a Petition to the High and Honourable Court of Parliament, by Marcellus Rivers and Oxenbridge Foyle Gentlemen, on the Behalf of Themselves and Three-Score and Ten More Free-Born English-Men Sold (Uncondemned) into Slavery. London: n.p., 1659.

An Epistle of Caution and Advice, Concerning the Buying and Keeping of Slaves. Philadelphia: James Chattin, 1754.

Estwick, Samuel. *Considerations on the Negroe Cause Commonly So Called, Addressed to the Right Honourable Lord Mansfield.* London: J. Dodsley, 1773.

Evans, Caleb. *A Reply to the Rev. Mr. Fletcher's Vindication of Mr. Wesley's Calm Address to Our American Colonies.* Bristol: W. Pine, [1775].

Ewald, Johann. *Diary of the American War: A Hessian Journal.* Translated and edited by Joseph P. Tustin. New Haven, Conn.: Yale University Press, 1979.

The Farmer's and Monitor's Letters to the Inhabitants of the British Colonies. Williamsburg, Va.: William Rind, 1769.

Fithian, Philip Vickers. *Journal and Letters of Philip Vickers Fithian, 1773–1774: A Plantation Tutor of the Old Dominion.* New ed. 1900; Williamsburg, Va.: Colonial Williamsburg, 1957.

Fletcher, John. *A Vindication of the Rev. Mr. Wesley's "Calm Address to Our American Colonies": In Some Letters to Mr. Caleb Evans.* London: The Foundry, [1775].

Foote, Samuel. *The Nabob: A Comedy in Three Acts.* London: Mr. Colman, 1778; reprint, New York: D. Longworth, 1813.

Ford, Worthington C., ed. *Journals of the Continental Congress, 1774–1789.* 34 vols. Washington, D.C.: U.S. Government Printing Office, 1904–37.

Fortescue, J. W., ed. *The Correspondence of King George the Third from 1760 to December 1783: Printed from the Original Papers in the Royal Archives at Windsor Castle.* 6 vols. London: Macmillan, 1927–28.

Fox, George. *A Journal or Historical Account of the Life, Travels, Sufferings, Christian Experiences, and Labour of Love in the Work of the Ministry, of ... George Fox.* 2 vols. Philadelphia: Marcus T. C. Gould and Isaac T. Hopper, 1831.

Fox, George. *To the Ministers, Teachers, and Priests, (So Called and So Stileing Your Selves) in Barbadoes*. London: n.p., 1672.
Franklin, Benjamin. *Benjamin Franklin's Letters to the Press, 1758–1775*. Edited by Verner W. Crane. Chapel Hill: University of North Carolina Press, 1950.
Franklin, Benjamin. *Papers of Benjamin Franklin*. Edited by Leonard W. Labaree et al. 42 vols. to date. New Haven, Conn.: Yale University Press, 1967–.
Freneau, Philip. *The Poems of Philip Freneau, Poet of the American Revolution*. Edited by Fred Lewis Pattee. 3 vols. Princeton, N.J.: Princeton University Library, 1902–7.
Freneau, Philip. *The Prose of Philip Freneau*. Edited by Philip M. Marsh. New Brunswick, N.J.: Scarecrow Press, 1955.
Gadsden, Christopher. *The Writings of Christopher Gadsden, 1746–1805*. Edited by Richard Walsh. Columbia: University of South Carolina Press, 1966.
Gee, Joshua. *The Trade and Navigation of Great-Britain Considered*. 4th ed. 1730; London: A. Bettesworth, C. Hitch, and S. Birt, 1738.
Gellman, David N., and David Quigley, eds. *Jim Crow New York: A Documentary History of Race and Citizenship, 1777–1877*. New York: New York University Press, 2003.
Gibbes, Robert W., ed. *Documentary History of the American Revolution: Consisting of Letters and Papers Relating to the Contest for Liberty, Chiefly in South Carolina*. 3 vols. New York: D. Appleton, 1853–55; reprint, Spartanburg, S.C.: Reprint Company, 1972.
Giunta, Mary A., et al., eds. *The Emerging Nation: A Documentary History of the Foreign Relations of the United States under the Articles of Confederation, 1780–1789*. 3 vols. Washington, D.C.: U.S. Government Printing Office, 1996.
Godwyn, Morgan. *The Negro's and Indians Advocate, Suing for Their Admission into the Church; or, A Persuasive to the Instructing and Baptizing of the Negro's and Indians in Our Plantations*. London: J. D., 1680.
Goldsmith, Oliver. *The Vicar of Wakefield: A Tale Supposed to Be Written by Himself*. Edited by Arthur Friedman. 1766; reprint, London: Oxford University Press, 1974.
Green, Jacob. *Observations on the Reconciliation of Great Britain and the Colonies. By a Friend of American Liberty*. New York: John Holt, 1776.
Greenblatt, Stephen, ed. *The Norton Anthology of English Literature*, vol. C, *The Restoration and the Eighteenth Century*. 9th ed. 1962; New York: Norton, 2012.
Greene, Jack P., ed. "'A Plain and Natural Right to Life and Liberty': An Early Natural Rights Attack on the Excesses of the Slave System in Colonial British America." *William and Mary Quarterly*, 3rd series, 57 (October 2000): 793–808.
Greene, Nathanel. *The Papers of General Nathanael Greene*. Edited by Richard K. Showman et al. 13 vols. Chapel Hill: University of North Carolina Press, 1976–2005.

Hair, P. E. H., ed. "Slavery and Liberty: The Case of the Scottish Colliers." *Slavery and Abolition* 21 (December 2000): 136–51.

Hall, Clayton Colman, ed. *Narratives of Early Maryland, 1633–1684*. New York: Barnes and Noble, 1910.

Hamilton, Alexander. *The Papers of Alexander Hamilton*. Edited by Harold C. Syrett et al. 27 vols. New York: Columbia University Press, 1961–87.

Hammon, Briton. *A Narrative of the Uncommon Sufferings, and Surprizing Deliverance of Briton Hammon, a Negro Man*. Boston: Green and Russell, 1760.

Hammon, Jupiter. *America's First Negro Poet: The Complete Works of Jupiter Hammon of Long Island*. Edited by Stanley Austin Ransom Jr. Port Washington, N.Y.: Kennikat Press, 1983.

Hampton, Christopher, ed. *A Radical Reader: The Struggle for Change in England, 1381–1914*. Nottingham, U.K.: Spokesman Books, 1984.

Hargrave, Francis. *An Argument in the Case of James Sommersett, a Negro, Lately Determined by the Court of King's Bench: Wherein It Is Attempted to Demonstrate the Present Unlawfulness of Domestic Slavery in England*. London: F. Hargrave, 1772.

Haynes, Lemuel. *Black Preacher to White America: The Collected Writings of Lemuel Haynes, 1774–1833*. Edited by Richard Newman. Brooklyn, N.Y.: Carlson, 1990.

Hoare, Prince. *Memoirs of Granville Sharp, Esq. Composed from His Own Manuscripts, and Other Authentic Documents in the Possession of His Family and of the African Institution*. London: Henry Colburn, 1820.

Holton, Woody, ed. *Black Americans in the Revolutionary Era: A Brief History with Documents*. Boston: Bedford/St. Martin's, 2009.

Hopkins, Samuel. *The Works of Samuel Hopkins, D.D., . . . with a Memoir of His Life and Character*. 3 vols. Boston: Doctrinal Tract and Book Society, 1854.

Hulton, Anne. *Letters of a Loyalist Lady: Being the Letters of Anne Hulton, Sister of Henry Hulton, Commissioner of Customs at Boston, 1767–1776*. Cambridge, Mass.: Harvard University Press, 1927.

Hutchinson, Thomas. *The Diary and Letters of His Excellency Thomas Hutchinson, Esq.* Edited by Peter Orlando Hutchinson. 2 vols. 1884–86; reprint, New York: Burt Franklin, 1971.

[Hutchinson, Thomas]. *Strictures upon the Declaration of the Congress at Philadelphia; in a Letter to a Noble Lord*. London: n.p., 1776.

Hyneman, Charles S., and Donald S. Lutz, eds. *American Political Writing during the Founding Era, 1760–1805*. 2 vols. Indianapolis: Liberty Fund, 1983.

"An Independent Whig." *The Revolution in MDCCLXXXII Impartially Considered*. London: J. Debrett, 1782.

Iredell, James. *The Papers of James Iredell*. Edited by Don Higginbotham. 2 vols. Raleigh, N.C.: Division of Archives and History, 1976.

Jay, John. *The Correspondence and Public Papers of John Jay, 1763–1826.* Edited by Henry Johnston. 4 vols. 1890–93; reprint, New York: Da Capo Press, 1971.
Jay, John. *The Selected Papers of John Jay.* Edited by Elizabeth M. Nuxoll et al. 7 vols. Charlottesville: University of Virginia Press, 2010–21.
Jay, William. *Life of John Jay: With Selections from His Correspondence and Miscellaneous Papers.* 2 vols. 1833; reprint, Freeport, N.Y.: Books for Libraries Press, 1972.
Jefferson, Thomas. *Notes on the State of Virginia, with Related Documents.* Edited by David Waldstreicher. 1787; Boston: Bedford/St. Martin's, 2002.
Jefferson, Thomas. *The Papers of Thomas Jefferson.* Edited by Julian P. Boyd et al. 48 vols. to date. Princeton, N.J.: Princeton University Press, 1950–.
Jensen, Merrill, ed. *Tracts of the American Revolution, 1763–1776.* Indianapolis: Bobbs-Merrill, 1967.
Johnson, Samuel. *The Letters of Samuel Johnson.* Edited by Bruce Redford. 5 vols. Princeton, N.J.: Princeton University Press, 1992–94.
[Johnson, Samuel]. *Taxation No Tyranny: An Answer to the Resolutions and Address of the American Congress.* 3rd ed. London: T. Cadell, 1775.
Johnson, Samuel. *The Yale Edition of the Works of Samuel Johnson.* Edited by E. L. McAdam Jr. et al. 23 vols. New Haven, Conn.: Yale University Press, 1958–.
Johnson, Samuel, and James Boswell. *A Journey to the Western Islands of Scotland; and the Journal of a Tour to the Hebrides.* Edited by Peter Levi. 1775, 1786; reprint, New York: Penguin, 1984.
Jones, Hugh. *The Present State of Virginia, from Whence Is Inferred a Short View of Maryland and North Carolina.* Edited by Richard L. Morton. 1724; reprint, Chapel Hill: University of North Carolina Press, 1956.
"Journal of a French Traveller in the Colonies, 1765, I." *American Historical Review* 26 (July 1921): 726–47.
"Journal of a French Traveller in the Colonies, 1765, II." *American Historical Review* 27 (October 1921): 70–89.
Journal of the House of Delegates of Virginia. Charlottesville, Va.: Dunlap and Hayes, [1781].
Kalm, Peter. *Peter Kalm's Travels in North America: The English Version of 1770.* Edited by Adolph B. Benson. 2 vols. New York: Wilson-Erickson, 1937.
Kearsley, G., ed. *American Gazette. Being a Collection of All the Authentic Addresses, Memorials, Letters, &c., Which Relate to the Present Disputes between Great Britain and Her Colonies.* 2nd ed. London: G. Kearsley, 1768–69.
Keir, Archibald. *Thoughts on the Affairs of Bengal.* London: n.p., 1772.
Keith, Sir William. *The History of the British Plantations in America.* London: S. Richardson, 1738.
Klingberg, Frank J., ed. *Codrington Chronicle: An Experiment in Anglican Altruism on a Barbados Plantation, 1710–1834.* Berkeley: University of California Press, 1949.

Krise, Thomas W., ed. *Caribbeana: An Anthology of English Literature of the West Indies, 1657–1777*. Chicago: University of Chicago Press, 1999.
Laurens, Henry. *The Papers of Henry Laurens*. Edited by George C. Rogers et al. 16 vols. Columbia: University of South Carolina Press, 1980–2003.
Lay, Benjamin. *All Slave-Keepers That Keep the Innocent in Bondage, Apostates Pretending to Lay Claim to the Pure & Holy Christian Religion*. Philadelphia: n.p., 1737.
[Lee, Arthur]. *An Appeal to the Justice and Interests of the People of Great Britain, in the Present Dispute with America. By Doctor Lee, of Virginia*. 4th ed. 1774; New York: James Rivington, 1775.
Lee, Arthur. *An Essay in Vindication of the Continental Colonies of America, from a Censure of Mr. Adam Smith, in His Theory of Moral Sentiments. With Some Reflections on Slavery in General. By an American*. London: T. Becket and P. A. DeHondt, 1764.
[Lee, Arthur]. *A Second Appeal to the Justice and Interests of the People, on the Measures Respecting America. By the Author of the First*. London: J. Almon, 1775.
Lee, Charles. *The Lee Papers*. 4 vols. New York: New York Historical Society Collections, 1871–74.
Lee, Richard Henry. *The Letters of Richard Henry Lee*. Edited by James Curtis Ballagh. 2 vols. New York: Macmillan, 1911–14.
Lee, Richard Henry. *Life of Arthur Lee, LL.D., Joint Commissioner of the United States to the Court of France, . . . with His Political and Literary Correspondence and His Papers*. 2 vols. Boston: Wells and Lilly, 1829.
Le Jau, Francis. *The Carolina Chronicle of Dr. Francis Le Jau, 1706–1717*. Edited by Frank J. Klingberg. Berkeley: University of California Press, 1956.
Leslie, Charles. *A New History of Jamaica, from the Earliest Accounts, to the Taking of Porto Bello by Vice-Admiral Vernon. In Thirteen Letters from a Gentleman to His Friend*. 2nd ed. London: J. Hodges, 1740.
Lesuire, Robert Martin. *The Savages of Europe. From the French*. Translated by James Pettit Andrews. London: T. Davies, 1764.
"The Letters of Hon. James Habersham, 1756–1775." *Collections of the Georgia Historical Society* 6 (1904): 9–245.
Ligon, Richard. *A True and Exact History of the Island of Barbadoes*. London, 1657; reprint, London: Frank Cass, 1970.
[Lind, John]. *Three Letters to Dr. Price, Containing Remarks on His Observations on the Nature of Civil Liberty, the Principles of Government, and the Justice and Policy of War with America*. London: T. Payne, J. Sewell, and P. Elmsly, 1776.
[Lind, John, and Jeremy Bentham]. *An Answer to the Declaration of the American Congress*. 5th ed. London: T. Cadell, 1776.
Locke, John. *Two Treatises of Government*. Edited by Mark Goldie. 1689; London: Everyman, 1993.

Lofft, Capel. *Reports of Cases Adjudged in the Court of King's Bench, from Easter Term 12 Geo. 3 to Michaelmas 14 Geo. 3 (Both Inclusive), 1772–1774*. London, 1776; reprint, n.p.: General Books, 2010.
[Long, Edward]. *English Humanity No Paradox; or, An Attempt to Prove, That the English Are Not a Nation of Savages*. London: T. Lowndes, 1778.
Long, Edward. *The History of Jamaica; or, General Survey of the Antient and Modern State of That Island*. 3 vols. 1774; reprint, London: Frank Cass, 1970.
Lovell, James. *An Oration Delivered April 2d, 1771. At the Request of the Inhabitants of the Town of Boston; to Commemorate the Bloody Tragedy of the Fifth of March, 1770*. Boston: Edes and Gill, 1771.
"A Lover of Constitutional Liberty." *The Appendix; or, Some Observations on the Expediency of the Petition of the Africans, Living in Boston, &c. Lately Presented to the General Assembly of this Province. . . . Likewise, Thoughts on Slavery*. Boston: E. Russell, 1773.
MacNicol, Donald. *Remarks on Dr. Samuel Johnson's Journey to the Hebrides*. London, 1779; reprint, New York: Garland, 1974.
Madison, James. *The Papers of James Madison*. Edited by William T. Hutchinson et al. 17 vols. Charlottesville: University Press of Virginia, 1962–91.
Mancall, Peter C., ed. *Envisioning America: English Plans for the Colonization of North America, 1580–1640*. 2nd ed. 1995; Boston: Bedford/St. Martin's, 2017.
Mandeville, Bernard. *The Fable of the Bees; or, Private Virtues, Publick Benefits*. Edited by F. B. Kaye. 2 vols. 1714–39; reprint, Oxford: Clarendon Press, 1924.
Marchant, Henry. *Journell of a Voyage from Newport in the Colony of Rhode Island to London, Travels thro' Many Parts of England and Scotland—Began July 8th 1771*. Microfilm. Rhode Island Historical Society, Providence.
Martin, Joseph Plumb. *A Narrative of a Revolutionary Soldier: Some of the Adventures, Dangers, and Sufferings of Joseph Plumb Martin*. 1830; reprint, New York: Signet Classics, 2010.
Martin, Samuel. *An Essay upon Plantership*. London: A. Millar, 1765.
Martin, Samuel, Sr. *A Short Treatise on the Slavery of Negroes in the British Colonies*. Antigua: Robert Mearns, 1775.
Mason, Matthew, and Nicholas Mason, eds. *The History of the Life and Adventures of Mr. Anderson*. Plymouth, U.K.: Broadview, 2009.
[Mather, Increase]. *The Declaration, of the Gentlemen, Merchants, and Inhabitants of BOSTON, and the Countrey Adjacent. April 18th. 1689*. Boston: Samuel Green, 1689.
Mayhew, Jonathan. *The Snare Broken. A Thanksgiving-Discourse, Preached at the Desire of the West Church in Boston, N.E. Friday May 23, 1766, Occasioned by the Repeal of the Stamp Act*. Boston: R. and S. Draper, 1766.
McDonald, Forrest, ed. *Empire and Nation*. Indianapolis: Liberty Fund, 1999.
Middleton, Arthur. "Correspondence of Hon. Arthur Middleton, Signer of the Declaration of Independence." Edited by Joseph W. Barnwell. *South Carolina*

Historical and Genealogical Magazine 26 (October 1925): 183–213; 27 (January 1926): 1–29; 27 (April 1926): 51–80; 27 (July 1926): 107–55.

Millar, John. *The Origin of the Distinction of Ranks; or, An Inquiry into the Circumstances Which Give Rise to Influence and Authority, in the Different Members of Society*. 1771; reprint, Indianapolis: Liberty Fund, 2006.

Molyneux, William. *The Case of Ireland Stated*. 1698; reprint, Dublin: Cadenus Press, 1977.

Montesquieu, Charles de Secondat, Baron de. *The Spirit of the Laws*. Translated and edited by Anne M. Cohler, Basia Carolyn Miller, and Harold Samuel Stone. 1748; reprint, Cambridge: Cambridge University Press, 1989.

Moore, Frank, ed. *Songs and Ballads of the American Revolution*. 1855; reprint, Port Washington, N.Y.: Kennikat Press, 1964.

Morgan, Edmund S., ed. *Prologue to Revolution: Sources and Documents on the Stamp Act Crisis, 1764–1766*. Chapel Hill: University of North Carolina Press, 1959.

[Morgann, Maurice]. *A Plan for the Abolition of Slavery in the West Indies*. London: William Griffin, 1772.

Morison, Samuel Eliot, ed. *Sources and Documents Illustrating the American Revolution, 1764–1788, and the Formation of the Federal Constitution*. 2nd ed. 1923; Oxford: Oxford University Press, 1929.

Murray, James. *Letters from America, 1773 to 1780: Being the Letters of a Scots Officer, Sir James Murray, to His Home during the War of American Independence*. Edited by Eric Robson. Manchester, U.K.: Manchester University Press, 1951.

Neville, Sylas. *The Diary of Sylas Neville, 1767–1788*. Edited by Basil Cozens-Hardy. London: Oxford University Press, 1950.

Nicholls, John. *Recollections and Reflections, Personal and Political, as Connected with Public Affairs, during the Reign of George III*. 2nd ed. 2 vols. London: Longman, Hurst, Rees, Orme, and Brown, 1822.

[Nisbet, Richard]. *Slavery Not Forbidden by Scripture; or, A Defence of the West-India Planters, from the Aspersions Thrown Out against Them, by the Author of a Pamphlet, Entitled, "An Address to the Inhabitants of the British Settlements in America, upon Slave-Keeping." By a West-Indian*. Philadelphia: n.p., 1773.

Oldmixon, John. *The British Empire in America, Containing a History of the Discovery, Settlement, Progress and Present State of All the British Colonies, on the Continent and Islands of America*. 2 vols. London: John Nicholson, 1708.

Paine, Thomas. *Thomas Paine: A Collection of Unknown Writings*. Edited by Hazel Burgess. New York: Palgrave Macmillan, 2010.

Paine, Thomas. *Thomas Paine: Collected Writings*. Edited by Eric Foner. New York: Library of America, 1995.

Paine, Thomas. *The Thomas Paine Reader*. Edited by Michael Foot and Isaac Kramnick. New York: Penguin, 1987.

Paine, Thomas. *The Writings of Thomas Paine.* Edited by Moncure Daniel Conway. 4 vols. New York: AMS Press, 1967.
Paley, William. *The Principles of Moral and Political Philosophy.* 2nd ed. 1785; London: J. Davis, 1786.
The Pamphlet, Entitled "Taxation No Tyranny," Candidly Considered, and It's Arguments, and Pernicious Doctrines, Exposed and Refuted. London: W. Davis and T. Evans, [1775].
Parker, Thomas. *Evidence of Our Transactions in the East Indies: With an Enquiry into the General Conduct of Great Britain to Other Countries, from the Peace of Paris in 1763.* London: Charles Dilly, 1782.
The Parliamentary Register; or, History of the Proceedings and Debates of the House of Commons. 17 vols. London: J. Almon, 1775–80.
The Patriots of North-America: A Sketch. With Explanatory Notes. New York: n.p., 1775.
Peabody, Sue, and Keila Grinberg, eds. *Slavery, Freedom, and the Law in the Atlantic World: A Brief History with Documents.* Boston: Bedford/St. Martin's, 2007.
Peckham, Howard H., ed. *Sources of American Independence: Selected Manuscripts from the Collections of the William L. Clements Library.* 2 vols. Chicago: University of Chicago Press, 1978.
Pendleton, Edmund. *The Letters and Papers of Edmund Pendleton, 1734–1803.* Edited by David John Mays. 2 vols. Charlottesville: University Press of Virginia, 1967.
Pepys, Samuel. *The Diary of Samuel Pepys.* Edited by Richard Le Gallienne. New York: Modern Library, 2003.
Personal Slavery Established, by the Suffrages of Custom and Right Reason. Being a Full Answer to the Gloomy and Visionary Reveries, of All the Fanatical and Enthusiastical Writers on that Subject. Philadelphia: John Dunlap, 1773.
Philbrick, Norman, ed. *Trumpets Sounding: Propaganda Plays of the American Revolution.* New York: Benjamin Blom, 1972.
Porter, Dorothy, ed. *Early Negro Writing, 1760–1837.* Boston: Beacon Press, 1971.
[Postlethwayt, Malachy]. *The National and Private Advantages Considered: Being an Enquiry, How Far It Concerns the Trading Interest of Great Britain, Effectively to Support and Maintain the Forts and Settlements in Africa, Belonging to the Royal African Company of England.* London: John and Paul Knapton, 1746.
Price, Richard. *The Correspondence of Richard Price.* Edited by W. Bernard Peach and D. O. Thomas. 3 vols. Durham, N.C., and Cardiff: Duke University Press and University of Wales Press, 1983–94.
Price, Richard. *Richard Price: Political Writings.* Edited by D. O. Thomas. Cambridge: Cambridge University Press, 1991.
Priestley, Joseph. *An Address to Protestant Dissenters of All Denominations, on the Approaching Election of Members of Parliament, with Respect to the State*

of Public Liberty in General, and of American Affairs in Particular. London: Thomas and John Fleet, 1774.

Priestley, Joseph. *Political Writings*. Edited by Peter N. Miller. Cambridge: Cambridge University Press, 1993.

Proceedings of the Massachusetts Historical Society. 3rd series, 48 (October 1914–June 1915).

Quincy, Josiah, Jr. *Observations on the Act of Parliament Commonly Called the Boston Port-Bill; with Thoughts on Civil Society and Standing Armies*. Boston: Edes and Gill, 1774.

Quincy, Josiah, Jr. *Portrait of a Patriot: The Major Political and Legal Papers of Josiah Quincy Junior*. Edited by Daniel R. Coquillette and Neil Longley York. 6 vols. Boston: Colonial Society of Massachusetts, 2005–14.

Ramsay, David. *History of South Carolina from Its First Settlement in 1670 to the Year 1808*. 2 vols. 1809; reprint, Spartanburg, S.C.: Reprint Company, 1959.

Ramsay, David. *An Oration on the Advantages of American Independence; Spoken before a Publick Assembly of the Inhabitants of Charlestown in South-Carolina, on the Second Anniversary of that Glorious Aera*. Charleston, S.C.: John Wells, 1778.

Rhodehamel, John, ed. *The American Revolution: Writings from the War of Independence*. New York: Library of America, 2001.

Rose, Willie Lee, ed. *A Documentary History of Slavery in North America*. New York: Oxford University Press, 1976.

Rush, Benjamin. *The Autobiography of Benjamin Rush, His "Travels through Life," Together with His Commonplace Book for 1789–1813*. Edited by George W. Corner. Princeton, N.J.: Princeton University Press, 1948.

Rush, Benjamin. *Letters of Benjamin Rush*. Edited by L. H. Butterfield. 2 vols. Princeton, N.J.: Princeton University Press, 1951.

Saberton, Ian, ed. *The Cornwallis Papers: The Campaigns of 1780 and 1781 in the Southern Theatre of the American Revolutionary War*. 6 vols. East Sussex, U.K.: Naval and Military Press, 2010.

Sancho, Ignatius. *The Letters of the Late Ignatius Sancho, an African to Which Are Prefixed Memoirs of His Life by Joseph Jekyll, Esq., M.P.* 1782; reprint, London: Dawsons of Pall Mall, 1968.

Sandoz, Ellis, ed. *Political Sermons of the American Founding Era, 1730–1805*. 2 vols. 2nd ed. 1991; Indianapolis: Liberty Fund, 1998.

Schaw, Janet. *Journal of a Lady of Quality: Being the Narrative of a Journey from Scotland to the West Indies, North Carolina, and Portugal, in the Years 1774 to 1776*. Edited by Evangeline Walker Andrews and Charles McLean Andrews. Lincoln: University of Nebraska Press, 2005.

Seabury, Samuel. *Letters of a Westchester Farmer (1774–1775). By the Reverend Samuel Seabury (1729–1796)*. Edited by Clarence H. Vance. White Plains, N.Y.: Westchester County Historical Society, 1930.

Serle, Ambrose. *The American Journal of Ambrose Serle, Secretary to Lord Howe, 1776–1778*. Edited by Edward H. Tatum. San Marino, Calif.: Huntington Library, 1940.
[Serle, Ambrose.] *Americans against Liberty; or an Essay on the Nature and Principles of True Freedom, Shewing that the Designs and Conduct of the Americans Tend Only to Tyranny and Slavery*. London: J. Mathews, 1775.
A Sermon, on the Present Situation of the Affairs of America and Great-Britain, Written By a Black, and Printed at the Request of Several Persons of Distinguished Characters. Philadelphia: Bradford and Hall, 1782.
[Sewall, Jonathan Mitchell]. *Gen. Washington, a New Favourite Song, at the American Camp*. N.p.: n.p., [1776].
Sharp, Granville. *A Declaration of the People's Natural Right to a Share in the Legislature, Which Is the Fundamental Principle of the British Constitution of State*. Philadelphia: John Dunlap, 1774.
Sharp, Granville. *An Essay on Slavery, Proving from Scripture Its Inconsistency with Humanity and Religion*. Burlington, N.J.: Isaac Collins, 1773.
Sharp, Granville. *The Just Limitation of Slavery in the Laws of God, Compared with the Unbounded Claims of African Traders and British American Slaveholders. With a Copious Appendix*. London: B. White, 1776.
Sharp, Granville. *The Law of Liberty; or, Royal Law, by Which All Mankind Will Certainly Be Judged! Earnestly Recommended to the Serious Consideration of All Slaveholders and Slavedealers*. London: B. White, 1776.
Sharp, Granville. *The Law of Retribution; or, A Serious Warning to Great Britain and Her Colonies, Founded on Unquestionable Examples of God's Temporal Vengeance against Tyrants, Slave-Holders, and Oppressors*. London: W. Richardson, 1776.
Sharp, Granville. *A Representation of the Injustice and Dangerous Tendency of Tolerating Slavery; or of Admitting the Least Claim to Private Property in the Persons of Men, in England*. London: Benjamin White and Robert Horsfield, 1769.
A Short Appeal to the People of Great-Britain; upon the Unavoidable Necessity of the Present War with Our Disaffected Colonies. London: G. Kearsly, 1776.
Simmons, R. C., and P. D. G. Thomas, eds. *Proceedings and Debates of the British Parliaments Respecting North America, 1754–1783*. 6 vols. to date. Millwood, N.Y.: Kraus, 1982–.
Smith, Adam. *The Theory of Moral Sentiments*. London: A. Millar, 1759.
Smith, Billy G., and Richard Wojtowicz, eds. *Blacks Who Stole Themselves: Advertisements for Runaway Slaves in the Pennsylvania Gazette, 1728–1790*. Philadelphia: University of Pennsylvania Press, 1989.
Smith, Paul H., comp. *English Defenders of American Freedoms, 1774–1778: Six Pamphlets Attacking British Policy*. Washington, D.C.: Library of Congress, 1972.

Smith, Paul H., et al., eds. *Letters of Delegates to Congress, 1774–1789*. 26 vols. Washington, D.C.: Library of Congress, 1976–2000.

Some Fugitive Thoughts on a Letter Signed Freeman, Addressed to the Deputies, Assembled at the High Court of Congress in Philadelphia. By a Back Settler. Charleston, S.C.: n.p., 1774.

Stock, Leo Francis, ed. *Proceedings and Debates of the British Parliaments Respecting North America*. 5 vols. Washington, D.C.: Carnegie Institution of Washington, 1924–41.

Swan, James. *A Dissuasion to Great-Britain and the Colonies, from the Slave-Trade to Africa. Shewing the Injustice Thereof, &c. Revised and Abridged*. Boston: J. Greenleaf, 1773.

Taylor, Robert J., ed. *Massachusetts, Colony to Commonwealth: Documents on the Formation of Its Constitution, 1775–1780*. Chapel Hill: University of North Carolina Press, 1961.

Thomas, Sir Dalby. *An Historical Account of the Rise and Growth of the West-India Collonies, and of the Great Advantages They Are to England, in Respect to Trade*. London: Jo. Hindmarsh, 1690.

Thomas, Peter D. G., ed. *The English Satirical Print, 1600–1832: The American Revolution*. Cambridge: Chadwyck-Healey, 1986.

Tinling, Marion, ed. *The Correspondence of the Three William Byrds of Westover, Virginia, 1684–1776*. 2 vols. Charlottesville: University Press of Virginia, 1977.

[Trelawny, Edward]. *An Essay Concerning Slavery, and the Danger Jamaica Is Expos'd to from the Too Great Number of Slaves, and the Too Little Care That Is Taken to Manage Them, and a Proposal to Prevent the Further Importation of Negroes into That Island*. London: Charles Corbett, [1746?].

Trenchard, John, and Thomas Gordon. *Cato's Letters; or, Essays on Liberty, Civil and Religious, and Other Important Subjects*. Edited by Ronald Hamowy. 4 vols. in 2. Indianapolis: Liberty Fund, 1995.

The Triumph of the Whigs; or, T'Other Congress Convened. New York: James Rivington, 1775.

Trumbull, John. *The Poetical Works of John Trumbull, LL.D. Containing M'Fingal, a Modern Epic Poem*. 2 vols. Hartford, Conn.: Lincoln & Stone, 1820.

[Tryon, Thomas]. *Friendly Advice to the Gentlemen-Planters of the East and West Indies in Three Parts . . . by Philotheos Physiologus*. London: Andrew Sowle, 1684.

[Tucker, Josiah]. *A Series of Answers to Certain Popular Objections, against Separating from the Rebellious Colonies, and Discarding Them Entirely; Being the Concluding Tract of the Dean of Glocester, on the Subject of American Affairs*. Gloucester, U.K.: T. Cadell, 1776.

Tucker, Josiah. *Tract V. The Respective Pleas and Arguments of the Mother Country, and of the Colonies, Distinctly Set Forth; and the Impossibility of a Compromise of*

Differences, or a Mutual Concession of Rights, Plain Demonstrated. 2nd ed. 1775; London: T. Cadell, 1776.
Tyranny Unmasked. An Answer to a Late Pamphlet, Entitled Taxation No Tyranny. London: W. Flexney, 1775.
Van Horne, John C., ed. *Religious Philanthropy and Colonial Slavery: The American Correspondence of the Associates of Dr. Bray, 1717–1777*. Urbana: University of Illinois Press, 1985.
Van Schreeven, William J., and Robert L. Scribner, eds. *Revolutionary Virginia: The Road to Independence*. 7 vols. Charlottesville: University Press of Virginia, 1973–83.
Verelst, Harry. *A View of the Rise, the Progress, and the Present State of the English Government in Bengal: Including a Reply to the Misrepresentations of Mr. Bolts, and Other Writers*. London: J. Nourse, 1772.
Wallace, George. *A System of the Principles of the Law of Scotland*. 2 vols. Edinburgh: G. Hamilton and J. Balfour, 1760.
Walvin, James, ed. *The Black Presence: A Documentary History of the Negro in England, 1555–1860*. New York: Schocken Books, 1971.
Warren, Joseph. *An Oration Delivered March 5th, 1772. At the Request of the Inhabitants of the Town of Boston; to Commemorate the Bloody Tragedy of the Fifth of March, 1770*. Boston: Edes and Gill, 1772.
Warren, Joseph. *An Oration; Delivered March Sixth, 1775. At the Request of the Inhabitants of the Town of Boston; to Commemorate the Bloody Tragedy of the Fifth of March, 1770*. Boston: Edes and Gill, 1775.
Washington, George. *George Washington's Barbados Diary, 1751–52*. Edited by Alicia K. Anderson and Lynn A. Price. Charlottesville: University of Virginia Press, 2018.
Washington, George. *The Papers of George Washington: Colonial Series*. Edited by W. W. Abbot et al. 10 vols. Charlottesville: University Press of Virginia, 1983–95.
Washington, George. *The Papers of George Washington: Confederation Series*. Edited by W. W. Abbot et al. 6 vols. Charlottesville: University Press of Virginia, 1992–97.
Washington, George. *The Papers of George Washington: Revolutionary War Series*. Edited by W. W. Abbot et al. 30 vols. to date. Charlottesville: University Press of Virginia, 1985–.
Washington, George. *The Writings of George Washington from the Original Manuscript Sources, 1745–1799*. Edited by John C. Fitzpatrick. 39 vols. Washington, D.C.: U.S. Government Printing Office, 1931–44.
[Wells, Richard]. *A Few Political Reflections Submitted to the Consideration of the British Colonies. By a Citizen of Philadelphia*. Philadelphia: John Dunlap, 1774.
Wesley, John. *A Calm Address to Our American Colonies*. London: R. Hawes, 1775.

Wesley, John. *A Calm Address to the Inhabitants of England*. London: J. Fry, 1777.
Wesley, John. *Political Writings of John Wesley*. Edited by Graham Maddox. Bristol, U.K.: Thoemmes Press, 1998.
Wesley, John. *Thoughts upon Slavery*. London: Joseph Crukshank, 1774.
Wesley, John. *The Works of John Wesley*. Edited by Frank Baker et al. 27 vols. to date. Oxford: Oxford University Press, 1975–.
Wharton, Francis, ed. *The Revolutionary Diplomatic Correspondence of the United States*. 6 vols. Washington, D.C.: U.S. Government Printing Office, 1889.
Wheatley, Phillis. *Complete Writings*. Edited by Vincent Carretta. New York: Penguin, 2001.
Whitefield, George. *Three Letters from the Reverend Mr. G. Whitefield: Viz . . . Letter III. To the Inhabitants of Maryland, Virginia, North and South-Carolina, Concerning Their Negroes*. Philadelphia: B. Franklin, 1740.
[Wilkes, John]. *The North Briton, from No. I. to No. XLVI. Inclusive . . . Corrected and Revised by a Friend to Civil and Religious Liberty*. 1763; reprint, New York: A.M.S. Press, 1976.
Willard, Margaret Wheeler, ed. *Letters on the American Revolution, 1774–1776*. Boston: Houghton Mifflin, 1925.
Winchester, Elhanan. *The Reigning Abominations, Especially the Slave Trade, Considered as Causes of Lamentation, Being the Substance of a Discourse Delivered in Fairfax County, Virginia, December 30, 1774*. London: H. Trapp, 1788.
Wood, Marcus, ed. *The Poetry of Slavery: An Anglo-American Anthology, 1764–1865*. Oxford: Oxford University Press, 2004.
Woods, John A., ed. "The Correspondence of Benjamin Rush and Granville Sharp, 1773–1809." *Journal of American Studies* 1 (April 1967): 1–38.
Woolman, John. *Considerations on Keeping Negroes: Recommended to the Professors of Christianity of Every Denomination. Part Second*. 1762; reprint, New York: Grossman, 1976.
Woolman, John. *The Journal and Major Essays of John Woolman*. Edited by Phillips P. Moulton. New York: Oxford University Press, 1971.
Woolman, John. *Some Considerations on the Keeping of Negroes: Recommended to the Professors of Christianity of Every Denomination*. 1754; reprint, New York: Grossman, 1976.
York, Neil L., ed. *The Crisis: A British Defense of American Rights, 1775–1776*. Indianapolis: Liberty Fund, 2016.
Young, Arthur. *Political Essays Concerning the Present State of the British Empire*. London: W. Strahan and C. Cadell, 1772.
Young, Jeffrey Robert, ed. *Proslavery and Sectional Thought in the Early South, 1740–1829: An Anthology*. Columbia: University of South Carolina Press, 2006.

Zubly, John J. *"A Warm and Zealous Spirit": John J. Zubly and the American Revolution, a Selection of His Writings*. Edited by Randall M. Miller. Macon, Ga.: Mercer University Press, 1982.

Secondary Sources

Adams, Thomas R. *American Independence: The Growth of an Idea*. Providence, R.I.: Brown University Press, 1965.
Adams, Willi Paul. *The First American Constitutions: Republican Ideology and the Making of the State Constitutions in the Revolutionary Era*. Translated by Rita and Robert Kimber. Chapel Hill: University of North Carolina Press, 1980.
Adelman, Jeremy. "An Age of Imperial Revolutions." *American Historical Review* 113 (April 2008): 319–40.
Alden, John Richard. "John Stuart Accuses William Bull." *William and Mary Quarterly*, 3rd series, 2 (July 1945): 315–20.
"The American Revolution from Two Perspectives: A Debate." Massachusetts Historical Society, https://www.masshist.org/events/american-revolution-two-perspectives-debate.
Amussen, Susan Dwyer. *Caribbean Exchanges: Slavery and the Transformation of English Society, 1640–1700*. Chapel Hill: University of North Carolina Press, 2007.
Anderson, Fred. *Crucible of War: The Seven Years' War and the Fate of Empire in British North America, 1754–1766*. New York: Random House, 2000.
Andrews, K. R., N. P. Canny, and P. E. H. Hair, eds. *The Westward Enterprise: English Activities in Ireland, the Atlantic, and America, 1480–1650*. Liverpool: Liverpool University Press, 1978.
Anstey, Roger. *The Atlantic Slave Trade and British Abolition, 1760–1810*. London: Macmillan, 1975.
Armitage, David. *Civil Wars: A History in Ideas*. New York: Knopf, 2017.
Armitage, David. *The Declaration of Independence: A Global History*. Cambridge, Mass.: Harvard University Press, 2007.
Armitage, David. *The Ideological Origins of the British Empire*. Cambridge: Cambridge University Press, 2000.
Armitage, David. "John Locke, Carolina, and the 'Two Treatises of Government.'" *Political Theory* 32 (October 2004): 602–27.
Armitage, David. "A Patriot for Whom? The Afterlives of Bolingbroke's Patriot King." *Journal of British Studies* 36 (October 1997): 397–418.
Armitage, David, and Michael J. Braddick, eds. *The British Atlantic World, 1500–1800*. 2nd ed. 2002; New York: Palgrave Macmillan, 2009.
Asaka, Ikuko. *Tropical Freedom: Climate, Settler Colonialism, and Black Exclusion in the Age of Emancipation*. Durham, N.C.: Duke University Press, 2017.

Baer, Friederike. *Hessians: German Soldiers in the American Revolutionary War.* Oxford: Oxford University Press, 2022.
Bailyn, Bernard. *Barbarous Years: The Peopling of North America: The Conflict of Civilizations, 1600–1675.* New York: Knopf, 2012.
Bailyn, Bernard. *Faces of Revolution: Personalities and Themes in the Struggle for American Independence.* New York: Random House, 1990.
Bailyn, Bernard. *The Ideological Origins of the American Revolution.* Enlarged ed. 1967; Cambridge, Mass.: Belknap Press of Harvard University Press, 1992.
Bailyn, Bernard. *The Ordeal of Thomas Hutchinson.* Cambridge, Mass.: Belknap Press of Harvard University Press, 1974.
Bailyn, Bernard, and Philip D. Morgan, eds. *Strangers within the Realm: Cultural Margins of the First British Empire.* Chapel Hill: University of North Carolina Press, 1991.
Bannister, Jerry, and Liam Riordan, eds. *The Loyal Atlantic: Remaking the British Atlantic in the Revolutionary Era.* Toronto: University of Toronto Press, 2012.
Barrow, Thomas C. *Trade and Empire: The British Customs Service in Colonial America, 1660–1775.* Cambridge, Mass.: Harvard University Press, 1967.
Baseler, Marilyn C. *"Asylum for Mankind": America, 1607–1800.* Ithaca, N.Y.: Cornell University Press, 1998.
Basker, James G. "'The Next Insurrection': Johnson, Race, and Rebellion." *Age of Johnson* 11 (2000): 37–51.
Basker, James G. "Samuel Johnson and the African-American Reader." *New Rambler* (1994–95): 47–57.
Bate, W. J. *Samuel Johnson.* New York: Harcourt, Brace, Jovanovich, 1975.
Beatty, Jacqueline. *In Dependence: Women and the Patriarchal State in Revolutionary America.* New York: New York University Press, 2023.
Beaumont, Andrew D. M. *Colonial America and the Earl of Halifax, 1748–1761.* Oxford: Oxford University Press, 2015.
Beckles, Hilary McD. *White Servitude and Black Slavery in Barbados, 1627–1715.* Knoxville: University of Tennessee Press, 1989.
Beeman, Richard R. *The Varieties of Political Experience in Eighteenth-Century America.* Philadelphia: University of Pennsylvania Press, 2004.
Bell, Karen Cook. *Running from Bondage: Enslaved Women and Their Remarkable Fight for Freedom in Revolutionary America.* Cambridge: Cambridge University Press, 2021.
Bemis, Samuel. *The Diplomacy of the American Revolution.* Revised ed. 1935; Bloomington: Indiana University Press, 1957.
Bender, Thomas, ed. *The Antislavery Debate: Capitalism and Abolitionism as a Problem in Historical Interpretation.* Berkeley: University of California Press, 1992.
Berger, Carl. *Broadsides and Bayonets: The Propaganda War of the American Revolution.* Revised ed. 1961; San Raphael, Calif.: Presidio Press, 1976.

Bickham, Troy. *Making Headlines: The American Revolution as Seen through the British Press.* DeKalb: Northern Illinois University Press, 2009.

Bilder, Mary Sarah. *The Transatlantic Constitution: Colonial Legal Culture and the Empire.* Cambridge, Mass.: Harvard University Press, 2004.

Black, Jeremy. *George III: America's Last King.* New Haven, Conn.: Yale University Press, 2006.

Blackburn, Robin. *The American Crucible: Slavery, Emancipation and Human Rights.* London: Verso, 2011.

Blackburn, Robin. *The Overthrow of Colonial Slavery, 1776–1848.* London: Verso, 1988.

Blanton, John N. "This Species of Property: Slavery and the Properties of Subjecthood in Anglo-American Law and Politics, 1619–1783." PhD diss., City University of New York, 2016.

Blassingame, John W. "American Nationalism and Other Loyalties in the Southern Colonies, 1763–1775." *Journal of Southern History* 34 (February 1968): 50–75.

Bonwick, Colin. *English Radicals and the American Revolution.* Chapel Hill: University of North Carolina Press, 1977.

Bowen, H. V. "British Conceptions of Global Empire, 1756–83." *Journal of Imperial and Commonwealth History* 36 (September 1998): 1–27.

Bowen, H. V., Elizabeth Mancke, and John G. Reid, eds. *Britain's Oceanic Empire: Atlantic and Indian Ocean Worlds, c. 1550–1850.* Cambridge: Cambridge University Press, 2012.

Bradburn, Douglas, and John C. Coombs, eds. *Early Modern Virginia: Reconsidering the Old Dominion.* Charlottesville: University of Virginia Press, 2011.

Bradley, Patricia. *Slavery, Propaganda, and the American Revolution.* Jackson: University Press of Mississippi, 1998.

Breen, T. H. *Tobacco Culture: The Mentality of the Great Tidewater Planters on the Eve of Revolution.* 2nd ed. 1975; Princeton, N.J.: Princeton University Press, 2001.

Breen, T. H. *The Will of the People: The Revolutionary Birth of America.* Cambridge, Mass.: Belknap Press of Harvard University Press, 2019.

Brewer, Holly. "Creating a Common Law of Slavery for England and Its New World Empire." *Law and History Review* 39 (November 2022): 765–834.

Brewer, Holly. "Slavery, Sovereignty, and 'Inheritable Blood': Reconsidering John Locke and the Origins of American Slavery." *American Historical Review* 122 (October 2017): 1038–78.

Brewer, John. *Party Ideology and Popular Politics at the Accession of George III.* Cambridge: Cambridge University Press, 1976.

Brookes, George S. *Friend Anthony Benezet.* Philadelphia: University of Pennsylvania Press, 1937.

Brown, Christopher Leslie. *Moral Capital: Foundations of British Abolitionism.* Chapel Hill: University of North Carolina Press, 2006.

Brown, Christopher Leslie, and Philip D. Morgan, eds. *Arming Slaves: From Classical Times to the Modern Age*. New Haven, Conn.: Yale University Press, 2006.

Brown, Kathleen M. *Good Wives, Nasty Wenches, and Anxious Patriarchs: Gender, Race, and Power in Colonial Virginia*. Chapel Hill: University of North Carolina Press, 1996.

Brown, Vincent. *Tacky's Revolt: The Story of an Atlantic Slave War*. Cambridge, Mass.: Belknap Press of Harvard University Press, 2020.

Bruns, Roger, ed. *Am I Not a Man and a Brother: The Antislavery Crusade of Revolutionary America, 1688–1788*. New York: Chelsea House, 1977.

Bruns, Roger. "Anthony Benezet's Assertion of Negro Equality." *Journal of Negro History* 56 (July 1971): 230–38.

Burnard, Trevor. *Creole Gentlemen: The Maryland Elite, 1691–1776*. London: Routledge, 2002.

Burnard, Trevor. *Jamaica in the Age of Revolution*. Philadelphia: University of Pennsylvania Press, 2020.

Burnard, Trevor. "Powerless Masters: The Curious Decline of Jamaican Sugar Planters in the Foundational Period of British Abolitionism." *Slavery and Abolition* 32 (June 2011): 185–98.

Burnard, Trevor. *Writing Early America: From Empire to Revolution*. Charlottesville: University of Virginia Press, 2023.

Burnard, Trevor, and John Garrigus. *The Plantation Machine: Atlantic Capitalism in French Saint-Domingue and British Jamaica*. Philadelphia: University of Pennsylvania Press, 2016.

Burstein, Andrew. *Sentimental Democracy: The Evolution of America's Romantic Self-Image*. New York: Hill and Wang, 1999.

Butler, Jon. *Becoming America: The Revolution before 1776*. Cambridge, Mass.: Harvard University Press, 2000.

Calhoon, Robert M., et al. *Tory Insurgents: The Loyalist Perception and Other Essays*. Revised and expanded ed. 1989; Columbia: University of South Carolina Press, 2010.

Cameron, Christopher. *To Plead Our Own Cause: African Americans in Massachusetts and the Making of the Antislavery Movement*. Kent, Ohio: Kent State University Press, 2014.

Campbell, Kenneth L. *Ireland's History: Prehistory to the Present*. London: Bloomsbury, 2014.

Canale, Joshua. "'When a State Abounds in Rascals': New York's Revolutionary Era Committees for Public Safety, 1775–1783." *Journal of the Early Republic* 39 (Summer 2019): 203–38.

Canizares-Esguerra, Jorge, and Erik R. Seeman, eds. *The Atlantic in Global History, 1500–2000*. Upper Saddle River, N.J.: Pearson, 2007.

Canny, Nicholas P., ed. *The Oxford History of the British Empire*, vol. 1, *The Origins of Empire*. Oxford: Oxford University Press, 1998.

Canny, Nicholas P., and Anthony Pagden, eds. *Colonial Identity in the Atlantic World, 1500–1800.* Princeton, N.J.: Princeton University Press, 1987.

Carey, Brycchan. *British Abolitionism and the Rhetoric of Sensibility: Writing, Sentiment, and Slavery, 1760–1807.* Basingstoke, U.K.: Palgrave Macmillan, 2005.

Carey, Brycchan. *From Peace to Freedom: Quaker Rhetoric and the Birth of American Antislavery, 1657–1761.* New Haven, Conn.: Yale University Press, 2012.

Carey, Brycchan, Markman Ellis, and Sarah Salih, eds. *Discourses of Slavery and Abolition: Britain and Its Colonies, 1760–1838.* Houndsmills, U.K.: Palgrave Macmillan, 2004.

Carretta, Vincent. *Phillis Wheatley: Biography of a Genius in Bondage.* Athens: University of Georgia Press, 2011.

Chakravarty, Urvashi. *Fictions of Consent: Slavery, Servitude, and Free Service in Early Modern England.* Philadelphia: University of Pennsylvania Press, 2022.

Chopra, Ruma. *Unnatural Rebellion: Loyalists in New York City during the Revolution.* Charlottesville: University of Virginia Press, 2011.

Clark, J. C. D. *The Language of Liberty. 1660–1832: Political Discourse and Social Dynamics in the Anglo-American World.* Cambridge: Cambridge University Press, 1994.

Clark, J. C. D. *Samuel Johnson: Literature, Religion and English Cultural Politics from the Restoration to Romanticism.* Cambridge: Cambridge University Press, 1994.

Clark, J. C. D. *Thomas Paine: Britain, America, and France in the Age of Enlightenment and Revolution.* Oxford: Oxford University Press, 2018.

Clark, Jennifer. *The American Idea of England, 1776–1840: Transatlantic Writing.* Farnham, U.K.: Ashgate, 2013.

Coffey, J. "'Tremble, Britannia!' Fear, Providence, and the Abolition of the Slave Trade." *English Historical Review* 77 (2012): 844–81.

Colley, Linda. *Britons: Forging the Nation, 1707–1837.* New Haven, Conn.: Yale University Press, 1992.

Cone, Carl B. *Torchbearer of Freedom: The Influence of Richard Price on Eighteenth Century Thought.* Lexington: University of Kentucky Press, 1952.

Conway, Stephen. *The British Isles and the War of American Independence.* Oxford: Oxford University Press, 2000.

Conway, Stephen. "From Fellow-Nationals to Foreigners: British Perceptions of the Americans, circa 1739–1873." *William and Mary Quarterly,* 3rd series, 59 (January 2002): 65–100.

Conway, Stephen. *The War of American Independence, 1775–1783.* London: E. Arnold, 1995.

Craton, Michael. *Testing the Chains: Resistance to Slavery in the British West Indies.* Ithaca, N.Y.: Cornell University Press, 1982.

Crawford, Michael J. *The Having of Negroes Is Become a Burden: The Quaker Struggle to Free Slaves in Revolutionary North Carolina.* Gainesville: University Press of Florida, 2010.

Crosby, David L. "Anthony Benezet's Transformation of Anti-Slavery Rhetoric." *Slavery and Abolition* 23 (December 2002): 39–58.

Crow, Jeffrey J., and Larry E. Tise, eds. *The Southern Experience in the American Revolution.* Chapel Hill: University of North Carolina Press, 1978.

Curley, Thomas M. "Johnson and America." *Age of Johnson* 6 (1994): 31–73.

David, James Corbett. *Dunmore's New World: The Extraordinary Life of a Royal Governor in Revolutionary America.* Charlottesville: University of Virginia Press, 2013.

Davidson, Philip. *Propaganda and the American Revolution, 1763–1783.* Chapel Hill: University of North Carolina Press, 1941.

Davis, David Brion. *The Problem of Slavery in the Age of Revolution, 1770–1823.* Ithaca, N.Y.: Cornell University Press, 1975.

Davis, David Brion. *The Problem of Slavery in Western Culture.* Ithaca, N.Y.: Cornell University Press, 1966.

Devlin, Rachel. *A Girl Stands at the Door: The Generation of Young Women Who Desegregated America's Schools.* New York: Basic Books, 2018.

Dirks, Nicholas B. *The Scandal of Empire: India and the Creation of Imperial Britain.* Cambridge, Mass.: Belknap Press of Harvard University Press, 2006.

Donoghue, John. *Fire under the Ashes: An Atlantic History of the English Revolution.* Chicago: University of Chicago Press, 2013.

Donoghue, John, and Evelyn P. Jennings, eds. *Building the Atlantic Empires: Unfree Labor and Imperial States in the Political Economy of Capitalism, ca. 1500–1914.* Leiden: Brill, 2016.

Donoghue, Norman E., II. *Prisoners of Congress: Philadelphia's Quakers in Exile, 1777–1778.* University Park: Pennsylvania State University Press, 2023.

Donoughue, Bernard. *British Politics and the American Revolution: The Path to War, 1773–1775.* London: Macmillan, 1964.

Dorsey, Peter A. *Common Bondage: Slavery as Metaphor in Revolutionary America.* Knoxville: University of Tennessee Press, 2009.

Dowd, Gregory Evans. *Groundless: Rumors, Legends, and Hoaxes on the Early American Frontier.* Baltimore: Johns Hopkins University Press, 2015.

Drescher, Seymour. *Abolition: A History of Slavery and Antislavery.* Cambridge: Cambridge University Press, 2009.

du Rivage, Justin. *Revolution against Empire: Taxes, Politics, and the Origins of American Independence.* New Haven, Conn.: Yale University Press, 2017.

Duval, Kathleen. *Independence Lost: Lives on the Edge of the American Revolution.* New York: Random House, 2015.

Duval, Lauren. "Mastering Charleston: Property and Patriarchy in British-Occupied Charleston, 1780–82." *William and Mary Quarterly,* 3rd series, 75 (October 2018): 589–622.

Dzurec, David J., III. *Our Suffering Brethren: Foreign Captivity and Nationalism in the Early United States.* Amherst: University of Massachusetts Press, 2019.

Edwardes, Michael. *The Nabobs at Home.* London: Constable, 1991.
Egerton, Douglas R. *Death or Liberty: African Americans and Revolutionary America.* New York: Oxford University Press, 2009.
Enfield, N. J. *Language vs. Reality: Why Language Is Good for Lawyers and Bad for Scientists.* Cambridge, Mass.: MIT Press, 2022.
Essig, James D. *The Bonds of Wickedness: American Evangelicals against Slavery, 1770–1808.* Philadelphia: Temple University Press, 1982.
Ewen, Misha. *The Virginia Venture: American Colonization and English Society, 1580–1660.* Philadelphia: University of Pennsylvania Press, 2022.
Fenn, Elizabeth A. "Biological Warfare in Eighteenth-Century North America: Beyond Jeffery Amherst." *Journal of American History* 86 (March 2000): 1552–80.
Ferguson, Moira. *Subject to Others: British Women Writers and Colonial Slavery, 1670–1834.* New York: Routledge, 1992.
Fisher, Samuel. "Fit Instruments in a Howling Wilderness: Colonists, Indians, and the Origins of the American Revolution." *William and Mary Quarterly,* 3rd series, 73 (October 2016): 647–80.
Flavell, Julie. *When London Was Capital of America.* New Haven, Conn.: Yale University Press, 2010.
Fletcher, F. T. H. "Montesquieu's Influence on Anti-Slavery Opinion in England." *Journal of Negro History* 18 (October 1933): 414–25.
Fliegelman, Jay. *Prodigals and Pilgrims: The American Revolution against Patriarchal Authority, 1750–1800.* Cambridge: Cambridge University Press, 1982.
Flower, Milton E. *John Dickinson: Conservative Revolutionary.* Charlottesville: University Press of Virginia, 1983.
Foster, Stephen, ed. *British North America in the Seventeenth and Eighteenth Centuries: The Oxford History of the British Empire Companion Series.* Oxford: Oxford University Press, 2013.
Foy, Charles R. "Seeking Freedom in the Atlantic World, 1713–1783." *Early American Studies* 4 (Spring 2006): 46–77.
Foy, Charles R. "'Unkle Sommerset's' Freedom: Liberty in England for Black Sailors." *Journal for Maritime Research* 13 (May 2011): 21–36.
Fredrickson, George M. *Racism: A Short History.* Princeton, N.J.: Princeton University Press, 2002.
Frey, Sylvia R. *Water from the Rock: Black Resistance in a Revolutionary Age.* Princeton, N.J.: Princeton University Press, 1991.
Fruchtman, Jack, Jr. *The Apocalyptic Politics of Richard Price and Joseph Priestley: A Study in Late Eighteenth-Century English Republican Millennialism.* Philadelphia: American Philosophical Society, 1983.
Fryer, Peter. *Staying Power: The History of Black People in Britain.* London: Pluto Press, 1984.

Furstenberg, François. "Beyond Slavery and Freedom: Autonomy, Agency, and Resistance in Early American Political Discourse." *Journal of American History* 89 (March 2003): 1295–330.

Gabriele, Matthew, and David M. Perry. *The Bright Ages: A New History of Medieval Europe.* New York: HarperCollins, 2021.

Gallagher, Sean. "Black Refugees and the Legal Fiction of Military Manumission in the American Revolution." *Slavery and Abolition* 43, no. 1 (2022): 140–59.

Gallay, Alan, ed. *Indian Slavery in Colonial America.* Lincoln: University of Nebraska Press, 2009.

Gallay, Alan. *The Indian Slave Trade: The Rise of the English Empire in the American South, 1670–1717.* New Haven, Conn.: Yale University Press, 2002.

Gallup-Diaz, Ignacio, Andrew Shankman, and David J. Silverman, eds. *Anglicizing America: Empire, Revolution, Republic.* Philadelphia: University of Pennsylvania Press, 2015.

Gauci, Perry. *William Beckford: First Prime Minister of the London Empire.* New Haven, Conn.: Yale University Press, 2013.

Gellman, David N. *Emancipating New York: The Politics of Slavery and Freedom, 1777–1827.* Baton Rouge: Louisiana State University Press, 2006.

Gellman, David N. *Liberty's Chain: Slavery, Abolition, and the Jay Family of New York.* Ithaca, N.Y.: Three Hills, 2022.

Gerbner, Katharine. "'We Are against the Traffik of Men-Body': The Germantown Quaker Protest of 1688 and the Origins of American Abolitionism." *Pennsylvania History* 74 (Spring 2007): 149–72.

Gigantino, James J., II. *The Ragged Road to Abolition: Slavery and Freedom in New Jersey, 1775–1865.* Philadelphia: University of Pennsylvania Press, 2015.

Gilbert, Alan. *Black Patriots and Loyalists: Fighting for Emancipation in the War for Independence.* Chicago: University of Chicago Press, 2012.

Glasson, Travis. "'Baptism Doth Not Bestow Freedom': Missionary Anglicanism, Slavery, and the Yorke-Talbot Opinion, 1701–30." *William and Mary Quarterly*, 3rd series, 67 (April 2010): 279–318.

Glasson, Travis. *Mastering Christianity: Missionary Anglicanism and Slavery in the Atlantic World.* Oxford: Oxford University Press, 2012.

Glover, Lorri. *Founders as Fathers: The Private Lives and Politics of the American Revolutionaries.* New Haven, Conn.: Yale University Press, 2014.

Gordon-Reed, Annette, and Peter S. Onuf. *"Most Blessed of the Patriarchs": Thomas Jefferson and the Empire of the Imagination.* New York: Liveright, 2016.

Gosse, Van. "'As a Nation, the English Are Our Friends': The Emergence of African American Politics in the British Atlantic World, 1772–1861." *American Historical Review* 113 (October 2008): 1003–28.

Gosse, Van. *The First Reconstruction: Black Politics in America from the Revolution to the Civil War.* Chapel Hill: University of North Carolina Press, 2021.

Gosse, Van. "Patchwork Nation: Racial Orders and Disorder in the United States, 1790–1860." *Journal of the Early Republic* 40 (Spring 2020): 44–81.

Gough, Robert J. "The Myth of the 'Middle Colonies': An Analysis of Regionalization in Early America." *Pennsylvania Magazine of History and Biography* 107 (July 1983): 393–419.

Gould, Eliga H. *Among the Powers of the Earth: The American Revolution and the Making of a New World Empire*. Cambridge, Mass.: Harvard University Press, 2012.

Gould, Eliga H. *The Persistence of Empire: British Political Culture in the Age of the American Revolution*. Chapel Hill: University of North Carolina Press, 2000.

Gould, Eliga H. "Zones of Law, Zones of Violence: The Legal Geography of the British Atlantic, circa 1772." *William and Mary Quarterly*, 3rd series, 60 (July 2003): 471–510.

Gragg, Larry. *Englishmen Transplanted: The English Colonization of Barbados, 1627–1660*. Oxford: Oxford University Press, 2003.

Greene, Jack P., ed. *The American Revolution: Its Character and Limits*. New York: New York University Press, 1987.

Greene, Jack P. *Evaluating Empire and Confronting Colonialism in Eighteenth-Century Britain*. Cambridge: Cambridge University Press, 2013.

Greene, Jack P., ed. *Exclusionary Empire: English Liberty Overseas, 1600–1900*. Cambridge: Cambridge University Press, 2010.

Greene, Jack P. "Liberty, Slavery and the Transformation of British Identity in the Eighteenth-Century West Indies." *Slavery and Abolition* 21 (April 2000): 1–31.

Greene, Jack P. *Peripheries and Center: Constitutional Development in the Extended Polities of the British Empire and United States, 1607–1788*. Athens: University of Georgia Press, 1986.

Gregory, James. *Mercy and British Culture, 1760–1960*. London: Bloomsbury, 2022.

Griffin, Patrick, ed. *Experiencing Empire: Power, People, and Revolution in Early America*. Charlottesville: University of Virginia Press, 2017.

Griffin, Patrick. *The Townshend Moment: The Making of Empire and Revolution in the Eighteenth Century*. New Haven, Conn.: Yale University Press, 2017.

Griffin, Patrick, et al., eds. *Between Sovereignty and Anarchy: The Politics of Violence in the American Revolutionary Era*. Charlottesville: University of Virginia Press, 2015.

Guasco, Michael J. *Slaves and Englishmen: Human Bondage in the Early Modern Atlantic World*. Philadelphia: University of Pennsylvania Press, 2014.

Hall, Catherine, and Sonya O. Rose, eds. *At Home with the Empire: Metropolitan Culture and the Imperial World*. Cambridge: Cambridge University Press, 2006.

Hamilton, David J. *Scotland, the Caribbean and the Atlantic World, 1750–1820.* Manchester, U.K.: Manchester University Press, 2005.
Hammond, John Craig. "Slavery, Settlement, and Empire: The Expansion and Growth of Slavery in the Interior of the North American Continent, 1770–1820." *Journal of the Early Republic* 32 (Summer 2012): 175–206.
Hanley, Ryan. *Beyond Slavery and Abolition: Black British Writing, c. 1770–1830.* Cambridge: Cambridge University Press, 2019.
Hannah-Jones, Nicole, et al., eds. *The 1619 Project: A New Origin Story.* New York: One World, 2021.
Hardesty, Jared Ross. *Black Lives, Native Lands, White Worlds: A History of Slavery in New England.* Amherst, Mass.: Bright Leaf, 2019.
Hardesty, Jared Ross. *Unfreedom: Slavery and Dependence in Eighteenth-Century Boston.* New York: New York University Press, 2016.
Harlow, Vincent T. *The Founding of the Second British Empire, 1763–1793.* 2 vols. London: Longmans, Green, 1952–64.
Harris, J. William. *The Hanging of Thomas Jeremiah: A Free Black Man's Encounter with Liberty.* New Haven, Conn.: Yale University Press, 2009.
Hattem, Michael D. *Past and Prologue: Politics and Memory in the American Revolution.* New Haven, Conn.: Yale University Press, 2020.
Heerman, M. Scott. "Abolishing Slavery in Motion: Foreign Captivity and International Abolitionism in the Early United States." *William and Mary Quarterly,* 3rd series, 77 (April 2020): 245–72.
Helg, Aline. *Slave No More: Self-Liberation before Abolitionism in the Americas.* Chapel Hill: University of North Carolina Press, 2019.
Herring, George C. *From Colony to Superpower: U.S. Foreign Relations since 1776.* New York: Oxford University Press, 2008.
Higginbotham, Don. "Some Reflections on the South in the American Revolution." *Journal of Southern History* 73 (August 2007): 659–70.
Higgins, W. Robert, ed. *The Revolutionary War in the South: Power, Conflict and Leadership.* Durham, N.C.: Duke University Press, 1979.
Higman, B. W. "The Sugar Revolution." *Economic History Review* 53, no. 2 (2000): 213–36.
Hinderaker, Eric. *Boston's Massacre.* Cambridge, Mass.: Belknap Press of Harvard University Press, 2017.
Hoffman, Ronald. *A Spirit of Dissension: Economics, Politics, and the Revolution in Maryland.* Baltimore: Johns Hopkins University Press, 1973.
Hoffman, Ronald, and Peter J. Albert, eds. *Peace and the Peacemakers: The Treaty of 1783.* Charlottesville: University of Virginia Press, 1986.
Holton, Woody. *Forced Founders: Indians, Debtors, Slaves, and the Making of the American Revolution in Virginia.* Chapel Hill: University of North Carolina Press, 1999.

Holton, Woody. *Liberty Is Sweet: The Hidden History of the American Revolution.* New York: Simon and Schuster, 2021.

Hoock, Holger. *Scars of Independence: America's Violent Birth.* New York: Crown, 2017.

Horne, Gerald. *The Counter-Revolution of 1776: Slave Resistance and the Origins of the United States of America.* New York: New York University Press, 2016.

Horne, Gerald. *Negro Comrades of the Crown: African Americans and the British Empire Fight the U.S. before Emancipation.* New York: New York University Press, 2012.

Hudson, Nicholas. "'Britons Never Will Be Slaves': National Myth, Conservatism, and the Beginnings of British Antislavery." *Eighteenth-Century Studies* 34 (Summer 2001): 559–76.

Hudson, Nicholas. "From 'Nation' to 'Race': The Origin of Racial Classification in Eighteenth-Century Thought." *Eighteenth-Century Studies* 29 (Spring 1996): 247–64.

Hudson, Nicholas. *Samuel Johnson and the Making of Modern England.* Cambridge: Cambridge University Press, 2003.

Hulsebosch, Daniel J. *Constituting Empire: New York and the Transformation of Constitutionalism in the Atlantic World, 1664–1830.* Chapel Hill: University of North Carolina Press, 2005.

Hulsebosch, Daniel J. "Nothing but Liberty: 'Somerset's Case' and the British Empire." *Law and History Review* 24, no. 3 (2006): 647–57.

Huston, James L. *The American and British Debate over Equality, 1776–1920.* Baton Rouge: Louisiana State University Press, 2017.

Hutchins, Zachary McLeod, ed. *Community without Consent: New Perspectives on the Stamp Act.* Hanover, N.H.: Dartmouth College Press, 2016.

The Impact of the American Revolution Abroad. Washington, D.C.: Library of Congress, 1976.

Isaac, Rhys. *Landon Carter's Uneasy Kingdom: Revolution and Rebellion on a Virginia Plantation.* New York: Oxford University Press, 2004.

Jackson, Maurice. *Let This Voice Be Heard: Anthony Benezet, Father of Atlantic Abolitionism.* Philadelphia: University of Pennsylvania Press, 2009.

James, Francis Godwin. *Ireland in the Empire, 1688–1770: A History of Ireland from the Williamite Wars to the Eve of the American Revolution.* Cambridge, Mass.: Harvard University Press, 1973.

James, Lawrence. *Raj: The Making and Unmaking of British India.* New York: St. Martin's Griffin, 1997.

James, Lawrence. *The Rise and Fall of the British Empire.* New York: St. Martin's Griffin, 1994.

Janis, Mark Weston. *America and the Law of Nations, 1776–1939.* Oxford: Oxford University Press, 2010.

Jasanoff, Maya. *Liberty's Exiles: American Loyalists in the Revolutionary World.* New York: Knopf, 2011.

Jones, Brad A. *Resisting Independence: Popular Loyalism in the Revolutionary British Atlantic.* Ithaca, N.Y.: Cornell University Press, 2021.

Jones, T. Cole. *Captives of Liberty: Prisoners of War and the Politics of Vengeance in the American Revolution.* Philadelphia: University of Pennsylvania Press, 2020.

Jones, T. Cole. "'The Dreadful Effects of British Cruilty': The Treatment of British Maritime Prisoners and the Radicalization of the Revolutionary War at Sea." *Journal of the Early Republic* 36 (Fall 2016): 435–65.

Jordan, Will R., ed. "When in the Course of Human Events": *1776 at Home, Abroad, and in American Memory.* Macon, Ga.: Mercer University Press, 2018.

Jordan, Winthrop D. *White over Black: American Attitudes toward the Negro, 1550–1812.* Baltimore: Penguin, 1969.

Kaplan, Sidney, and Emma Nogrady Kaplan. *The Black Presence in the Era of the American Revolution.* Amherst: University of Massachusetts Press, 1989.

Kelly, Joseph. *Marooned: Jamestown, Shipwreck, and a New History of America's Origin.* New York: Bloomsbury, 2018.

Kendi, Ibram X. *Stamped from the Beginning: The Definitive History of Racist Ideas in America.* New York: Nation Books, 2016.

Kilbride, Daniel. *Being American in Europe, 1750–1860.* Baltimore: Johns Hopkins University Press, 2013.

Klooster, Wim, ed. *The Cambridge History of the Age of Atlantic Revolutions,* vol. 1, *The Enlightenment and the British Colonies.* Cambridge: Cambridge University Press, 2023.

Klooster, Wim. *Revolutions in the Atlantic World: A Comparative History.* New York: New York University Press, 2009.

Klose, Fabian. *In the Cause of Humanity: A History of Humanitarian Intervention in the Long Nineteenth Century.* Cambridge: Cambridge University Press, 2022.

Knott, Sarah. *Sensibility and the American Revolution.* Chapel Hill: University of North Carolina Press, 2009.

Kupperman, Karen Ordahl, ed. *America in European Consciousness, 1493–1750.* Chapel Hill: University of North Carolina Press, 1995.

Kupperman, Karen Ordahl. *Providence Island, 1630–1641: The Other Puritan Colony.* Cambridge: Cambridge University Press, 1993.

Kurtz, Stephen G., and James H. Hutson, eds. *Essays on the American Revolution.* Chapel Hill: University of North Carolina Press, 1973.

LaCroix, Alison L. *The Ideological Origins of American Federalism.* Cambridge, Mass.: Harvard University Press, 2010.

Langford, Paul. *A Polite and Commercial People: England, 1727–1783.* Oxford: Oxford University Press, 1989.

Larson, Edward J. *American Inheritance: Liberty and Slavery in the Birth of a Nation, 1765–1795.* New York: Norton, 2023.
Lascelles, E. C. P. *Granville Sharp and the Freedom of Slaves in England.* 1928; reprint, New York: Negro Universities Press, 1969.
Lauber, Almon Wheeler. *Indian Slavery in Colonial Times within the Present Limits of the United States.* 1913; reprint, New York: AMS Press, 1969.
Lawson, Philip, and Jim Phillips. "'Our Execrable Banditti': Perceptions of Nabobs in Mid-Eighteenth Century Britain." *Albion* 16 (Autumn 1984): 225–41.
Lee, Wayne. *Barbarians and Brothers: Anglo-American Warfare, 1500–1865.* Oxford: Oxford University Press, 2011.
Lepore, Jill. *The Name of War: King Philip's War and the Origins of American Identity.* New York: Knopf, 1998.
Linebaugh, Peter, and Marcus Rediker. *The Many-Headed Hydra: Sailors, Slaves, Commoners, and the Hidden History of the Revolutionary Atlantic.* Boston: Beacon Press, 2000.
Littlefield, Daniel C. "John Jay, the Revolutionary Generation, and Slavery." *New York History* 81 (2000): 91–132.
Litto, Fredric M. "Addison's Cato in the Colonies." *William and Mary Quarterly,* 3rd series, 23 (July 1966): 431–49.
Lockridge, Kenneth A. *The Diary, and Life, of William Byrd II of Virginia, 1674–1744.* Chapel Hill: University of North Carolina Press, 1987.
Lockwood, Matthew. *To Begin the World Over Again: How the American Revolution Devastated the Globe.* New Haven, Conn.: Yale University Press, 2019.
Lynch, James. "The Limits of Revolutionary Radicalism: Tom Paine and Slavery." *Pennsylvania Magazine of History and Biography* 123 (July 1999): 177–99.
Lynd, Staughton, and David Waldstreicher. "Free Trade, Sovereignty, and Slavery: Toward an Economic Interpretation of American Independence." *William and Mary Quarterly,* 3rd series, 68 (October 2011): 597–630.
Lyons, Benjamin. "The Law of Nations and the Negotiation of the Treaty of Paris (1783)." *Journal of the Early Republic* 42 (Summer 2022): 205–25.
Mackesy, Piers. *The War for America, 1775–1783.* Lincoln: University of Nebraska Press, 1964.
MacLeod, Duncan J. *Slavery, Race and the American Revolution.* Cambridge: Cambridge University Press, 1974.
Macleod, Emma. *British Visions of America, 1775–1820: Republican Realities.* London: Pickering and Chatto, 2013.
Macleod, Emma. "A Proper Manner of Carrying on Controversies: Richard Price and the American Revolution." *Huntington Library Quarterly* 82 (Summer 2019): 277–302.
MacMaster, Richard K. "Arthur Lee's 'Address on Slavery': An Aspect of Virginia's Struggle to End the Slave Trade, 1765–1774." *Virginia Magazine of History and Biography* 80 (April 1972): 141–57.

Major, Andrea. *Slavery, Abolitionism and Empire in India, 1772–1843.* Liverpool: Liverpool University Press, 2012.

Mandler, Peter. *The English National Character: The History of an Idea from Edmund Burke to Tony Blair.* New Haven, Conn.: Yale University Press, 2006.

Marshall, P. J. *"A Free though Conquering People": Eighteenth-Century Britain and Its Empire.* Aldershot, U.K.: Ashgate, 2003.

Marshall, P. J. *The Making and Unmaking of Empires: Britain, India, and America, c. 1750–1783.* Oxford: Oxford University Press, 2005.

Marshall, P. J., ed. *The Oxford History of the British Empire*, vol. 2, *The Eighteenth Century.* Oxford: Oxford University Press, 1998.

Marston, Jerrilyn Greene. *King and Congress: The Transfer of Political Legitimacy, 1774–1776.* Princeton, N.J.: Princeton University Press, 1987.

Mason, Keith. "A Loyalist's Journey: James Parker's Response to the Revolutionary Crisis." *Virginia Magazine of History and Biography* 102 (April 1994): 139–66.

Mason, Matthew. "A Missed Opportunity? The Founding, Postcolonial Realities, and the Abolition of Slavery." *Slavery and Abolition* 35 (June 2014): 199–213.

Mason, Matthew. "North American Calm, West Indian Storm: The Politics of the Somerset Decision in the British Atlantic," *Slavery and Abolition* 41, no. 4 (2020): 723–47.

Mason, Matthew. *Slavery and Politics in the Early American Republic.* Chapel Hill: University of North Carolina Press, 2006.

Mason, Matthew. "Slavery, Servitude, and British Representations of Colonial North America." *Southern Quarterly* 43, no. 4 (Summer 2006): 109–25.

Massey, Gregory D. *John Laurens and the American Revolution.* Columbia: University of South Carolina Press, 2000.

Massey, Gregory D. "The Limits of Antislavery Thought in the Revolutionary Lower South: John Laurens and Henry Laurens." *Journal of Southern History* 63 (August 1997): 495–530.

Mayer, Henry. *A Son of Thunder: Patrick Henry and the American Republic.* New York: Grove, 1991.

Mayer, Holly A., ed. *Women Waging War in the American Revolution.* Charlottesville: University of Virginia Press, 2022.

McConville, Brendan. *The King's Three Faces: The Rise and Fall of Royal America, 1688–1776.* Chapel Hill: University of North Carolina Press, 2006.

McDonnell, Michael A. *The Politics of War: Race, Class, and Conflict in Revolutionary Virginia.* Chapel Hill: University of North Carolina Press, 2007.

Menard, Russell R. *Sweet Negotiations: Sugar, Slavery, and Plantation Agriculture in Early Barbados.* Charlottesville: University of Virginia Press, 2006.

Molineux, Catherine. *Faces of Perfect Ebony: Encountering Atlantic Slavery in Imperial Britain*. Cambridge, Mass.: Harvard University Press, 2012.

Molineux, Catherine. "Pleasures of the Smoke: 'Black Virginians' in Georgian London's Tobacco Shops." *William and Mary Quarterly*, 3rd series, 64 (April 2007): 327–76.

Moniz, Amanda. *From Empire to Humanity: The American Revolution and the Origins of Humanitarianism*. New York: Oxford University Press, 2016.

Monod, Paul Kleber. *Imperial Island: A History of Britain and Its Empire, 1660–1837*. Chichester, U.K.: Wiley-Blackwell, 2009.

Moore, Sean D. *Slavery and the Making of Early American Libraries: British Literature, Political Thought, and the Transatlantic Book Trade, 1731–1814*. Oxford: Oxford University Press, 2019.

Moots, Glenn A., and Phillip Hamilton, eds. *Justifying Revolution: Law, Virtue, and Violence in the American War of Independence*. Norman: University of Oklahoma Press, 2018.

Morgan, Edmund S. *American Slavery, American Freedom: The Ordeal of Colonial Virginia*. New York: Norton, 1975.

Morgan, Edmund S., and H. M. Morgan. *The Stamp Act Crisis: Prologue to Revolution*. Chapel Hill: University of North Carolina Press, 1953.

Morgan, Philip D., and Sean Hawkins, eds. *Black Experience and the Empire*. Oxford: Oxford University Press, 2004.

Morris, Richard B. *The Peacemakers: The Great Powers and American Independence*. New York: Harper and Row, 1965.

Morton, Louis. *Robert Carter of Nomini Hall*. Charlottesville: University Press of Virginia, 1941.

Muller, Hannah Weiss. "Bonds of Belonging: Subjecthood and the British Empire." *Journal of British Studies* 53 (January 2014): 29–58.

Mullin, Gerald W. *Flight and Rebellion: Slave Resistance in Eighteenth-Century Virginia*. New York: Oxford University Press, 1972.

Murrin, John M. *Rethinking America: From Empire to Republic*. Oxford: Oxford University Press, 2018.

Musselwhite, Paul. *Urban Dreams, Rural Commonwealth: The Rise of Plantation Society in the Chesapeake*. Chicago: University of Chicago Press, 2019.

Musselwhite, Paul, Peter C. Mancall, and James Horn, eds. *Virginia 1619: Slavery and Freedom in the Making of Early America*. Chapel Hill: University of North Carolina Press, 2019.

Muthu, Sankar. *Enlightenment against Empire*. Princeton, N.J.: Princeton University Press, 2003.

Nechtman, Tillman W. *Nabobs: Empire and Identity in Eighteenth-Century Britain*. Cambridge: Cambridge University Press, 2010.

Nedelhaft, Jerome. *The Disorders of War: The Revolution in South Carolina*. Orono: University of Maine at Orono Press, 1981.

Nelson, Eric. "Patriot Royalism: The Stuart Monarchy in American Political Thought, 1769–75." *William and Mary Quarterly*, 3rd series, 68 (October 2011): 533–72.

Nelson, Paul David. *William Tryon and the Course of Empire: A Life in British Imperial Service*. Chapel Hill: University of North Carolina Press, 1990.

Newman, Richard, and James Mueller, eds. *Antislavery and Abolition in Philadelphia: Emancipation and the Long Struggle for Racial Justice in the City of Brotherly Love*. Baton Rouge: Louisiana State University Press, 2011.

Newman, Simon P. *Freedom Seekers: Escaping from Slavery in Restoration London*. London: University of London Press, 2022.

Newman, Simon P. *A New World of Labor: The Development of Plantation Slavery in the British Atlantic*. Philadelphia: University of Pennsylvania Press, 2013.

Nyquist, Mary. *Arbitrary Rule: Slavery, Tyranny, and the Power of Life and Death*. Chicago: University of Chicago Press, 2013.

Okoye, F. Nwabueze. "Chattel Slavery as the Nightmare of the American Revolutionaries." *William and Mary Quarterly*, 3rd series, 37 (1980): 3–28.

Oldfield, J. R. *Transatlantic Abolitionism in the Age of Revolution: An International History of Anti-Slavery, c. 1787–1820*. Cambridge: Cambridge University Press, 2013.

Olson, Alison Gilbert. *Making the Empire Work: London and American Interest Groups, 1690–1790*. Cambridge, Mass.: Harvard University Press, 1992.

Olwell, Robert A. "'Domestick Enemies': Slavery and Political Independence in South Carolina, May 1775–March 1776." *Journal of Southern History* 56 (February 1989): 21–48.

Olwell, Robert, and Alan Tully, eds. *Cultures and Identities in Colonial British America*. Baltimore: Johns Hopkins University Press, 2006.

Olwell, Robert A., and James M. Vaughn, eds. *Envisioning Empire: The New British World from 1763 to 1773*. London: Bloomsbury Academic, 2020.

Onuf, Peter, and Nicholas Onuf. *Federal Union, Modern World: The Law of Nations in an Age of Revolutions, 1776–1814*. Madison, Wis.: Madison House, 1993.

Orr, Bridget. *Empire on the English Stage, 1660–1714*. Cambridge: Cambridge University Press, 2001.

Oshatz, Molly. *Slavery and Sin: The Fight against Slavery and the Rise of Liberal Protestantism*. Oxford: Oxford University Press, 2012.

O'Shaughnessy, Andrew Jackson. *An Empire Divided: The American Revolution and the British Caribbean*. Philadelphia: University of Pennsylvania Press, 2000.

O'Shaughnessy, Andrew Jackson. *The Men Who Lost America: British Leadership, the American Revolution, and the Fate of the Empire*. New Haven, Conn.: Yale University Press, 2013.

Pagden, Anthony. *Lords of All the World: Ideologies of Empire in Spain, Britain and France, c. 1500 to c. 1800*. New Haven, Conn.: Yale University Press, 1995.

Paley, Ruth, Christina Malcolmson, and Michael Hunter, eds. "Parliament and Slavery, 1660–c. 1710." *Slavery and Abolition* 31 (June 2010): 257–81.
Parent, Anthony S., Jr. *Foul Means: The Formation of a Slave Society in Virginia, 1660–1740*. Chapel Hill: University of North Carolina Press, 2003.
Parkinson, Robert G. *The Common Cause: Creating Race and Nation in the American Revolution*. Chapel Hill: University of North Carolina Press, 2016.
Parkinson, Robert G. "War and the Imperative of Union." *William and Mary Quarterly*, 3rd series, 68 (October 2011): 631–34.
Peabody, Sue. "An Alternative Genealogy of the Origins of French Free Soil: Medieval Toulouse." *Slavery and Abolition* 32 (September 2011): 341–62.
Peabody, Sue. *"There Are No Slaves in France": The Political Culture of Race and Slavery in the Ancien Regime*. Oxford: Oxford University Press, 1996.
Pestana, Carla Gardina. *The English Atlantic in the Age of Revolution, 1640–1661*. Cambridge, Mass.: Harvard University Press, 2004.
Pestana, Carla Gardina. *Protestant Empire: Religion and the Making of the British Atlantic World*. Philadelphia: University of Pennsylvania Press, 2009.
Pettigrew, William A. *Freedom's Debt: The Royal African Company and the Politics of the Atlantic Slave Trade, 1672–1752*. Chapel Hill: University of North Carolina Press, 2013.
Philyaw, L. Scott. "A Slave for Every Soldier: The Strange History of Virginia's Forgotten Recruitment Act of 1 January 1781." *Virginia Magazine of History and Biography* 109, no. 4 (2001): 367–86.
Piecuch, Jim. *Three Peoples, One King: Loyalists, Indians, and Slaves in the Revolutionary South, 1775–1782*. Columbia: University of South Carolina Press, 2008.
Pincus, Steven. "Rethinking Mercantilism: Political Economy, the British Empire, and the Atlantic World in the Seventeenth and Eighteenth Centuries." *William and Mary Quarterly*, 3rd series, 69 (January 2012): 3–34.
Polgar, Paul J. *Standard-Bearers of Equality: America's First Abolition Movement*. Chapel Hill: University of North Carolina Press, 2019.
Potts, Louis W. *Arthur Lee, a Virtuous Revolutionary*. Baton Rouge: Louisiana State University Press, 1981.
Pulis, John W., ed. *Moving On: Black Loyalists in the Afro-Atlantic World*. New York: Garland, 1999.
Pulsipher, Jenny Hale. *Subjects unto the Same King: Indians, English, and the Contest for Authority in Colonial New England*. Philadelphia: University of Pennsylvania Press, 2005.
Pulsipher, Jenny Hale. *Swindler Sachem: The American Indian Who Sold His Birthright, Dropped Out of Harvard, and Conned the King of England*. New Haven, Conn.: Yale University Press, 2018.
Pybus, Cassandra. *Epic Journeys of Freedom: Runaway Slaves of the American Revolution and Their Global Quest for Liberty*. Boston: Beacon Press, 2006.

Quarles, Benjamin. *The Negro in the American Revolution*. 1961; reprint, Chapel Hill: University of North Carolina Press, 1996.

Rabin, Dana Y. *Britain and Its Internal Others, 1750–1800: Under Rule of Law*. Manchester, U.K.: Manchester University Press, 2017.

Rael, Patrick. *Eighty-Eight Years: The Long Death of Slavery in the United States, 1777–1865*. Athens: University of Georgia Press, 2015.

Ragsdale, Bruce. *A Planters' Republic: The Search for Economic Independence in Revolutionary Virginia*. Madison, Wis.: Madison House, 1996.

Reid, John Phillip. *The Concept of Liberty in the Age of the American Revolution*. Chicago: University of Chicago Press, 1988.

Rezek, Joseph. *London and the Making of Provincial Literature: Aesthetics and the Transatlantic Book Trade, 1800–1850*. Philadelphia: University of Pennsylvania Press, 2015.

Richardson, David. *Principles and Agents: The British Slave Trade and Its Abolition*. New Haven, Conn.: Yale University Press, 2022.

Rivers, Isabel, and David L. Wykes, ed. *Joseph Priestley, Scientist, Philosopher, and Theologian*. Oxford: Oxford University Press, 2008.

Roberts, Justin. *Slavery and the Enlightenment in the British Atlantic, 1750–1807*. Cambridge: Cambridge University Press, 2013.

Robertson, James. "An Essay Concerning Slavery: A Mid-Eighteenth Century Analysis from Jamaica." *Slavery and Abolition* 33 (March 2012): 65–85.

Robinson, Donald L. *Slavery in the Structure of American Politics, 1765–1820*. New York: Harcourt Brace Jovanovich, 1971.

Rodgers, Nini. *Ireland, Slavery, and Antislavery: 1612–1865*. Basingstroke, U.K.: Palgrave Macmillan, 2007.

Rosenberg, Phillippe. "Thomas Tryon and the Seventeenth Century Dimensions of Anti-Slavery." *William and Mary Quarterly*, 3rd series, 16 (October 2004): 609–42.

Royle, Edward, and James Walvin. *English Radicals and Reformers, 1760–1848*. Brighton, U.K.: Harvester Press, 1982.

Rozbicki, Michal Jan. *The Complete Colonial Gentleman: Cultural Legitimacy in Plantation America*. Charlottesville: University Press of Virginia, 1998.

Rozbicki, Michal Jan. *Culture and Liberty in the Age of the American Revolution*. Charlottesville: University of Virginia Press, 2011.

Ruddiman, John A. "'Is This the Land of Liberty?': Continental Soldiers and Slavery in the Revolutionary South." *William and Mary Quarterly*, 3rd series, 79 (April 2022): 283–314.

Rugemer, Edward B. *Slave Law and the Politics of Resistance in the Early Atlantic World*. Cambridge, Mass.: Harvard University Press, 2018.

Runciman, David. *Political Hypocrisy: The Mask of Power, from Hobbes to Orwell and Beyond*. Princeton, N.J.: Princeton University Press, 2008.

Rushton, Peter, and Gwenda Morgan. *Treason and Rebellion in the British Atlantic, 1685–1800*. London: Bloomsbury, 2020.
Sachse, William L. *The Colonial American in Britain*. Madison: University of Wisconsin Press, 1956.
Saillant, John. "Slavery and Divine Providence in New England Calvinism: The New Divinity and a Black Protest, 1775–1805." *New England Quarterly* 68 (December 1995): 584–608.
Sainsbury, John. *Disaffected Patriots: London Supporters of Revolutionary America, 1769–1782*. Montreal, Ont.: McGill-Queen's University Press, 1987.
Sassi, Jonathan. "With a Little Help from the Friends: The Quaker and Tactical Contexts of Anthony Benezet's Abolitionist Publishing." *Pennsylvania Magazine of History and Biography* 135 (January 2011): 33–71.
Schama, Simon. *Rough Crossings: Britain, the Slaves and the American Revolution*. New York: HarperCollins, 2006.
Sesay, Chernoh M., Jr. "The Revolutionary Black Roots of Slavery's Abolition in Massachusetts." *New England Quarterly* 87 (March 2014): 99–131.
Shaffer, Jason. *Performing Patriotism: National Identity in the Colonial and Revolutionary American Theater*. Philadelphia: University of Pennsylvania Press, 2007.
Shankman, Andrew. "Toward a Social History of Federalism: The State and Capitalism to and from the American Revolution." *Journal of the Early Republic* 37 (Winter 2017): 615–53.
Shankman, Andrew, ed. *The World of the Revolutionary American Republic: Land, Labor, and the Conflict for a Continent*. New York: Routledge, 2014.
Shannon, Timothy. "A 'Wicked Commerce': Consent, Coercion, and Kidnapping in Aberdeen's Servant Trade." *William and Mary Quarterly*, 3rd series, 74 (July 2017): 437–66.
Sharples, Jason T. *The World That Fear Made: Slave Revolts and Conspiracy Scares in Early America*. Philadelphia: University of Pennsylvania Press, 2020.
Sheridan, Richard B. "The Jamaican Slave Insurrection Scare of 1776 and the American Revolution." *Journal of Negro History* 61 (July 1976): 290–308.
Shields, David S., and Fredrika J. Teute. "The Meschianza: Sum of All Fetes." *Journal of the Early Republic* 35 (Summer 2015): 185–214.
Shyllon, Folarin. *Black People in Britain, 1555–1833*. London: Oxford University Press, 1977.
Shyllon, Folarin. *Black Slaves in Britain*. Oxford: Oxford University Press, 1974.
Silverman, Kenneth. *A Cultural History of the American Revolution: Painting, Music, Literature, and the Theatre in the Colonies and the United States from the Treaty of Paris to the Inauguration of George Washington, 1763–1789*. New York: Thomas Y. Crowell, 1976.
Sinha, Manisha. *The Slave's Cause: A History of Abolition*. New Haven, Conn.: Yale University Press, 2016.

Sinha, Manisha. "To 'Cast Just Obliquy' on Oppressors: Black Radicalism in the Age of Revolution." *William and Mary Quarterly*, 3rd series, 44 (January 2007): 149–60.

Sirota, Brent S. *The Christian Monitors: The Church of England and the Age of Benevolence, 1680–1730.* New Haven, Conn.: Yale University Press, 2014.

Slaughter, Thomas P. *The Beautiful Soul of John Woolman, Apostle of Abolition.* New York: Macmillan, 2008.

Smith, Craig Bruce. *American Honor: The Creation of the Nation's Ideals during the Revolutionary Era.* Chapel Hill: University of North Carolina Press, 2018.

Sparks, Randy J. *The Two Princes of Calabar: An Eighteenth-Century Atlantic Odyssey.* Cambridge, Mass.: Harvard University Press, 2004.

Spector, Robert M. "The Quock Walker Cases (1781–1783): Slavery, Its Abolition, and Negro Citizenship in Early Massachusetts." *Journal of Negro History* 53 (January 1968): 12–32.

Spero, Patrick, and Michael Zuckerman, eds. *The American Revolution Reborn.* Philadelphia: University of Pennsylvania Press, 2016.

Stahr, Walter. *John Jay: Founding Father.* New York: Hambledon and London, 2005.

Stamatov, Peter. *The Origins of Global Humanitarianism: Religion, Empires, and Advocacy.* Cambridge: Cambridge University Press, 2013.

Stanwood, Owen. *The Empire Reformed: English America in the Age of the Glorious Revolution.* Philadelphia: University of Pennsylvania Press, 2011.

Steinfeld, Robert J. *The Invention of Free Labor: The Employment Relation in English and American Law and Culture, 1350–1870.* Chapel Hill: University of North Carolina Press, 1991.

Stovall, Tyler. *White Freedom: The Racial History of an Idea.* Princeton, N.J.: Princeton University Press, 2021.

Suranyi, Anna. *Indentured Servitude: Unfree Labour and Citizenship in the British Colonies.* Montreal, Ont.: McGill-Queen's University Press, 2021.

Swaminathan, Srividhya. *Debating the Slave Trade: Rhetoric of British National Identity, 1759–1815.* London: Ashgate, 2009.

Swaminathan, Srividhya. "Developing the West Indian Proslavery Position after the Somerset Decision." *Slavery and Abolition* 24 (December 2003): 40–60.

Swingen, Abigail L. *Competing Visions of Empire: Labor, Slavery, and the Origins of the British Atlantic Empire.* New Haven, Conn.: Yale University Press, 2015.

Sword, Kirsten. "Remembering Dinah Nevil: Strategic Deceptions in Eighteenth-Century Antislavery." *Journal of American History* 97 (September 2010): 315–43.

Sword, Kirsten. *Wives Not Slaves: Patriarchy and Modernity in the Age of Revolutions.* Chicago: University of Chicago Press, 2021.

Taylor, Alan. *American Colonies.* New York: Penguin, 2001.

Taylor, Alan. *American Revolutions: A Continental History, 1750–1804*. New York: Norton, 2016.
Taylor, Alan. *The Internal Enemy: Slavery and War in Virginia, 1772–1832*. New York: Norton, 2013.
Taylor, Alan. "Introduction: Expand or Die: The Revolution's New Empire." *William and Mary Quarterly*, 3rd series, 74 (Oct. 2017): 619–32, and *Journal of the Early Republic* 37 (Winter 2017): 599–614.
Taylor, William Harrison. *Unity in Christ and Country: American Presbyterians in the Revolutionary Era, 1758–1801*. Tuscaloosa: University of Alabama Press, 2017.
Thomas, P. D. G. *The House of Commons in the Eighteenth Century*. Oxford: Clarendon Press, 1971.
Tiedemann, Joseph S., et al., eds. *The Other Loyalists: Ordinary People, Royalism, and the Revolution in the Middle Colonies, 1763–1787*. Albany: SUNY Press, 1987.
Tomlins, Christopher. *Freedom Bound: Law, Labor, and Civic Identity in Colonizing English America, 1580–1865*. Cambridge: Cambridge University Press, 2010.
Tycko, Sonia. "The Legality of Prisoner of War Labour in England, 1648–1655." *Past and Present* 246 (February 2020): 35–68.
Van Buskirk, Judith L. *Generous Enemies: Patriots and Loyalists in Revolutionary New York*. Philadelphia: University of Pennsylvania Press, 2002.
Van Buskirk, Judith L. *Standing in Their Own Light: African American Patriots in the American Revolution*. Norman: University of Oklahoma Press, 2017.
Van Cleve, George William. "Mansfield's Decision: Toward Human Freedom." *Law and History Review* 24, no. 3 (2006): 665–71.
Van Cleve, George William. *A Slaveholders' Union: Slavery, Politics, and the Constitution in the Early American Republic*. Chicago: University of Chicago Press, 2010.
Van Cleve, George William. "'Somerset's Case' and Its Antecedents in Imperial Perspective." *Law and History Review* 24, no. 3 (2006): 601–45.
Vaughn, James M. *The Politics of Empire at the Accession of George III: The East India Company and the Crisis and Transformation of Britain's Imperial State*. New Haven, Conn.: Yale University Press, 2019.
Voelz, Peter M. *Slave and Soldier: The Military Impact of Blacks in the Colonial Americas*. New York: Garland, 1993.
Wahrman, Dror. "The English Problem of Identity in the American Revolution." *American Historical Review* 106 (October 2001): 1236–62.
Waldstreicher, David. "Ancients, Moderns, and Africans: Phillis Wheatley and the Politics of Empire and Slavery in the American Revolution." *Journal of the Early Republic* 37 (Winter 2017): 701–33.

Waldstreicher, David. "The Changing Same of U.S. History." *Boston Review*, 10 November 2021, https://www.bostonreview.net/articles/the-changing-same-of-u-s-history/.

Waldstreicher, David. "The Hidden Stakes of the 1619 Controversy." *Boston Review*, 24 January 2020, https://www.bostonreview.net/articles/david-waldstreicher-hidden-stakes-1619-controversy/.

Waldstreicher, David. *The Odyssey of Phillis Wheatley*. New York: Farrar, Straus and Giroux, 2023.

Waldstreicher, David. *Runaway America: Benjamin Franklin, Slavery, and the American Revolution*. New York: Hill and Wang, 2004.

Waldstreicher, David. *Slavery's Constitution: From Revolution to Ratification*. New York: Hill and Wang, 2009.

Walvin, James. *Black and White: The Negro in English Society, 1555–1945*. London: Allen Lane, the Penguin Press, 1973.

Walvin, James. *England, Slaves, and Freedom, 1776–1838*. Houndsmills, U.K.: Macmillan, 1986.

Walvin, James. *The Zong: A Massacre, the Law and the End of Slavery*. New Haven, Conn.: Yale University Press, 2011.

Warren, Wendy. *New England Bound: Slavery and Colonization in Early America*. New York: Liveright, 2016.

Weimer, Adrian Chastain. *A Constitutional Culture: New England and the Struggle against Arbitrary Rule in the Restoration Empire*. Philadelphia: University of Pennsylvania Press, 2023.

Weiss, Gillian. "Infidels at the Oar: A Mediterranean Exception to France's Free Soil Principle." *Slavery and Abolition* 32 (September 2011): 397–412.

Whiting, Gloria McCahon. "Emancipation without the Courts or Constitution: The Case of Revolutionary Massachusetts." *Slavery and Abolition* 41, no. 3 (2020): 458–78.

Wickwire, Franklin, and Mary Wickwire. *Cornwallis: The American Adventure*. Boston: Houghton Mifflin, 1970.

Wiecek, William M. "*Somerset*: Lord Mansfield and the Legitimacy of Slavery in the Anglo-American World." *University of Chicago Law Review* 42, no. 1 (1974): 86–146.

Wiencek, Henry. *An Imperfect God: George Washington, His Slaves, and the Creation of America*. New York: Farrar, Straus and Giroux, 2003.

Wilentz, Sean. *No Property in Man: Slavery and Antislavery at the Nation's Founding*. Cambridge, Mass.: Harvard University Press, 2018.

Wilson, Kathleen. *The Island Race: Englishness, Empire and Gender in the Eighteenth Century*. New York: Routledge, 2003.

Wilson, Kathleen. *The Sense of the People: Politics, Culture, and Imperialism in England, 1715–1785*. Cambridge: Cambridge University Press, 1995.

Wilson, Lee B. *Bonds of Empire: The English Origins of Slave Law in South Carolina and British Plantation America, 1660–1783.* Cambridge: Cambridge University Press, 2021.
Wineman, Walter Ray. *The Landon Carter Papers in the University of Virginia Library: A Calendar and Biographical Sketch.* Charlottesville: University of Virginia Press, 1962.
Wood, Gordon S. *The American Revolution: A History.* New York: Modern Library, 2002.
Wood, Gordon S. *The Idea of America: Reflections on the Birth of the United States.* New York: Penguin, 2011.
Wood, Gordon S. *Power and Liberty: Constitutionalism in the American Revolution.* Oxford: Oxford University Press, 2021.
Wood, Gordon S. *The Radicalism of the American Revolution.* New York: Vintage Books, 1991.
Wood, Gordon S. *Revolutionary Characters: What Made the Founders Different.* New York: Penguin, 2006.
Wood, Peter H. *Black Majority: Negroes in Colonial South Carolina from 1670 through the Stono Rebellion.* New York: Norton, 1974.
Working, Lauren. *The Making of an Imperial Polity: Civility and America in the Jacobean Metropolis.* Cambridge: Cambridge University Press, 2020.
York, Neil Longley. *Neither Kingdom nor Nation: The Irish Quest for Constitutional Rights, 1698–1800.* Washington, D.C.: Catholic University of America Press, 1994.
Young, Alfred F., ed. *The American Revolution: Explorations in the History of American Radicalism.* DeKalb: Northern Illinois University Press, 1976.
Young, Alfred F., ed. *Beyond the American Revolution: Explorations in the History of American Radicalism.* DeKalb: Northern Illinois University Press, 1993.
Zelnik, Eran. "Self-Evident Walls: Reckoning with Recent Histories of Race and Nation." *Journal of the Early Republic* 41 (Spring 2021): 1–38.

INDEX

abolitionists, 2, 85, 88, 103–4, 107, 120, 137, 154, 157, 177–79, 187–201, 203, 207–11, 215, 217; historiography of, 18–19, 28, 38, 44, 205–6, 217, 220–21n9, 224n37, 225n17, 226n32, 228n72, 228–29n81, 233n7
Adams, Abigail, 202
Adams, John, 134, 144, 146–52, 155, 168, 182, 199, 202
Adams, Samuel, 144–45, 156
Allen, Ethan, 70
Allen, John, 192, 262n43
Allen, William, 76
Allinson, Samuel, 188, 198
American Revolution: historiography of, 2–6, 54–57, 157–58, 161, 173–77, 205–7, 213, 216–17, 220–21n9, 232n3, 239n25, 247n51, 265n81, 265n86, 268n102, 269n118, 272nn6–7, 273n17, 274–75n35, 279n87, 282n126, 284nn2–3; stakes of, 1, 54, 59–74, 197; War of the, 60–61, 64–66, 69–71, 80, 85–86, 91, 93, 96–97, 99–100, 110–11, 139, 144–45, 147–48, 150, 157–58, 163–64, 174, 177–80, 198–200, 205–9, 213, 216, 283n136
Anglicans, 23–25, 37, 39, 46, 73, 76, 93, 101, 105, 225n17
Atkins, Josiah, 129–30, 196
atrocities, politics of wartime, 92, 94, 98, 100, 111–19, 126–30, 135–37, 141, 148–49, 152–54, 250n77, 254–55n137
Attucks, Crispus, 152

Barbados. *See* West Indies, British
Barlow, Joel, 194
Barre, Isaac, 63, 149
Beckford, William, 29, 90, 145–46
Belinda (enslaved woman), 195, 280n91

Benezet, Anthony, 37–41, 187–88, 190, 193, 197, 280n99
Bentham, Jeremy, 81, 253n124
Black writers and freedom seekers. *See* slave resistance
Board of Trade, 42, 44, 48, 120, 223n19
Bolts, William, 103, 108
Boston Massacre, 68–69, 78, 143–44, 151–52, 196
Boswell, James, 104–5
British Empire: debates over nature of, 9–11, 14–15, 21–24, 101–3, 122–23, 205–13, 217; distribution of sovereignty within, 44, 47–49, 61–64, 68, 90, 107–10; government support for slavery and slaving in, 42–44, 47–48, 207–8, 212; historiography of, 9, 14–15, 157–62, 186–87, 205–7, 217, 221n3; metropolitan images of, general, 10–11, 77, 100–103, 105–6, 114–15, 128, 140, 147, 149–50, 202, 221n3; slavery and images of, 11, 20–21, 24–29, 31, 39, 47–48, 53–54, 79–80, 103–7
Bull, Fenwick, 131
Bull, Stephen, 127
Burgoyne, John, 91
Burke, Edmund, 23, 27, 49, 61, 74, 93, 104, 116–17, 121, 126–27, 135, 147
Burnaby, Andrew, 77, 158
Byrd, William, II, 29–31, 43

Campbell, Alexander, 116
Campbell, Lord William, 87, 123, 162
Carleton, Sir Guy, 164–72, 185–86, 206–7, 211–12
Carolina, 20–21, 25, 39, 43, 66, 77, 81–82, 87, 97, 101, 104, 122–23, 132–33, 136, 162, 178, 182–87, 195–96, 204–5, 211, 229n96

Carter, Landon, 29, 84, 98, 107, 126, 131, 144, 183–84, 257n165
Carter, Robert, 30, 132
Carter, Robert Wormeley, 76
Catholics. See Protestantism, cause of
Cave, Edward. See Gentleman's Magazine
Chauncy, Charles, 178, 274n21
Church of England. See Anglicans
Clinton, Sir Henry, 124, 131, 133, 137, 160, 163–64, 166, 169
Coercive Acts, 60, 67–69, 144, 149, 178
Congress, declarations and acts of, 69–70, 84, 92, 94, 110, 116, 120, 156, 172, 199. See also Declaration of Independence
consistency, value of in politics. See hypocrisy, charges of
Constitution: British, 35, 63–66, 72, 76, 78, 89–90, 93, 96–97, 102, 108, 143, 188, 202, 210; US, and slavery, 186–87, 216–17
Cornwallis, Lord, 66, 118–19, 124, 129–30, 136, 154
Cresswell, Nicholas, 80, 100, 104
Crèvecoeur, Hector St. John de, 72
Cromwell, Oliver, 12, 246–47n38
Cushing, William, 195, 280n92

Dana, Francis, 112
Dartmouth, Earl of, 87, 94–95, 114
Day, Thomas, 179
Deane, Silas, 127–28
Declaration of Independence, 55, 61, 80–81, 111, 121–22, 140, 150, 167, 182, 204, 253n124
De Lancey, Oliver, 169
Dickinson, John, 41, 67–68, 113, 143, 147, 264n69
Dissenters, religious, 26, 35, 72, 75–77, 88, 90, 103–4, 136, 179–81, 209
Dunmore, Lord, 61, 122, 152, 164, 224n4, 266n90; Proclamation of, 55, 69, 81, 89, 94–98, 125–38, 152–54, 157–67, 181–87, 213, 216, 244n97, 268n106

East India Company. See India
English Civil War and Revolution, 12–14, 16–17, 33, 43, 45, 54, 85, 89–91

English Empire. See British Empire
Enlightenment, 26–28, 53, 99, 104, 107, 111, 210
evacuations of North America by British forces, 129, 133, 163–72, 184–87, 205–7, 211–12

Fairfax, Bryan, 203
Florida, 35, 39, 118, 159, 226n21
Fox, Charles James, 93, 141, 211–12
France, alliance with US, 61–62, 85, 118, 134, 137, 140–41, 157–58, 167–68, 181. See also Protestantism, cause of
Franklin, Benjamin, 69, 82, 88–89, 110, 126, 134–35, 140–41, 149, 170, 182, 283n148
Freneau, Philip, 154

Gadsden, Christopher, 45, 67, 202–3, 205
Gage, Thomas, 78–79, 94, 115
Gates, Horatio, 144
gender, 56, 100, 154, 164–66, 184, 190, 251n90, 263n67, 269n116, 276n46
Gentleman's Magazine, 27, 29, 31–32, 63–64, 81, 86, 101–4, 123, 136, 210–11, 245n11
George III, 61–63, 71, 81, 86, 91–93, 97, 119, 121–22, 126, 128, 132, 134, 139, 141, 163, 208
Georgia, 39, 87, 184, 192
German mercenaries, 116–17, 135, 137, 148–49, 155, 158, 165, 185, 254–55n137
Glorious Revolution, 17, 23, 32–33, 48–49, 65–66, 91–93, 157
God, favor and punishment from, 1, 10, 25, 37–39, 75–76, 92, 137, 163, 178–80, 197–200, 207–9, 280n98
Godwyn, Morgan, 24, 225nn18–19
Goldsmith, Oliver, 76
Gordon, Thomas, 35, 46
Greene, Nathanael, 66, 113, 129, 195
Grenville, George, 59–60, 146
Grenville, James, 126
Gwynn, Peggy, 164–65

Hamilton, Alexander, 172
Harrison, Benjamin, 129

Hartley, David, 134–35, 210, 283n148
Haynes, Lemuel, 199
Henry, Patrick, 68, 97, 178, 198
Hillsborough, Earl of, 122, 224n4
honor: ideal of, 54, 63, 70, 82, 102–3, 112, 130, 139–72, 188, 200–201, 205–7, 211–12; personal and national, defined, 139–41, 165, 259n1
Hopkins, Samuel, 177, 199
Hopkins, Stephen, 203
Howe, William, 165
humanity: defined, 99–100, 165, 244n1; ideal of, 27–28, 32, 37, 54, 66, 70, 76, 81–82, 88, 99–142, 146, 153–54, 168, 171, 178–79, 181–82, 192, 199–200, 208–9, 211–12, 215
Huntingdon, Countess of, 162
Hutchinson, Thomas, 78, 87, 119, 122, 238n14
hypocrisy, charges of, 12, 40, 74–98, 123, 130–32, 147, 170, 179, 187–200, 202, 209–11

India, 10, 22, 61–62, 100–105, 107–8, 115, 140, 179, 207, 209, 245n13
Indigenous people, 10–12, 20–21, 23–24, 35, 39, 77, 81, 107, 151, 182, 189, 194, 209, 252n98; as British military allies, 56, 116–18, 128–29, 134–37, 142, 148–49, 158, 160–61, 174, 251n91, 254–55n137
Innes, Alexander, 160
Innes, William, 80
Ireland, 10–12, 14, 21, 23–24, 42, 45, 46, 62, 71, 93–94, 101, 103, 105, 152, 221n3
Izard, Ralph, 172, 186

Jackson, Judith, 164
Jacobites, 65, 93. *See also* Scottish influence, fear of
Jamaica. *See* West Indies, British
Jay, John, 112, 167–68, 263n67
Jefferson, Thomas, 121–22, 126, 131, 190, 204
Jeremiah, Thomas, 87, 123, 162

Johnson, Samuel, 61, 73, 79–80, 83, 88, 95, 99, 104–6, 109, 126, 158, 241n57, 247n48
Johnstone, George, 118, 126, 181

King, Boston, 163–64

Lafayette, Marquis de, 126, 177–78, 274n19
Laurens, Henry, 92, 121, 127, 132–33, 149, 153, 168–69, 178, 183, 203, 270n129
Laurens, John, 132–33, 155, 196–97, 204–5, 253–54n130, 257n167
law of nations. *See* atrocities, politics of wartime
Lay, Benjamin, 40
Lee, Arthur, 68, 109–10, 112, 143, 153, 155, 178, 192, 204, 252–53n111
Lee, Charles, 91, 184
Lee, Francis Lightfoot, 75, 126, 131
Lee, Richard Henry, 152–53, 175–76, 252–53n111
Lee, William, 144, 176
Leslie, Alexander, 167, 169, 186
Lind, John, 81, 123–24, 253n124
Livingston, Robert R., 112, 114, 169–70
Locke, John, 18, 68, 77, 92
Long, Edward, 99–100, 106–7, 136–37, 246n36
Lowndes, Rawlins, 184–85
Luttrell, Temple, 65–66, 93, 179–80, 212
Lyttelton, Lord William Henry, 118, 136

Madison, James, 171, 184, 196
Magna Carta, 13
Mansfield, Lord, 64, 78, 89, 106, 109, 148, 186–88, 196, 207, 238n14
Margrett, David, 162
maroons. *See* slave resistance
Maryland, 15, 30, 190
Massachusetts, Revolutionary legislative resolutions of, 119–20, 194–95
Massachusetts Gazette, 77, 80, 84
Middleton, Arthur, 186
Millar, John, 104, 191–92
Montesquieu, Baron de, 27–28
Morris, Gouverneur, 134

New England, 20, 42–43, 45, 75, 80, 107, 120, 146, 158, 194, 203
North, Lord, 60–62, 66, 73, 91, 113, 116–17, 136, 141, 207
North Carolina. *See* Carolina

Oldmixon, John, 31, 33
Oliver, Andrew, 91
Oliver, Peter, 118
Otis, James, 107, 192, 203

Paine, Thomas, 54–55, 70, 112, 128–29, 245n13
Parliament, authority of, 48–49, 59–60, 62–65, 79, 106, 109–10, 190, 192
patriotism, appeals to and contests over, 32–37, 39, 44–45, 54, 75, 82–86, 99, 191–93, 202
Pendleton, Edmund, 70, 131–32, 171
Pennsylvania, and servitude and slavery, 39–40, 47–48, 193–95, 199, 279n86
Pepys, Samuel, 16
Pitt, William ("the Elder"), 110, 141
Price, Richard, 64, 71–72, 92, 94, 123–24, 180–81, 274n31
Priestley, Joseph, 90
prisoners of war. *See* atrocities, politics of wartime
property rights, 68–69, 85, 97, 159, 168–72
proslavery arguments, 15–16, 30–35, 85, 101, 107, 181, 246n36
Protestantism, cause of, 10, 12, 21–25, 32–33, 35, 40, 49, 71, 151, 201, 202
Providence. *See* God, favor and punishment from

Quakers, 6, 37–41, 43, 75, 77, 178, 183, 198, 228–29n81, 275n42
Quincy, Josiah, 142–44, 149, 202

race and racism: attacks on, 24–26, 31, 37, 77, 194, 262n45, 279n87; developing ideas of, 14–15, 20–21, 30–31, 46, 100, 107, 117, 130, 142–45, 148–60; historiography of, 54–55, 174, 177, 205, 262n45

radicals and reformers, British and European, 35, 45–47, 64–66, 70–71, 83, 87–93, 109, 126–27, 134–36, 147, 179–82, 190–91, 210, 212
rebellion, politics of, 75, 80, 89–98, 111, 146, 215, 243n87
regional distinctions on slavery, 37, 41–43, 47–48, 88, 201–5, 229n96
Richmond, Duke of, 114, 135–36
Rockingham, Marquess of, 70–71
Royal African Company. *See* slave trade, transatlantic
Rush, Benjamin, 53, 110, 112, 120, 178–79, 191, 195, 198, 204, 246–47n38
Rutledge, Edward, 118–19

Sancho, Ignatius, 209
Sandwich, Earl of, 87, 116, 141
Schaw, Janet, 101
Scottish influence, fear of, 46–47, 97–98, 105, 125, 135, 144, 155
Seabury, Samuel, 84
servitude, 16, 20–21, 46, 180, 212, 224n4; debates over, 12–15, 21; indentured, 13–14, 47–48, 69, 78–79, 94–95, 125, 250n82; kidnapping and, 11–12; penal, 11–14, 77, 88–89, 105, 110, 119, 121
Seven Years' War, 34, 36–39, 49, 62, 101–2, 149, 225n15, 264n69
Sharp, Granville, 120, 179, 188, 190–91, 193, 197–98, 208
Shelburne, Earl of, 93, 117, 140–41
slave resistance, 25–27, 31, 33, 36–40, 42–43, 48, 69, 81, 94–98, 105, 123–38, 145, 149, 151–54, 158, 161–72, 174, 176, 181–87, 189–90, 192–94, 197–98, 200, 213, 215, 228n72, 265n86, 268n106, 281n105
slavery, rhetoric of political, 15–19, 32–33, 44–46, 53, 66–74, 76, 79, 83–86, 90, 92, 96, 113, 118–19, 134, 156, 173, 175–82, 189–91, 193, 201–3, 230n106, 235n43, 264n69
slave trade, transatlantic: British participation in, 12, 33–35, 160–61; debates

over, attempts to restrict, 32–37, 42–44, 119–22, 145; in the politics of the American Revolution, 87–89, 115, 119–22, 126, 132, 145, 178–79, 187–88, 190, 194–99, 202, 204, 206–12, 216–17, 252n104, 252–53n111
slavishness, fear of, 17–18, 46–47, 67, 69–70, 134–35, 142–48, 152, 173, 202–3
Smith, Adam, 27, 100, 142–43
Society for the Propagation of the Gospel. *See* Anglicans
Somerset v. Steuart, 78, 89, 106, 108–9, 148, 162, 186–88, 196, 207–8, 238n14, 245n19
South Carolina. *See* Carolina
Spain, US alliance with, 112, 157–58, 167. *See also* Protestantism, cause of
Stamp Act, 1, 53, 59, 63–64, 66–68, 84, 109–10, 145–47, 151, 176, 198, 201, 204
Stiel, Murphy, 163
Stuarts, 16–18, 33, 48–49, 91–92, 225n18
Sugar Act, 1, 53, 66, 145, 203

Tories (British political party), 17, 33, 46, 65–66, 92, 105
Townshend, Charles, 90
Trenchard, John, 35, 46
Tucker, Josiah, 73, 77, 80–81, 142, 209–10
Turkey, Turks, 13, 39–41, 45–46, 78–79, 93, 126, 201

Virginia: laws and resolutions of, 14, 68–69, 95–96, 98, 110, 119, 125–27, 131, 133, 156, 190, 253–54n130; metropolitan images of, 10–11, 24, 29–31, 43

Wallace, George, 27–28, 36
Ward, Joseph, 140
Ward, Samuel, 67–68, 175, 178
Warren, James, 152
Warren, Joseph, 68–69
Washington, George, 43, 61, 66–67, 70, 86, 113–16, 125, 129, 134–35, 156, 163, 170–71, 184, 196, 200, 203, 211, 229–30n101, 265n81
Wayne, Anthony, 128
Wesley, John, 72, 103–4, 179, 209
West Indies, British, 12–13, 160; antislavery in, 36, 39, 41; image and influence of in the metropolis, 14–15, 18, 23–24, 26–31, 33, 36, 42, 61, 69, 99–101, 103–7, 145, 160–61, 179, 203–4, 210–13, 217, 245n19; North American Patriots and, 84, 88, 98, 115, 127–28, 131–33, 145–47, 179, 187, 203; relations with British North America, 20, 41–43, 145; slavery and slave law in, 14–15, 20, 31, 34, 36, 98, 108–9
Wheatley, Phillis, 77, 189–90, 193
Whigs (British political party), 17, 23, 33, 46, 48–49, 65–66, 77, 92, 105
Whitefield, George, 1, 25
Wilberforce, William, 187
Wilkes, John, 35, 46–47, 64–66, 83, 114, 116–17, 128, 176, 181
Woodford, William, 98, 152
Woolman, John, 37–38, 40
Wright, Sir James, 87, 133

Young, Arthur, 62–63

www.ingramcontent.com/pod-product-compliance
Lightning Source LLC
Chambersburg PA
CBHW031451170925
32739CB00002B/15